STUDIES IN ORIENTAL CULTURE   NUMBER 2

Chinese Government in Ming Times:

SEVEN STUDIES

TILEMANN GRIMM, RAY HUANG, JUNG-PANG LO,

 JOHN MESKILL, JAMES B. PARSONS,

ROMEYN TAYLOR, LIEN-SHENG YANG

Chinese Government in Ming Times SEVEN STUDIES

EDITED BY CHARLES O. HUCKER

Columbia University Press   1969   New York and London

STUDIES IN ORIENTAL CULTURE
Edited at Columbia University

Board of Editors

Contributors

TILEMANN GRIMM *Professor of Chinese History,*
Ruhr-University Bochum, Bochum, Germany

RAY HUANG *Associate Professor of History, New Paltz University College,*
State University of New York, New Paltz, New York

CHARLES O. HUCKER *Professor of Chinese, Chairman, Department of*
Far Eastern Languages and Literatures, The University of Michigan,
Ann Arbor, Michigan

JUNG-PANG LO *Associate Professor of History,*
University of California, Davis, Davis, California

JOHN MESKILL *Associate Professor of Chinese and Japanese,*
Barnard College, Columbia University, New York, New York

JAMES B. PARSONS *Professor of History,*
University of California, Riverside, Riverside, California

ROMEYN TAYLOR *Associate Professor of History,*
University of Minnesota, Minneapolis, Minnesota

LIEN-SHENG YANG *Harvard-Yenching Professor of Chinese History,*
Harvard University, Cambridge, Massachusetts

Preface

The year now beginning as I write, 1968, marks the six hundredth anniversary of the formal establishment of China's Ming dynasty (1368–1644). Since the China of Ming times distinguished itself in book production and in scholarship, it seems particularly appropriate for a scholarly volume to be presented in celebration of this occasion; and all those concerned with production of the symposium volume in hand consequently hope it may be received as a worthy contribution to the world-wide observance of the Ming anniversary.

Following a century of Mongol dominance, the Ming dynasty gave China renewed independence and pride, political and social stability, and previously unparalleled preeminence in East Asian affairs. Then, after two and a half centuries, Ming gave way to conquering Manchus, under whom China was eventually to feel the impact of modern Europe's expansionism and imperialism. Thus falling between two eras of dramatic turmoil that were of special interest to the outside world, and inevitably falling victim to the Manchus' need to paint their predecessors in unflattering lights, the Ming period long suffered scholarly neglect. Chinese and Japanese scholars were content to think of Ming times only as the setting for the famous Neo-Confucian philosopher Wang Yang-ming, and Western scholars were content to think of Ming times only as the setting for Matteo Ricci and his fellow Christian missionary pioneers.

The past twenty years, however, have witnessed a strong upsurge of scholarly interest in all aspects of Ming China, among Chinese, Japanese, and Westerners alike; and there is increasingly evident a realization that the Ming period was at once the mature culmination of China's ages-old institutional and cultural traditions and, from the opposite point of view, the seedbed from which the institutions and culture of today's China have grown. One major consequence of this burgeoning interest has been the organization in 1963 of a cooperative international Ming Biographical History Project for the purpose of producing a substantial and authoritative reference work on China in Ming times. Under the auspices of the Association for Asian Studies and with financial support from a host of sources (including the Association for Asian Studies itself, the American Council of Learned Societies, the Ford Foundation, the Rockefeller Foundation, the National Endowment for the Humanities, more than twenty American colleges and universities, and cooperating groups in Taiwan, Hong Kong, Japan, and Korea), a headquarters staff in New York directed by Dr. L. Carrington Goodrich is focusing the research of scores of scholars in America, Europe, and Asia on Ming topics and problems.

Rising interest in Ming times early intersected another theme of scholarly interest in China—long-developed interest in China's governmental traditions. And the volume in hand, while coincidentally contributing to observance of the Ming anniversary, grows directly out of a research conference convened in 1965 to exploit the confluence of these scholarly currents. Called the Research Conference on Ming Government, it met for the better part of a week in August, 1965, under the joint sponsorship of the Committee on Studies of Chinese Civilization of the American Council of Learned Societies and the Ming Biographical History Project Committee of the Association for Asian Studies, and enjoying the generous hospitality of the University of Illinois.

Participants in the 1965 conference were Professors Robert B. Crawford of the University of Illinois, Wm. Theodore de Bary of Columbia University, S. N. Eisenstadt of the Hebrew University of Jerusalem, Chao-ying Fang of the Ming Biographical History Project, Wolfgang Franke of Hamburg University, L. Carrington Goodrich of the Ming Biographical History Project, Tilemann Grimm of Bochum University, Ping-ti Ho of the University of Chicago, Ray Huang of the Southern Illinois University at Alton (now of the State University of New York at New Paltz), Charles O. Hucker of the University of Michigan, James T. C. Liu of Princeton University, Jung-pang Lo of the University of California at Davis, John Meskill of Barnard College, James B. Parsons of the University of California at Riverside, Romeyn Taylor of the University of Minnesota, Ssu-yü Teng of Indiana University, Denis Twitchett of the University of London, and Lien-sheng Yang of Harvard University, and Mr. Chihua Wu of Academic Sinica, Taiwan. Conference *rapporteurs* were Messrs. John Dardess and Silas Wu of Columbia University and James Millinger of Yale University.

Twelve research papers on different aspects of Ming government were prepared to serve as bases for discussion at the conference. Among them were early drafts of the seven papers now gathered together for publication in this volume. All these papers break new research ground and will influence the further course of Ming studies and studies of China's governmental traditions more generally. Although they were originally written by specialists for specialists, they need not daunt the nonspecialist reader, who should find in them gratifying glimpses into the detailed workings of a strange governmental system grappling with universally understandable problems. For a generalized overview of the system in its entirety, if such is desired, the uninitiated reader might do well to consult my booklet *The Traditional Chinese State in Ming Times (1368–1644)* (Tucson, 1961).

The papers that follow are largely pioneering efforts to explore problem areas that have long blocked the way toward fuller understanding of Ming government. One such problem area is local government. Whereas the organization and operation of the Ming central government have become fairly well known, little has previously been done to clarify such matters as the selection, the perquisites, the functions, the powers, and in general all the various conditions of service of local officials. In the first paper of this volume Professor Yang addresses himself to these problems, within the larger context of discussing the traditional Chinese problem of, and Chinese thinking about, finding an appropriate balance between centralization and decentralization of political power.

Few aspects of the Ming state system have been as neglected as its military aspect, and both Professor Taylor and Professor Lo offer pioneering contributions in this realm. Professor Taylor focuses on institutional problems, exploring the ways in which the Ming dynasty's distinctive hereditary military establishment evolved out of antecedent Mongol institutions and customs. Professor Lo focuses on functional aspects—how the Ming government reacted to a sequence of military-diplomatic crises—in a broad analysis, using the techniques and approaches of modern behavioral scientists, of the procedures through which important state decisions were arrived at.

Professor Huang grapples with equally neglected problems of Ming government: whence came government revenues, and how were they expended? This is probably the most complicated research realm of all those represented in this volume, and Professor Huang explores it with boldness, patience, and skill, opening up innumerable byways for further investigation.

The next two papers, Professor Grimm's and Professor Meskill's, deal with the educational system through which the Ming government attempted to establish moral standards and to prepare good men for state service. Professor Grimm, concentrating on a particular type of government office called the education intendancy, analyzes the changing attitudes of the Ming state toward education and morality and the government's ways of establishing its predominance in this realm; whereas Professor Meskill explores the interrelationships of privately established schools and the government, giving special attention to the entanglement of such schools in political controversies.

Professor Parsons' painstakingly researched paper examines, in an unprecedentedly exhaustive way, a variety of problems relating to the geographical and social origins and the career patterns of the Ming officialdom. This relates not only to clarification of the nature of the Ming government, but also to continuing scholarly controversies about social mobility and class relations throughout traditional Chinese history as a whole. Professor Parsons' paper, alone among those included here, has already appeared in print elsewhere, in the journal *Monumenta Serica*, vol. XXII, fasc. 2 (dated 1963, issued 1966), pp. 343–406. I am greatly indebted both to Professor Parsons and to the editors of *Monumenta Serica* for permission to include it here.

Explorations as varied as these into diverse aspects of the Ming governmental system are not easily condensed into generalizations about new insights gained or vistas opened. But I believe all participants in the 1965 research conference felt, and I hope all readers of this volume will feel, that these papers well represent the kinds of research work being done on the frontiers of our knowledge of the Ming state and open exciting avenues for furtherance of the work. I am sure I speak for all participants in the conference, and especially for the contributors to this volume, in expressing gratitude to those agencies that made the conference possible and to Columbia University Press for now making these studies available to a wider audience.

The use of official titles and governmental terms throughout the volume generally follows the usage in my article "Governmental

Organization of the Ming Dynasty," *Harvard Journal of Asiatic Studies*, XXI (1958), pp. 1–66, and its index in XXIII (1960–61), pp. 127–51. (Both the article and the index have just been reprinted in a volume entitled *Studies of Governmental Institutions in Chinese History*, published by the Harvard University Press.) The volume now in hand does not incorporate relevant Chinese characters into the text or notes, but following the notes there is a glossary giving Chinese characters for all special terms that appear in romanized form in the text and notes.

Charles O. Hucker

Ann Arbor, Michigan
January, 1968

Contents

Preface   CHARLES O. HUCKER   vii

Ming Local Administration   LIEN-SHENG YANG   1

Yüan Origins of the Wei-so System   ROMEYN TAYLOR   23

Policy Formulation and Decision-Making on Issues Respecting Peace and War   JUNG-PANG LO   41

Fiscal Administration During the Ming Dynasty   RAY HUANG   73

Ming Education Intendants   TILEMANN GRIMM   129

Academies and Politics in the Ming Dynasty   JOHN MESKILL   149

The Ming Dynasty Bureaucracy: Aspects of Background Forces JAMES B. PARSONS   175

Notes   233

Glossary   273

Index   277

Chinese Government in Ming Times:

SEVEN STUDIES

Local Administration

FEUDALISM AND CENTRALISM IN THE CHINESE TRADITION

In Chinese usage, the term normally rendered "feudal system" (*feng-chien*) refers to the monarch's establishment or recognition of feudal states in which the position of the state ruler is hereditary. In contrast, the "prefectural system" (*chün-hsien*) refers to division of the empire into prefectures and districts, to which the central government appoints prefects and district magistrates as governors, each for a limited period of time. In simplified terms, the former system corresponds to a federation of feudal states and the latter to a consolidated empire. The contrast between the two systems was so sharp in the minds of scholars in traditional China that they often discussed the advantages and disadvantages of both with great zeal, without recognizing any problem of definition. The two systems, however, need not be viewed as two completely contradictory modes of government. In reviewing the history of political institutions, it seems more meaningful to treat the two traditionally accepted models as two polarities with a wide spectrum of shades of colors between them.

A mixed system was tried as early as the second century B.C. when the Han dynasty (202 B.C.–A.D. 220) divided the empire into both "commanderies" (*chün*, corresponding to *fu* or prefectures in Ming and Ch'ing times) and "principalities" or "kingdoms" (*kuo*). During the first Han decades, some hereditary princes became as powerful as the feudal lords in Late Chou China. Only after suppression of a rebellion of seven kingdoms in 154 B.C. did the imperial government assume effective control of the principalities, most of which were then reduced to the size of commanderies. To each principality the central government sent a chancellor (*kuo-hsiang*) as the real governor, thus reducing the princes to nominal heads of their states.

Large-scale enfeoffment of imperial princes with real power was practised again in Western Chin times (265–317). But eight powerful princes allied with and fought against each other in turn and created a period of chaos, which occasioned invasions and uprisings of barbarian groups in the first part of the fourth century. In the following period of disunion, the prefectural system was on the whole maintained under both the Northern and Southern Dynasties. From Sui (581–618) and T'ang (618–907) times on, it was even more firmly established as the basic pattern for the unified empire. But toward the end of the T'ang period regional commanders wielded so much power that they have been compared to the heads of feudal states in ancient China. This abuse was corrected (in the opinion of many scholars, overcorrected) from the Sung dynasty (960–1279) on by various measures to assure centralized imperial control.

The Han combination of commanderies and principalities was criticized by the great neo-Confucianist Chu Hsi (1130–1200) as being "no institution." [1] Nevertheless, more recent dynasties, especially during their early periods, tended to establish princes or generals with hereditary titles and privileges—and, more importantly, hereditary power and authority—particularly in newly incorporated areas or on the frontier. Ming T'ai-tsu (1368–98) set up several of his sons on the northern frontier. One of them, the Prince of Yen, eventually dethroned his nephew and declared himself emperor (Ch'eng-tsu, 1402–1424). From the early years of the Ming dynasty, General Mu Ying and his descendants were allowed to govern hereditarily a considerable portion of Yunnan Province. Under both Yüan and Ch'ing, newly surrendered Chinese generals were enfeoffed as kings or marquises, although they were soon removed to make possible a more consolidated empire.

As a minor variant of the feudal system, when foreign groups or aborigines were incorporated into the empire, their chieftains were often allowed to retain their hereditary power and authority. Such territories were known under T'ang and Sung as "prefectures under loose rein" (*chi-mi fu-chou* or *chi-mi chou*), and such chieftains were known as "chieftains serving as local officials" (*t'u-ssu*) under Ming and Ch'ing. The long term trend was the replacement of the chieftain system by the normal prefectural system (called *kai-t'u kuei-liu*). Interestingly enough, one method adopted by the Ming government to control the aboriginal chieftains was to send term appointees (*liu-kuan*) to be their subordinate officials, especially chiefs of police (*li-mu*), very much as the Han dynasty sent chancellors to control the principalities.[2]

In connection with the enfeoffment of imperial princes, it should be noted that Chinese tradition also recognized nominal enfeoffment to be part of the "feudal system." Under this term historians have recorded people's receiving titles of nobility with corresponding emoluments and privileges more or less hereditarily, although with neither territory nor power. For instance, Ma Tuan-lin (*c.* 1250–1319) in his great encyclopedia *Wen-hsien t'ung-k'ao* (Comprehensive inquiry into documentary sources) devoted several chapters of his "Study on Feudalism" to this type of feudalism.[3] The Ming system of nobility has been well summarized by Professor Charles O. Hucker.[4] One point he fails to clarify, however, is that both the position of imperial prince (*ch'in-wang*) and that of prince of the second degree (*chün-wang*) were hereditary, that is, to be inherited by one son in each instance. This point helps to explain the large number of princes in the later years of the dynasty, who became a serious drain on state revenues.

The contrast between the feudal system and the prefectural system points sharply to the problem of centralization. Of course, it is difficult to strike a happy balance between the centrifugal and centripetal forces of a society. As for the governmental system, various dynasties in Chinese history tried to learn lessons from earlier experience, and indeed they had many lessons to learn. In this exploratory essay, a historical survey will be made of traditional Chinese views of the feudal and prefectural systems. This will be followed by some general remarks on topics in Ming local government on various levels. These remarks, it should be noted, are based on a preliminary and incomplete survey of the materials and are intended only to stimulate discussion and further research and investigation.

TRADITIONAL ARGUMENTS ABOUT THE FEUDAL SYSTEM AND THE PREFECTURAL SYSTEM

The collected works of the great late Ming scholar Ku Yen-wu (1613–82) contain a series of nine essays entitled *Chün-hsien lun*

(Discourses on the prefectural system), of which the first and most important essay has been translated into English. Some excerpts follow:

If we understand why the feudal system changed into the prefectural system, we will also understand that as the prefectural system in turn falls into decay it too must change. Does this mean that there will be a return to feudalism? No, this is impossible. But if some sage were to appear who could invest the prefectural system with the essential meaning of feudalism, then the world would attain order . . . . The fault of feudalism was its concentration of power on the local level, while the fault of the prefectural system is its concentration of power at the top. The sage-rulers of antiquity were impartial and public-minded in their treatment of all men, parceling out land to them and dividing up their domains. But now the ruler considers all the territory within the four seas to be his own perfecture, and is still unsatisfied. He suspects every person, he handles every affair that comes up, so that each day the directives and official documents pile higher than the day before. On top of this, he sets up supervisors, provincial governors and governors-general, supposing that in this way he can keep the local officials from tyrannizing over and harming the people. He is unaware that these officials in charge are concerned only in moving with utmost caution so as to stay out of trouble until they have the good fortune to be relieved of their posts, and are quite unwilling to undertake anything of profit to the people . . . . If, however, the position of local officials is accorded its proper dignity, and such officials are granted fiscal and administrative authority, if the post of supervisor is discontinued, the enticement of hereditary office held out to officials, and a method whereby they may select their own subordinates put into effect, this will achieve the goal of imbuing the prefectural system with the essential meaning of feudalism, and the decay that has come about in the last two thousand years can be remedied . . . .[5]

Professor Wm. Theodore de Bary explains this contrast by the dichotomy between Legalism and Confucianism, which similarly are terms to be understood as polarities permitting numerous shades of colors in between.

Ku Yen-wu was a utilitarian thinker and a solid scholar. Some of his views may look reactionary to the trends of the time (a fact Ku himself realized); they are nevertheless respectable because they are based on historical research and personal observation and are often marked by a high degree of sophistication. His penchant for the historical approach led him to many discoveries, including the early origins of the prefectural system, a thesis further developed by Ch'ing scholars and more recently by scholars of our own time.[6]

In order to understand fully the significance of Ku's slogan "imbuing the prefectural system with the essential meaning of feudalism" (*yü feng-chien yü chün-hsien*), it is necessary to go back some two thousand years.

When the prefectural system was first applied to the whole unified empire of Ch'in in 221 B.C., the sole argument was that feudal states tended to wage wars against each other as in Late Chou times and the Son of Heaven would find it difficult to control them. In the words of the First Emperor of Ch'in, "To establish states again would mean a planting of weapons," i.e., sowing the seeds of war. Following similar reasoning, Chia I under Han Wen-ti (179–157 B.C.) proposed a policy of "establishing many states while keeping their power small," so that the country could be governed "like the body's control of arms and the arm's control of fingers." This policy, though not adopted immediately, was realized step by step after the rebellion in 154 B.C. Thus, control became the paramount principle of government in Ch'in and Han times.

Under the succeeding Wei dynasty (220–64), the control of imperial clansmen was quite rigid. According to Ts'ao Chiung, a clansman who in 243 wrote an essay advocating a return to the feudal system,[7] clansmen had to begin their military or civil service careers very low, and even the brilliant had to serve first as a centurion or magistrate of a small district. Ts'ao admitted that one should avoid the situation of "having so large a tail that one cannot wag it." Nevertheless, he advocated the enfeoffment of both imperial princes and worthies of other families in order to maintain the time-honored principles of keeping one's relatives close (*ch'in ch'in*) and of recognizing the worthy as they deserve (*hsien hsien*). The help of relatives and the worthy is necessary to the emperor because despotism (*tu-chih*, or governing by oneself) cannot last long. The long-lived Chou dynasty and the short-lived Ch'in dynasty are cited as contrasting examples.

Early in the Chin period (265–317), Lu Chi, a brilliant literary figure from South China, wrote an essay on enfeoffment.[8] Granting that even good institutions cannot avoid abuse and that no government patterns can be laid down for eternity, he chooses the feudal system as the better of the two because it permits a slow decline and downfall. In contrast, an empire practising the prefectural system may collapse suddenly in the face of a mass rebellion or may have the central power usurped from within. Lu also points out that both state rulers and prefects can be either good or bad. In theory, a state ruler could be concerned more with his governmental duties because what he governed was a kind of family property, whereas prefects and magistrates would tend to place their own promotions and other self-ish interests before the welfare of the people. Consequently, according to Lu, good rulers would do more good than good prefects and stupid rulers would do less harm than stupid prefects—which appears to be a possibility though not a probability. At about the same time, the statesman Liu Sung also advocated substantial enfeoffment. It is not clear how much these third-century advisers influenced the Chin enfeoffment policy. Ironically, Lu Chi served under two of the eight powerful princes who fought against each other, and he lost his life in 303.

In the Chen-kuan era (627–49), T'ang T'ai-tsung invited his court officials to discuss a possible revival of the feudal system.[9] The discussion was inconclusive and added no important arguments on either side. One argument advanced was that the length of a dynasty was predestined and was not related to the practice of either system. Although this argument was made by Li Po-yao in defense of the prefectural system, later it was severely criticized by Tu Yu, author of the important encyclopedia *T'ung tien* (Comprehensive canon), who also favored the prefectural system.[10] Tu points out that the Han dynasty lasted four hundred years—in other words, as long as the ancient Hsia dynasty—although Hsia practiced the feudal system and Han practiced the prefectural system. More important, Tu declares that rulers were set up by Heaven to shepherd the people. The great increases in population realized under Han, Sui, and T'ang should be taken as evidence of the superiority of the prefectural system. Elsewhere Tu asserts that, other things being equal, a country that can feed more people must be considered more successful than one that can feed fewer.[11] Altogether this seems a rather progressive view. It is no wonder that Chu Hsi labels Tu's writings as "approving the modern but criticizing the ancient" (*shih-chin fei-ku*).[12]

Arguing against the point that it was easy for an empire to collapse, Tu says that it also takes only a short time for an empire to be reunified. The periods of chaos that preceded reunification under the Former Han, the Later Han, and the T'ang, according to his count, took eight, thirteen, and ten years respectively. As a statesman-scholar, Tu in general favored honoring the sovereign, strengthening the trunk and weakening the branches, and establishing stable institutions and appropriate instructions, causing the people to multiply and become rich and the ruling dynasty to last long.[13]

Tu's progressive view was matched by a younger contemporary, the brilliant essayist Liu Tsung-yüan (773–814), who wrote probably the most eloquent exposition on the prefectural system. In his *Feng-chien lun* (Discourses on the feudal system),[14] Liu declares his opinion that the feudal system was not formed by the wish or design of the sage rulers of antiquity, as was argued by many traditional scholars, but was a historical necessity forced on them by social development. In struggling for life and gain in a primitive society, it was natural for small tribal groups to develop into a large group or to be controlled by another group. Similarly, in later times, it was natural for large tribal groups to form a feudal state or be absorbed into another feudal state. It was natural for the position of a chieftain or feudal lord to be hereditary because he was the leader of the group by consent. Finally, it was natural for a king to rise over and above the feudal states. After conquest, the founders of the ancient Shang and Chou dynasties continued enfeoffment because they were obliged to reward their assistants.

A corollary to this thesis is that to practice the feudal system was to be partial to one's relatives and friends. In contrast, although the prefectural system was based on partiality to the selfish interests of the despot, it also contained germs of great impartiality by allowing the worthy to govern the people, instead of relying on hereditary nobles. It was difficult to remove a bad feudal lord but easy to replace a bad prefect or magistrate.

Comparing the disadvantages of the two systems, Liu applied what may be termed "the rebellion test." Toward the end of the Ch'in dynasty there were rebellious people but not rebellious governors because, although the people could no longer stand the tyrannical government, the governors were still under control. The Han dynasty experienced rebellious principalities but not rebellious commanderies. The T'ang dynasty had rebellious generals but not rebellious prefectures. These data prove the superiority of the prefectural system.

As has already been observed by Professor Hsiao Kung-ch'üan, Liu's theory on the origins of the feudal system, however historical in basis, was unorthodox.[15] Many later scholars have criticized Liu for his lack of respect for the ancient sage rulers.[16] Nonetheless, they tend to praise his eloquence. In addition, one is tempted to conjecture about the possible linkage between Liu's advocacy of nonhereditary aristocracy (in the sense of government by the best citizens) and his own social background and political connections.[17]

Among Liu's enthusiastic supporters, the most notable were Su Shih (1036–1101) and Yang Shen (1488–1559), both celebrated literary figures of their times. Su Shih added an argument against enfoeffment by pointing out that jealousy of hereditary fortunes often brought members of the nobility to miserable ends.[18] This argument, though not particularly strong, reminds us of the warnings later given by Huang Tsung-hsi (1610–95) about the inescapable destiny of complete destruction waiting for the despot and his descendants.[19] For his part, Yang Shen tried to justify the prefectural system by citing cases of beneficial replacement of aboriginal chieftains by appointed officials under the Ming dynasty.[20] Both Su and Yang considered Liu's arguments conclusive.

The other camp also had reinforcements, particularly in the Sung period, which has been generally recognized as an extraordinarily creative era. In addition to its remarkable contributions to philosophy, art, and literature, in the realm of learning the era is marked by historical scholarship and the development of protoscience, in natural sciences and social sciences alike. The Sung understanding of institutional history was deepened by an awareness of the interdependence of various institutions and a broad application of the concepts of "body" (t'i: substance, structure and principle as sources of energy) and "functions" (yung).[21] Another obvious point is that by now the Chinese people had accumulated sufficient experience to permit a more sophisticated analysis.

The abuse of overcentralization under the Sung was criticized by several scholars including Chu Hsi, Ch'en Liang (1143–94), and Yeh Shih (1150–1223), although they had rather divergent views on philosophy and other theories of government.[22] Lo Pi, another scholar of the twelfth century, however, should be singled out as the most effective debater on the side of decentralization. His *Lu-shih* (Great history) contains *Feng-chien Hou-lun* (Further discourses on the feudal system) and other sections advocating the spirit of the feudal system, especially the establishment of many states of limited size.[23] In his opinion hereditary chieftains were successful in maintaining peace and order in the "prefectures under loose rein." Sung T'ai-tsu (960–75) permitted several of his generals on the frontier to have considerable fiscal and administrative power and allowed them to stay in their posts for many years. This excellent policy was enfeoffment in reality although not in name. Arguing against Su Shih, Lo took pains to trace the fates of various nobles under the two Han dynasties and found out that the great majority lost their fortunes when they lost imperial favor, whereas only a few were killed by insubordinate slaves. On the other hand, bureaucrats or their descendants also could lose their fortunes through jealous attacks, although such cases were not often recorded in histories because the historians considered such events trivial.

Lo lists as many as ten advantages of a feudal state the size of a district. These include easy maintenance of peace and defense and ready promotion of welfare and education. He even asserts that all good institutions had their bases in the feudal system. Although this may be an overstatement, Lo must not be judged as a conservative on this basis. Actually, he was quite progressive in many of his views. For instance, he observed that there are necessary and irreversible trends in history and cited the development of weapons as one example. "Weapons cannot be done away with; they can only become more destructive." It must be remembered that he was thinking of enfeoffment in spirit with various modifications in practice. If we leave out the point about hereditary rulers, he was almost arguing for self-government on the district level. This reminds us of the community contracts (*hsiang-yüeh*) introduced in the eleventh century by the Lü brothers in Lan-t'ien, Shensi, and subsequently modified and promoted by the celebrated Confucian scholar Chu Hsi (1130–1200).

The Lü family's community contracts exerted some influence in later times and even outside of China. Unfortunately, as has been pointed out by Hsiao Kung-ch'üan, these contributed mainly to systems of rural control and failed to pave the way to local self-government.[24]

The end of the Yüan dynasty saw a remarkable commentator on the feudal system in Wu Lai (1297–1340). Following the Sung tradition, he stressed the close relationship between enfeoffment and the legendary well-field *(ching-t'ien)* system: "Well-fields were small enfeoffment; enfeoffment was large well-fields." One institution cannot be revived without the other.[25] Since Wu was the master of the early Ming minister Sung Lien, it seems possible that some of Wu's views may have influenecd Ming T'ai-tsu in his enfeoffment policies and his establishment of military colonies *(t'un-t'ien)*, generally considered a modified version of well-fields for soldiers. Wu also lamented the lack of power on the part of prefects and magistrates under the Yüan dynasty. These local governors were not allowed to employ their own subordinate officials and had very little fiscal, administrative, or military power. His penetrating essay on these points is quoted almost *in toto* in Ku Yen-wu's *Jih-chih lu* (Record of daily learning).

From the above discussion it becomes clear that Ku's slogan "imbuing the prefectural system with the essential meaning of feudalism" was in the tradition of a line of scholars protesting against over-centralization. Nor was he alone in his own time. Huang Tsung-hsi, who shared many of Ku's views, even seriously proposed in his *Ming-i Tai-fang Lu* (A plan for the prince) the establishment of independent governors on the frontier after the T'ang model.

SOME ASPECTS OF MING LOCAL GOVERNMENT

In the spirit of the traditional scholars who compared the feudal system and the prefectural system in history, let us make a few comparisons of Ming local government with local government under earlier dynasties, especially Han, T'ang, and Sung. Occasionally it is also necessary to compare Ming and Ch'ing, because, although local governments in these two periods resemble each other so much that most of the descriptions and discussions of Professor T'ung-tsu Ch'ü

in his *Local Government in China under the Ch'ing* are applicable
also to the Ming, certain differences deserve attention.

One basic principle of the prefectural system was that all head
officials in the local government were agents of the central government. With intensified application of the system in the latest
dynasties, this principle became paramount. In Ming times government at the provincial level was dominated by three appointed
officials each bearing the title "commissioner" or "envoy" (*shih*), a
term that had assumed importance as early as the T'ang dynasty.
These were an administration commissioner (*pu-cheng shih*), a surveillance commissioner (*an-ch'a shih*), and a regional military commissioner (*tu chih-hui shih*). On the local administrative levels the
head officials were prefects (*chih-fu*), subprefectural magistrates (*chih-
chou*), and district magistrates (*chih-hsien*). These titles, which can
be traced back to Sung times, literally mean "[He who is sent] to be
in charge of the governmental affairs of" a prefecture, a subprefecture,
or a district—in other words, an agent of the central government.
The term for province (*sheng*, rather informally used in Ming times)
was shortened from the term Branch Secretariat (*hsing-sheng*, meaning a field headquarters of the metropolitan Secretariat). The institution was borrowed from the Yüan system for a brief period at the
very beginning of the Ming dynasty. The Yüan dynasty in its turn
had borrowed the term from earlier dynasties, but in Yüan times it
had been applied systematically for the first time to the whole empire.
The basic principle of the prefectural system is thus clearly revealed
in the literal meaning of these terms.

Officials on the provincial or supervisory level also had their origins
in the early imperial era, but they became regularly established only
in Sung times, when there were four parallel commissioners in charge
of military, judicial, financial, and transportation (revenue-forward-
ing) affairs in areas roughly comparable to the provinces of later
times. These Sung commissioners were forerunners of the Ming provincial authorities described above. Since in Ming times there were
both a right administration commissioner and a left administration
commissioner, there were also four top officials in the three Ming
offices. In addition, the emperor appointed a censor as regional inspector (*hsün-an*) to make annual tours of inspection in each province.

Later Ming emperors also delegated high-ranking officials to be grand coordinators (*hsün-fu*, literally, "touring pacifiers") in provinces or strategic areas, and still later there appeared supreme commanders (*tsung-tu*) with major military responsibilities extending over several provinces. The appointment of the grand coordinators and supreme commanders to the provinces or the frontier was intended to achieve more control and coordination, but not infrequently it led to over-lapping and confusion of authority. From the middle decades of the fifteenth century, grand coordinators became increasingly common and powerful. In 1456 it was ordered that both administration com-missioners and surveillance commissioners should be subject to special evaluation (*k'ao-ch'a*) by the regional inspectors and grand co-ordinators (collectively known as *fu-an*).[26] In 1540 the emperor ap-proved a proposal to permit these supervisors, without first sending in memorials of impeachment, to arrest greedy, cruel, and unlawful local government officials of the sixth rank or below.[27] Thus the regional inspectors and grand coordinators formed a superstructure over the provincial officials. The supreme commanders, however, re-mained irregular appointees. Only under the Ch'ing dynasty did they and the grand coordinators become regularly established governors-general or viceroys and provincial governors, respectively.

In the Ming period, under these various provincial authorities but above prefects and magistrates were a large number of major assistant officials known as intendants of circuits (*tao*). Their duties had either functional or regional limitations, as was indicated in their various titles. Contemporary records make it clear that they were not always effective in Ming times and became still less so in the Ch'ing period. According to Lü K'un, writing in 1592, certain intendants of his time served merely as companions to higher surveillance officials during their tours of inspection, and they themselves were expert in seizing opportunities to demand banquets and theatrical entertainments from the districts and to seize public funds to make gifts to each other.[28] Nevertheless, since many intendants had specified duties connected with military preparations, education, salt-inspection, etc., it seems likely that altogether the intendants also played a substantial role on a sublevel of Ming local government.

Not all the commissioners and provincial authorities were bureaucrats. Corresponding to officials on the provincial or a slightly lower level, senior eunuchs (*t'ai-chien*) were sent as special commissioners for such purposes as supervision of military defense, extraction of special revenues, and direction of imperial manufactories. As confidential servants of the emperor, they exercised much power and aroused no little hatred among officials and people alike, excepting those who collaborated with them for selfish interests. The post of senior eunuch serving as grand defender (*chen-shou*) was even compared by contemporaries to that of the grand coordinator.[29] Fortunately, it existed only sporadically and appears to have existed for all thirteen provinces for less than a decade prior to 1435. The appointment of eunuch commissioners made the multi-level system of local government even more complicated and of course did little to enhance the prestige or authority of the prefects and magistrates as shepherds of the people. However, although such eunuch appointees may have been comparable otherwise to alien governors under dynasties of conquest, such as Northern Wei or Yüan, they did not reach the local administrative level.[30]

Such considerations should not be interpreted to mean that the Ming emperors completely failed to heed ancient lessons about paying special attention to the selection and treatment of prefects and magistrates. Under the conscientious early Ming emperors the records of local officials were carefully noted in the capital, and prefects who had satisfactorily completed nine-year terms of service were often given ranks and salaries and reassigned to remain in their posts for nine more or even eighteen more years. But imperial attention to such matters waned. Of 120 model local officials noted in the *Ming-shih* (Ming history), more than 100 served in the early era between 1368 and 1435; fewer than 20 served between 1436 and 1566, only two served between 1567 and 1619, and none served thereafter.[31] Stable local government is naturally reflected in the general dynastic configuration.

As for the qualifications of subprefectural and district magistrates, it is well known that under Ming and Ch'ing dynasties the majority were degree holders. Professor T'ung-tsu Ch'ü has pointed out, in the case of subprefectural and district magistrates serving in 1745 and in 1850, that persons with status as metropolitan graduates (*chin-shih*), provincial graduates (*chü-jen*), and National University students (*chien-sheng*), in that order, were dominant among district magistrates whereas, conversely, National University students, provincial graduates, and metropolitan graduates, in that order, were dominant among subprefectural magistrates. Both metropolitan and provincial graduates were winners of higher degrees, but National University students in Ch'ing times were commoners who purchased such status. Professor Ch'ü points out the interesting phenomenon that "more *chou* magistrates came from the commoner *chien-sheng* than from the *chin-shih* group," but makes no further comment.[32] I believe an explanation can be found by differentiating between officials who were located in the frontier areas and those in the interior, and also by finding out what posts the magistrates were promoted to and from. It is likely that the metropolitan and provincial graduates, and especially the metropolitan graduates, tended to be appointed to the preferable interior subprefectures and districts. In terms of promotion, although the post of a subprefectural magistrate was on the whole higher than that of a district magistrate, the difference was so small that district magistrates with metropolitan degrees would be promoted to higher posts.

Similar but less complete information on subprefectural and district magistrates can be gathered from Ming gazetteers. For instance, the *Hsing-ning-hsien Chih* (Gazetteer of Hsing-ning district) compiled by the literatus-artist-official Chu Yün-ming (1460–1526) lists 25 magistrates from 1390 to 1516 for his rather small district in Kwantung Province. Of these, two were metropolitan graduates, one was of a special recommendation category (*jen-ts'ai*, "talent"), 11 were National University students, and 11 were provincial graduates, the last group including Chu himself.[33]

As has been pointed out by Professor Ping-ti Ho,[34] students of the National University in early Ming times constituted a group especially favored and trusted by the emperor and thus enjoyed unusual opportunities for official appointments of all kinds. From about the middle of the fifteenth century, however, their status began to deteriorate; there were already complaints that students tended to be too old, often over fifty or sixty, by the time they had completed their required training in public offices in the capital and their long period of waiting at the Ministry of Personnel.[35] Those who could no longer bear to wait might seek to be appointed as officials on the frontier, a practice known as "abandoning oneself to barren areas" (*t'ou-huang*). Many simply wanted to line their pockets quickly and retire.[36]

Another complaint in the later part of the Ming period was about overdifferentiation between metropolitan and provincial graduates. In both appointment and gradation the metropolitan graduates were by far the favored group. This discrimination made many provincial graduates reluctant to take appointments in local government but willing to continue to try their luck in the metropolitan examinations even at an advanced age.[37] As a check to this trend, a rule in 1571 prohibited appointment of provincial graduates who were over fifty as subprefectural or district magistrates and limited them to miscellaneous posts.[38]

For an over-all picture, convenient sources are memorials by Ko Shou-li (1505–78), a notable literatus-official from Shantung.[39] According to him, sometime in the third quarter of the sixteenth century, among the approximately 2,000 subprefectural and district magistrates, less than 200 were metropolitan graduates. A large province in the interior would have from several to more than a dozen; a province on the northern or southern frontier might not have even one or two. In the central province Honan, there were 108 subprefectures and districts. Among their magistrates in a particular year, he counted 62 provincial graduates and 28 National University students but only four metropolitan graduates. The posts of two subprefectural magistrates and twelve district magistrates in Honan were vacant at the time. Ko's explanation was that in recent years the quota of triennial metropolitan graduates was limited to 300, and most of the successful candidates preferred appointments in the capital. The situation underlines the age-old problem of balance between inner and outer bureaucrats.

In terms of their authority there seems to be little significant difference between the prefects and magistrates of Ming and those of Ch'ing times. A clear contrast, however, has been made by both traditional and modern scholars between these local officials in later times and their counterparts in earlier times, especially those of the Han dynasty. As head of an independent office, the commandery governor or district magistrate in Han times had the authority to select his own subordinate officials. This practice, continued for three to four centuries after the fall of the Han dynasty, tended to create lord-vassal relationships between the head official and his subordinates, a tendency that able emperors would and did attempt to correct. Authority to employ one's own staff members was taken away in Sui and T'ang times; at least, subordinate officials in civil offices were all to be appointed by the central government.[40] This restriction, together with other factors such as the ancient principle of avoidance (hui-pi, i.e., not to serve in one's native place) [41] and the more recent requirement of special skill in composing the eight-legged essay at the expense of more useful knowledge to pass the examination, led to the development of private secretaries in local government on various levels in Ming and Ch'ing times.[42] As privately engaged advisers, these secretaries were outside the governmental system. Nevertheless, the Yung-cheng emperor (1722–35) required governors and viceroys to submit information on their private secretaries. Although the order was issued on the pretext that these advisers might qualify for official appointments, obviously the major purpose was to exercise a measure of control.[43]

A related matter is the head official's authority to discipline his subordinates. In T'ang times flogging of a registrar, chief of police, or other subordinate official by the head official was commonplace. Flogging became less common in Sung times but very common under the Chin and notoriously common under the Yüan rulers.[44] In Ming and Ch'ing times prefects and magistrates were not allowed to flog their subordinate officials. According to Ming rules, the head official (cheng-kuan) in any office should not freely sentence his principal subordinates (shou-ling kuan) even if the latter were clearly guilty. Disciplinary measures should be left to the proper judicial authorities.[45] Of course, even so prefects and magistrates had the authority to flog clerks and runners.

As for judicial power, it has been noted that Han governors and magistrates could execute criminals without seeking imperial approval. This power became somewhat restricted in Sui and T'ang times and more severely restricted in the Sung era. Scholars have found scattered examples of such freedom to execute even in Sung times, but the laws even then required that all cases involving the death penalty be reviewed by provincial and imperial authorities.[46] In Ming and Ch'ing times flogging was the only lawful punishment that could be administered by a prefect or magistrate. Rules issued in early Ming times authorized flogging with a light stick up to 50 blows for a district magistrate and flogging with a heavy stick up to 80 blows for a sub-prefectural magistrate and up to 100 blows for a prefect.[47]

In reality, as sole judges of the courts of primary jurisdiction, the prefects and magistrates remained very powerful in judicial matters. The *Ming-shih* records as not uncommon cases in which people died under floggings that were administered either as a punishment or as a means to extract confession.[48] According to a rule proposed in 1493, only when a prefect or magistrate had 20 or 30 such cases against his record would he be subject to demotion or more severe punishment.[49] The phrase "family-breaking district magistrate and household-extinguishing prefect" (*p'o-chia hsien-ling, mieh-men tz'u-shih*), which had earlier versions, was still proverbial in the Ming period.[50] The use of elders and community leaders to settle disputes on the village level does not seem to have dissipated the judicial power of the magistrate materially.

As for military power, it has been pointed out that the Han commandery governor was military commander as well as civil governor. The "military governor" (*chün-wei*) was only his assistant.[51] With the development of military authorities on the provincial level, the authority of the prefect and magistrate tended to be limited to local police and militia. This was the situation under the Ming and Ch'ing dynasties. Nevertheless, as heads of local government, prefects and magistrates could be held accountable for all kinds of failures, responsibility or accountability being a dominant principle of Chinese tradition in government and society. The Ming code specifies that if a prefect or magistrate should press the people to rebellion by maladministration and thereby lose his city, his head should be chopped off.[52]

In matters of education and rituals, the Han commandery governor had the authority and responsibility to recommend to the central government yearly a number of the "filial and incorruptible" (*hsiao-lien*) as candidates for office, the number being proportional to the population in the commandery. He also had discretionary authority to honor and decorate citizens in the area under his jurisdiction. In Ming and Ch'ing times, although the magistrate and prefect were responsible for the first and second qualifying tests (*hsien-shih* and *fu-shih*) set for the candidates for the first degree (*sheng-yüan*), the final examinations and the degree itself, which qualified the candidate to become a student in the local government school, were to be given by educational authorities on the provincial level. The decoration (*ching-piao*) of chaste widows or filial sons and the inclusion of names of celebrated officials or native worthies among those to be honored in local shrines were matters that involved bonded petitions (from neighbors, local gentry, etc.) and checking and rechecking ordered by officials on various levels—a process of red tape that benefited mainly the clerks who handled the matter. Normally, the decision was made on the provincial level, but it was to be reported to the imperial court because the Son of Heaven was the source of all grace.[53]

In the realm of public finance the long-term trend from T'ang and Sung times on was for the prefecture and district to forward more and more funds to the provincial authorities and beyond to the central government or to the emperor himself. The prefect or magistrate spent much of his energy fulfilling levy quotas set for the area under his jurisdiction. The local expenditures depended mainly on surtaxes, minor local levies such as fees for the registration of real estate deeds, and fines, booty, and confiscated property. Many expenses, regular or irregular, were apportioned to the population at large.[54]

Closely related to the problem of local finance is that of the income of the head officials and their subordinates. Although the prefectural system assumes a salaried bureaucracy, the forms of salary payment varied considerably from dynasty to dynasty. In the T'ang period, for instance, the two important sources of official income were rent from "land pertaining to office" (*chih-fen t'ien*), also known as "office land" (*chih-t'ien*), and payment received from state-provided servants, guards, and attendants in lieu of actual service.[55] In addition, the state provided for various offices "land for public administration" (*kung-hsieh t'ien*) or "funds for the public administration" (*kung-hsieh ch'ien*), from which rent or interest was drawn for the maintenance of office buildings, entertainments, and other office expenses, thus providing a kind of joint expense account for the officials in a yamen. From Sung times on, public land became less important as a source of salary and office expenses. Ming T'ai-tsu attempted to revive the system of "office land" but soon abandoned it.[56] For office expenses and entertainments, the Sung dynasty had an arrangement known as "treasury for public expenses" (*kung-shih k'u*), a system greatly appreicated by contemporary bureaucrats but discontinued in Ming and Ch'ing times.[57]

In Ming times official salaries were figured in bushels of grain. Actual payments, however, were made only partly in grain, the rest being converted to paper money, copper cash, or commodities under complicated rules which varied according to the rank of the official and changed from time to time.[58] With the spread of silver economy in the middle Ming period, the trend was to convert salary payments to silver. The official and actual rates of conversion varied considerably, and not infrequently to the advantage of the recipient official.

Besides receiving official salaries, local government officials enjoyed certain fringe benefits and opportunities to collect all kinds of legal or extralegal fees, known mostly as "standard practice" (*ch'ang-li*) in Ming times. A major fringe benefit was that the state provided the head official and a few of his top subordinates each with an official residence behind their yamen. They were obliged to live there because the law prohibited them from buying real estate in the area under their jurisdiction while they were in office. In addition, they were provided furniture and utensils, firewood, attendants, and brooms.[59] These were obviously remnants of similar privileges in T'ang, Sung, and earlier times. Under the Ming, however, the practice was for the official to receive monetary payments for most of these items.

The head official, subordinate officials, and sometimes even clerks all had their share in the surtaxes collected on land, on adult males (*ting*), and often also on salt, and in the fees charged on such occasions as the appointments of state-sanctioned community leaders and tax-collectors [60] or the rechecking of the registers for soldiers or artisans.[61] Travel expenses for prefects and magistrates, particularly for their triennial court audiences (*ch'ao-chin*), were borne also by the people.[62] The court audience was an occasion to present gifts to various officials in the capital, who regarded that year as their year of harvest or year to collect rents.

Custom permitted all kinds of gift-making on other occasions such as the birthdays of the head officials, his parents, and his wife.[63] On arrival at his new post, the prefect or magistrate was to be dined and presented some bolts of silk. Normally, some delegated clerks would have gone to meet him at his old post. Clerks selected from among the peasants were to make a "paper contribution" (chih-shu), again often commuted to money, when they first reported for duty, and they were to make a still larger contribution when actually assigned to one of the sections in the local government.[64] Such contributions went to the local treasury and, together with fines, booty, and confiscated property,[65] constituted what was loosely known as "harmless [to use]" funds (wu-ai, i.e., unearmarked funds),[66] which tended to be shared by the personnel of the office concerned. Sometimes such funds were also used for public services and public works, usually as a contribution by an official taken from his share. A provincial official might also ask a prefect or magistrate to make a gift on his behalf to a member of the gentry, and the sum might then be charged against the provincial official's share of the unearmarked funds.[67] Finally the central government became interested in the "harmless funds"; in 1564 it was ordered that of the fines, booty, and confiscated property belonging to the offices of the regional inspectors and other censors on duty in the provinces 40 percent should be delivered to the Ministry of Revenue and 40 percent to the Ministry of Works.[68]

The abuse of overcentralization of financial power in general, and its effect on public services and public works in particular, have been criticized by scholars since Sung times.[69] The following observations by Ku Yen-wu bear especially on the point:

From my personal experience in the empire, all the prefectures that date back to the T'ang dynasty have inner and outer walls of good size as well as straight streets and alleys. All the offices and official residences that were built in T'ang times occupy large and spacious grounds. Of those created since the Sung dynasty, the more recent the less decent . . . . The reason why all construction works have come to a complete stop nowadays is exactly because the state takes all the revenues from the prefectures and districts and has every penny forwarded to the central government, and the local officials and the people are both pressed to exhaustion and thus have no funds for construction.[70]

This situation permitted members of the gentry and wealthy men to play a significant role in public services and public works in the last dynasties, a thesis already known to traditional scholars and further developed by modern scholars.[71] This role of the gentry and the local wealthy improved their reputation and also their influence. Many members of the Ming and Ch'ing local elite could be called benevolent magnates, but perhaps as many if not more could be classified as wicked magnates. Benevolent or wicked, these magnates became natural targets of attack in times marked by class struggle, particularly during the servant and tenant revolts in late Ming and early Ch'ing times.[72]

ROMEYN TAYLOR 明 *Yüan Origins*

of the Wei-so System

The regular army of the Ming dynasty was organized in guards (*wei*) and chiliads (*ch'ien-hu so*). As a basis for frontier defense, their declining efficiency eventually made necessary the use of supplementary auxiliaries. The *wei* and *so*, however, not only persisted throughout the dynasty but grew in manpower, albeit irregularly,[1] and by the beginning of the seventeenth century they controlled for their own use about one quarter or one fifth of all the agricultural land reported in the empire.[2]

The *Ming-shih* (Ming history) treats this vast and richly endowed guard system as having been created *de novo* by the Ming.[3] The Yüan military system was said to have been abolished and a new one created in consequence of a memorial presented in 1368 by the scholar Liu Chi, then a vice censor-in-chief.[4] These statements were cited by Wu Han in 1938 without explicit disagreement.[5] But this account is probably not correct. The guard system had already been established within Chu Yüan-chang's regime at Nanking before he became the founding emperor of the Ming dynasty and during the period of his nominal subordination to the short-lived state of Sung that was controlled by the White Lotus Society. Moreover, the *Ming Shih-lu* (True records of the Ming dynasty) does not record any such memorial by Liu Chi. On the contrary, it gives the main credit for the Ming governmental institutions to Chang Ch'ang, a former minister of revenue in the Yüan government, who defected to Chu Yüan-chang and served him until 1367, when Chang was executed for treason.[6] This points to the possibility of a high degree of institutional continuity from Yüan to Ming. Moreover, as Henry Serruys has already observed, the Ming guard system may have been a particularly important instance of Mongol influence in China *via* the Yüan military system, not only in its grouping by multiples of ten, but in its reliance upon a separate registration category of military service families and a hereditary officer class.[7] Others have pointed out continuity in the use by the two dynasties of military population registers,[8] in the use of colony-fields (t'un-t'ien) to support the military establishment,[9] and in the Censorate.[10]

It has also been noted that the wei-so system in some important respects resembled the fu-ping of the Western Wei, Sui, and early T'ang periods. In both cases, the units were composed of conscripts who were expected to divide their time between military service and productive labor and were rotated to interior and frontier garrisons that made use of t'un-t'ien. I do not intend here to dispose of the possibility that the military institutions common to the Yüan and Ming may have been influenced by knowledge of the T'ang system, although it has been suggested that these may be an instance of parallelism rather than a reflection of influence.[11] Rather, I shall deal with the question of the continuity of Yüan and Ming institutions and suggest some implications for the social history of the period that may be found in such continuity.

While the successive Ch'i-tan, Nü-chen, and Mongol conquerors in China were, in varying degree, influenced by the culture of their subjects, some Chinese institutions appear to have been reshaped in the direction of the culture and social norms of the conquerors. This was especially true in military organization. The invaders arrived in China organized as armies, and those of them who remained generally lived in military communities surrounded by the subject population. While the civil administrations of the defeated states were partially, and in the case of the Southern Sung largely, left intact, their military establishments were supplanted by those of the invaders and their native auxiliaries. Serruys believes that the privileged status of the Mongol elite during the Yüan period not only encouraged Mongols to retain their own culture, but caused some imitation of Mongol culture by Chinese subjects.[12] Supposing this to have been true, it follows that the Mongol military communities must have been reservoirs of Mongol culture in China. If much of the Yüan military system was later adopted by the Ming, one should expect to find here evidence of relatively strong alien influence.

EVOLUTION OF THE MONGOL
MILITARY SYSTEM

The origins of certain non-Chinese features of the Yüan military system may be found in the steppes, where Chinggis Khan exploited changes taking place in Mongol society in order to transform the existing hierarchy of clans into a nomadic feudalism. The attachment of warriors to a leader as his companions, not on the basis of clan relationships but as individual associates in military service, created the possibility of replacing the clans by a feudal hierarchy independent of clan ties and unified by the single authority of the khan.[13] After he was acclaimed khan, Chinggis standardized the designations of Mongol communities according to their size as permanently registered tens, hundreds, chiliads, and myriads.[14] Most of the units did not correspond to clan divisions, and their very creation and continuance undermined clan authority.[15] Each unit of a thousand or more with its people and its grazing and hunting rights constituted a fief,[16] which was conferred on a military companion.[17] The new units roughly formed a pyramid with the smallest grouped into units of the next larger kind, and so on. The whole structure was tied together by infeudation and subinfeudation of the new aristocrats (*noyan*, masters) by the khan and his princes down at least to the chiliarch.[18] Although the *noyan* were subject to promotion, demotion, or dismissal, their fiefs normally passed by inheritance from father to son. This means that even before their conquest of North China they had adopted the patrilineal type of inherited privilege that distinguished the Nü-chen and Mongols from the Ch'i-tan, who used collectively held clan privilege (Chinese *shih-hsüan*, hereditary selection) in their Liao state.[19]

The institution of the khan's personal guard (*kesig*, Chinese *ch'ieh-hsieh*) added weight to the imperial authority. This elite corps was drawn from the families of the *noyan*, who also ruled the myriads.[20]

Under this system of control, there were two groups of aristocracy: the great lords or enfeoffed princes on one hand, and on the other the *noyan,* who were the myriarchs, chiliarchs, and sometimes centurions. Subject to the aristocracy were the ordinary soldiers, who were bound on pain of death to the service of the chiliarchs under whom they were registered. Farther down the scale were plebeians who were attached to the Mongol communities often as the result of defeat in war. The lowest class was that of slaves, which comprised domestic slaves and artisans, and farmers among conquered sedentary peoples.[21]

The expansion of the Mongol empire west and south resulted in the settlement of many Mongol communities among much more numerous sedentary populations, especially in China. After the Mongols had conquered the Nü-chen Chin state in 1234, part of the defeated population, together with its property, was divided among the leading Mongol aristocrats. The rest belonged directly to the khan.[22] Since, unlike other spoils of war, the North China farmers could not be transported to the steppe without rendering both them and their lands practically valueless, they had to be exploited in their own fields. This necessitated a migration of the Mongol communities into North China.

Although the Chin bureaucracy was not destroyed and the Chin law code was kept in force until 1271,[23] there was at first little integration of the Mongols with the bureaucracy. Even the collection of taxes was farmed out to Muslim merchant companies.[24] And after Kubilai as first emperor of the Yüan dynasty (r. 1260–94) integrated the Mongol and foreign elite with a greatly strengthened and still largely Chinese bureaucracy, the Yüan military system remained the chief institutional home of the alien elite and a reservoir of Mongol society and culture on Chinese soil. Elite units guarded the capital. These included the *kesig* and the many *wei* or guards, the first five of which—right, left, front, center, and rear—were established by Kubilai. These were still myriads; their designation as *wei* possibly was to mark their elite character. Other units, still called myriads *(wan-hu),* were assigned to garrison other cities. Most or all of the latter consisted of non-Mongol auxiliaries with Mongol and other non-Chinese officers.

Military prestige during the Yüan period must have been greatly fortified by the rough equivalence of elite status and the military vocation. Even in civil offices, the head officials *(daruhaci,* Chinese *ta-lu-hua-ch'ih*) were generally chosen from among the *noyan* of the guards and myriads.[25]

The formal arrangement of local military offices is fairly clear. Civil circuits *(lu)* were frequently garrisoned by myriads and counties *(hsien)* by chiliads.[26] Since there were 185 civil circuits and 1,127 counties,[27] however, it is clear that this pattern was not strictly observed. The myriads and chiliads were classed as superior, ordinary, or inferior according to their approximate troop strengths of 7,000, 5,000, or 3,000 and 700, 500, or 300, respectively.[28]

The highest central military agency was the Bureau of Military Affairs *(shu-mi yüan)*, which directed all units except the *kesig*, which was responsible only to the emperor. Between the Bureau of Military Affairs and the capital guards was the Chief Military Commission *(ta tu-tu fu)*.[29] Not a regular part of the military hierarchy, but occasionally functioning as additional levels of command between the Bureau of Military Affairs and the myriarchs were regional offices of various kinds, most of them temporary. Branch Secretariats *(hsing chung-shu sheng)* constituted a direct and, eventually, permanent extension of the authority and presence of the metropolitan Secretariat to between 11 and 15 areas of provincial scale.[30] Military as well as civil affairs were within their competence. In case of some emergency, the Bureau of Military Affairs might set up a branch bureau temporarily to bring its authority directly to the scene. A branch bureau *(hsing shu-mi yüan)* might in turn set up a subbranch bureau *(fen shu-mi yüan)*. Additional offices were established in pacification circuits *(hsüan-wei tao)* to communicate between the Branch Secretariats and the lower offices, civil and military. When local troops had to be used, the pacification circuit offices doubled as (local) military commands *(yüan-shuai fu)*.[31] Routine administration of the military system was overseen by the Ministry of War *(ping-pu)*.[32] The Censorate *(yü-shih t'ai)* with its branch offices *(hsing yü-shih t'ai)* and its 22 circuit *(tao)* offices *(su-cheng lien-fang ssu)* investigated abuses in the military as in the civil sphere.[33]

The Yüan military communities were of diverse ethnic background. Some, the *kesig* and probably all the guards, were predominantly Mongol. Some or all of the myriads garrisoning the northern civil circuits may have been elements of the *T'an-ma-ch'ih* army of Ch'i-tan, Nü-chen, and Chinese troops who served Chinggis and Ogodei against the Chin state.[34] The southern circuits were garrisoned by *wan-hu* of the Han army. "Han" in this context does not mean Chinese but denotes the whole population of the old Chin state, including Ch'i-tan, Nü-chen, Chinese, and Koreans. The Han army conscripted from this population, therefore, was also of mixed origins.[35] The Han army in the south was supplemented by myriads of the "newly submitted army." These were soldiers of the Southern Sung dynasty who had surrendered to the Yüan and whose families were now permanently enrolled as liable for military service. Control of the Mongol military communities generally remained in the families of the *noyan*. When an officer was removed from his hereditary post to serve in some other office, the next family member in line would take his place.[36] State control of non-Mongol units was guarded by the presence in each myriad and chiliad of a *ta-lu-hua-ch'ih* who was usually a Mongol. Even centuries of the larger type were commanded jointly by a Mongol and another non-Chinese.[37]

The military communities of soldiers and their own households were supported by colony-fields *(t'un-t'ien)*. These were not new in China, having been used mainly, though not exclusively, in frontier defense at least since the Former Han era. They were used on a larger and increasing scale in the interior of China by the Ch'i-tan, Nü-chen, and Mongol conquerors. The intruders from the north had to garrison China in order to exploit their conquest, and they were mostly unused to agriculture. The Nü-chen chiliads and centuries that occupied the north of China during the Chin period were provided with large and continuous blocks of land at the rate of 40 *mou* per adult male. The Mongols, especially in the reign of Kubilai, further increased the number and total area of the agricultural colonies.[38] In 1308 there were more than 120 of them, with a total area of 172,000 *ch'ing*.[39] This provided at least part of the support required for an establishment of about 720,000 soldiers.[40]

The guards (*wei*) of the capital army established and administered their own colonies through colony-field chiliad offices (*t'un-t'ien ch'ien-hu so*). Where the labor came from that was used in the fields is not always clear, but for at least some units it was at first supplied entirely by Han army and "newly submitted army" soldiers. For each soldier-farmer about 50 *mou* of land were provided.⁴¹ The myriads and chiliads that garrisoned places outside the capital region were not intended to control their own colony-fields. Instead, the Branch Secretariats organized agricultural colonies of Chinese military and civilian households, and these provided food for the military communities. But they were under the direct control of local civil offices, usually colony-field myriad offices *(t'un-t'ien wan-hu fu)* established in the civil circuits.⁴² In practice, some additional labor was furnished by the regular soldiers' household members.⁴³ Beginning in 1304, even the *wei* were ordered to use half their soldiers in the fields.⁴⁴

The largely alien aristocracy's continued enjoyment of its privileged status in China depended on the military communities. If these became ineffective, or lost their identity with the conquest dynasty, the Yüan regime would either lose much of its alien and aristocratic character, becoming virtually Chinese, or would risk being overthrown. The grant of colony-fields to these communities at first enabled the foreign soldiers to avoid becoming full- or part-time farmers without, at the same time, becoming a charge on the state tax revenues. This was not enough, however, to ensure their survival. Several administrative measures were adopted to separate them from the rest of the population and keep them up to strength.

One such measure was the use of hereditary population registers to freeze communal and occupational status. The Yüan subject's privileges and obligations vis-à-vis the state depended upon his religion, his ethnic or geographic origin, and his occupation. The Yüan census erected a permanent administrative obstacle to diffusion of the alien elite into the mass of the subject population and provided an extremely detailed inventory of skills in order that these might be forever placed at the service of the state. The categories by origin were: Mongols *(Meng-ku)*, classified peoples *(Se-mu jen)* who were mainly central and west Asians, *Han-jen,* who were descendant of the Chin state and its subjects, and *Nan-jen,* people indigenous to the domain of the Southern Sung.⁴⁵ Categories by occupation cut across those by origin. Originally all able-bodied Mongol men were soldiers registered in the chiliads. In China, Mongol soldiers' households were entered on the military registers and required to furnish soldiers from among their men in the proportion of one to two or one to three.[46] The Han army was permanently registered, and the Han military households were subject to variable demands for conscripts.[47] Finally, the "newly submitted army" was entered on the military rolls in 1290.[48] By origin, the descendants of the *T'an-ma-ch'ih* soldiers and *Han* soldiers were registered as *Han-jen* and the "newly submitted army" as *Nan-jen*.[49] Except for the southern auxiliaries, therefore, the military communities were distinguished from the rest of the population by registration according to origin and according to occupation. Furthermore, in order to make certain that the military communities reproduced themselves, nature was assisted by a law of 1286 requiring local officials to see to it that the men of military households were married.[50]

Within the military communities there was a clear social division between the officers and the ordinary soldiers, even in units that were homogeneous in point of origin. Military offices were normally hereditary, and the office-holding families were the old aristocracy of the steppe regime supplemented by later additions.[51] All officers of the *kesig* during most of the Yüan era and most officers of the *wei* were Mongols.[52] The officers of the myriads were mainly non-Chinese. Nearly all the myriarch *ta-lu-hua-ch'ih* were Mongols. A few were "classified people," but Chinese were extremely rare. Most of the lower-ranking officers were "classified people." [53] The proportion of Chinese officers was held down by a rule that when a Chinese officer was promoted to a higher office he should be replaced by someone not of his own family.[54] Where the soldiers were Chinese, the social gap was further widened by legal discrimination on the basis of origin. A law of 1285 required that arms of inferior quality be destroyed, those of ordinary quality be issued locally to Mongols only, and those of superior quality be placed in storage under the control of provincial officials or non-Chinese local officials.[55] Mistrust on the part of the alien elite is also reflected in a law of 1290 forbidding any Chinese to have access to the military registers, which were considered to be highly secret.[56] Separate community-registration units *(she)* were established for Mongols lest this institution result in a mixing of Mongols and Chinese.[57]

The relation between the military aristocracy and ordinary soldiers was also influenced by the sedentary agricultural milieu of the military communities. Officers often became landowners either by gifts of land from the state or by expropriation of private or public land.[58] A law forbidding officers to use their soldiers or state-owned oxen on their own estates reflects this state of affairs.[59] A report of 1277 paints a picture of unrestrained exploitation of soldiers and their families by the officers.[60] The original feudal tie binding the ordinary Mongol soldier to his chiliad was thus eroded or perhaps wholly destroyed, and desertions occurred on a large scale.[61] Similar trouble with the Han soldiers is reflected in an order of 1281 that Han soldiers who ran away were to be executed and their families wiped out.[62]

The destruction of the original feudal solidarity of the military communities of the Mongols and of the auxiliaries contributed to popular unrest and undermined the ability of the Yüan to cope with widespread revolt during the 1350s. As early as 1330 it was found necessary to supplement the regular conscription by hiring soldiers.[63] When the final wave of rebellions got under way mainly under messianic leaders of the White Lotus Society, such defense as the dynasty had in the Huai and Yangtze valleys was provided largely by hastily recruited militia (*i-ping*).[64] The main Yüan forces, the *wei*, were little used against the rebels until it was much too late, because of political rivalries among the Mongol aristocrats in the North.

EVOLUTION OF THE MING MILITARY SYSTEM

The Ming military system and, indeed, the entire Ming regime had its specific origin in a military office established in 1352 in Hao-chou, on the south bank of the Huai, by followers of the White Lotus Society. The office was a *yüan-shuai fu*, which as we saw in the Yüan system was a temporary headquarters within a *hsüan-wei ssu*. Hao-chou itself was within the jurisdiction of a *fen yüan-shuai fu* established by the Yüan in 1352 at An-feng lu to direct the suppression of the rebels.[65] The chief *yüan-shuai* at Hao-chou, striving as *primus inter pares* to assert his authority over four unruly fellow *yüan-shuai*, was Kuo Tzu-hsing. In 1352 Chu Yüan-chang entered his service as a soldier and, at almost the same time, entered his household as the husband of his adopted daughter, surnamed Ma.

The Ming regime in the year of its imperial fulfillment, 1368, already had behind it a history of 16 years, during which time its institutional structure had gradually evolved. Chu Yüan-chang's personal prospects were markedly advanced by the death of his father-in-law in 1355, less than four years after the start of the uprising at Hao-chou. Chu then disregarded the principle of hereditary office, which he later built into his own military system, and defied the authority of the White Lotus Society leaders in order to elbow aside Kuo's son and heir. He shortly led a force across the Yangtze, took T'ai-p'ing, usurped full title to his brother-in-law's military patrimony, and set up his headquarters in the newly fallen city. From this time until 1363 he represented himself as an official of Sung despite his effective independence. In that year he reduced the Sung pretender Han Lin-erh to the role of a mere figurehead, and he may have been responsible for Han's death in 1366.

The history of the creation of the Ming military system may be divided into two main stages. During the first stage, or until the third month of 1364, the typical Sung local military administrative unit was the *yüan-shuai fu*. These offices were then replaced in the second stage by *wei*, similar to those of the main army of the Yüan. The pattern of the first period was established at T'ai-p'ing in 1355. The T'ai-p'ing civil circuit *(lu)* was dissolved and a prefecture *(fu)* created in its place. Alongside the prefectural civil office, a local military command *(yüan-shuai fu)* was installed in the same city with Chu Yüan-chang as its head.[66] This process was repeated again and again during the next eight years. The reason for the liquidation of the Yüan civil circuits is not clear. Perhaps it was felt that officials of this intermediate level were too closely associated with the central government and that their severance from it might be emphasized in this way. The reasons for setting up the *yüan-shuai fu* seem clear enough. This simply followed Yüan precedent in creating temporary local commands where fighting was expected or in progress. Moreover, Chu generally tried to preserve local civil administration intact, removing only unpopular or untrustworthy officials, whereas the *yüan-shuai* officers were usually chosen from among his own followers rather than from among the officers of the defeated garrison. The local military officials, therefore, could be relied on to guard against any attack from without or treachery within.

From the third to the sixth month of 1356 Chu's forces captured three more seats of civil circuits: Chin-ling (Nanking), Chen-kiang, and Kuang-te. In each of these he followed the same procedure as at T'ai-p'ing, except that the new military headquarters at Nanking was of higher rank, a *ta* (superior) *yüan-shuai fu.* In the sixth month, he also established a Branch Bureau of Military Affairs at T'ai-p'ing (nominally an extension of the Bureau of Military Affairs established in the White Lotus Society's Sung government).[67] In the seventh month Chu assumed the title Duke of Wu and in his Nanking metropolis organized his regime as the Kiangnan Branch Secretariat of the Ta Sung government. Under its military aspect, his new government included a Kiangnan Branch Bureau of Military Affairs and a "commandery before the tent in charge of the personal guard" *(chang-ch'ien tsung-chih ch'in-ping tu chih-hui shih ssu).*[68] He also established five *yüan-shuai fu* for the right, left, front, center, and rear "wings" (*i*), which suggests a five-fold division of his main army. Still another office, the *ping-ma chih-hui (shih) ssu,* was charged with ferreting out seditious activity. This office was identical in name with one long considered to be the Yüan antecedent of the notorious secret-service-like Embroidered-uniform Guard (*Chin-i wei*) of Ming times.[69] The arrangement of Chu's central military offices remained unchanged until 1361 except for the addition in the twelfth month, 1358, of a capital force called the "corps for defense of the center" *(yü-chung chün),* which was composed of men selected from wealthy families of Wu-chou.[70]

In the third month of 1361 Chu announced the reorganization of his Branch Bureau of Military Affairs into a Chief Military Commission *(ta tu-tu fu).* The effect of this change was to replace the branch bureau in its function of directing all forces, capital and outer, with an office which in the Yüan system, under the identical name, had regulated only the *wei* (other than the *kesig*). This pointed toward the later universalization of the *wei* as the standard unit of all Ming forces. The organization of the Chief Military Commission took place over a considerable period of time, however. A full complement of offices was not specified until the third month of 1364.[71] Many officials of the superseded branch bureau, meanwhile, had continued to use their old official titles.

The number of local military offices had grown during the same period. By 1364 at least 22 yüan-shuai fu had been created, including the five at the capital controlling the five wings of the main army. Of the remaining 17, three were associated with subprefectures (chou) and the rest with former civil circuits that had been converted to prefectures. To facilitate control of the yüan-shuai fu, Chu had opened five subbranch bureaus (fen shu-mi yüan).[72]

The second stage in the organization of the Ming military system was reached early in 1364. A crushing victory over the rival state of Han during the fall of 1363 ended the main threat to Chu's state and occasioned his elevation to the rank of prince. His regime now took on many of the attributes of imperial sovereignty, despite the fact that he continued to use the Ta Sung calendar until 1367. The Branch Secretariat became a full Secretariat, and offices were established that were proper only to an imperial government. In the third month of 1364, as we have noted, he filled out the offices of the Chief Military Commission. At the same time Chu reorganized the capital army in 17 personal-army guards (ch'in-chün wei), corresponding to the wei of the Yüan metropolitan forces. Further, he ordered the conversion of all the local yüan-shuai fu into wei, thereby progressing from a manifestly temporary kind of office to a permanent type. All the wei, metropolitan and other, were now directly subordinate to the Chief Military Commission.[73] One difficulty in carrying out this reorganization soon became apparent. Many of Chu's officers had defected from the Yüan on the promise that they would be allowed to retain their original ranks. On the plea that continued adherence to this promise would cause intolerable confusion, these officers were given ranks in the new wei system appropriate to the sizes of forces under their command.[74] Although this reorganization was probably about completed by the end of 1364, new yüan-shuai fu were occasionally created for newly occupied places after this time.[75]

Consistently with the replacement of the Bureau of Military Affairs by the Chief Military Commission in the capital, the provincial-level branch bureaus were replaced first by Branch Military Commissions *(hsing tu-tu fu)* and then by Regional Military Commissions *(tu wei chih-hui shih ssu,* abbreviated in 1375 to *tu chih-hui shih ssu).*[76]

ELEMENTS OF CONTINUITY FROM
YÜAN TO MING

The formal arrangement of military offices with which Chu began his imperial reign was, as we have seen, clearly derived from that of the Yüan, although much simplified. The Yüan had had two basic types of local military administration, the ordinary *wan-hu fu* in the circuits and the *wei* of the metropolitan elite force. The Ming adopted only the *wei,* which were then used both in the capital area and in the outer prefectures. The Chief Military Commission now commanded all imperial forces except for the personal troops *(ch'in chün)* which, like the Mongol *kesig,* were the emperor's own. The Mongol practice of separating command of forces actually guarding and fighting from the everyday management of the military communities was continued by the Ming, which replaced the now-vanished *yüan-shuai* with regional commanders *(tsung-ping kuan)* or grand defenders *(chen-shou).*[77]

That the Yüan models were closely followed in the creation of corresponding Ming offices can be seen by comparing Chu Yüan-chang's *ta tu-tu fu* of 1364[78] and 1367[79] with that of the Yüan,[80] or the Ming *wei*[81] with that of the Yüan.[82] The principal differences in the case of the *wei* were that the Ming guard commander was a *chih-hui shih* whereas his Yüan counterpart had been a *tu chih-hui shih* (the title of a Ming regional military commissioner) and that the Ming *wei* after 1367 had five instead of ten chiliads.[83] The units of 100, 1,000, and 10,000 had been in use among Chu's forces from the beginning, as is shown by the career of one of his officers who was successively a centurion *(po-hu),* a chiliarch *(ch'ien-hu),* and a myri-arch *(wan-hu)* during the period 1352–54.[84] The reduction of the *wei* to five chiliads, however, conformed to the strength of an ordinary Yüan myriad which, despite its name, was expected to maintain only 5,000 soldiers.[85] This reduced the *wei* to a size appropriate to replace the myriads in the prefectures.

The use of colony-fields (*t'un-t'ien*) by Chu Yüan-chang lagged behind his creation of military offices, although he made it clear very early that he thought them important. When he organized his Kiangnan Branch Secretariat in 1356, it included an office called *ying-t'ien ssu*, which was to concern itself with the promotion of agriculture.[86] K'ang Mao-ts'ai, a trusted military officer, was appointed in 1358 to head this office.[87] In the same year another officer had already achieved self-sufficiency in food for his five thousand men by creating colony-fields.[88] Apparently other commanders were expected to do the same, but in the second month of 1363 Chu reproached his officers with having failed whereas K'ang Mao-ts'ai, on land that was no better than theirs, had produced on his colony-fields 15,000 *tan* for his troop rations and still had a surplus of 7,000 *tan*. He then bluntly ordered them in season to put their soldiers to work on the land.[89] Devastated areas in the middle Yangtze region were restored to production as military colony-fields in 1365.[90] All *wei* were subsequently required to establish colony-fields, but throughout the first Ming reign laggard units were still striving to comply.[91]

In their uses of colony-fields, the Ming *wei* conformed roughly to the practice of the Yüan *wei*. The colony-fields were not under civil management as had been the case for the Yüan *wan-hu fu*, but were managed internally by the military units themselves. This was consistent with Chu's intention to reform the Yüan system. He insisted that the military colony-fields were intended to relieve the civil population of the burden of supplying the army. Whereas the Yüan *wei* had been ordered to put half their soldiers in farming, the Ming regulations called for a proportion of about seven tenths. Since the average land allotment was still fifty *mou* per soldier-farmer, as in the Yüan *wei*, the area in colony-fields had to be greatly expanded. Figures in the *Ta-Ming Hui-tien* (Collected statutes of the Ming dynasty) for *t'un-t'ien* total 893,188 *ch'ing* (*mou* were excluded from the addition) for the "original quota" (1368?) and 2,138,407 *ch'ing* for the "present quota" (Wan-li reign, 1573–1620). [92] Another difference was the more complete integration of the agricultural function with the military. Whereas the Yüan *wei* had specialized *t'un-t'ien* chiliarchs,[93] the Ming chiliarchs were responsible for both functions.

Continuity with the Yüan can also be shown in the use of population registers to separate and control a hereditary military class. Not only was the method similar in principle, but households on the Yüan military registers were retained in that category as far as possible by Chu Yüan-chang. In an instruction of 1365 he declared that persons submitting to him who had once been soldiers would continue to be used in that capacity. Any who had been ordinary civilians should present themselves to the civil authorities for peaceful employment in agriculture.[94] A similar order was issued in 1370.[95] In 1368, moreover, Chu ordered military officers to search out Yüan census registers and submit them for use in the capital.[96]

As it evolved during a decade of experimentation, the Ming census was much simpler than that of Yüan. The communal categories were dropped and the occupational categories had been reduced to three main ones: ordinary civilians *(min)*, soldiers *(chün)*, and artisans *(chiang)*. Still, however, the form of each household's obligatory service to the state was determined by its permanent census category.[97]

This brings us to the most striking and significant element of continuity with the Yüan regime. In the context of a Chinese society that had, in the Sung era, in selecting officials given strong emphasis to the principle of merit as proven in open competitive examinations, the Mongols' practice of a hereditary aristocracy of office-holders was distinctly anomalous. This practice was most uniform in the military system; civil-service heirs were given offices of lower rank,[98] and civil service examinations were temporarily revived. Chu Yüan-chang restored the examinations and restricted hereditary privilege in civil offices, but he continued Yüan practice in making the management of the military communities hereditary in the families of the officers. He expressed dissatisfaction with the way in which the examination system, even in civil administration, had worked prior to the Mongol conquest and served notice of his intention to take a direct hand in its functioning.[99] Moreover, he filled most of the highest civil offices of the central government with his new military aristocrats.[100]

Military offices were classed as "hereditary" or "circulating." The former included the commander, vice-commander, and assistant commander of the *wei*, chiliarch and assistant chiliarch, military judges in the *wei* and chiliads, and centurions with substantive or acting appointments.[101] Capital and provincial offices were "circulating."

These, however, were appointed from the ranks of the hereditary officers, so that the military officers collectively were a self-perpetuating elite.

We have seen that the Ming military officers inherited from their Yüan counterparts a clearly defined official function as hereditary managers of the military communities. It also seems that the Yüan military aristocrats had become widely unpopular because of the ways in which they abused their authority at the expense of the civil population and because of their failure to control their soldiers. Along with his attempts to reform the military system by making it responsible to the state and economically self-sustaining, Chu tried to preserve the elite status of his officers. The officers were his old comrades-in-arms, often his fellow townsmen, and they shared with him in building the new regime. As long as there were great disorders, Chu's relatively well-disciplined forces could stake a claim to public support as the best hope for a return to peace. With internal peace largely restored and the civil administration resuming its usual primacy in day-to-day government, the prestige of the military was again threatened.

One element of prestige in the Chinese context was education. Even the Yüan *wei* maintained Mongolian and Chinese teaching officials. During the first Ming reign, at least some of the guards were provided with classical academies *(ju-hsüeh)* to train the officers' sons and younger brothers.[102] Presumably civil academies were used where none was provided in the guard. When in 1377 the Ministry of Rites proposed the establishment of specialized military academies and the use of a military examination system, Chu rejected the idea and insisted on the principle, honored in antiquity, that education was indivisible, providing everything that was proper for all.[103] His apprehension was well founded, because the military academies that were established some sixty years later offered a watered-down literary curriculum, which must have reacted badly upon the status of military officers. The training of officers was reinforced by severe laws that prohibited unbecoming behavior. A law of 1390 provided that officers or soldiers who studied singing would have the tips of their tongues cut off, those who played chess would lose their hands, those who played soccer would lose their feet, and those who engaged in trade would be banished to the frontiers.[104] The status of military officers was also supported by their virtual monopoly of the hereditary titles of nobility (62 of 64) that were awarded with annual stipends during the first reign.[105] Chu's partiality may also be reflected in the provision that military officers should have precedence over their civil colleagues in the performance of local sacrifices. Later in his reign, however, this practice was dropped as ritually improper.[106]

As in Yüan there was, moreover, in Ming a deep division between the military elite and the ordinary soldiers. While the officers were well rewarded, their soldiers were often disaffected. Between 1367 and 1380 nearly 48,000 desertions were recorded. To check this dissipation of imperial power, the census procedures relating to families on the military register were greatly elaborated.[107]

What was the origin of this new military elite? Of the 62 officers who were given hereditary titles of nobility, 45 were old soldiers who had served Chu since before 1360.[108] The veterans, whom he favored in granting appointments and titles, were nearly all uneducated men of the Kiang-Huai region of his birth and early career. They were both a heavily regional group and, by education, a group not normally qualified for public office.[109] The proportion of Mongols among them is difficult to determine because many may at this time have chosen expediently to adopt Chinese names. Serruys believes that, at least after 1368, the number may have been considerable.[110]

RECAPITULATION

The origin of the Ming guard system may be briefly recapitulated. The disintegrating clan society of the steppes was replaced by a feudal hierarchy of peoples organized in hundreds, chiliads, and myriads. These were adapted to Chinese conditions by the adoption of certain Chinese institutions and techniques. The now-sedentary military communities of the Mongol and allied conquerors were supported throughout China by colony-fields, which were already a Chinese institution and had been spread throughout the North China Plain by the Nü-chen Chin dynasty. The military communities and their associated *t'un-t'ien* were subjected to a Chinese-style code of law that derived its authority from a khan who ruled in China as a Chinese

emperor. The old registers of the Mongol communities were supplanted by a Chinese-style, but uniquely complicated, census machinery, and the management of the communities was invaded by
censorial and administrative agencies of the central government and
its regional extensions. What remained of the original patrimony of
the *noyan* was clearly no longer a feudal fief. The aristocracy had
become, in effect, a gentry whose status was confirmed by inherited
privileges. Chu Yüan-chang, in creating the Ming regime, fashioned
his military system after the elite *wei* of Yüan and created a new
military elite of hereditary office- and title-holders from among his
rude soldier companions. At the same time, however, he made clear
his intention to reform the system by subjecting it to effective state
control, as the Yüan had tried but failed to do.

Why did Chu Yüan-chang perpetuate the essentially non-Chinese
institution of a hereditary elite of military officers? Part of the answer
may be found in the fact that Chu, originally within the rebel Sung
regime and, later, on his own, built his government out of materials
already provided by the old regime, and thereby minimized the dis-
ruption of the society he sought to rule. Moreover, he was intimately
advised by ex-officials of the Yüan who, under the pressure of events
during the rebellion, must have found it necessary to stick fairly close
to the prescriptions they knew from experience. It also seems possible
that Chu Yüan-chang and some of his followers were favorably impressed by the Yüan military organization as a means of supporting
their new regime.[111]

JUNG-PANG LO 明 *Policy Formulation*

and Decision-Making on Issues Respecting

Peace and War

DECISION-MAKERS AND THE SCOPE OF THEIR POWERS

It is generally recognized that the formulation of state policies and the making of decisions are among the functions and responsibilities of any government. But the processes by which state policies are formed and decisions on courses of action are adopted, the factors which determine the choice of options, and the roles and competences of the various men who make the decisions still remain to be fully analyzed. One line of approach which has attracted scholarly attention in the field of political science during the past decade is that of the decision-making studies which apply the techniques and methodology of sociology and social psychology to the study of political dynamics.[1]

In the behavioral approach, inquiry is focused on the personalities and the experience, the social and economic status, and the states of mind of the "decision-makers"—that is, those public officials who bear responsibility for forming policies of state and making crucial decisions. "The analysis of international politics," wrote Richard C. Snyder, "should be centered, in part, in the behavior of those whose action is the action of the state, namely, the decision-makers."[2] Next, consideration is given to the impersonal forces which influence the action and the conduct of the decision-makers, e.g., historical movements, ideology, rules and precedents, government systems, sources of information, and public opinion. Decisions are the product of the interaction involved in the relations of the leaders and the interplay of the external forces upon them.

"The decision-making approach to the study of politics," declares

Professor Snyder, "clearly belongs to the category of dynamic, as distinct from static, analysis. . . . Relatively speaking, dynamic analysis is process analysis. By process is meant here, briefly, time plus change —change in relationships and conditions. Process analysis concerns a sequence of events, i.e. behavioral events."[3] It stands in contrast to structural or static analysis, which treats hierarchical relationships.

The dynamic approach is particularly apposite to the study of Chinese political institutions. The Chinese have a penchant for organizational schemes of government, from the ancient *Chou-li* (Rites of the Chou dynasty) down to the modern *Organic Law of the Central People's Government*, which assign titles, functions, and duties to various officials. But the functions and duties of many officials have often existed only on paper, and others have changed markedly during the passage of time and under the pressure of circumstances. Moreover, in the Chinese tradition, authority has not been equated with power, nor position with rank.

Political scientists, deploring the lack of useful typologies in the analysis of foreign policy, define the task of decision-making studies to be the devising of conceptual formulas to reconstruct the situation confronting the decision-makers.[4] They criticize the historical approach as being concerned with the unique and anecdotal, diverting scholars from attempts to test theories.[5] But the lack of typologies cannot be laid at the door of Chinese writings on political history, which have been described as being too heavily inclined toward typology. Since in China history is considered to be not only a record of change but also an agent of change, the characters, behavior, and acts of public men are often stereotyped to conform with the subjective judgment of the writers, to serve as object lessons for posterity. A strong aggressive emperor may be typed as a tyrant,[6] and his forward or positive foreign policy may be categorized as engaging in "exhaustive wars in pursuit of military glory" (*ch'iung-ping tu-wu*).

Thus rulers and their policies were arbitrarily typed and labeled, and thus the titles, ranks, positions, and duties of government leaders, which may have been envisaged or may have been in effect at one time but not at another, were prescribed, giving the impression that the power and authority assigned to these leaders were permanently concomitant with their ranks and positions. The acceptance of some of the selected types of rulers as representative and the extemporaneous assignment of authority as permanent are the pitfalls of many studies of China's political system of the past. And when writers, using a modicum of Chinese sources, approach the studies from the viewpoint of Marxist dialectics, garnishing them with interpretations of Max Weber, and coloring them with the antimonarchical emotion of recent years, the result is *chinoiserie* rather than an accurate portrayal of China's social and political institutions.

One example may be found in the exposition of the theory of oriental despotism, which attributes unlimited powers to rulers. As K. A. Wittfogel defines absolutism, "A government is absolutist when its rule is not effectively checked by non-government forces. The ruler of an absolutist regime is an autocrat when his decisions are not effectively checked by intra-governmental forces. The absolutist regimes of hydraulic societies are usually headed by a single individual in whose person is concentrated all the power over major decisions." [7] Without outside control and internal balance, he continues, there develops a cumulative tendency of unchecked power, which permits the holder of the strongest position to expand his authority. His power is not negated by his delegation of administrative duties to assistants or by his leaning for advice on trusted and carefully selected officials; nor does it cease to be absolutist "because the center of decision-making temporarily shifts to persons or groups below the ruler." [8]

Wittfogel's main interest is China, and in China, to be sure, there were monarchs who concentrated all decision-making powers in themselves and by the force of their personalities were able to overawe their ministers. But to write about these instances as though they were the norm conjures up in the mind of casual readers a fantasm of a government by ukase; of potentates who could plunge the empire into war on a whim; of obsequious, groveling functionaries who carried out their masters' commands without question; and of a people cowering under the knout and milked by corrupt officials. This is a warped picture, a caricature, no less, of China's political institutions of the past. A deeper probe beneath the prescribed functions and the high-sounding titles and an examination of the kaleidoscopic changes in the actual working of government institutions in China would reveal that there was a wide variation of power—actual power, that is, not formal power—held by the emperors and a constant shift of the center of decision-making.

In accordance with the ancient and unquestioned Chinese doctrine that political stability derives from the elevation of one man to be head of state,[9] the Chinese emperor traditionally assumed supreme authority over state affairs.[10] But it should certainly not be thought that the power of the emperor was wholly unbalanced by other constitutional agencies and that his dictates were unchallenged. The actions of the emperor were restricted by various conventions and traditions,[11] by public opinion and the concept of *li* (propriety) serving as a kind of unwritten constitution,[12] by the guidance of his close relatives, and by the advice and warnings of his ministers. But the main counterpoise to the weight of imperial authority was the bureaucracy.

In early times the edicts of the emperor on state policy were subject to review by the chief councilor (*ch'eng-hsiang*) or prime minister (*tsai-hsiang*) and the remonstrating officials (*chien-kuan*) who, if necessary, could return them for reconsideration. This practice, known as *feng-po* (sealed dissent), constituted a modified form of veto. The officials of the bureaucracy, chancellors and remonstrators alike, not only had responsibility for advising and counseling the emperor as regards planning and policy formulation, but also countermanded imperial decrees which they considered not in the best interest of the empire.[13] Admittedly, the system was rudimentary, but in combination with other safeguards it served in some measure to keep the authority of the emperor within reasonable bounds. Nor were the officials servile minions. There were among them upright men of principles and responsibility, men who were proud of the tradition and dignity of their office, men of independent views who did not hesitate to express them freely and boldly, and men with the interest of the state and of the people at heart who were not afraid to defy the will of tyrannical rulers. The relinquishment of administrative duties by many emperors left the chief councilor the *de facto* head of government and often the center of law-making and decision-making machinery.

While the chief councilor and his subordinate agencies handled routine matters of government, the formulation of policy and the making of decisions on major questions of war and state (*chün kuo ta-shih*) required the careful deliberation and exchange of views of many men. There were memorials which poured into the capital from officials and commoners in the empire, there were proposals by ministers in the capital, there were meetings at ministerial level and in the court, and from this range of opinion a consensus was reached. In the Han period, and possibly in later times, the decisions were based on majority vote, which the emperor generally, though not always, followed.[14] In the T'ang period the teamwork of the Three Departments—the Secretariat (*chung-shu sheng*) for the collation of proposals, planning, and the initiation of a course of action; the Chancellery (*men-hsia sheng*) for policy review and the rejection of any improper line of action; and the Department of State Affairs (*shang-shu sheng*) for the execution of policy—and joint sessions of the officers of the Three Departments in the Hall of State Affairs (*cheng-shih t'ang*) combined to check abuses of imperial authority and also to widen the exercise of decision-making powers.[15]

Power—actual power—was not the monopoly of one political group. It seesawed between the imperial faction and the bureaucratic faction, fluctuating with the personalities of the political leaders. One noticeable phenomenon in Chinese history was the periodic slide of power centers from the side of the emperor to the side of the bureaucracy. The chief councilors, the supervising secretaries (*chi-shih-chung*), the officials of the Three Departments, and even officials of the Bureau of Military Affairs (*shu-mi yüan*) of late T'ang and Sung times—all were originally members of the emperor's personal staff, but they eventually evolved into powerful spokesmen of the bureaucracy. Periodically, too, there were diminutions of imperial power. In early Sung, in an attempt to halt the gravitation of power to the bureaucracy at the expense of the imperial court, the emperors assumed all decision-making power. The chief councilor, who shared with the emperor the responsibility of government, was reduced to the function of an executive secretary. The Chancellery, which reviewed decisions, was abolished, although remonstrating officials such as supervising secretaries were retained. But gradually, under less executive-minded emperors, the chief councilors came back to their former status.

At the beginning of the Ming period the founding emperor, T'ai-tsu (1368–98), perpetuated the system of chief councilors. Then in 1380, to assert imperial power and to curb the influence of the bureaucracy, he abolished the office of the chief councilor and the Secretariat and assumed direct control over the six ministries, which now constituted the executive branch of the government. He had secretaries from the Hanlin Academy to assist him in clerical work but "at the time, the emporor personally held the reins of power, and the secretaries seldom participated in deliberations or decisions." [16]

In the formulation of his policies, T'ai-tsu conscientiously sought the views of many men: he listened to the advice of his ministers and, in the manner of dictators who regard themselves as the champions of the people, he made a show of seeking popular opinion. But final judgment on the course of action to adopt was reserved for himself.

Ch'eng-tsu (1402–24) initiated the practice of asking a few Hanlin grand secretaries, including Yang Shih-ch'i and Yang Jung, to join him in confidential discussion of state affairs.[17] The responsibility of the grand secretaries increased during the succeeding reigns so that in the 1430s "all matters of state, important or not, were referred to Yang Shih-ch'i and the other grand secretaries for decision." [18] They became "*de facto* prime ministers" *(chen tsai-hsiang)*.[19] The later grand secretaries Hsia Yen and Yen Sung, who dominated the political scene during Shih-tsung's reign (1521–66), and Chang Chü-cheng early in Shen-tsung's era (1572–1620) were also spoken of as "*de facto* prime ministers." [20]

A reason for the shift of power from the imperial faction to the bureaucratic faction was abdication of power by the emperors themselves. Power, as Harold Lasswell defines it, is participation in the making of decisions.[21] During the minority of Ying-tsung (1435–49, 1457–64), decisions about state affairs were made by his grandmother, the empress dowager, in consultation with the ministers Yang Shih-ch'i, Chang Fu, and others, but the intimate meetings of the emperor with his grand secretaries were abolished.[22] Several attempts were made by the ministers to revive the custom. When Shih-tsung came to the throne in 1521, Hsia Yen, then a supervising secretary, submitted a long memorial in which he urged the emperor to be sure to consult his ministers. "After your daily court sessions, when your majesty retires to the Wen-hua Hall to read reports and memorials, you should summon the ministers of the Grand Secretariat to meet with you and to decide matters with you. Important matters should be handed down to an assembly of court ministers for decision. You should not issue decrees on the advice of the people near you. Even when your sagacious mind has made a decision, it should be referred to the Grand Secretariat for discussion before it is carried out." [23] But this plea, like many others, went unheeded. The emperors detached themselves from the government and for 164 years, from 1465 to 1627, they rarely had audience with their ministers.[24] The grand secretaries carried out the normal operation of government, acting on their own initiative in the handling of routine affairs and summoning meetings of other officials of the bureaucracy to deliberate important issues. The emperors were still the source of authority but, as Professor Lasswell points out, authority alone is power of low weight and when control (effective power) and authority (formal power) are in the same hands, a weakening of one leads to the weakening of the other.[25]

In such circumstances it became customary for memorials and reports—requests and proposals from officials in the capital and in the provinces—having been channeled through the ministries and processed in the Office of Transmission (*t'ung-cheng ssu*) and the Offices of Scrutiny (*k'o*) of the supervising secretaries, eventually to be dealt with by the grand secretaries. Considering the frequent mention of conferences, it is probable that the various grand secretaries met to discuss important issues. They then drafted "suggested rescripts" (*t'iao-chih* or *p'iao-i*) which, upon the emperor's approval, would be promulgated as imperial decrees. The emperor could approve, reject, or request a revision as he deemed wise.[26] But, so detached had emperors become, they would often passively acquiesce in the views and policies of their chief ministers. Some merely left matters to the discretion of their personal eunuch attendants, most notably the eunuch director of ceremonials (*ssu-li t'ai-chien*); and some eunuchs became so bold as to draft decrees themselves, so that "the prime minister's power came to be held by the eunuchs." [27]

The political influence of eunuchs grew out of the concentration of authority in the person of the emperor and was a symptom of the malfunctioning of the Ming political system. T'ai-tsu had warned against the employment of eunuchs. He had also perpetuated many institutional features from the past to forestall possible abuses of power, irresponsible actions, or errors of judgment on the part of all those entrusted with authority. How effective they were is another matter. The fact remains that they existed.

One feature was the widening of channels for the expression of public opinion. When he created the Office of Transmission in 1377, T'ai-tsu declared: "Political ideas are like water and should constantly flow. This is why this office is to be named *t'ung-cheng* [to facilitate the flow of political views]."[28] Under the Ming system every one in the empire, officials and commoners alike, could theoretically submit memorials without restriction and without fear, to criticize the ruler and the government or to make suggestions on issues of the day. As late as the 1430s, it was said, memorials submitted by any humble citizen in a side street in the morning could reach the emperor deep in the seclusion of his palace by nightfall.[29] Through the expression of popular opinion, even though it represented largely the views of the literate class, it was hoped that the ruler would be able to gauge the pulse of the empire. While the ruler was by no means constrained to accept such advice and suggestions, popular opinion when forcibly presented and representing large segments of the empire often did constitute political pressure of sorts which the ruler could not ignore.

More importantly, the reports, the preliminary estimates of the situation, and the proposals and requests for courses of action that flowed in from officialdom provided the rough casts from which policies were shaped and refined in the capital. Problems that required special attention were referred to the proper ministry in charge, where they were discussed in meetings (*pu-i*), and recommendations were sent to higher levels for further deliberation. Matters respecting relations with foreign states which involved possibilities of military action were deliberated in joint meetings of the officials of the Ministry of Rites and the Ministry of War. Major issues of war and of state were reviewed and weighed in plenary court conferences (*t'ing-i*) which were attended by the heads of the six ministries, the

Censorate, the Office of Transmission, and the Grand Court of Revision, and by supervising secretaries and investigating censors. Decisions of these conferences were then submitted to the emperor.[30] Sometimes the grand secretaries would convene such meetings and participate in the deliberations.[31] The influence of court conferences on state policies varied widely in the Ming period. During the 1440s conferences were frequent and well attended, but throughout the second reign of Ying-tsung (1457–64) no court conferences were convened. During the Shih-tsung and Shen-tsung reigns, when powerful ministers dominated the political scene, court sessions consisted merely of colloquies among the ranking officials, while everyone else sat in silence,[32] often leaving the conference room without knowing what had been discussed.[33] But in the last years of the Ming dynasty court conferences were often scenes of bedlam when the participants argued over the issue of peace or war with the invading Manchus, presenting no consensus of opinion on which the government might base a policy.[34] Despite the weakness of the system, the meetings at ministerial level as well as the court conferences provided the state with organs for deliberation, thus broadening the area of decision-making.

The development of a line of action from nebulous suggestions through adjustments and compromises to concrete decisions was watched over, step by step, by the supervising secretaries. They kept check also on the process by which a line of action was translated from deliberation and decision to execution. Operating in six Offices of Scrutiny, they maintained surveillance over officials and also had the responsibility of remonstrating with the emperor.[35] They could not only send back proposals of the officials with their "sealed dissents" (*feng-po*); they could even return decrees of the emperor for reconsideration.[36] In a directive issued in 1426 Hsüan-tsung (1425–35) ordered that, in particular, all decrees transmitted through eunuch attendants should be confirmed by the supervising secretaries before they were acted upon.[37] By the use of their modified veto power and by their remonstrances, the supervising secretaries served as the voice of official disapproval of the dictates of the emperor. Ku Yen-wu (1613–82), writing at the end of the Ming period with stories of tyranny and oppression by rulers and eunuchs still fresh in his mind, remarked: "For rulers of men, there is no greater harm than to have everyone concurring with them and no one to contradict them." [38] Theoretically, the supervising secretaries, acting as watchmen over the welfare of the empire and its people, could thwart the emperor. The great Sung dynasty statesman Ou-yang Hsiu (1007–87) had written, "When the Son of Heaven says yes, the remonstrators can say no; when the Son of Heaven says 'This must be done,' the remonstrators can say 'This must not be done.' To stand on the front terrace of the palace and to argue right and wrong with the Son of Heaven, this is the duty of the remonstrating officials." Ch'iu Chün (1418–95), referring to the words of Ou-yang Hsiu, noted that while the supervising secretaries of his time did not reach Ou-yang Hsiu's ideal, they did not shirk their responsibility to speak freely on the administration of the empire.[39]

By Ch'iu Chün's time, the avenues for the flow of opinion (yen-lu) were already shrinking. Whereas early rulers felt secure enough to invite advice and remonstrances, later monarchs regarded any questions about their behavior as personal affronts; they regularly imprisoned, beat, demoted, and exiled their critics. Intimidated and browbeaten, many officials played it safe by keeping quiet or by innocuously criticizing clerical errors in documents. Some formed cabals and sniped at each other over trivial matters.[40] The reluctance of officials to express their views freely was, as Huang Tso (1490–1566) remarked, quite "contrary to the behest of the sagacious founders." But after all, Huang asked rhetorically in a mixed metaphor, "Who would want to stroke the dragon's scales the wrong way and bring displeasure to the divine countenance?" [41] Even in this oppressive atmosphere, however, there were courageous, outspoken men who did not hesitate to say and do what they considered to be right at the risk of offending those in power. According to Ku Yen-wu, it was these remonstrating officials, working behind the scenes and using their power of feng-po (sealed dissent) discreetly during the Shih-tsung and Shen-tsung reigns, who nipped in the bud many an ill-advised measure and thus enabled the Ming government to function during the difficult days of dynastic decline.[42]

HISTORICAL PRECEPTS AND
STRATEGIC CONSIDERATIONS

When confronted with problems, anyone might first of all do well to resort to past experience in search of ready-made formulas. This pragmatic attitude occurs particularly to the Chinese mind, which is steeped in literary tradition and which places great stock on the guidance of history. In the conduct of foreign affairs, as in social intercourse, there were maxims and precedents that were so constantly quoted that they became clichés and, like political slogans, exerted an influence in the shaping of policy and the making of decisions.

Some of the apothegms were repeated over and over again in Ming documents. When T'ai-tsu remarked in 1376, "As to the control of the barbarians of the four quarters, we have only to be militarily prepared and to attend to our frontier defenses. Resist them when they invade us but do not pursue them relentlessly when they withdraw," [43] he was giving expression to one of these adages and its corrollary. The grand secretary Yang Shih-ch'i also cited two well-known sayings when he declared in 1438, "The principles by which the emperors and kings control the barbarians are only to let the barbarians of the four quarters maintain defenses for us (*shou-tsai ssu-i*) [44] and to employ the barbarians to fight barbarians." [45] The first saying in Yang's statement is a part of the much-quoted aphorism: "The Son of Heaven who has the right principles maintains his defenses in the land of the barbarians of the four quarters." The word *shou* can be interpreted as the maintenance of military defenses strategically far from the frontiers of China, but commentators interpreted it to mean that, by a policy of benevolence, the barbarians could be won over to defend China's frontiers for her.[46] By extension, it came to mean that China's cultural influence would suffice and there was no need to resort to arms.

Such axioms culled from the pages of history and literature were often quoted, but more often quoted and more authoritative as guidelines were the dicta of the founder of the dynasty. The ideas expressed in an address by T'ai-tsu have often been cited as the main principles of the foreign policy of the Ming government. On the morning of

October 30, 1371 (*hsin-wei* in the 9th month of the 4th year of Hung-
wu), T'ai-tsu convened the officials of the Secretariat, the Chief Military Commission, and the Censorate for a full-scale meeting at the
Feng-t'ien Gate and, climbing up to the gate tower, he made a speech
on foreign policy in which he said, *inter alia:*

> We should chastise the barbarian states beyond our frontiers (*hai-wai*)
> which threaten China but we should not take arms against those
> which do not threaten us. The ancients have a saying: "The expansion
> of territory is not the way to [achieve] enduring peace, and the over-
> burdening of the people is a cause of unrest." For example, the Sui Em-
> peror Yang sent his forces to invade Liu-ch'iu, killing and injuring the
> foreign people, setting fire to their palaces and homes, and taking several
> thousand of their men and women as prisoners. Yet the land which he
> gained was not enough to furnish him with supplies and the people he
> enthralled could not be made to serve him. For vain glory he exhausted
> China. This is told in history, and he has been derided by later genera-
> tions.
> As for the little barbarian states beyond our frontiers, over the moun-
> tains and across the sea, located in far corners [of the world], it is my
> view that if they do not menace China we should not invade them. But
> the nomadic barbarians (Hu and Jung) of the west and the north have
> for generations been a danger to China; we have no alternative but to be
> on guard against them. You ministers should bear these words in mind
> and know my desire.[47]

The caution against indulging in military adventurism and the
exhortation to be always on guard against intrusions from the north
were reiterated in the *Tsu-hsün* (Ancestral Instructions) which, in
final form, was promulgated in 1395.[48] Enlarging on the theme of his
speech about not invading the small states beyond the sea, T'ai-tsu in
these Instructions listed 15 states which China would not invade.
These were Korea, Japan, Greater and Lesser Liu-ch'iu, Annam, Cam-
bodia, Champa, Samudra, Siam, Java, Brunei, Pahang, Sri Vijaya,
Hsi-yang (?), and Pai-hua (?).[49] The Instructions have been cited ex-
tensively by Ming officials and historians as the basis of China's
foreign and strategic policy.[50]

In his speech T'ai-tsu warned his ministers and officers against
embarking on wars for the sake of conquest, and in his Instructions
he enjoined his "descendants of later generations not to rely on the
wealth and power of China to seek the temporary glory of war or to

wage wars without good cause." In both he stressed that China's chief danger came from the north and urged strong defenses and the stationing of large garrisons on the northern frontier.

In voicing his concern about the danger from the north T'ai-tsu was underlining what has been a basic fact of life to the Chinese from the beginning of their history. The threat from the north to the security of China was always regarded as greater than any other. T'ai-tsu himself declared in 1372, "The eastern barbarians [Japanese] are not, like the northerners, a danger to our heart and stomach. They are no more than mosquitos and scorpions." [51] Ku Ch'eng, military commandant of Kweichow Province, in a memorial in 1403 said that the barbarians on the frontiers of Yunnan, Kwangtung, and Kwangsi Provinces were but wasps and scorpions and that Japanese pirate incursions were sporadic, whereas the main danger came from the north.[52] Summing up the strategic considerations of the time, the Ming manual of war, the *Wu-pei chih* (Treatise on military preparations, 1617), rated foreigners in terms of the dangers they posed to China. At the top of the list were the northern barbarians, followed by the Japanese, the Hsi-fan (Tibetans?), the tribes of Hami (Chinese Turkestan), the peoples from Outremer (i.e., the Portuguese, etc.), the Annamese, and finally the Koreans.[53]

Aware of China's central location and dominant position in East Asia, the first Ming emperor frequently declared that peace in his world depended on the political stability and security of China.[54] In 1373 he said, "From ancient times it has been necessary to stress frontier defense. When the frontier regions are secure, China is untroubled and can keep the barbarians of the four quarters under control." [55] He therefore constantly stressed armed vigilance. "One must possess a military spirit before one can speak of turning away from military pursuits," he said, "and when the empire is at peace is the time to prepare against all eventualities." [56] The emphasis on defense against the warlike peoples of the north was thus a part of larger international policy.

But why should he single out 15 maritime states and proclaim that they would not be invaded by China? The epexegeses confuse the problem further by indicating that T'ai-tsu severed diplomatic relations with some of them, including Japan, because of involvement in the Hu Wei-yung conspiracy of 1379. If he found them to be recalcitrant, why should he assure them that they would be safe from punitive action by China? If it was a diplomatic maneuver, why should he restrict his freedom of action, and that of his successors, by such an unequivocal announcement? Ho Ch'iao-yüan (*chin-shih* in 1586) expressed the view of many Ming scholars by explaining that T'ai-tsu did not wish to attack these states because they were the first to submit and were the most submissive.[57] A modern historian, Wu Han, believes that, after the exhaustive war which culminated in the expulsion of the Mongol rulers in 1367, T'ai-tsu was reluctant to be drawn into wars in the south and east.[58] Neither of these explanations is wholly persuasive. Some of the states mentioned were far from submissive. Twice, in 1370 and 1380, T'ai-tsu actually threatened to send fleets against Japan.

Since the published text of the Ancestral Instructions was promulgated in 1395, it is likely that the list of 15 states was added as an afterthought and appended to the manifesto, which in content bears close resemblance to the speech in 1373. If this announcement of special treatment for the 15 maritime states was made about 1395, we may speculate that it was part of a deliberate policy suited to that particular time. For, although the Eastern Mongols had been destroyed and scattered, a greater menace now threatened. From across the steppes came alarming news that a new scourge, Tamerlane, emboldened by conquests in Western Asia and Eastern Europe, aimed to restore the great Mongol Empire. The Ming emperor was not unaware of the peril. Two of his emissaries to Samarkand had been detained, possibly as suspected spies.[59] The proclamation to the 15 states of the south and the east could very possibly have been intended to win their good will so that China would be safe from the seaward side and T'ai-tsu could concentrate his attention on defense of the northwestern frontier. A recent article by Hsü Yü-hu suggests that such considerations explain why T'ai-tsu dispatched envoys to the states of the south and east late in his reign and why Ch'eng-tsu, on the eve of Tamerlane's invasion of China in 1404, launched the series of South Seas naval expeditions that made the eunuch admiral Cheng Ho famous.[60] The objective must have been, by a combination of diplomacy and naval power, to induce the maritime nations to befriend

China during China's impending clash with the Timurid Khanate. Fortunately for China, Tamerlane's invasion was aborted by the khan's death early in 1405.

SOME SAMPLE CASES OF DECISION-MAKING

Of the wars in which Ming China came to be entangled, many do not offer opportunities for decision-making analyses. The long struggles with the Mongols in T'ai-tsu's reign were inherited from the past, and there was never any question of continuing or discontinuing them. Many other wars just happened, as border skirmishes escalated into larger-scale fighting without any clear decision to make war ever having been taken. In such instances, political leaders had to concern themselves with ways of conducting the wars but did not consider whether or not to engage in them. In other instances, however, political leaders found themselves confronted with situations offering alternative possibilities of action, when choices were made. Although the extant historical materials often limit the kinds of analyses that are possible, these situations can be explored for insights into Ming China's decision-making processes.

1. Intervention in Annam in 1406

Relations between China and Annam became strained when Le Qui-ly seized power in Annam, exterminated the Tran ruling house, waged war on Champa, and in 1395 occupied the region of Ssu-ming on the China-Annam frontier. T'ai-tsu was furious but, not desiring to go to war, he recognized the new regime by accepting tribute from it.[61] In 1402 Le Qui-ly (who changed his name to Ho Qui-ly) placed his son, Le Han-th'u'ong (or Ho Han-th'u'ong) on the throne and, in the following year, requested investiture from the Ming court. Ch'eng-tsu, who in 1403 had just made himself ruler of China by ousting his nephew, referred the question to the Ministry of Rites which, after a conference, recommended that the request be granted. But when the Chams sought aid from China, Ch'eng-tsu sent a squadron of nine warships which forced the Annamese fleet to withdraw from its investment of the Cham capital.[62]

In 1406 Ming policy changed, and Ch'eng-tsu decided to place a

Tran pretender, Tran Thien-binh, on the Annamese throne. The Chinese escort was ambushed and the pretender killed as soon as they crossed the frontier. Upon receipt of the news, Ch'eng-tsu angrily charged that the Ho (Le) regime had deceived him. "If we do not destroy them, what are our armies for?" he asked, and he "thereupon decided to go to war." [63] Ming armies crossed the frontier under the command of Chang Fu and in a six-month campaign defeated the Annamese and restored Annam as a Chinese province.

2. Expedition Against the Mongols in 1421

In the north, intermittent clashes with the Mongols continued. In 1409, when Aruqtai killed a Ming envoy and later wiped out a Chinese force, Ch'eng-tsu decided to lead a large expedition against the Mongols personally. There was no consultation with ministers. However, when Ch'eng-tsu planned his third expedition in 1421 and convened a meeting of his ministers to discuss the campaign, he was surprised to encounter dissident views among them. The minister of war Fang Pin, the minister of revenue Hsia Yüan-chi, and the minister of justice Wu Chung all advised against war on the grounds that China was economically exhausted from past campaigns, that supplies were short, that the army had suffered heavy losses of horses, and that it would be difficult to achieve success in the foreseeable future. The emperor flew into a rage. Fang Pin, in fear, committed suicide. Hsia Yüan-chi was arrested. The emperor then ordered Chang Fu, the victor of Annam, and others to discuss the issue, and they speedily mapped out plans for supplying the army.[64] The Chinese were victorious in their drive across the Gobi Desert and they were also successful in campaigns of 1422 and 1424, also personally led by Ch'eng-tsu; but the hope that by massive strikes they could destroy the enemy and make the frontier permanently secure was not realized.

3. Decision To Withdraw from Annam, 1426–27

In the south, the Ming government found itself mired in a protracted struggle from which it could not extricate itself. Thus Ming China was fighting wars on two distant fronts, which its long-term strategy had sought to avoid. In Annam, after Chang Fu's armies withdrew, leaving small garrisons and civilian administrators, native revolts broke out. Twice between 1408 and 1413 Chang Fu led armies into Annam to put down such insurrections, and did so with much brutality. When Chang Fu was finally recalled in 1416, large-scale rebellions broke out again in Annam under the leadership of Le Loi. The Ming commanders who succeeded Chang Fu were inept, and eunuchs who were sent out as army supervisors further inflamed the people by their outrageous demands. With economic distress in China, it became increasingly difficult to supply the expeditionary forces, and the Chinese troops with their heavy arms and equipment found it hard and frustrating to counter the hit-and-run guerrilla tactics of the rebels. In 1421 the Ming commander, Li Pin, reported that the two greatest problems confronting the Chinese army in Annam were a shortage of supplies, which had to be brought in from China both by sea and by long land routes, and the difficulty of coming to grips with an enemy who, whenever pressed, found refuge across the border in Laos.[65] Ming protests to the Laotian chieftains were of no avail. Neither were offers of amnesty to Le Loi, who continued to strike at Chinese garrisons and supply lines from his Laotian refuge.

Jen-tsung came to the Ming throne in 1424 with hopes for peace. He had actually suggested possible recognition of the regime of Le Loi.[66] Despite his private feelings, he acted to continue the war by reshuffling the top commanders of the Ming armies in Annam. Hsüan-tsung, who succeeded him in 1425, did the same. On May 8, 1426 (*i-ch'ou*, 4th month, 1st year of Hsüan-te), he appointed Wang T'ung commander in chief "to exterminate the rebels and to bring peace to that corner [of the empire]." But his action troubled him, he said, and that night he could not sleep. On the following day he spoke privately to the minister of personnel Chien I, the minister of revenue Hsia Yüan-chi, and the grand secretaries Yang Shih-ch'i and Yang Jung. He expressed his desire to withdraw from the war and to grant autonomy to Annam. He quoted the Ancestral Instructions' admonitions against offensive wars and said that the original intention of Ch'eng-tsu was not to make Annam a Chinese province but to restore the legitimate Tran rulers. Hsia Yüan-chi and Chien I both declared that a withdrawal from Annam would mean giving up twenty years of labor and would also impair China's prestige in the eyes of the world, and they urged that greater efforts be made to put down the rebellion. But Yang Shih-ch'i and Yang Jung endorsed the emperor's view, saying that at the time of the legendary emperors Yao and Shun and during the Hsia, Shang, and Chou epochs Annam was not a part of China, that since it had been annexed by China in the Han period it had been a liability, and that the abandonment of Chu-yai (Hainan Island) in 46 B.C. was a praiseworthy deed which the Ming government should emulate. "Your majesty should not stoop to contend with wolves and pigs." [67] Hsüan-tsung did not act as he wished, but on July 6, 1426 (*ping-shen*, 5th month, 1st year of Hsüan-te), he had another conversation with the two Yangs in which all three reassured each other that the original policy of Ch'eng-tsu was not to establish a province in Annam and that their views regarding a pull-out from Annam were justified.[68]

That winter the Annamese under Le Loi shifted from their guerrilla tactics to large-scale frontal assaults on the Chinese garrisons. Wang T'ung was defeated in a battle in which he sustained from 20,000 to 30,000 casualties. Thanhhoa in the south was evacuated. At the end of the year the Ming court sent another army, under Liu Sheng, to reinforce Wang T'ung. On February 12, 1427 (*i-ssu*, 1st month, 2d year of Hsüan-te), the emperor had another conversation with Yang Shih-ch'i and Yang Jung during which he complained about Hsia Yüan-chi and Chien I, who wanted to continue the war. The emperor cited another historical case to support his argument: In antiquity, when Cheng Shu assassinated Duke Ling of Ch'en, the Viscount of Ch'u killed Cheng Shu and made Ch'en a province (in 534 B.C.), but four years later Ch'u restored the state of Ch'en. The withdrawal of Chinese troops from Annam, Hsüan-tsung stated, would enable the peoples of China and Annam both to enjoy the blessings of peace. The two Yangs concurred and added that withdrawal would be a virtuous deed.[69] They agreed to send Huang Fu to explore the possibility of a truce.

When Ming reinforcements under Liu Sheng reached the frontier, Le Loi wrote a letter to the Ming court asking for an armistice. He claimed that he had found a descendant of the Tran line, a certain Tran Cao, whom he would acknowledge as king if the Chinese would grant Annam autonomy. A few weeks later, when Liu Sheng crossed the frontier in the vicinity of Langson, he suffered a crushing defeat, losing 70,000 men. When report of the disaster reached Wang T'ung, he agreed to the terms of armistice laid down by Le Loi and, without waiting for instructions from Peking, pulled out his troops.

Le Loi's letter reached Peking more than a month before the news of the military reverses. On November 16 (*jen-wu*, 10th month, 2d year of Hsüan-te), Hsüan-tsung summoned his ministers for a meeting. While both official annals and unofficial histories agree about the outcome of the conference, they differ markedly in their description of the roles of the participants. According to the terse account in the *Ming Shih-lu* (True records of the Ming dynasty), the emperor passed Le Loi's letter around to his counselors, saying that the original purpose of the twenty years of warfare had been to restore the legitimate Tran rulers to the throne of Annam. "Now that a descendant of the Tran line has been found, shall we or shall we not accede to the request for truce?" The assembled ministers all agreed that peace would conform to the will of Heaven and that China should agree to Le Loi's request.[70]

Unofficial histories so far consulted all differ from the *Ming Shih-lu* in their description of what took place at the meeting. Although they contain discrepancies in details—some say that the emperor summoned the ministers one by one and sought their views in private, and others say that he met them together as a group—these accounts are in agreement as to the views expressed by the ministers. The version in the *Shu-yü Chou-tzu Lu* (Compendium of reports on foreign lands) by Yen Ts'ung-chien (*chin-shih* in 1559) is representative: Upon receipt of Le Loi's letter, the emperor showed it to Chang Fu. Chang Fu declared: "Our officers and men have endured years of hardship to conquer [Annam]. This petition is a ruse by Le Loi. We should send more troops to wipe out the rebels." Both Chien I and Hsia Yüan-chi said that to hand over the territory to Le Loi without any justifiable reason would be a revelation of China's weakness to the world. The emperor then turned to the other ministers. Yang Jung pointed to the misery and distress brought about by the war and urged acceptance of the peace proposals. "We may turn disaster into good fortune. The suggestion to send in more troops should not be adopted," he said. Yang Shih-ch'i repeated the argument that the original intention of

Ch'eng-tsu was to restore the throne to the Tran line and not to make Annam a province, and that as the abandonment of Chu-yai (Hainan Island) by the Han Emperor Yüan (in 46 B.C.) was a glorious deed, so would be a present withdrawal from Annam. On the following day the emperor summoned an assembly of his entire court and announced his decision to accept Le Loi's proposal.[71] Three days later a commission was appointed to proceed to Annam to negotiate the armistice. Upon reaching Annam, however, the commissioners met with rebuff from Le Loi who, flushed with victory, refused to step down in favor of the Tran scion. He said Tran Cao had died. He also refused to permit the repatriation of the bulk of the Chinese administrators and troops.

This was a great diplomatic defeat for China and a revelation of China's weakness that had far-reaching repercussions. Even though the decision to withdraw was made before news of the military disasters reached Peking, the timing was unfortunate, for it gave the impression that mighty China had been humbled by tiny Annam. While the annals of Hsüan-tsung's reign in the *Ming Shih-lu* (edited by Yang Shih-ch'i and Chang Fu) credited the emperor with being the chief advocate of peace, later Ming historians regarded Yang Shih-ch'i and Yang Jung as the pacifists who by their sophistry, flattery, and cajolery guided the emperor on his disastrous course of action. The loss of Annam, wrote Yen Ts'ung-chien, "stemmed from the wrong policy of the chief ministers. The two Yangs . . . lacked the far-sightedness of Chien and Hsia." [72] The abandonment of the land and people of Annam, said Ku Ying-t'ai (*chin-shih* in 1647), "exposed China to the contempt of the barbarians and lost to China her prestige and power. . . . The two Yangs were peacetime prime ministers. . . . In time of crisis and decision they were found wanting." [73]

4. Lu-ch'uan and Burma, 1441–48

The impact of China's retreat from Annam was felt by many non-Chinese peoples on the perimeter of the empire. Among these were the Maw Shans, a Burman tribe on the Yunnan frontier which soon involved China in a long and costly war. In 1437 Ssu-jen-fa (identified as Thonganbwa),[74] the sawbwa of Lu-ch'uan, revolted, defeated provincial troops sent against him, and proclaimed himself king of Tien.

The military commandant of Yunnan Province asked for an army of 120,000 to put down the revolt, but it was not till 1441 that a court conference was convened to consider the situation, now increasingly critical. Chang Fu and others favored suppression of the revolt. The vice minister of justice Ho Wen-yüan argued that, since Lu-ch'uan was only a tiny plot of land and the Maw Shans a small tribe, a benevolent policy would be sufficient to induce the rebels to lay down their arms and that there was no need for a punitive expedition. Yang Shih-ch'i strongly supported Ho's view. But Chang Fu retorted that unless firm measures were taken the neighboring tribes would be encouraged to break away. "To reveal our weakness to the barbarians is not the right policy." The new, young emperor Ying-tsung gave his approval and authorized the mobilization of 150,000 men for the campaign. Liu Ch'iu, a Hanlin reader-in-waiting, then submitted a memorial pointing out that since Lu-ch'uan was far away, it mattered little whether it remained Chinese territory or whether it broke away, but the Mongols were threatening the northern frontier. "To ignore the wolves in order to beat the dogs and pigs, to neglect the danger at our front gate and courtyard in order to wage a war in the distance is not the best policy." He suggested that the expedition be canceled. But his memorial was ignored because, it was said, the palace eunuch Wang Chen "was at this time in power and wanted to display [China's] military power to foreign lands." [75]

Ying-tsung was said to have approved the war plans, but he was then only fifteen years old and deferred to his grandmother and to the high ministers on all matters of state. The eunuch director of ceremonials, Wang Chen, did not openly assert his pernicious influence on Ming politics until the death of the empress-dowager in the following year.[76] Of the ministers, Yang Jung had passed away and Yang Shih-ch'i was in semiretirement, and the new grand secretaries still lacked standing. Who then made the decision to go to war?. The prime movers were probably the militarists led by Chang Fu, and the decision was made after careful consideration. The minister of war Wang Chi was said to have favored armed intervention in the conference debates, seeking to please Wang Chen, who he saw was rising in power. Yet the war was not undertaken solely for the sake of military glory. The historian Ku Ying-t'ai refuted Liu Ch'iu's argument that

Lu-ch'uan, being small and far away, could be abandoned. Had the Ming court failed to act, the infection would have spread, he pointed out, and China's southwestern provinces would have been endangered.[77]

Ming armies defeated Thonganbwa in a month-long winter campaign and drove the Maw Shans from their base in Lu-ch'uan. In pursuit of Thonganbwa, who had fled into Upper Burma, the Chinese crossed the frontier, thus precipitating a war with the Burmans. Although defeated in 1445, the Ming forces invaded Burma again in the following year and were before the walls of the Burmese capital, Ava, when the Burmans surrendered the body of Thonganbwa. Then a son of the Maw Shan chieftain rallied his men and resumed resistance, and it was not till 1448 that the Maw Shans were subjugated. By this time the Kalmuck Mongols under Essen were encroaching on the northern frontier. Events moved swiftly, culminating in the hasty decision by Ying-tsung, on Wang Chen's advice, to lead an expedition personally against the enemy and in a famous debacle in the battle of T'u-mu in 1449.

5. Consideration of Annam in 1480

Another case in which eunuchs were charged with interference in foreign affairs occurred in 1480, when the eunuch Wang Chih was in power. After the Annamese invasion and occupation of most of Champa in 1470, the Chams who still held out in the south sent mission after mission to the Ming court to appeal for succor. Their pleas fell on deaf ears until they won Wang Chih to their cause. When Wang Chih's plan for intervention in Annam was referred to the court ministers for deliberation, Lu Jung, director of the Bureau of Operations in the Ministry of War, advised caution. His views were supported by other ministers, and the plan was shelved. Later, Wang Chih, still desirous of intervention in Annam, sent for the records of troop mobilization used in the time of Ch'eng-tsu. Liu Ta-hsia, then director of the Bureau of Operations, hid the files and persuaded the minister of war Yü Tzu-chün to send in a strong memorandum against the proposal. Again Wang Chih was frustrated.[78]

This was the incident which later historians have mistakenly described as the burning of the sea charts used in the Cheng Ho expeditions. In blocking Wang Chih's plan, officials in the Ministry of War were guided by strategic considerations. By his rude and arrogant actions, Wang Chih had offended the Mongols and the Jurchens, and there was desultory fighting on the northern and northeastern frontiers. A conflict with Annam would have involved China in wars on three frontiers and, as one Ming writer remarked, "one cannot foretell what would have been the fate of the empire." [79]

6. Decision To Intervene in Annam, 1537–40

In 1522 an adventurer named Mac Dang-dung seized power in Annam. In 1529, after ousting the last of the Le kings, he made his son Mac Dang-doanh king and sent a mission to Peking to request investiture. The Ming court replied that it would make an investigation first. At this time Le Ninh, claiming to be the son of the last Le ruler, had raised an army and, operating from bases in Cham states in the south and in Laos, had invaded Annam in an effort to restore the Le dynasty. Since civil war was raging, the Ming court waited for the situation to clarify.

It was not until 1536 that the Chinese gave serious attention to Annam. The occasion was the birth of the heir apparent. It was customary to announce such an auspicious event to neighboring countries, and the question arose whether or not to send a mission to Annam. Hsia Yen, who as minister of rites was in charge of foreign affairs, had just been made grand secretary. In a memorial he pointed out that Annam had not sent tribute for twenty years and that Mac Dang-dung and his son were usurpers who had tyrannized over the people and plunged the country into civil strife. "It is our moral obligation to chastise the rebels and suppress the rebellion," he concluded. "This is the way for China, as suzerain, to control the barbarians of the four quarters." [80] Emperor Shih-tsung asked that the ministers of rites, war, and personnel confer and discuss the question. At their meeting Hsia Yen strongly recommended the dispatch of a punitive expedition against Annam and, to forestall arguments, he pointed out that the Ancestral Instructions of T'ai-tsu about not invading Annam applied only to the Tran rulers, who were submissive, and not to the subsequent regimes of the Le and Mac usurpers.[81] Chang Tsan, the minister of war, spoke in favor of Hsia Yen's proposal. The other conferees agreed but suggested that a commission be sent to Annam first to find out the true state of affairs. The Ministry of War also held a series of meetings to map out mobilization plans.[82]

The war preparations provoked loud protests from many segments of the bureaucracy. The supreme commander of Yunnan Province, Mu Shao-hsün, wrote that there was no assurance of success in a campaign against Annam because of the rugged terrain there and that it would be costly in men and materiel.[83] The vice minister of revenue T'ang Wei submitted a seven-point memorandum early in 1537 urging a halt to the preparations. He argued that the Ancestral Instructions expressly forbade any invasion of Annam, that the government should follow Hsüan-tsung's example in forsaking Annam, that China had suffered heavy losses in past wars with Annam, and that the cost of another expedition was prohibitive. "When the barbarians abroad fight among themselves it is China's good fortune," he declared. Since the outbreak of civil war in Annam, the frontier of Kwangtung Province had been free of depredations. Finally, he concluded, it would be unwise to neglect the danger in the north to plunge into a war in the south.[84] Chang Tsan, the minister of war, agreed that these views merited consideration.

In the summer of 1537 an embassy from Le Ninh arrived and, in an elegantly phrased petition, sought China's aid in the war to expel the Mac usurpers. Yen Sung, Hsia Yen's fellow provincial and his arch rival, had newly become minister of rites and, in an effort to discredit Hsia Yen's policy, he expressed doubt about the legality of Le Ninh's claims and the credentials of Le Ninh's envoy. Chang Tsan tended to support Yen Sung. However, the emperor Shih-tsung appeared to be under Hsia Yen's influence. A decree was issued that the Ministries of Rites and War should review the question. Yen Sung and Chang Tsan both changed their tunes and voiced a strong recommendation to send an army into Annam against Mac Dang-dung. Not all of the officials gave their approval. The vice minister of war P'an Chen maintained that it was a dangerous policy to overlook the Mongols in the north. "To let the robbers into our front courtyard while we involve ourselves in a war in a miasmic land far away is not a desirable policy." [85] His kinsman P'an Tan, supreme commander of Kwangtung

Province, and Chang Yüeh, prefect of Lien-chou, submitted protests against war, saying that Mac Dang-dung was ready to submit. Their views were ignored. Both Yen Sung and Chang Tsan advised against acceptance of Mac Dang-dung's overtures because Le Ninh appeared to be winning in Annam. During the meetings the censor Hsü Chiu-kao and the supervising secretary Hsieh Ting-i submitted memorials advocating a suspension of the war preparations, and the emperor himself also suggested further study of the situation. As a result, troop movements were halted.

In the eighth month the grand coordinator of Yunnan Province, Wang Wen-sheng, reported the arrest of Mac Dang-dung's spies and the capture of some of Mac's documents with contumelious wording. Along with his report Wang also sent war plans suggested by Le Ninh's adherents for the conquest of Annam. Upon receipt of these papers the Ming court issued instructions to the frontier officials to resume mobilization. The regional inspector of Kwangtung, Yü Kuang, who advised against war, was deprived of his salary for a year, and P'an Tan was replaced by Chang Ching (alias Ts'ai Ching) as supreme commander of Kwangtung.

In the spring of 1538 Mac Dang-dung asked for the terms of peace. Officials of the Ministry of War, summoned to a conference in court to deliberate the question, charged that Mac Dang-dung's overture was a ruse. They decided on the dispatch of expeditionary forces. But they suspended action when the frontier commander Chang Ching reported that the campaign would require 300,000 men, 1,600,000 piculs of rice per year, and a special allocation of 700,000 taels for the construction of warships, the manufacture of arms, and the purchase of equipment and horses.[86]

The issue of war and peace split the ranks of the bureaucracy. Early in 1539 Weng Wan-ta, deputy commissioner for Kwangsi in charge of war preparations, advised caution. He pointed out that the war would be costly, that the provinces of Kwangtung and Kwangsi were impoverished, that there was no assurance of victory, and that the founding emperor, in a similar situation, had not thought it necessary to unseat a Korean usurper.[87] On the other hand, Lin Hsi-yüan, prefect of Ch'in-chou near the frontier of Tongking, submitted four memorials outlining an amphibious campaign which he guaranteed would succeed in destroying the Mac regime. The plan called for a two-pronged drive by land coordinated with an attack from the south by Cham forces assisted by naval units from Kwangtung and Fukien. The Ministry of War, unable to decide, requested a court conference. The emporer chided his ministers for privately stating that China should not embark on the war and urged them to reach a decision for the welfare of the state. In spite of his hint, however, they voted to call off the invasion.[88] The dismissal of Hsia Yen, the chief proponent of the war, may perhaps have been a reason.

But hopes of peace were shattered in the tenth month of 1539 when Mac Dang-dung rejected Chinese demands that he recognize Le Ninh as king. Reports came that he was planning to invade Kwangsi. Once again a conference was convened in Peking. Shih-tsung rebuked the ministers for being too much swayed by the influence of one man, Hsia Yen. He bade them reach a decision: "Should we abandon this country or should we intervene? There should be a definite decision." [89] The ministers decided to launch the invasion to punish the Mac regime, and the emperor gave his approval. In the sixth month of 1540, with 120,000 Chinese troops massed on the Kwangsi frontier, Mac Dang-dung walked into the Chinese camp barefooted and with a rope around his neck in token of his submission. After a court discussion in Peking, Annam was made a Chinese protectorate and Mac Dang-dung made hereditary protector. As for Le Ninh, his cause was quietly brushed aside with the excuse that his claim to the Annamese throne lacked legal support.

7. Attempted Recovery of the Ordos, 1546–48

After the loss of the Ordos, at the northern bend of the Yellow River, to the Chakhar Mongols in 1462, there were repeated requests from Chinese residents and local officials in the frontier regions for its recovery. The requests were referred to the Ministry of War but no action was taken. In 1546 Tseng Hsien, the supreme commander of the Three Frontiers (san-pien), proposed the dispatch of an army of 60,000 men with a large artillery train to strike and to destroy the enemy bases. By ample use of firearms, in which the Chinese were superior, and by hitting at the enemy heavily year after year, he argued, the Chinese could recover the strategic region. The plan was handed down to the Ministry of War for deliberation. With the support of Hsia Yen, who had returned to power that year, the plan was adopted.[90] Shih-tsung gave his approval, and the Ministry of War appropriated thirty million taels for the campaign.

In the summer of 1547 Tseng Hsien led his forces into the Ordos and scored a victory, capturing large stores of arms and large herds of horses and camels, and compelling the enemy to withdraw to the north. He was commended and rewarded by the emperor. Later in the year he presented his plan for a second expedition. In a top-level court conference the minister of war Wang I-chi said it was a good plan, and the emperor gave his endorsement. When the plan was referred to the officials of the Ministry of War for further study, the emperor told them "to consider carefully with the interest of the state at heart, and when you have decided on a course of action report to me." [91] But the emperor did not receive any report of their decisions and, when he inquired about this, Yen Sung used the opportunity to condemn Hsia Yen's policy.

In spring of 1548, when Altan Khan of the Tumed Mongols made one of his forays across the frontier, Yen Sung charged that warlike acts of Tseng Hsien and Hsia Yen had provoked the enemy incursion resulting in the massacre of several thousand inhabitants of Yenan. Moreover, Yen complained that Tseng had used funds appropriated to him for military expenses to bribe Hsia Yen to support his scheme. Tseng was summarily executed and Hsia Yen was dismissed from office. Yen Sung then had his creatures submit a barrage of memorials accusing Hsia Yen of recommending Tseng and of various malfeasances, so that Hsia was also executed.[92] Wang I-chi, the minister of war, was transferred, and all who spoke in favor of the plan to recover the Ordos were deprived of their salaries.

Yen Sung's way was to do nothing, to drift. Not only did he silence all talk of offensive operations; he also discouraged any action that might be construed by the enemy as provocative. His timidity only emboldened Altan Khan, whose horde penetrated to the very gates of Peking in 1550. Frantically, the emperor summoned his ministers for a series of emergency meetings in the court to decide on a course of action. But before any decision was reached the Tumeds, laden with spoils, withdrew. Yen Sung came under bitter attack from his critics. After his downfall conferences and discussions continued to be held periodically as the Ming government vacillated between policies of peace and war toward the Tumed Mongols.

8. Secret Peace Overtures to the Manchus in 1642

Late in the dynasty, with the Manchus pressing down from the north and with rampant banditry and insurrections in the south, the Ming government found itself caught between two fires. In this dilemma, there were officials in the Ming court who believed that peace with the Manchus could be arranged so that the Ming armies could concentrate their efforts on suppressing the domestic rebellions. One of these men was Yang Ssu-ch'ang, a confidant of the last emperor, Chuang-lieh-ti (r. 1627–44), and a leader of an influential group which subscribed to the view that friendly gestures and concessions were sufficient to turn back aggression. In 1638, when he was minister of war, he proposed, with the emperor's support, a plan of buying peace from the Manchus by cession of land and the establishment of trade relations. The plan aroused considerable opposition and, although many censors and supervising secretaries such as Lin Lan-yu and Ho Chieh who protested were demoted or transferred, it was not adopted.[93]

After reverses suffered by the Ming armies in the summer of 1641, Yang Ssu-ch'ang's protégé and his successor as minister of war, Ch'en Hsin-chia, secretly sent emissaries to the Manchu camp to ask for terms of peace. The grand secretary Hsieh Sheng reported Ch'en's activities to the emperor, adding that the explorations were harmless and might possibly bring peace. Summoned before the emperor, Ch'en admitted his activities. The emperor told him to carry on with his efforts, but cautioned him to be careful in keeping his activities secret. But the news leaked out. When the supervising secretaries and censors Fang Shih-liang, Ni Jen-chen, Chu Hui, and others questioned Hsieh Sheng, Hsieh replied, "His majesty is praying in the Feng-hsien Hall. He has made up his mind to discuss peace. Gentlemen, please do not speak about this matter any more." His response stirred up a furor and, as a result of denunciations submitted by the supervising secretaries and censors, Hsieh Sheng was dismissed. The censorial officials suspected that Ch'en Hsin-chia was also in communication with the enemy, but they had no proof. Moreover, Ch'en had powerful friends in court, including the eunuch director of ceremonials, Wang Te-hua.

Having entrusted Ch'en with the task of conducting secret talks with the Manchus, Chuang-lieh-ti exchanged scores of notes with Ch'en. The emperor's messages, written in his own hand, were delivered by the director of the Bureau of Operations in the Ministry of War, Ma Shao-yü. Repeatedly the emperor warned Ch'en that the messages were confidential and not to be divulged. But one day, after Ma's visit, Ch'en Hsin-chia left the emperor's message on his desk. His servant, thinking it was a routine report, sent it through the usual channel so that it was published in the *Ti-pao* (Peking Gazette). The disclosure caused an immediate uproar. Led by Fang Shih-liang, censors and supervising secretaries deluged the emperor with memorials attacking the peace move. The emperor, as Chao I described the incident, was very annoyed and embarrassed. Under pressure from the majority of the officials, he reprimanded Ch'en Hsin-chia and ordered his arrest. At his trial Ch'en made things worse by boasting about his action. Following more memorials from the remonstrating officials, he was thrown in prison and later executed. From then on, the emperor did not dare to propose peace with the Manchus.[94] Two years later, Peking fell to rebels and the Ming dynasty came to an end.

THE DECISION-MAKING PROCESS: A RECAPITULATION

"War is a major affair of the state," wrote the ancient Chinese strategist Sun-tzu. "It is a matter of life and death, the road to survival or destruction." [95] Throughout history Chinese thinkers by the scores have insisted that the utmost care and prudence must be exercised in determining courses of action that might involve the country in hostilities, and their admonitions in this regard have repeatedly been called to the attention of Chinese statesmen confronted by crises. Moreover, since the Chinese have been fully committed to the view that politics is a matter of human relations rather than of impersonal institutions, it is not surprising that wide participation in important decision-making procedures has always been sought, especially in regard to such weighty issues as peace and war.

Even in the Ming period, when absolutism was at one of its heights in China and when members of the bureaucracy were often browbeaten, intimidated, and persecuted, the principle of consultation prevailed. Even the tyrannical early emperors T'ai-tsu and Ch'eng-tsu made shows of consulting their ministers, and strong-willed Hsüantsung, though personally committed to withdraw from Annam, acted to withdraw only after encouraging his ministers to argue out the problem in his presence and giving careful consideration to differences of view among them. From Hsüan-tsung's time on, in an uneven development, the center of decision-making power as regards major issues gradually shifted from the emperor to the high-ranking ministers. Emperors might hint and threaten, and court favorites might coerce and intimidate, but court conferences persisted as the forum in which important issues were resolved. And when rulers or their favorites planned unpopular courses of action, officialdom found it possible to block them by collective action.

Not only were many men thus involved in decisions about war and peace; their decisions were usually arrived at only after long deliberations in which proposals and their consequences were carefully studied and chances of success were carefully calculated.[96] The procedure did not substantially differ from that followed by modern states.

1. Intelligence

Information on developments in neighboring states was obtained from reports of diplomatic officials, spies, and informers and from observations by travelers and "experts." The courier service operated by the Ministry of War was fast and efficient in transmitting such information to the capital.

2. Appraisal

The assessment of the situation was made by officials in the regions close to the scenes of action and by responsible agencies in the capital, particularly by the Ministry of Rites, which had charge of foreign relations, and the Ministry of War.

3. Recommendation

The evaluation of the situation was usually accompanied by suggestions regarding courses of action. Since proposals were based on
information received, which often was fragmentary or erroneous, and
on appraisals that were subjective and influenced by the proponents'
own experience and knowledge, they could often be wrong. The Ming
court, for example, was uncertain about Le Ninh's status, and this
prevented a quick decision regarding Annam in 1537–40.

4. Judgment

Memoranda were processed and channeled through the Office of
Transmission, the Offices of Scrutiny, and the respective ministries.
If not discarded or pigeonholed, they then reached the court for study
by the grand secretaries who made preliminary decisions on the
courses to adopt, subject to the final approval of the emperor. Major
issues, such as peace or war, were referred to the respective ministers
or, at higher level, to a plenary conference in court for deliberation
and debate. Since appraisals of the same situation and solutions recommended by different men were bound to vary, the responsibility of
the decision-makers was the selection of a course of action from whatever options confronted them. In their deliberations, they were guided
by (a) intelligence reports, (b) suggestions by local officials, (c) their
own experience and knowledge, (d) historical precepts, past precedents, ancestral instructions, etc., (e) instructions from the emperor
and views of influential personages, and (f) external factors such as
requests for succor or demands and threats by foreign governments.
Concern for the welfare of the state was matched against the personal
interests and ambition of the leaders, and domestic politics were
juxtaposed with foreign relations.

5. Decisions

The participants voted by writing out their opinions. Each of them
apparently had an equal voice and unanimity was hoped for. "When
there was unanimity, custom apparently dictated that the assembly's
decision was binding on the Emperor." [97] When the assembled ministers were unable to reach a decision, the cases were sometimes referred

back to the emperor, along with the minutes of the debates, for him to decide. For emperors who made their own decisions the views of the ministers served as bases for consideration. Others were willing to let their ministers help them to make up their minds or make decisions for them. Imperial sanction could mean that the choice of courses of action had been personally studied and approved by the emperor himself or that the approval was rubber-stamped in his name by other individuals wielding *de facto* power. Thus decisions on such vital issues as war and peace, even under the absolutism of the Ming period, generally represented the consensus of many men and the result of careful calculation of the risks involved. They were seldom impulsive acts born of the whim and caprice of any single individual.

RAY HUANG 明 *Fiscal Administration*

During the Ming Dynasty

The financial history of a Chinese imperial dynasty spanning more than 270 years cannot be easily summarized in a single article. Yet an attempt at a general survey has been growing increasingly desirable. The lack of such a basic outline has been a serious handicap to students of Ming economic history. Inasmuch as the Ming bureaucrats and contemporary writers regarded each fiscal problem as a separate issue, they tended to dismember a variety of subjects. Cross references were rare in their writing. The interplay of one element with another was simply disregarded in most cases. Nowhere in the contemporary sources can we find a broad and general study which treats the fiscal administration as an entity. This may be a blessing to those scholars who are well adjusted to the demand for area specialization—an element much emphasized in modern historiography. But without seeing the operation of the whole, it is difficult to evaluate the functions of the parts. The awesome volumes of data and the numerous subtleties inherent in Ming governmental organization present another stumbling block. They discourage researchers from probing into far corners outside their specialized areas, because once such an investigation starts there is no end to it. We therefore run the risk of becoming unknowingly influenced by the compartmented perspectives of contemporary sources.

Marianne Rieger, a bold soul by any historian's standard, undertook over thirty years ago to outline the Ming fiscal administration. Her effort produced a glossary of taxation and administrative terminology during the Ming period, with many annotated observations.[1] While the general definitions offered by the writer remain useful to this date, for the most part her interpretation of the fiscal operation

In preparing this paper, the author was aided by a generous grant from Southern Illinois University. Gayle Huang helped in consolidating the figures used in the paper and in making the English text presentable.

has been outdated and invalidated by modern research. Besides, her presentation is limited to a frontal view of the Ming fiscal structure; little is said about the functional operations of the fiscal machinery.

This paper endeavors to carry the effort somewhat further. My objective is twofold: To review the fiscal institutions and usages of the Ming dynasty, and to investigate the causes of its financial crisis in the early seventeenth century. From my point of view these two subjects are closely interrelated; it is hardly possible to work on one without touching the other. My presentation will attempt to cover both formal structures and functional practices. Certainly, my findings cannot be anything but a preliminary outline. I have no illusion that the analysis that follows will be thorough and complete, or that it will stand permanently unrevised. Nevertheless, it is my hope that the sketch may be of some reference value to current students of Ming government and of Ming economic history.

THE INFLUENCE OF TRADITIONAL THOUGHT AND PRACTICES ON FISCAL ADMINISTRATION

In traditional China statecraft and Confucian humanism usually went hand in hand. No regime could win public approval unless it was identified with the classical spirit, and concern for benevolence often preoccupied the minds of the bureaucrats. The Ming civil administrators in particular were willing to bend their policies and procedures to suit the concept of government by virtue, sometimes at the expense of legality and administrative efficiency. In the numerous official documents written by Ming bureaucrats we rarely find a writer tackling his problem with businesslike directness. Instead, we find that official memoranda, even on fiscal matters, are developed into lengthy essays in which the key issues are subordinated to ethical considerations. This general attitude was a serious handicap in the empire's fiscal administration. A few examples may help to clarify the point.

In 1521 a man named Shao Ching-pang was appointed tax collector at the inland port Ching-chou. Although the commodity tax was collected according to a prescribed ad valorem schedule, the court also assigned an annual quota to each port, basically as a general target of collection. In three months, Shao's collections had fulfilled the quota. He therefore suspended the taxation altogether. For the rest of the year commercial vessels were allowed to call at the port free of duty.[2] In 1565 Yang Shih-ch'iao, another collector, established an honor system at Hang-chou, by which the tax assessment was based entirely on each merchant's own declaration; no official inspection was ever conducted.[3] From our point of view, the two officials were guilty of laxity and of courting personal favor among the taxed. But no such charge was brought against them by their contemporaries. On the contrary, they were commended by Ming historians as having been model officials who had extended the emperor's magnanimity to the people.

In 1590 Shen Pang, a magistrate in Peking, discovered a racketeering ring operating in the imperial capital. The offenders had made several bogus official seals and sold forged tax receipts on real estate transfers for fees which consisted of only fractions of the normal tax. Many residents in Peking had dealt with the racketeers. As a result, the tax revenue had dwindled drastically. Once the offenders were under arrest, Shen posted a public notice, demanding that those who had purchased the falsified papers pay the taxes which they had thus far evaded. On those who failed to turn up voluntarily he imposed a stiff fine. Before the year ended Shen was impeached by an imperial censor, on the charge that he was a "greedy official." The impeachment further charged that Shen's punishments had been tyrannical, improperly imposed upon "ignorant and pitiful subjects." Another censor appointed to investigate the case cleared Shen of being greedy, since he had not tried to benefit from the matter personally. But in the final analysis this investigator still blamed him for being too strict in administering the law, which was a clear departure from the Confucian concept of good government.[4]

Regarding tax revenue as "blood and sweat of the people," Ming officials tended to treat governmental funds with extreme care. The striving for exactness often reached the point of being impractical. As a rule, governmental incomes and expenditures, at least on paper, were broken down into figures carrying more than ten digits beyond the decimal point. The land tax collectable from Wan-p'ing County in Peking was listed in official reports as 3,668.7526548666125 taels of silver in 1592.[5] The 1620 edition of the tax handbook of Hui-chou Prefecture listed the poll tax within the prefecture as 0.1054117712 taels of silver per person. In the same prefecture the tax quota on winter wheat, when commuted to monetary payments, was calculated at the ratio of 0.3247275302 taels of silver to the picul.[6] This cumbersome system remained universal throughout the dynasty. After the Manchus took over, for some time they followed the same practice. It was only in 1685 that the K'ang-hsi emporor finally proclaimed that all petty figures beyond the fourth digit after the decimal point should be eliminated.[7]

In theory, being a member of the bureaucracy was a matter of honor rather than an opportunity for materialistic compensation. It involved more duties than privileges. The scholar-officials were expected to live in puritanical austerity. Following this principle, the emoluments of the Ming bureaucracy were fixed at a low level. The minister of revenue, for instance, drew an annual salary of 732 piculs of grain. The pay scale was graduated all the way down to 60 piculs annually for the lowest member of the bureaucracy.[8] Eventually the payments were made partially in commodities such as cotton cloth, pepper, and devalued paper currency, further reducing the actual compensation of civil servants. Consequently, payment of imperial officials constituted only an insignificant item in the national expenditure.[9] Rations and salaries of officials in Peking handled by the imperial treasury in 1578 totaled less than 50,000 piculs of grain and about 44,000 taels of silver.[10] A report dated 1629 disclosed that the annual cost of maintaining all civil offices in the capital, in addition to an unspecified amount of subsidies paid to imperial clansmen residing in Peking, amounted then to about 150,000 taels of silver.[11] This accounted for less than one percent of the state expenditure.

As the ideal spirit of classical humanism could not always be realized, compromises and backstage manipulations of the prescribed order had to be accepted. The aforementioned pay scale of the bureaucracy was obviously an important factor leading to irregular practices and official corruption in the later part of the dynasty. The enormous assets confiscated from many impeached officials clearly evidenced that the top bureaucrats were supplementing their meager allowances with illegitimate and quasi-legitimate incomes. In fact,

the Ming fiscal administration is noted for embracing two irrecon-
cilable extremes: the unbending commitment to a rigid order in
principle and the widespread violation of the same principle in reality.

Most of the Ming state institutions, as handed down to the later
part of the dynasty, had grown out of customary usages rather than
creative legislation. Once an important precedent was established by
the emperor, it had a certain binding effect on his successors. Since
Ming officials adopted a static concept of the economy, they took it
for granted that fiscal policies established by their forebears were
applicable to their own times as well. Deviations from early practices
were avoided in all but exceptional circumstances, and statesmen
rarely dared to suggest full-scale revamping of the existing system.
Improvised modifications were introduced merely as temporary substitutes for a perfect order. Ironically, as time went on such makeshift
revisions also gained respectability and were honored no less than
earlier precedents. The code of Ming administrative procedures,
Ta-Ming Hui-tien (Collected statutes of the Ming dynasty), contains
a vast body of such precedents. In it many entries under fiscal administration are inconsistent, incoherent, and even contradictory of one
another. The lack of periodical and systematic reforms remained an
underlying weakness of Ming government. Its vital institutions were
too rigidly structured to accommodate any change of circumstances.

THE MINISTER OF REVENUE AND THE
MINISTRY OF REVENUE

The minister of revenue during the Ming dynasty rarely functioned
as a policy maker. Most of the time he was a fiscal adviser to the
crown. He was empowered to supervise routine fiscal matters; but as
regards any action deviating even slightly from the established procedure he had to seek approval from the emperor. While submitting
recommendations to the emperor, the minister of revenue was not
immune to criminal charges. In 1441 Liu Chung-fu was imprisoned
merely because he had petitioned that the palace horses be entrusted
to civilian stables for maintenance. This harmless suggestion was
considered offensive enough for prosecution. Court circles recom-

mended death sentences for both Liu and his vice-minister, since they had dared to advocate departure from "the established laws of the dynastic founders." Pardoned by Emperor Ying-tsung (1435–49, 1457–64), Liu was ordered to carry a lance and guard the palace gate for sixteen days before returning to ministerial duty.[12] This case shows the extremely restricted freedom in action of the ministerial officials.

Of the eighty-nine officials appointed ministers of revenue during the dynasty, twenty-five left office through retirement, twenty-two were transfered to other duties, sixteen were dismissed, seven died in office, seven resigned because of illness and mourning, three were executed, two were banished with their names removed from the civil service register, one was exiled, one left office without authorization, one was killed in battle, and one committed suicide at the fall of the dynasty. The remaining three are not accounted for; the reasons for their leaving office cannot be ascertained from the sources currently available.[13] An analysis of the list gives further evidence that the ministers of revenue were very much dependent upon the whims of their autocratic masters.

The founding emperor, T'ai-tsu (1368–98), was a ruthless despot. Of the twelve ministers of revenue who served him only three are known to have left office gracefully. The rest were jailed, dismissed, banished, or executed. Furthermore, the emperor seemed to value his ministerial officials' meticulousness more than their administrative talents. As a rule, the minister of revenue under his reign was a career bureaucrat who had risen to the top position after years of service in the ministry and was expected to be a master of details. Yu Hsing was promoted to the post in 1393 because, when questioned by the emperor, he was able to produce vital statistics on taxation and population offhand.[14] The demand that the minister of revenue be preoccupied with details seems to have continued in later years. In 1441 the same hapless Liu Chung-fu who was mentioned above was sentenced to death because during a confrontation with the emperor he had failed to recall the number of horses and camels that Oirat tribes had turned in as tribute.[15] On the other hand, Hsia Yüan-chi (appointed 1402) and Wang Ch'iung (appointed 1513) were cited as having been brilliant administrators because of their infallible memories. The latter in particular managed to remember the granary reserves in the various installations and military supplies at different army posts down to the exact figure.[16]

Ch'eng-tsu (1402–24) busied himself in military campaigns. His minister of revenue for 20 years, Hsia Yüan-chi, accompanied him in the field and gained enough of the monarch's confidence to become his chief adviser. Yet in 1421, merely for trying to dissuade Ch'eng-tsu from taking personal command of an expedition into the Mongolian desert, Hsia was arrested and disgraced.[17] Perhaps the only minister of revenue during the dynasty who exercised notable initiative and authority was Ko Tse, who was said to have countermanded Jen-tsung's (1424–25) directives to reduce the land tax.[18] Ko was able to defy the sovereign largely because he had been minister regent when Jen-tsung was still crown prince. Also, Jen-tsung was a monarch of unusual tolerance and leniency. After Hsüan-tsung (1425–35) succeeded Jen-tsung, Ko was reappointed minister of revenue. In 1432 Hsüan-tsung complained that his orders to lighten the tax burdens of the population had been repeatedly disregarded by the Ministry of Revenue;[19] the incident seems to suggest that the senior statesman continued to handle his ministerial affairs with autonomy. But Ko's defiance of the crown by no means broadened the authority of his office. In 1451 Chin Lien tried to follow in Ko's footsteps and failed. That year Emperor Ching-ti (1457–64) had ordered a one third across-the-board tax cut. Chin, apparently trying to bring state revenue in line, interpreted the decree as applying to tax in kind only and decided that monetary payments should not be covered by the reduction. Before his directives to the provincial officials could be put into effect, he found himself imprisoned.[20]

After the mid-fifteenth century, ministers of revenue appeared to fare better. As the civil service matured, appointments to the ministry of revenue were given only to men of some experience, usually provincial governors and frontier administrators whose ability had been widely recognized. The death penalty, still claiming lives among ministerial officials throughout the dynasty, was never again meted out to the empire's chief fiscal administrator. Even imprisonment of a minister of revenue was seldom ordered. Of the forty-six ministers of revenue who served after ascension of the emperor Shih-tsung in

1521, eleven terminated their terms through retirement, fourteen were transferred, and seven resigned. Even though nine ministers of revenue were formally dismissed, only Wang Kou (in 1547) and Pi Tzu-yen (in 1633) are known to have been arrested while in office.[21] This record may create an impression that in the later part of the dynasty occupants of the office were better received by the crown; the minister of revenue was permitted to serve with some measure of dignity. But the authority of the office was hardly increased.

The steady rise of eunuch power in and after the reign of Wu-tsung (1505–21) is a well-known phenomenon of Ming history. As more and more palace attendants were appointed to purchase missions and to supervisory positions over service and supply installations, a conflict of interest with the Ministry of Revenue became inevitable. Again and again a minister of revenue found that his security in office depended upon his willingness to cooperate with, to compromise with, and to give deference to powerful eunuchs. Many a minister of revenue, including several who seemingly had retired according to normal civil service procedure, were in fact removed from office because they objected to appropriations alloted to eunuch commissioners. After fighting losing battles with eunuchs, Ch'in Ching retired in 1527, Ma Shen in 1569, Wang Yin-chiao in 1622; Pi Chiang resigned in 1586, and Wang Lin was transferred in 1585.[22]

Factional quarrels among court officials, which became intense in later years, also handicapped the operation of the ministry. The Ming governmental system required the emperor to give audience to a great number of court officials, both senior and junior. Memorials for imperial scrutiny were submitted by large numbers of censors, supervising secretaries, and ministerial officials down to divisional heads and sectional chiefs. Remonstrances and criticisms on fiscal policies could be initiated by almost anyone, regardless of his area of specialization and current assignment. Such criticisms were often motivated by personal likes and dislikes as factions in the court developed. Frequently opinions expressed in the memorials reflected mere partisan and doctrinal polemics, while fiscal technicalities might be completely ignored. The minister of revenue was required to answer all the charges. Yin Cheng-mou requested retirement in 1578 and Chao Shih-ch'ing left office without authorization in 1611, both as victims of partisan controversies.[23]

The adverse effect of such criticisms on fiscal administration was obvious. The requirement that the chief fiscal administrator answer charges from various quarters could absorb a great deal of his energy. Pi Tzu-yen, minister of revenue between 1629 and 1633, is described by his biographer as having composed all his own memoranda, daily producing several thousand words.[24] In the extant documents left by him we seldom see the minister analyze his problems in clearcut and specific terms. Again and again the tone of his papers is forensic and the topic under discussion diffuse. This undoubtedly reflects the general practice of the time. Sun Ch'eng-tse, a supervising secretary in the Office of Scrutiny for Revenue in the later part of the last Ming reign, that of Chuang-lieh-ti (1627–44), disclosed that memoranda for the emperor handled by his section increased 50 percent as compared with the volume submitted in the late 1620s, and 70 percent as compared with the volume in the 1610s. In conclusion, Sun, an official whose own prescribed duty was remonstrance, observed: "The more are the opinions offered, the less energy is left [for official business] . . . The more topics are opened for debate, the less talented are the men remaining [in office]. The drawback [of the present system] is that too many pitfalls and camouflages are dressed up within the abundant suggestions." [25]

By our standard, the organization of the Ministry of Revenue could be summarized as hopelessly understaffed. Under the minister were two vice-ministers. But these deputies were usually given field assignments such as superintendent of imperial granaries, commissioner in charge of the Grand Canal, and commissioner for military supplies to Manchuria. Normally the minister had no executive officer, no comptroller, no chief statistician, no full-time treasurer, and no planning staff. He dealt directly with the heads of 13 territorial bureaus within the ministry.[26] Even though the table of organization provided the minister with a "business assistant" and a "document checker," those officers seldom acted as undersecretaries. When the minister of revenue Ni Yüan-lu promoted a brilliant but hitherto unknown student as his business assistant and placed under him five staff members to take charge of office routine, the step was considered a novelty.[27] Within each territorial bureau there were supposed to be three or four staff members of civil service status, but the positions were not always filled. Even when they were filled, the occupants were frequently detailed to the provinces to administer field installations, and therefore remained absent from the ministry for long periods of time. In the 1570s the staff members were not even required to report to the ministry; they held official positions on an inactive and honorary basis. The appointments merely enabled them to acquire seniority for promotions. The bureau heads carried on the heavy load of office work with the help of some 165 lesser functionaries, who were basically clerks. It was Wang Kuo-kuang, minister from 1572 to 1576, who first demanded that all personnel assigned to the ministry report to the office daily.[28] In the 1610s even the positions of bureau heads were left vacant. Minister Li Nü-hua acted concurrently as head of several bureaus under his own command. In such circumstances the ministry simply did not have the necessary manpower to make over-all estimates, to coordinate interdepartmental activities, or even to consolidate current data.

The lack of central planning in the fiscal operation finally became glaringly apparent. The bulk of the ministry's business was carried out by earmarking certain specific revenues for particular purposes, matching the receivables with expenditures item by item. The proceeds from the commodity tax from a certain inland port were routed to a certain government-owned dockyard for ship construction; land taxes collected from a particular prefecture were delivered to a specific frontier post. Cash transactions normally were carried out in the provinces between delivery agents and corresponding receiving offices. The system resembles numerous strands of wire running through a switchboard whose operator is not a conversing party. As time went on it became extremely cumbersome, especially when new expenditures were incurred and the rerouting of funds became necessary. In 1592 the magistrate of the Wan-p'ing County in Peking reported that he was required to make cash deliveries to 27 depots and agencies designated by the central government. Yet the total amount involved was less than 2,000 taels of silver; most cases involved less than 50 taels, and some only one or two taels.[30] Each official in the Ministry of Revenue was assigned to supervise such cash flows within his designated geographical area. Understandably, he would have difficulty in maintaining a clear view of those transactions, let alone be able to evaluate the effectiveness of the spending.

The Ming fiscal system made no clear-cut differentiation between state income and local income. All tax revenues were imperial incomes. The parceling of funds for imperial and local expenses did not follow any broadly conceived principle. The terms by which funds were categorized, *ch'i-yün* and *ts'un-liu*, literally mean "checked-out" and "staying-in." The former denotes items delivered to vaults and depots outside the territory in which they were originally collected, while the latter refers to those items dispensed within the territory. Normally the "checked-out" funds were earmarked to support the imperial capital and the imperial army, and to finance many kinds of state projects, while the "staying-in" items could be considered primarily as local funds and regional reserves. But the demarcation was by no means so definite. The "checked-out" funds from a county, when delivered outside the county's boundary, could be disbursed to support prefectural and provincial governments and to finance local relief. Conversely, the "staying-in" funds were sometimes spent to defray imperial expenditures. For example, the two county magistrates in Peking were jointly responsible for providing money, food, and stationery for the triennial civil service examinations held in the capital—a case wherein an imperial function was financed by local funds.[31] What is more, surpluses derived from both "staying-in" and "checking-out" funds could be disbursed only by decree of the emperor. All deposits in the numerous granaries and vaults across the country were theoretically imperial reserves. The whole system required the central government to direct the fiscal operation of the local government in greatest detail. This made efficient administration all but impossible.

The Ministry of Revenue never composed a budget as such. In the early years of the dynasty, the court did require the several provinces to submit reports on the next year's incomes and expenditures. The budgetary control never became effective; in part this was because the local officials were simultaneously tax-collectors and fund-disbursers. And the remote provinces could not turn in their reports until two thirds of the fiscal year had already elapsed. After 1513 the annual report was discontinued; in its place a decennial report was submitted.[32] But this could be no more than a rough estimate. After 1583 the decennial reports submitted by the provinces and prefectures included also the commuted *corvée* labor incomes and the expenditures of the funds so derived. They became the so-called *Fu-i ch'üan-*

shu (Comprehensive book on taxation and services).[33] On a national level a *K'uai-chi Lu* (Fiscal records) was composed. Despite the enormous volumes of information provided by those handbooks, the data therein were not arranged in a logical, integrated fashion. Commodities of all kinds, such as grain, cotton, hemp, silk fabrics, dates, and sesame seeds, were listed together. Cash items including taels of silver, strings of copper cash, and government notes of depreciated value were never converted into a common standard and consolidated. The breakdown of the expenditures showed such minute details as the maintenance of ferry boats, the vermilion pigment for official seals, and wages for trumpeters by the day. Even with the aid of today's business machines, we find the figures simply unmanageable, because neither the conversion ratio nor the units and measurements are at all clear, not to mention the surcharges and delivery allowances. It is extremely doubtful that before the early seventeenth century Ming officials could have digested the volume of fiscal information available and given it a logical interpretation. In 1632 Minister of Revenue Pi Tzu-yen submitted a memorandum for Chuang-lieh-ti in which tax arrears across the country were listed. The list covers four and a half pages of fine print in its present reproduced form. Among many other items, the minister brought to the emperor's attention certain overdue payments from Wu-hsien which were supposed to have been paid in lieu of the county's annual tribute of honey to the court. Their total value was less than twenty-eight taels of silver; and this took place when the nationwide tax arrears exceeded tens of millions of taels! [34] In all, we can say that such practices are the natural results of the basic Ming fiscal system, which relied on a decentralized administration within a centralized ministry. Since the vision of the administrators remained localized and stationary, they tended to give emphasis to the minor and inconsequential.

The greatest weakness of the system was that few officials could make over-all estimates and forecasts. As a matter of fact, Ming officials generally avoided anticipating future problems and foretelling an enlarged budget. They would rather wait until tax delinquencies and fiscal deficits actually occurred, and then seek remedies as best they could.

In the Ming governmental organization, several ministries and departments and imperial agencies in Peking and the combined offices in Nanking maintained their separate incomes, which were derived from special commodity taxes, regular land tax, and commutation of labor service, etc. While this will be spelled out in more detail later, it may be mentioned here that the minister of revenue, even within his limited authority as the chief fiscal administrator, exercised no control over these state funds collected and disbursed autonomously by his colleagues.

Not all Ming contemporaries were unaware of the institutional weaknesses outlined above. Ni Yüan-lu, the last minister of revenue of the dynasty, a man of remarkable financial insight, apparently attempted many reforms during his administration.[35] In his memoranda for the emperor, he suggested that state incomes and expenditures be consolidated and integrated. In the later part of 1643 he even prepared a military budget, anticipating annual military expenditures of 21,221,486 taels of silver. With a projected income of 15,845,027 taels, the deficit would be 5,376,460 taels. To make up for the deficit he planned to resort to issuing government notes.[36] At the same time he also suggested a concentration of fiscal responsibility, complete commutation of taxes in kind, revival of coastal transport between north and south, liberalization of business control, and elimination of tax farmers. All these proposals came too late: the next year the dynasty collapsed and Ni himself perished with the court.

MAJOR SOURCES OF STATE REVENUE

Land Taxes

As could have been expected, the Ming court derived a dominant proportion of its income from land taxes. Yet it never instituted a consistent land-tax system. Revenue derived from land, confusingly but interchangeably called *tsu-fu* (rent and tribute), *liang* (grain tax), or *k'o* (impositions), included ordinary land tax, the *corvée* labor service related to it, the grain production quotas of military colonies, and rents from government land. With all pomp and elaboration, the Ming court established a highly organized civil service; but it never employed a salaried staff to administer the land tax. From the early military-conquest years of the dynasty, the collection of land taxes

was left to civilian agents called *liang-chang* (tax captains), who were
to deliver consignments of grain to strategic points designated by the
court. This procedure, growing out of wartime policy, remained in
practice throughout the entire duration of the dynasty.[37]

Apparently Ming T'ai-tsu had intended to establish a uniform rate
of land taxes. But even during his own reign this was not accomplished, and as time went by the central government had less and less
control over the actual collection. A tax quota was established for each
county and each prefecture. In theory, such quotas were to be revised from time to time upon periodical land surveys. But the survey
was rarely conducted, and the quota became permanent or semiper-
manent. It has been pointed out by a Ch'ing scholar that from 1391
to 1533 the cultivated land of two counties in Honan, Hsi-hua and
Yung-ch'eng, increased ten and seventeen times respectively, but the
tax quotas of the two counties were never upgraded.[38] Since the early
years of the dynasty, it had been a common practice that certain
counties and prefectures counted several *mou* of land as one fiscal
mou, giving taxpayers with inferior landholdings a hidden advantage.[39]
In December, 1580, under the astute statesman Chang Chü-cheng, a
nationwide land survey was conducted, aiming at the elimination of
abuses and irregular practices.[40] It was decided that one standard *mou*
measurement was to be universally adopted. The program fell far
short of its goal. Chang died in 1582, and the final result of the survey
seems never to have been tabulated and published. But even from the
incomplete returns we can see that the cultivated acreages in several
provinces had previously been grossly underreported. Notably, the
taxable land in Kweichow Province before the survey was listed as
186,000 *mou*, but after the survey it was reported as 328,000 *mou*,
showing an increase of over 70 percent.[41] Likewise, the cultivated
land of Shantung before the survey was 76,300,000 *mou*, but after the
survey it was 112,700,000 *mou*; the increase was close to 50 percent.[42]
The court, while facing an annual deficit, accepted the new figures
without revising the total tax payments of these two provinces.
Records show only that the tax quotas of Hukwang Province, several
prefectures in the Northern Metropolitan Area, and two military districts in Shansi were revised upward upon the completion of the land
survey.[43]

The effect of the quota system on the government's fiscal management was profound. It limited its income from land to an established ceiling. In the later period when the court combed the country for revenue, additional land taxes had to be collected as extra-schedule levies, and under most difficult conditions. When the central government tried to reassert the principle that tax quotas should be revised to reflect population growth and increased acreage under cultivation, local magistrates simply resubmitted their districts' earlier data as current returns. Those districts whose population and economic activities had actually remained at a standstill also suffered, since now the central government could do little to lighten their tax burdens.

The total land tax assessment in terms of piculs of grain—the basic standard of the dynasty—was rather stable throughout the period until the seventeenth century. Summarizing the unedited data of the *Ta-Ming Hui-tien*, I conclude that the total assessment of 1393 was 29,776,426 units; that of 1502 was 26,792,259 units; and that of 1578 was 26,638,412 units.[44] The last two figures may have been slightly underestimated, since in the later part of the dynasty some of the tax obligations were assessed in commodities other than grain. But such assessments, based upon actual crops produced on land, were relatively small in amount. (They differed from commutation payments, which meant tax payments made in substitute items that bore no connection with the actual crop.) My calculation shows that the total value of such assessments in 1578 could not have exceeded two percent of all land taxes.

Under the quota system the county remained the basic unit for tax collection. The tax captains were as a rule appointed by the county magistrate. Even though on provincial and prefectural levels there were officials designated as tax supervisors, their major functions were coordinating and supervisory. Basic fiscal responsibility rested on the county magistrate. When administrative officials were frequently punished for tax delinquencies during the later part of the dynasty, it was the county magistrates who suffered most. On the other hand, provincial governors and prefects seem to have had certain unspecified authority over tax administration. By issuing executive orders they could regulate and modify tax procedures within their districts. The so-called single whip method (*i-t'iao-pien fa*), which consolidated the tax payments, miscellaneous collections, and *corvée* labor services in the later part of the sixteenth century, was for the most part initiated by the prefects. These officials could not revise the tax quotas charged to counties; but on many occasions they took the initiative of re-apportioning the different classes of taxes to the several counties. (For different classes of taxes, see below.) Thus they redistributed the tax burdens of the counties without altering their nominal quotas. The administrative orders so issued, after remaining in effect for a considerable length of time, often entered respective local histories and attained the force of customary law. This clearly shows the lack of uniformity within the tax administration.

The accounting of the land taxes was further complicated by a number of factors. First of all, in most cases a surcharge was added to the basic assessment. This followed the principle that taxpayers were obligated to transport the grain payments to granaries and depots designated by the court, sometimes hundreds or even thousands of miles away. Unless the payment fell into the category of "staying-in" items, in which case the taxpayers could possibly make the delivery themselves, they had to rely for transportation upon the special army corps operating on the Grand Canal, or upon tax captains. In both cases transportation costs and service charges had to be prepaid. The actual amount depended upon the distance of the haul, road hazards, and transfers en route. For grain payments which originated in the lower Yangtze valley and were designated for Peking, for instance, a surcharge over 80 percent of the basic assessment was not uncommon. In some cases the surcharges could exceed the basic payment.[45]

Commutation of tax or service obligations into monetary payments and other commodities did not simplify the procedure. When tax payments were converted to silver, there was not a uniform conversion ratio to follow. Rather, each time a consignment was commuted it was handled as an individual case. Consideration was given to whether the original payment was a "staying-in" or "checked-out" item, the kind of transportation obligation attached to it, and the prevailing food price and transportation cost at the time of commutation. Only after the commutation was put into effect was the conversion ratio permanently applied to the particular tax consignment. The local history of Yang-chou Prefecture indicated that in the 1550s grain payments from the prefecture for northward dispatch were payable in silver ranging from 0.7 taels of silver per picul to 1.2 taels per picul, the disparities being created by successive commuting orders.[46] There were times, however, when the court waived the above considerations altogether and arbitrarily set up a conversion ratio; the application was limited to certain payments specified in the commutation order. An outstanding case occurred in 1436, when Ying-tsung decreed that some four million piculs of tax grain collectable from several provinces should be permanently commuted at 0.25 taels of silver per picul. This covered all "checked-out" payments from Kwangtung, Kwangsi, and Fukien Provinces, and portions of land taxes in Chekiang, Kiangsi, and Hukwang Provinces and the Southern Metropolitan Area around Nanking. The total proceeds of this commutation, 1,012,729 taels of silver per annum, were later designated as *chin-hua-yin* (Gold-Floral-Silver) and became the emperor's personal expense account.[47] Its implications will be discussed later. From a tax administration point of view, the most objectionable feature of this series of settlements was that commutations were handed out piecemeal; too many times *ad hoc* decisions were permitted to modify the permanent tax structure. The inconsistencies in effect created many different classes of land tax for taxpayers. The price of husked rice in the Yangtze valley was about one tael of silver per picul in the later fourteenth century; it slipped to 0.5 or 0.6 taels per picul in the sixteenth and seventeenth centuries.[48] Yet some taxpayers were paying 1.2 taels per picul, or more than double their share, while others were paying 0.25 taels per picul, or half their share.

Contrary to general belief, cash generated from land taxes and made available to the Ministry of Revenue in Peking consisted of only a relatively small amount. This is explained by Table 1. It may be noted that most supplies and funds were earmarked as "staying-in" funds or were delivered directly to the frontier posts or to Nanking. What remained for delivery to the imperial capital constituted only a little over one third of all tax revenue. Of the four million piculs of grain delivered to imperial granaries (referred to as "grain tribute" by many scholars), only a small portion was distributed as emoluments to civil officials. The bulk was rationed to capital garrisons, construction laborers, palace cooks, artisans, etc. The surplus was to build up a granary reserve. The actual annual central-government expenditure in the 1580s was within the range of 2.2 million to 2.6 million piculs.[49] The Court of Imperial Entertainments received 210,000 piculs annually.[50] This court operated then as the world's largest grocery store and dining hall. It employed 6,300 cooks in 1425,[51] and toward the

TABLE 1 *Estimated Collection and Distribution of Land Taxes ca. 1578* (*Unit: picul and/or equivalent*)

Collection

Summer tax	4,600,000
Autumn tax	22,000,000
Total	26,600,000

Distribution

Earmarked as "staying-in" funds and supplies		11,700,000
Delivered to frontier posts directly by taxpayers		3,300,000
Delivered at Nanking		1,500,000
Delivered to Peking		9,530,000
In grain at imperial granaries	4,000,000	
In grain to Court of Imperial Entertainments & other agencies	210,000	
Commuted to cotton cloth & other palace supplies	900,000	
Commuted to Gold-Floral-Silver	4,050,000	
Otherwise permanently commuted	370,000	
Miscellaneous (subsidies to imperial clansmen, appropriations for royal manufacture, etc.)		570,000
Total		26,600,000

end of the dynasty the staff grew larger. The Court distributed meat and alcoholic beverages, provided free meals to officials on various occasions, and rationed groceries to the palace attendants. From the number of wine jars delivered to this agency and the amount of salt consumed by it, it can be estimated that its kitchen service must have served from 10,000 to 15,000 persons daily.[52] This does not even cover the numerous sacrificial services that were handled by the Court of Imperial Sacrifices. Cotton cloth and other supplies took up another

900,000 piculs because of the enormous number of attendants who staffed the Ming palace. It has been estimated that around 1600 there were possibly 70,000 palace eunuchs and some 9,000 palace women.[53] Also, cotton cloth was sometimes rationed to army personnel. The four million odd piculs of grain commuted to Gold-Floral-Silver, as was mentioned above, had become the emperor's personal income. Out of the annual proceeds totaling one million odd taels of silver, the emperor distributed 100,000 taels to senior military commanders and the rest was spent for his personal grants and purchases, over which the Ministry of Revenue had no control.[54] This left only the 370,000 piculs permanently commuted to silver payments available to the ministry. Generally at 0.7 taels per picul, this consignment in 1578 yielded 247,613 taels.[55] But in this very year Shen-tsung (1572–1620) decreed that thereafter each year the ministry was to surrender 200,000 taels to supplement the expense account of the crown,[56] practically depleting even this last resource.

Later sixteenth-century accounts nevertheless show that the Ministry of Revenue received large sums of money from the land taxes. Whence was this income derived? The cash was generated from two sources. On one hand, it included supplies delivered to the frontier posts directly by taxpayers. At 3.3 million piculs per annum, the supplies were commuted into silver payments in 1487 and 1492.[57] After 1558, and especially after the decrees of 1573, most of those silver payments were handled through the Ministry of Revenue.[58] As soon as the payments were received by the ministry they were forwarded to appropriate consignees in the several frontier posts. What was involved, then, was no more than a procedural change. On the other hand, the ministry's income included portions of the grain within the four-million-picul quota that was supposed to be delivered at imperial granaries (grain tribute). In the mid-seventeenth century, granary reserves in Peking had been built up to last for more than ten years. On the recommendations of Wang Kou, minister of revenue, and Wan Piao, commander in chief of the Army Transportation Corps, unscheduled commutations, with quotas rotating among the several provinces, were authorized.[59] From then on, the annual delivery at Peking seldom reached the four-million-picul mark. In most cases the delivery was less than three million piculs.[60] The amount of cash produced from the one million odd piculs varied from year to year, since the conversion ratio was often adjusted to effect tax relief for areas suffering from natural disasters. There were also occasions when portions of the consignment were remitted, as in the case of famine. It is estimated that the Ministry of Revenue derived an annual income of 500,000 taels of silver from the unscheduled commutations. And this sum, it may be emphasized, constituted the only major cash item that the ministry received from regular land taxes.

Another item of state income, though derived from land, was audited separately. This was the animal fodder that was submitted by tax-paying subjects. The collection of hay was initiated in 1370 in the prefectures near Nanking. The levy was assessed upon landowners at the basic rate of sixteen bundles of hay per hundred *mou* of land. The collection was later extended to Chekiang, Shantung, Shansi, and Honan Provinces and the Northern Metropolitan Area.[61] The 1578 record indicates that the court received 338,419 taels of silver as commuted payments from this imposition, not counting the 9,602,305 bundles of hay actually delivered by taxpayers.[62] Had the delivered portion been equally commuted at the prevailing ratio of 0.03 taels of silver per bundle, it would have yielded another 288,069 taels. Thus the total worth of this income exceeded 626,488 taels. Even the commuted portion alone produced 10 to 15 percent of the silver payments received by the Ministry of Revenue. Though it seems a nuisance tax, the animal fodder levy contributed substantially to the state revenue.

The service levy, which included *corvée* labor, militia service, the obligation of serving as guardsmen, orderlies, and postmen, and the requisition of many material supplies by several imperial agencies, was originally separated from the regular land tax in early Ming times. But after the sixteenth century it tended to overlap or be merged with the land tax. How it was handled varied from one district to another; there was no standard procedure to follow. In the category of labor service, for instance, the original imposition units, the *ting*, meant an able-bodied male. After the service was gradually commuted to monetary payments, however, the word lost its original meaning and became a flexible fiscal unit, devoid of any precise definition. Some districts assessed relatively few numbers of *ting*, but the payment for each was high. Others imposed more; conversely, the payment for each *ting* was lighter. The old method of assessing *ting* as a capitation with its quota distributed among the male population continued in many regions. When the commuted payments were insufficient to meet the rising costs of the required service, nevertheless, the general tendency was to make up the deficit by imposing a new surcharge on the regular land tax. When Hsün-te County, Kwangtung Province, in 1584 found its original *ting* quota no longer sufficient to cover the expenses, it did not raise the commuting payment, but created an additional number of *ting* by demanding that each 50 *mou* of taxable land furnish an extra *ting*.[63] As time went by the portion of revenue derived from land gradually exceeded the portion derived from the poll tax.[64] Hsiang-ho County in the Northern Metropolitan Area in the early seventeenth century derived 60 percent of its service levy from land and only 40 percent from the poll tax.[65]

Adoption of the single whip method did not eliminate the diversity of standards. The single-whip money (*t'iao-pien-yin*), as it is called, was originally designed to enable the land owners to meet their tax obligations with a single payment. But in the majority of cases this aim was never accomplished, many districts continuing to leave some items out of the consolidated payment. Furthermore, while the method partially consolidated the collection, it did little to modify the tax structure. In other words, while the payments under many different headings were added up for each taxpayer in one bill, the varied headings were rarely simplified and were by no means totally eliminated. In the tax bill (*yu-t'ieh*) the basic land tax, with the picul as its fiscal unit, was always separated from the service levy, with the *ting* as its unit. Some counties retained a score or so of subtitles under these two general headings, each following a particular commuting ratio.

It is usually assumed that the service levy was a local tax. This is only partially true. It was a local tax to the extent that it was locally assessed and accounted for, that the central government had virtually no control over it, and that the bulk of the payments was retained for local expenses. But funds derived from the service levy were also used for hiring laborers to maintain the Grand Canal and to operate its water gates, in the case of those districts wherein the waterway was located. The carriers of the imperial postal system were likewise paid with the proceeds from the service levy. And practically every county had to dispense a part of its revenue from the service levy to purchase supplies for its scheduled contribution to the imperial palace. The more common items thus contributed were botanical medicines for the Imperial Academy of Medicine, local delicacies for the Court of Imperial Entertainments, and quilted uniforms for the Ministry of War. Some districts contributed writing brushes and sweeping brooms. The quantities were huge and the list was virtually endless. In the early seventeenth century the monetary value of such material ran close to four million taels of silver, not to mention the transportation costs.[66]

In general, the service levy was heavier south of the Yangtze than in northern counties and prefectures, reflecting the more intense commitment in militia service and the higher degree of sophistication of local government in the southern region. In the data of 30 counties and prefectures that I have sampled, the collection in many northern communities was equivalent to about 30 percent of the land tax assessment, while an equivalent of 50 or 60 percent in the south was not uncommon. But several counties in the north as well as in the south, such as Wen-shang County of Shantung Province, Ch'ang-hua County of Chekiang Province, and Hsün-te County of Kwangtung Province, made collections equivalent to or exceeding 100 percent of the respective counties' land taxes.[67]

Salt Revenue

Revenue derived from the state salt monopoly constituted the second largest item of state income. Under the monopoly system, all salt producing areas across the empire were organized into thirteen distribution commissions and superintendencies.[68] Each of those offices was assigned a production quota and a distribution region. Families engaged in salt manufacturing were registered in the respective areas. By law, each male member of those families was required to turn in 3,200 catties of salt each year, or about two short tons annually. During T'ai-tsu's reign, the total production quota was set at 459,316,400 catties, or about 306,000 short tons.[69]

The actual manufacture required little governmental supervision. The salt-producing families owned their homesteads. Where the salt was not produced through the sun-drying process, iron caldrons were furnished by the state. Fuel was collected from designated "grass land," sometimes consisting of marshes. To compensate the workers, the state authorized the commissions and superintendencies to distribute one picul of grain for every 400 catties of salt produced.[70] But this policy was never fully carried out. From the outset the government substituted paper currency for the grain payment. As the value of paper money plunged, compensation virtually stopped. The salt-producing personnel, however, were encouraged to reclaim waste public land, with land taxes reduced or omitted. At times the government subsidized the purchase of tools. Sometimes forced contributions were also exacted from salt merchants to provide relief. Toward the end of the dynasty the salt producers seemed to live mainly on the so-called non-quota salt produced by themselves.[71]

In the first century of the dynasty the court sold salt directly to the public on a rationed basis, and purchase was mandatory. Probably the direct sale never did more than partially meet public needs, since the amount rationed to the rural population (two catties and two ounces per person per year) could hardly be considered adequate. On the other hand the sale price (one string of cash in government notes per catty) also seems to be exorbitantly high. When the government notes continued to depreciate in value, the court discontinued salt distribution in 1474. Nevertheless, the collection of salt-purchase payments from the population was not suspended. The money so collected, unabashedly called "payment for rationed salt," was divided between the central government and the local governments.[72] Thus, since it delivered no salt, the court now virtually imposed a new poll tax on its population. The 1578 account indicates that 80,555 taels of silver were annually turned in to the imperial treasury as "payment for rationed salt." [73]

The bulk of the salt produced by the state was actually sold to commercial distributors. In the early years some form of barter system was practiced. Salt buyers were instructed to provide grain at frontier army posts designated by the court. Upon delivery, the authorities handed promissory notes to the merchants, which the latter cashed for salt in the producing areas. By this procedure the government relieved itself of all transportation obligations, and the revenue was channeled to supplement army supplies.[74] In the later part of the fifteenth century the barter system was replaced by cash transactions. In the sixteenth century, in an effort to resolve supply problems in the frontier regions, the barter system was partially revived.[75]

Since the salt producers were destitute and large numbers of them regularly deserted, the production quotas in the several commissions and superintendencies could not always be met. The government, furthermore, tended to oversell its promissory notes. The result was that many merchants, after having made cash or grain deliveries, found that they had to wait for future stock, sometimes for years or even decades. In early times the government promissory notes were not transferable; they must be cashed by the consignee in person. When a salt buyer died before the salt note had been cashed the promissory notes were often escheated.[76] This discouraged the merchants; at the same time, as the annual production was allocated merely to meet previous commitments, the revenue also dried up.

The court resorted to a new device in 1440. The annual salt production was classified into two categories. Eighty percent was called "regular stock" and the remaining 20 percent "reserve stock." Ostensibly, the former was kept in normal circulation and the latter stockpiled for emergency use, in preparation for urgent military demands. But no sooner had the classification been created than the reserve was made available at public auction. Since the delivery involved no waiting, this stock was sold for cash at higher prices. In the mid-sixteenth century the regular stock was reduced to 40 percent and the reserve stock increased to 60 percent.[77] Thus the general sale of salt from this point on always involved default on the part of the government. Spot delivery was transformed to futurity; the delivery date was repeatedly set back. The proceeds of the sale always included advances against future stock. Sometimes the salt administrators, in order to boost the revenue, even forced on merchants who had contracted to purchase from the reserve stock a proportional amount from the future-delivery regular stock.

Still more complicated was the handling of the nonquota salt. As a result of population growth and the proliferation of salt-producing families in the sixteenth century, both the demand for and the supply of salt were substantially increased. Nevertheless, because of managerial weaknesses, the official quota for each commission or superintendency could not be proportionately upgraded. This created a large amount of nonquota salt, perhaps twice as much as the official quota. According to early regulations, the government should require the producers to surrender the stock, with compensation of 0.25 piculs of grain for every 200 catties of surplus salt. Since the government could no longer pay, the nonquota salt was not collected. Yet the producers were not free to sell it to the public. Only when a merchant purchased an amount of official salt from a government agency was he issued a license which permitted him to enter the restricted area to purchase from the producers a proportional amount of nonquota salt, either equivalent to his official purchase, or, sometimes, twice as much.[78] When the salt cleared the check point the merchant surrendered the license and paid the government a fee, which in reality developed into an excise tax. The rate as set in the Huai River region in the late sixteenth century was 0.8 taels of silver for every 200 catties, or approximately six taels per short ton.[79]

The matter would have been much simpler if the court had been content with this revenue derived from a fixed rate on a variable volume. But instead, at the same time, it also demanded that fixed quotas of silver must be collected from this income. Quotas of "surplus-salt silver" were now assigned to the several commissions and the superintendencies. Each salt administrator, therefore, had to force the producers to manufacture more salt to meet his quota. In many instances, by fulfilling this extra demand, districts became delinquent in their regular production quotas.[80] As the system deteriorated, smuggling became rampant. Some influential merchants purchased the licenses from original legitimate traders; others held the same licenses and reused them over the years without surrendering them. Apparently many of them carried on armed smuggling or became affiliated with smugglers.

The details of the salt administration are too complicated to be presented in this outline. But we have not the slightest doubt that it represents one of the worst cases of a bureaucrat-managed economy. The state intended to monopolize the manufacture without financing it; it attempted to sell the salt directly to the consuming public without creating a centralized distribution agency. Dealing with merchants, the government seldom carried out its obligations faithfully. Officials in charge were too anxious to produce an immediate profit, with regard neither for the future nor for the market situation. Laws protecting the monopoly were stringent but could not be enforced. In the reign of Wu-tsung, abuses by eunuchs and influential aristocrats virtually wrecked the whole operation. Despite reforms by later administrators, the monopoly was never put on a sound basis.

It must be noted that the salt monopoly could be enormously profitable. A memorial to the throne dated 1527 indicated that the retail price of salt in Nanking, a city adjacent to the producing area, was about 25 taels of silver per short ton.[81] The manufacturing cost, even at one picul of grain for every 400 catties of salt as allowed by the government, was less than two taels per short ton. From various references and estimates by contemporaries I conclude that the total annual production across the country by the later sixteenth century could not be less than one million short tons. If efficiently managed, the income from salt alone could consequently have solved all the financial problems of the Ming state.

Despite the abuses and uncertainties suffered by the producers and salt merchants, capitalization in salt manufacture and salt dealing began to take place in Ming times. Contemporary sources now and then mentioned the "affluent salt-producers." They were either from the original producing families or merely outsiders, who, from whatever sources they may have accumulated capital, were able to use their wealth to buy out some of the producers under official registration. As salt producers, they and their employees were exempted from paying land taxes and performing *corvée* labor to an extent proportionate to the production quota they fulfilled. The extra "grass lands" were rented out for income. With their family fortunes continually growing and their operations extending, they became the forerunners of the "factory merchants" who owned half of the salt-producing properties on the east coast by 1830.[82] As for trading in salt, at first an unofficial "franchise" developed. By the mid-fifteenth century "dealerships" began to be purchased and sold among the merchants.[83] By 1617 the "franchise" of wholesale dealers gained official recognition, and anyone whose name did not appear in the official register was excluded from the wholesale trade in the Huai River region.[84] It is not surprising that most of those remaining on the list and enjoying the trading privilege later amassed fabulous fortunes. The salt monopoly, therefore, enriched a few at the expense of the whole population, and, as we see now, did not benefit the state as much as it could have done.

The 1578 account indicates that the total production quota of the 13 commissions and superintendencies was 486,764,200 catties, or about 324,000 short tons.[85] The increase from the earlier figure had been minor. But the surplus-salt silver assessed to the thirteen units contributed to a total income of 1,200,363 taels of silver, 983,320 taels to be submitted to Peking and the remaining 217,043 taels to be delivered to several army posts.[86] In a memorandum addressed to Shen-tsung by Minister of Revenue Li Nü-hua in the 1610s it was discovered that the annual total of salt revenue, including salt, grain, and cash payments, was worth more than two million taels. But the minister acknowledged that the target was never met.[87] Another source indicates that in 1606 the commissions and superintendencies met only half of their production quotas.[88] In 1607 and 1621 imperial orders were issued to remit previous delinquencies hitherto charged to the 13 units.[89] It is evident that until the early seventeenth century the annual yield from the salt monopoly remained in the vicinity of 1.2 million taels of silver, with perhaps one million taels actually turned in at Peking. Additional income, such as grain payments to the frontier posts through the barter system, was sporadic and insignificant. There were instances where the annual income was pushed above the normal level, but this usually resulted in delinquencies and lower yields in the subsequent years.

Business Taxes

For most of the Ming dynasty, foreign trade was outlawed. The exclusion policy deprived the imperial government of all revenues that could have been derived from imports and exports. But the inland customs duty was a major source of governmental income. The customs duties were collected at Pei-hsin-kuan near Hang-chou, Hsü-yeh-kuan near Su-chou, Huai-an, Yang-chou, Lin-ch'ing, Ho-hsi-wu, the Ch'ung-wen Gate of Peking, and Chiu-chiang.[90] With the exception of the last-mentioned port, all collecting points were situated along the Grand Canal, which indicates the large volume of commerce carried on that north-south trunkline.

The inland duty originated as a toll. In the early years assessments were made according to the carrier's capacity and measurements; the cargo itself was not taxed.[91] Payments were made exclusively in government currency. Later the assessment was extended to merchandise. In the mid-sixteenth century, both silver and paper money were collected. Before the turn of the century, however, inland duty paid in silver became the rule, paper currency and copper cash constituting only small fractions of the income.[92] The collecting rates and procedures were meticulously codified. The custom regulations at Lin-ch'ing alone as published ran to 105 pages and consisted of 1,900 items and articles.[93] But contemporary sources reveal that the actual collection deviated considerably from the codification. For one thing, by assigning annual quotas of collection to the several ports, the court virtually demanded that certain levels of income be guaranteed by the officials in charge. It could not expect them at the same time to abide strictly by the prescribed rates.[94]

The annual quota of the eight ports was 342,729 taels of silver in 1599; it increased to 374,929 taels in 1621 and to 479,929 taels in 1624. In 1629 a 10 percent increment was added to the collection; in 1630 another 20 percent was imposed. In 1640 the annual quota was increased by an additional 200,000 taels.[95] But by then the canal zone was so devastated and governmental machinery so completely broken down that it is doubtful if even half of the quota was actually met.

A sales tax was also collected throughout the empire, mainly on commodities at minor ports and carried overland. In early times there were more than 400 collecting stations dotted over the country; officials in charge were court personnel. In the fifteenth and sixteenth centuries many stations were combined and abolished. In the seventeenth century only 112 remained.[96] The collection, in time, was taken over by local officials. In many instances prefectural and county judges acted concurrently as collectors. Because of the divergent standards applied to the collection, the total revenue from this source is difficult to estimate. My calculation shows that around 1500 the annual proceeds amounted to the equivalent of 138,000 taels of silver. The proceeds of 1578 were close to the equivalent of 150,000 taels.[97]

Unlike the inland customs duty, the sales tax was seldom delivered to the central government. From time to time the court did direct certain collecting stations to deliver small amounts of cash to various imperial agencies. On other occasions the proceeds were delivered to subsidize imperial clansmen. But such deliveries usually involved only several hundred taels of silver, and the payments were not regular.[98] The rest of the income was retained by the counties and prefectures for local expenses. In general, the sales tax administration was most decentralized and the proceeds least effectively audited. The contribution to imperial coffers from this source was only nominal.

Other Income

A special commodity tax was collected by the Ministry of Works. The taxable items included lumber, bamboo, iron, hemp, limestone, and tung oil. In the early years the tax was collected in kind; the material was delivered to government-owned shipyards. Since the government ship-construction program was also supervised by the Ministry of Works, the income and expenditure were considered to have canceled each other, and the accounts were not audited by the Ministry of Revenue. After the fifteenth century the collection was made in silver; but the proceeds continued to be handled by the Ministry of Works.[99] Funds derived from this source were usually dispatched to the several dockyards every season. While there were thirteen collection stations across the empire (four near Peking, one each at Nanking, Huai-an, Chen-ting, Lan-chou, Kuang-ning, Ching-chou, T'ai-p'ing, Wu-hu, and Hang-chou), we know only that in the early seventeenth century the combined annual revenue of the three major stations, namely Hang-chou, Wu-hu, and Huai-an, was 44,510 taels of silver.[100]

Also audited by the Ministry of Works were the funds collected for water control projects and the revenue derived from public land reclamation programs. The former was managed by the ministry's Bureau of Irrigation and Transportation; the latter, by the Bureau of State Lands.[101] Water control projects throughout the dynasty were supervised by imperial agencies; but individual provinces and prefectures furnished the labor and material, each assigned an annual quota. As those local obligations were gradually commuted to monetary payments, funds derived from this income were submitted to the Ministry of Works. Revenue from land reclamation was earmarked to furnish caps and gowns for court personnel, to supply charcoal to the palace, and to defray several other miscellaneous expenses.[102] The unedited data furnished by a ministerial official in the early seventeenth century suggest that the annual total of the former income was 139,150 taels of silver and that of the latter was 117,355 taels.[103] But in practice these funds were rarely placed under such strict central management as the regulations called for. In most cases local collectors, usually civilian agents, made periodical deliveries to their corresponding offices, sometimes without reporting to the ministry. There was one case where the local collectors in a prefecture near Peking pocketed the proceeds for six consecutive years before the embezzlement was discovered.[104] During the reign of Shen-tsung some of these funds were also appropriated for other uses. For instance, the water control funds from Chekiang Province and the land reclamation funds from An-ch'ing Prefecture were rerouted to finance the manufacture of imperial silk fabrics. At other times the revenue was reallocated to pay for lumber supplies to the palace.[105] While some cash payments from these incomes were delivered to Peking, the total amount was insignificant and irregular. But it seems that around 1600 the Ministry of Works was self-sufficient, its income remaining adequate to cover the expenditures handled by its various bureaus and agencies. Up to then the cash surplus of the ministry was occasionally handed over to the Ministry of Revenue. Thereafter the Ministry of Works itself ordinarily had a deficit. It had to "borrow" from other sources, mainly from the Court of the Imperial Stud.

Funds controlled by the Court of the Imperial Stud provided an important cash reserve for the empire. They were derived from commutation of service obligations of the civilian population. In the early years of the dynasty a number of households across the empire were assigned to maintain 100,000 army horses for the government. Each year 20,000 new horses were to be delivered from this pool. After 1466 such delivery was waived; rather the population was ordered to submit twelve taels of silver in place of each horse in the yearly quota. Thus the court had an annual income of 240,000 taels.[106] With these funds, the court was to purchase horses to fill army needs. But the purchase was seldom carried out, and the cash reserve continued to accumulate. Around 1580 the silver deposits exceeded four million taels.[107] This reserve was slowly expended around the turn of the century, first by consecutive "borrowings" by the Ministry of Revenue, the Ministry of Works, and the Court of Imperial Entertainments. By increasing the commutation ratio, the Court of the Imperial Stud increased its income to the range of 350,000 to 430,000 taels in the 1620s.[108] But by then the revenue was spent as soon as it was received; and delinquencies on the part of the paying population also began to occur.

There were several other miscellaneous items of income. The imperial pastures near Peking and Nanking were rented to the public in the later part of the dynasty, the rents yielding 80,000 taels per year.[109] Confiscations and fines produced 170,000 taels in 1578 [110] and 128,617 taels in 1580.[111] Commutation of miscellaneous labor services, sales of the imperial calendar, and collections at certain imperial shrines could have yielded 125,000 taels around 1600.[112] Thus the miscellaneous items were worth at least 350,000 taels of silver each year.

In enumerating these miscellaneous items, I have omitted rents collected from the several imperial estates, which were delivered to the palace and usually became expense accounts of empresses dowager. Nor have I mentioned monetary payments for supplies to imperial stables and zoos, where the income was spent on the purpose for which it was collected. Taxation on tea production is also not included in this analysis, because the tax, collected in kind, was traded for horses in the frontier regions. International trade is not discussed in this study, because it had comparatively little significance in the dynasty's fiscal administration. A large volume of the maritime trade was carried on by smugglers. When international trade was finally legalized, in the late sixteenth century, the ocean-going traffic was heavy. In 1594, when Yüeh-kang, Fukien Province, was opened for trade, the tariff collected at the port reached 29,000 taels of silver.[113] The funds were used for local military expenses. But the court almost immediately reverted to its exclusion policy. Tributary trade was not conducted for revenue purposes. Indeed, imported commodities, notably pepper and sapanwood, were utilized by the Ming court to pay civil officials and imperial clansmen. Then the emperor had to bestow on the tributary emissaries enormous quantities of gifts. In the seventeenth century when much palace construction was in progress, a forced contribution called *chu-kung* (aid to construction) was imposed on military and civil officials as well as wealthy merchants, and in 1625 this yielded 831,457 taels.[114] This, too, we would consider as an irregular income.

Summary

In summary, we find that the regular cash items receivable by the Ministry of Revenue from 1570 to 1600 remained approximately on the level of 2.6 million taels of silver per year. The sum is arrived at by adding the items found in Table 2.

TABLE 2 *Estimated Cash Receivables by the Ministry of Revenue, 1570–1600 (Unit: 1 tael of silver per year)*

Cash items derived from land taxes	500,000
Commutation of animal fodder	330,000
Payment for "rationed salt"	80,000
Salt revenue collected from commissions, etc.	1,000,000
Internal Custom Duty	340,000
Miscellaneous	350,000
Total	2,600,000

These receivables remained relatively stable throughout the period. This may seem strange to most students of Ming history, as they can find from various contemporary sources figures which differ drastically from this estimate. As a matter of fact, I have compared nine sets of such figures, all referring to annual receivables by the Ministry of Revenue. They vary from 2.3 million taels of silver to 5.4 million.[115] The discrepancies, however, are due to the use of different accounting methods. Some of the inflated figures have been arrived at by including several cash items which the Ministry of Revenue *handled* but did not actually *receive*, such as the Gold-Floral-Silver due to the crown, frontier subsidies to the army posts which originally were delivered directly by taxpayers, etc. In essence the imperial revenue neither increased nor decreased in any appreciable volume. Of this I feel reasonably certain, because in this period there was no significant alteration of the fiscal structure. The fiscal changes that appeared were procedural modifications only.

FISCAL ADMINISTRATION: UNTIL 1590

In the preceding sections I have emphasized that fiscal administration during the dyansty was subordinated to ideological principles; the Ministry of Revenue was greatly understaffed; the minister lacked sufficient authority to implement any policy; and state revenues were too rigidly tied to various expenditures to allow for freedom in fiscal planning. Yet I must also observe that the fiscal machinery as set up by the dyansty did remain workable for over two hundred years. Not until the later sixteenth century and the early seventeenth century did financial problems become insoluble.

In the reigns of T'ai-tsu and Ch'eng-tsu the country was ruled by the sword. Imperial power was at its height, and many administrative policies were enforced with the vigor of martial law. The whole population across the empire was under registration, with each family permanently confined to its registered domicile and occupation. Forced migrations involving large segments of the population were sometimes decreed. Because the only economic group that might conceivably resist the imperial power was the group of large landowners in the lower Yangtze valley, T'ai-tsu confiscated enormous tracts of land from this group, on the charge that they had previously supported a rival.[116] Although the confiscation was only halfheartedly enforced and the legal ownership of this land remained ambiguous, those who held the land had to pay heavily. In some cases the annual payments to the government exceeded two piculs of grain for each *mou* of land [117]—that is, about two thirds of the yield of the most fertile soil. Whether this levy was rent due to the crown or punitive tax is not at all clear. Yet this ambiguity was not a matter of great significance during the early part of the dynasty; it became a thorny issue only in the later years, when the central government lost its power and vigor.

The court did not limit its impositions to regular taxation. Materials and services were called for by acquisition. Military supplies such as bows, arrows, and winter garments, and palace supplies such as wax, tea, fresh food, dyes, charcoal, lumber, paper, and medicine, were all contributed by the people. Basic metals including copper and iron were either mined by the state or requisitioned from civilian sources. This virtually eliminated a great portion of the cost of governmental operation.[118]

During this period the annual silver payment received by the imperial treasury consisted of only 300,000 taels.[119] But even this cash income might not have been necessary, since by that time precious metals were forbidden in private transactions. The court rarely paid anyone in gold or silver. To defray its expenses it distributed the millions of piculs of grain that were at its disposal and supplemented such grain payments with paper currency, which was neither convertible nor backed up with valuables. The exact amount of paper currency in circulation was never recorded. We only know that by 1450 its value had depreciated 1,000 times.[120] Financial irresponsibility, it may be noted, started early in the dynasty. Nevertheless, in this early phase of the dynasty the court had abundant financial resources in its command to meet its fiscal problems. That is why Ming contemporaries often nostalgically referred to this period as one in which "all granaries and depots in the counties and prefectures were so overstocked that the deposits usually turned red and decomposed," [121] a situation that they regarded as highly desirable.

The early middle period, which covered the 80 years from 1425 to 1505, was a time of extensive consolidation and readjustment. Many Ming fiscal institutions attained their permanent features during this period. In these 80 years China experienced a prolonged period of peace and prosperity. Even though Mongols repeatedly raided the northern frontiers in the mid-fifteenth century and in 1449 even captured Emperor Ying-tsung, the fighting did not seriously damage the nation's economy. The Yellow River was successfully harnessed in the 1450s, the project having been accomplished by an efficient husbanding of the nation's resources. Despotism in the Ming court at the same time became more tempered. While still benefiting from the abundance of imperial incomes, fiscal administration during the period experienced a general relaxation of control, and great leniency was shown the taxpayers. The policy of considering government paper currency as the only legal tender had already proved to be unworkable, and in the 1430s the practice was formally abandoned.[122]

The Grand Canal connecting Peking and the Yangtze opened for traffic in 1415, and by decrees of 1431 and 1474 the transporting of tax grains was completely taken over by the army's special transportation corps operating on the waterway.[123] Thereafter, southern taxpayers were to deliver their consignments south of the Yangtze, with added surcharges. In 1436 the Gold-Floral-Silver was institutionalized, and in consequence, as was noted earlier, four million piculs of tax grain were permanently commuted to monetary payments at reduced rates. This measure alone depreciated the total value of the receivables from land taxes by one tenth.

Still more far-reaching in effect was a drastic reduction of land tax quotas in the Yangtze delta. Although T'ai-tsu had confiscated many of the estates in this region, the landowners continued to hang on to the properties and, as imperial power began to wane, openly refused to pay the special high taxes. The tax delinquency in Su-chou Prefecture alone mounted to eight million piculs in 1430. The court commissioned Chou Sheng with a vice-minister's rank to "tour and soothe" the region. Chou virtually became a provincial governor of the district for the next 21 years. At his recommendation, land taxes in the several prefectures in the Yangtze delta were greatly reduced.[124]

Here the point involved is an issue of controversy, and from our point of view, a topic which deserves a more than casual examination. Many Ming contemporaries, some of them obviously speaking for local interests, vociferously protested the exorbitant taxes assessed upon the southeastern prefectures. They often pointed out that the quota of Su-chou alone was 2,700,000 piculs, more than the combined assessments of several remote provinces. Among the 159 Ming prefectures, they contended, this constituted a most unjust case. But in making such protests they failed to mention that in the fifteenth century the registered population of Su-chou was 3.84 percent of the national total, and also exceeded the combined population of the remote provinces cited.[125] Furthermore, the prefecture was situated within a well-developed area and received benefits from many government water-control projects. In productivity, its land was among the best of the country. A majority of its landowners belonged to the gentry class; they had the ability to pay. Moreover, their titles to the properties were challengeable. Lately this topic of heavy taxation in the lower Yangtze has attracted the interest of many scholars. Despite differences of opinion, none of them expresses any sympathy for the local gentry who were most responsible for the tax arrearages.[126] Even a contemporary source indicates that the basic cause for tax delinquency was that "affluent households refused to pay the surcharges, which had to be collected [exclusively] from the poor." [127]

Chou Sheng's solution seems to have pacified the local gentry. Not only was the tax quota of Su-chou reduced by 720,000 piculs to 2,050,000 piculs; no less than one third was to be paid in Gold-Floral-Silver, which favored the taxpayers with a special conversion ratio.[128] Similar reductions were granted to the several adjacent prefectures. Tax procedures were also changed and local rates of collection were revised, to ease the burden of the high-rate payers.[129] Immediately after the settlement the tax delinquencies in the region did seem to diminish; but in a few decades the arrearages again rose to prodigious figures. The problem not only plagued the tax administration throughout the Ming period, but also remained unsolved during the Ch'ing dynasty.[130] Recently historians seem to be in agreement that the fundamental issue behind the problem was the concentration of land ownership in this geographical section. The landed gentry, with their steadily increasing wealth, dared to resist what appeared to be an omnipotent imperial power.[131] Such resistance started in the rather early phases of the dynasty; as the imperial dynasty moved into decline it became more flagrant.

By making concessions to such local interests, the Ming court seriously diminished its own source of revenue, and once the tax quota of a locale was reduced it could not easily be increased to the earlier level. My calculation shows that the fifteenth-century tax reduction in the four critical prefectures in the lower Yangtze, namely Su-chou, Sung-chiang, Chen-chiang, and Ch'ang-chou, totaled close to one million piculs. Considering revenue losses due to commutation of the remaining payments at lower rates, the net loss of imperial income exceeded 1.9 million taels of silver in value.[132]

The magnanimity of the court was not limited to the realm of tax collection. By a decree of 1425 able-bodied male subjects assigned to the military colonies, who previously had been required to turn in all their grain surplus to the state, were now required to submit only half of that amount. Benevolent as it was, the decree seems to have permanently weakened the army supply system, since the loss of income that resulted was by no means compensated for by revenues derived elsewhere. Late Ming writers regarded this measure as a significant step toward the collapse of the military colony system.[133]

The only new revenue that the state instituted during the early middle period was the inland customs duty, which came into existence in 1429. Before long this duty, along with the sales tax, was substantially increased. However, the increase was not aimed at adding more revenue, but was an attempt to enforce the circulation of government notes. In the 1450s this policy was abandoned. About the same time the collection was reduced to about one third of the former rate.[134]

In general, it is clear that during this early middle period the Ming court voluntarily lessened its tax income from many sources. This is not a sign of lack of financial strength. On the contrary, by its decrees and policies the Ming court demonstrated its confidence in its fiscal management. While the empire's military strength was allowed to decline, while the power of the central government no longer remained unchecked, the dynasty's financial condition remained sound. Fundamentally, this was because under normal circumstances the Ming governmental machinery required very little maintenance. The numerous local funds and abundant requisitioned material and *corvée* labor were readily available for carrying out routine governmental operations. Imperial income, even with the aforementioned tax reductions, still developed a surplus each year. Toward the end of the fifteenth century silver deposits at the Ministry of Revenue's T'aits'ang Vault are said to have exceeded eight million taels.[135]

The fifteenth century also saw China's grain economy transformed into a monetary economy. The use of silver as the common standard of exchange became popularized. In the decade between 1487 and 1496 two more major items of government income were made payable in silver. This took place while two of the dynasty's most influential ministers of revenue, Li Ming and Yeh Ch'i, were in charge of fiscal administration. The former was responsible for the commutation of the military supplies forwarded to the frontier army posts by the northern prefectures; the latter was instrumental in deriving cash income from the salt monopoly.[136] But throughout the dynasty the

basic assessment of land tax remained in grain, with not even a suggestion that all payments might be converted to silver. Furthermore,
the gradual increase of receivables in silver by the court does not
reflect the widening of state revenue. On the contrary, the total value
of the receivables seems to have decreased after each commutation
order.

The years between 1505 and 1590 might be called the later middle
period. In this period China's economic growth made phenomenal
strides, the upsurge being accentuated in the nation's southeast sector.
Cotton and silk manufacturing, mining and smelting, and porcelain
industries in particular expanded with high speed.[137] International
trade was officially outlawed; but in fact it was carried out with the
connivance of local authorities.[138] Coinciding with the general prosperity was a rapid population growth. The inland sector, however,
did not as a whole benefit from such economic activities. The northwest sector even suffered some reverse effects. This region had few
products for export. Wool produced in this area was not a popular
commodity in humid south China, nor did its carpetmaking industry
generate any sizable volume of trade. At the same time the northwest
provinces, which had little grain surplus, had to purchase such necessities as salt, tea, and textile materials from outside, thus seriously
draining the amount of silver in circulation in this general area. Before
the close of the sixteenth century economic depression in the northwest became steadily more pronounced.[139]

The major fiscal problem that the Ming court faced was two-fold.
First, as the military colony system continued to degenerate, more
supplies for the armed forces had to be provided from civilian sources.
Previously these supplies had been furnished exclusively by the northern provinces; now this region could no longer shoulder the ever-
increasing burden. Second, as state expenditures continued to expand,
an appreciable increase in tax revenue in the south was not feasible
because of the resistance of deeply entrenched local interests and a
lack of enthusiasm among bureaucrats in the field, who, following their traditional line of thinking, regarded any increase in the
tax quota as evil and incompatible with their concept of good
government.

Marauding by Japanese pirates, who infested the southeastern seaboard during the mid-sixteenth century, caused the Ming court to make several readjustments. Campaigns against the pirates were financed through local resources. An emergency assessment of 400,000 taels of silver was added to the land taxes of the several affected provinces.[140] Other local levies were also increased to support a newly organized militia. Some of the increases were discontinued after the campaigns became successful; but a number of items, especially those added to the single-whip money, remained in force.[141] From those days on, the militia became an important local institution in the southeast section, and the several provinces enjoyed more fiscal autonomy.

Before the pirate problem was solved, the Mongol leader Altan Khan began invading the northwest frontier region. In the decades between 1550 and 1570 his invasions developed into a serious crisis. This was a time when the northern frontier was already in a state of decline, and the series of assaults by the invaders only served to aggravate the situation. Additional food and cash supplies had to be provided by the central government. Even after the crisis was over, a higher cost of army maintenance persisted.

Supplies furnished to the northern army posts in 1502 by Shantung, Honan, and Shansi Provinces and eleven prefectures of the Northern Metropolitan Area seem to have been close to 1.6 million piculs; those furnished in 1578 amounted to 3.3 million piculs.[142] Besides, the court also had to deliver to the army posts supplies derived from its own income. Before the 1520s such subsidies never exceeded 500,000 taels of silver for any single year.[143] In 1549, barely thirty years later, 3,178,354 taels had to be sent.[144] The 1578 account shows that the annual subsidies from Peking reached 3,186,348 taels, in addition to 645,015 taels derived from salt revenue.[145] The combined subsidies exceeded 3.8 million taels. Undoubtedly the imperial treasury was operating with an annual deficit.

Table 3 shows the total receivables and expenditures handled by the T'ai-ts'ang Vault in 1577, 1578, 1583, 1593, and 1607. (Note that the figures include the Gold-Floral-Silver and the commuted portions of military supplies furnished by the northern provinces; they there-fore appear to be somewhat larger than 2.6 million taels, which I have figured earlier to be the average annual income in this period.)

TABLE 3   *Net Surplus and Deficit of the T'ai-ts'ang Vault*[146]
(*Unit: 1 tael of silver*)

Year	Income	Expenditure	Net Surplus or Deficit
1577	4,355,400	3,494,200	+ 861,200
1578	3,559,800	3,888,400	− 328,600
1583	3,676,100	4,524,700	− 848,600
1593	4,512,000	5,465,000	− 953,000
1607	3,800,000	4,200,000	− 400,000

It is clear that toward the 1590s an annual deficit in the vicinity of one million taels was not uncommon. It seems that the bulk of the silver payments handled by the Ministry of Revenue, probably no less than 90 percent of such payments, was delivered for military expenditures in the border lands.

One noticeable feature of the fiscal administration until 1590 was that, in the face of enlarged expenditures, the court seldom attempted to increase tax revenue. Aside from the 400,000-tael additional assessment to support campaigns against Japanese pirates that was mentioned earlier, I can find evidence of only one more instance of such additional impositions. This happened in 1551 when, at the high point of Altan's invasion, an assessment totaling 1,200,000 taels of silver was added to the land taxes of southern provinces and prefectures.[147] Generally, deficits were met by calling in deposits from provincial vaults and treasuries and by withdrawing silver reserves from the T'ai-ts'ang Vault. By 1588 the silver reserve at the vault still remained on the six-million-tael level.[148] The Court of the Imperial Stud also had a reserve of some four million taels. Local reserves amounted to millions in many provinces.[149] As long as these cash reserves were on hand to balance the deficit, there was no threat of an imminent breakdown of the fiscal administration. Only when all these reserves were exhausted was there a genuine crisis. And this is what finally came about in the last decade of the sixteenth century.

FISCAL ADMINISTRATION: AFTER 1590

The long reign of Shen-tsung (1572–1620), and especially the period from 1590 to 1620, was the crucial phase of the Ming dynasty in almost all aspects. Many traditional historians blame Shen-tsung personally for all of China's troubles in his time, and it is true that his own indolence and extravagance were perhaps sufficient to topple any dynasty.[150] He did nothing to rehabilitate state finance. On the contrary, government funds were regularly reallocated to suit his personal desires and fancies. The imperial income of some one million taels in Gold-Floral-Silver could not keep pace with his spending, even though in 1578 he arbitrarily increased his personal account by 200,000 taels.[151] Thereafter there was no pretense of keeping state funds and crown income separate, and on numerous occasions large sums of cash were transferred from the T'ai-ts'ang Vault to the inner palace. Funds designated for water control purposes were diverted to the manufacture of imperial silk goods. Land taxes collected in the southern provinces were called in to support palace construction enterprises. Realizing that he was unable to command the respect of his civil servants, Shen-tsung chose to ignore them. He refused to give audience to his ministers, let important official vacancies go unfilled, and would not even conduct an inquiry when several of his top officials, including Minister of Revenue Chao Shih-ch'ing, left office without authorization. Government documents were often left pigeonholed in the palace, and bitter remonstrances went unanswered. Shen-tsung's cynicism went so far that, without reorganizing the official fiscal establishment, he dispatched trusted palace eunuchs to several key cities as special tax commissioners who actually supplanted the civil service. The business that they transacted simply bypassed the regular official channels. No governmental system, and especially none in which sound central leadership on the throne was as essential as in the traditional Chinese system, could remain unaffected by such persistent abuse. Even so, it would be a gross mistake to regard Shen-tsung's irresponsibility as the major cause of the dynasty's decline and eventual downfall. It must be recognized that cracks and strains in the Ming governmental machinery had developed even before the start of his misrule.

The inability of the central government to raise more funds remained an obvious weakness. Even before successive increases in land taxes were ordered, beginning in 1618, tax delinquencies had already accumulated alarmingly. A memorandum dated 1593 indicates that between 1586 and 1592 tax arrearages across the empire totaled

7,461,100 taels.[152] Another document discloses that in 1615 land tax arrearages reached 2,365,400 taels. The delinquencies in the next two years, 1616 and 1617, added another 2,869,410 taels.[153] Thus the government had not even been able to collect the regular revenue when it decided to undertake additional assessments. This held true for other state incomes. Although we do not have all the detailed figures, it has been mentioned that the inland customs duty produced only 260,000 taels of silver in 1601, out of an annual quota of 342,729 taels.[154] As was noted earlier in this paper, the salt production in 1606 met only half of the official quota.

Tax delinquencies were by no means a direct result of Shen-tsung's misgovernment. Rather, they were the product of the Ming governmental system, which was, in essence, to grant local gentry arbitrary power over an agrarian society. Since the tax administration never effectively penetrated the rural areas, the moment imperial power waned it fell a victim of the managerial class. Tax burden was no longer evenly distributed. Unauthorized collections became widespread. The single whip method, started as a reform by provincial officials in the sixteenth century to consolidate and simplify the chaotic levies and collections, ended with more abuses in many instances.[155] "The commutation also took numerous forms, sometimes numbering up to several items; the rates were so many and so complicated that even the petty officials in charge of the matter did not know them; yet they fixed upon whatever rate pleased them." [156] On top of all this, the benevolent policy of the Ming court to remit back taxes from time to time further sabotaged its own administration. Out of the spirit of royal benevolence, the emperor usually decreed upon his enthronement or the investiture of the crown prince or on other auspicious occasions that unpaid taxes up to a specified date were altogether canceled. Some theorize that this was no more than a noble gesture, since the back taxes might have become uncollectable under any circumstances. Nevertheless, such decrees clearly encouraged delinquency. There were times when local taxes had been collected and the funds were on the way to the imperial treasury and then a general remission was ordered. The tax captains therefore recalled the payments en route and pocketed the money. The bona fide taxpayers did not receive the benefit of remission at all.

A list compiled by a traditional historian shows that during the Ming dynasty such general remissions were ordered twenty-seven times. Such remissions were ordered nineteen times by the emperors preceding Shen-tsung. Shen-tsung himself ordered six remissions during his reign of forty-eight years. The remaining two remissions were ordered after his time.[157]

Rising costs of military expenses in the sixteenth and seventeenth centuries had no direct connection with governmental efficiency. Before the seventeenth century most of the Ming soldiers were sons from hereditary military families. The government paid their rations and allowances in grain. After 1600 recruitment took the place of conscription. Around 1620 an infantryman's basic pay was fixed at 18 taels of silver per year.[158] When soldiers were transferred from home stations to the combat zone, a bounty called "settle-the-family fee" at five or six taels per man was distributed. In addition, the family that the soldier left behind received 0.6 taels of silver per month.[159] Toward the end of the dynasty the Ming armies often involved more than half a million soldiers in active duty. In 1642 the authorized strength of the army reached 1,238,524 men.[160] Thus the basic pay of the troops alone should have exceeded 20 million taels of silver.

A combat horse cost 12 taels of silver in the seventeenth century. My calculation shows that its maintenance could not have been less than 0.8 taels per month. As firearms gained wide use on the battlefield, supplies of munitions also became more costly. The Ming Ministry of Works reported that during the four years between 1618 and 1621 the field armies in Manchuria had been delivered 1,134 pieces of heavy artillery, 1,253,000 missiles of all kinds, and 250 tons of sulphur. In addition, 261,589 sets of armor were sent.[161]

The Manchurian campaign that began in 1618 so easily shook the dynasty's foundation because it coincided with a low point in the Ming empire's fiscal position. Previously three major wars fought before the turn of the century had virtually emptied the silver deposits in Peking. A war in Inner Mongolia started in 1592. In the same year the Japanese warrior Toyotomi Hideyoshi invaded Korea. Ming forces met the invaders in the peninsula, and the war dragged on for seven years. Over and above all this, another expeditionary force had to be sent against rebellious aborigines in the southwest.

The costs of those three campaigns amounted to 12 million taels of silver—a sum unheard of in the dynasty's prior history.[162]

The expenses involved in the suppression campaign against the aborigines in the south were largely borne by Hukwang and Szechuan Provinces.[163] During the Korean campaign a special surtax was added on the land taxes in the Northern Metropolitan Area and Che-kiang.[164] The rest of the war fund was obtained by drawing from treasury reserves. The silver deposit at the T'ai-ts'ang Vault, which at one time had accumulated to eight to ten million taels, dwindled to 120,000 taels in 1618.[165] Cash held by the Court of the Imperial Stud was reduced to the vicinity of 1,200,000 taels in 1603 [166] and further depleted to 270,000 taels in 1607.[167]

Ironically, while the state coffer was practically empty, funds controlled by the emperor were rather abundant. Many historians have never forgiven Shen-tsung because in the crucial months after the Manchu attack in 1618 he held back the bullion in deposit at the Tung-yü Vault within the inner palace. This cash reserve had accumulated from Gold-Floral-Silver. As the emperor's personal savings, its amount was never publicly announced. After the Ming armies met early defeat, petitions for dispatching this reserve to Manchuria were submitted by ministers, supervising secretaries, provincial governors, and even by retired army generals and students.[168] Shen-tsung cynically replied that he did not have the money. In 1619 Minister of Revenue Li Nü-hua handed no fewer than six memorials to the emperor, requesting loans of two million taels from his personal account.[169] Only twice did the monarch open up his own purse, in 1618 handing over 100,000 taels to the Ministry of Revenue and the next year 396,173 taels.[170] Yet three days after his death in the summer of 1620 the Tung-yü Vault yielded two million taels for military supplies,[171] and after three more months 1,800,000 more taels were released from the same source.[172] In early 1621, after Hsi-tsung's accession, 500,000 more taels came out of the emperor's personal account to meet the expenses of the army.[173]

The Manchurian crisis in the early seventeenth century could not have been averted by prompter release of these four million taels of Gold-Floral-Silver. It must be borne in mind that by 1618 the civil and military administrators in Manchuria had lost control over the rural population. The armed forces could no longer be serviced in the field. Every ton of army supplies, including food, horse fodder, clothing, and equipment had to be shipped from the interior. The Ming court was not prepared for such an operation. The supply route from the interior to the frontier had been neglected for a long time. Transportation overland by ox-cart was prohibitively expensive. In 1619, when a supply command was established in Tientsin, it was discovered that transportation by sea could reduce the cost to one tael of silver for each picul of grain.[174] But the commissioner in charge of supplies reported that, to keep the army in Manchuria adequately fed, he needed 4,000 seafaring ships instead of the 700 then available.[175] The deplorable army supply situation was described in concrete terms by Hsiung T'ing-pi, governor general at Mukden in 1619:

In Liaotung [Manchuria] a bow costs two taels of silver, an arrow five to six tenths [of a tael]. Besides, it is difficult to locate a supplier. And now daily necessities such as armor, underwear, haversacks, bridles, and saddles all need to be replaced and mended. [But here] nothing, not even a piece of thread or a strip of leather, is inexpensive. I have personally seen soldiers selling their personal belongings to repair their equipment. [Some of them] even put on armor over their naked bodies, without any undergarments to speak of. At such times my heart bleeds and I wish I could take their place . . .[176]

To expose an army in a remote region under such distressing circumstances was to court disaster. When soldiers' pay was in arrears, discipline evaporated. Revolt erupted. Mass desertions occurred. There was a case in 1619 where a full regiment vanished overnight, as 700 out of its 1,000 soldiers broke ranks and ran away.[177] Now mounted soldiers butchered their own horses, in order to avoid taking part in suicidal cavalry charges.[178] Even with morale at such a low point, the army had yet to suffer more defeats. The Manchus were given an opportunity to digest and consolidate their conquests, and to grow in strength. The Ming court had to mobilize a larger army, which in turn required more military supplies. The whole sequence was a vicious cycle.

Military expenses continued to rise until the fall of the dynasty, since in its last decade the court faced the double threat of internal rebellion and foreign invasion. For the most part, the war costs were met with increased land taxes. Seven such emergency increases were ordered within two decades, each being put into effect on top of the previous accumulation. The dates and amounts of increase appear as follows: [179]

1618	0.0035	taels of silver on each *mou* of land
1619	0.0035	taels of silver on each *mou* of land
1620	0.002	taels of silver on each *mou* of land
1631	0.003	taels of silver on each *mou* of land
1635	1/10	increment added to regular land tax assessment
1637	0.0048	taels of silver on each *mou* of land under previous registration; 0.01409 taels of silver on each *mou* of land previously untaxed
1639	0.01	tael of silver on each *mou* of land

Thus by 1639 the total levy was 0.0268 taels of silver on each *mou* plus one tenth of the basic assessment. Indeed, it is difficult to ascertain what the basic assessment was. With surcharges added, in most cases the basic assessment might be close to 0.05 taels of silver per *mou*. Among the highest assessments, 0.5 taels per *mou* was not uncommon. The total increase, therefore, was 0.0318 taels per *mou* in the former case and 0.0796 taels per *mou* in the latter case.

From an administrative point of view, the most objectionable feature of the series of increases was their being ordered piecemeal. This might have been inevitable inasmuch as the nation, the fiscal machinery, and the psychology of the bureaucrats were unprepared for any drastic action. Only when compelled by circumstances did the court order the increases, and even then with reluctance. Furthermore, the state's ability to collect was doubtful. As it was, the gradual increases still resulted in delinquencies and large amounts of uncollectables in the provinces. The Ming civil officials and military commanders left volume after volume of documents referring to army pay in arrears, military supply needs unfilled, and funds delivered behind schedule in these critical years. It seems that after 1620 soldiers' pay being in arrears over six months was a commonplace. In view of the national crisis that the dynasty was facing, the slow and ineffective fiscal mobilization had a grave consequence; since the crucial situation was not dealt with squarely at the beginning, it tended to deteriorate further, and the belated remedies only proved more and more expensive. Evidently, none of the last three Ming emperors had the strength and character to save the situation. Kuang-tsung (1620) reigned for only a month. Hsi-tsung (1620–27) was an imbecile. He let the powerful eunuch Wei Chung-hsien run the government while the bureaucrats were hopelessly embroiled in partisan strife. The last monarch, Chuang-lieh-ti (1627–44), was impetuous and distrustful. He executed war ministers and field commanders by the dozen. An established dynasty in China usually demonstrated surprising endurance in time of crisis; the unflinching loyalty of the millions provided a unique reservoir of strength which often enabled the imperial dynasty to overcome imminent perils. In the first half of the seventeenth century the Ming central leadership had so thoroughly discredited itself that even this loyalty began to falter.

Yet, in the light of the dynasty's financial history, the importance of the role of personality should not be over-emphasized. The breakdown of the Ming fiscal system was the accumulated effect of many active and dormant factors in the background. In essence, fiscal administration over two hundred years had so followed a pattern that there was little free play left. At the same time, population growth, evolution from grain economy to monetary economy, uneven economic development in terms of geographical sections, higher costs of military expenses as a result of modern warfare, and the need of a better transportation system—all these either had not been or could not have been visioned by the dynastic founders—demanded that the Ming court take bold steps, engage itself in new areas of action, and assume new fiscal responsibilities. To these demands the court had failed to respond.

The increasing assessments in land taxes in the seventeenth century have been called "exorbitant" by many historians and have been regarded as the major cause that led to the dynasty's downfall.[180] There is little doubt that the collection of extras added new and additional strains to an already overworked fiscal machinery; it also imposed an unbearable burden on certain taxpayers. But whether or not additional quotas had been imposed beyond the nation's ability to pay remains a debatable question. The more I look into the details, the less am I inclined to believe that the rates were excessive. Nor had the extras been ruthlessly imposed on the population without due consideration. When the first increase was ordered in 1618 Kweichow Province was exempted. Even though the extra, at 0.0035 taels per *mou*, was charged to the other provinces and districts, each territorial unit was instructed to make adjustments to suit local conditions.[181] The over-all target of collection was set at slightly above two million taels, based on the land registration data of 1578.[182] More exemptions were allowed for the second and third increases. Consequently, when the accumulated rate reached 0.009 taels per *mou*, the account of 1623 shows that total proceeds were 4,491,481 taels,[183] implying that the rate had been applied to fewer than 500 million *mou* of land, out of more than 700 million *mou* under registration. The 1635 imposition was collected in the five central provinces for campaigns against internal rebellion. At first the extra started from basic tax payments in excess of ten taels of silver, and later it was extended to any payment of more than one tael.[184] The 1637 addition, at 0.0048 taels per *mou*, yielded 1,929,000 taels,[185] suggesting that the rate was applicable to some 402 million *mou* of taxable land, or merely 51 percent of the 783 million *mou* then registered. At the same time it was explicitly declared that "calamity areas were exempted." [186] The Ming land tax data are neither so complete nor so uniformly recorded as to allow us to derive an average at this stage. But, as was mentioned earlier, a basic assessment with added surcharges equivalent to 0.05 taels of silver per *mou* could be regarded as a typical case. *Corvée* labor and other obligations chargeable to landed properties might add 0.03 taels of silver to it. The aforementioned seven increments, at 0.0318 taels per *mou*, would make the over-all payments 0.1118 taels per *mou*. This was about 10 to 15 percent of the annual yield from land of modest fertility in central and south China. Though high by seventeenth-century standards, the rate was by no means intolerable.

After the seven consecutive increases, the total annual target of collection was some 21 million taels.[187] Within that amount, possibly 2.12 million taels were collected from reclaimed land, taxes on property transfers, savings in local government expenses, etc.[188] Direct income from land taxes could not have exceeded 20 million taels in any single year. But even this target was an unattainable goal. Nowhere can I find any evidence that this quota was fulfilled. I assume from reports on delinquencies that collections were considered quite successful if any year's proceeds came close to 70 percent of the projected quota. It is extremely doubtful that the actual collections in the 1640s ever met half of the assigned volume. Such evidence leads me to believe that the nation's resources had not been exhausted; rather, the fundamental problem derived from the central government's inability to mobilize the nation's financial sinews. Ming contemporaries were not entirely unaware of the situation. Supervising Secretary Wu Chih-yü commented: "I dare say that today the people are not impoverished, nor are the nation's resources dried up. Only the financial planners made them so." [189] Pi Tzu-yen, minister of revenue from 1624 to 1633, also put down on record: "The income derived from land taxes—what has actually been handed over to the imperial treasury and finally dispatched to the front for military expenses—is comparable to one hair taken off the body of a horse." [190]

How much was 21 million taels of silver? Briefly, it was the necessary appropriation to support half a million troops for a year in the mid-seventeenth century. Since by then the pay and rations of one infantryman cost eighteen taels annually, nine million taels were required to pay a force of such size. By any conservative standard, two or three million taels should be allowed for officers' pay. The remaining eight or nine million taels would not be an overabundant appropriation for combat horses, arms, uniforms, equipment, and transportation to support the troops. If the population of China by then had reached 150 million, as Professor Ping-ti Ho estimates,[191] supporting such a modest-sized army should not have become a problem. There should have been 300 persons standing behind each one bearing arms.

The notion that late Ming taxation was exorbitant is further disproved by the fact that the succeeding Manchu or Ch'ing dynasty required no less income even to maintain its normal operations. To be sure, when the Manchus took control of China in 1644, they immediately proclaimed that all extra assessments on land taxes were rescinded, and reduced commodity taxes and inland customs duties by half. But in reality large amounts of silver payments continued to flow into the imperial coffers. Presumably in the new dynasty's early years, when Ming loyalists in the south had to be suppressed, the revenue was raised largely through wartime confiscations and inquisitions. The details are not clarified by contemporary sources. But after 1651 useful statistics began to appear in state papers. The total revenues of the three subsequent years are listed as follows: [192]

1651:	Income in grain	5,739,424 piculs
	Income in silver	21,106,142 taels
1652:	Income in grain	5,628,711 piculs
	Income in silver	21,261,383 taels
	Additional income from salt revenue	2,122,014 taels
1653:	Income in grain	5,672,299 piculs
	Income in silver	21,287,288 taels
	Additional income from salt revenue	2,128,016 taels

In the 1680s income in grain further increased to seven million piculs, income in silver reached 27 million taels, and salt revenue reached 2.7 million taels.[193] Moreover, unscheduled impositions were also ordered by the Manchus. In 1650, to finance the construction of the summer palace in Jehol, 2.5 million taels were added to the regular land tax.[194] In 1661, when state income again was inadequate to meet expenditures, about 5,771,000 taels of silver were levied in addition to regular land taxes.[195]

It is interesting to note that the Manchus did little to reform the general fiscal structure left by their predecessors. Tax management on the local level continued to be influenced by the gentry.[196] National land surveys were ordered but not seriously pushed through. [197] But several items of income which previously had been handled by various departments were now transferred to the Ministry of Revenue, and the numerous impositions on the local level were somewhat integrated. Thus some degree of fiscal consolidation was achieved.

Tax delinquencies tended to reappear as soon as the new regime established itself. But the new dynasty seemed to be more firm in enforcing its tax laws. One report indicates that in 1661 13,517 persons in the lower Yangtze region were charged with tax delinquency, all of whom were cited as being "connected to military and civil service, or the silk-robed gentry." The emperor directed that those persons be duly punished.[198]

Two things now seem quite clear. First, in the seventeenth century China's level of economic activities had reached a higher plateau.

State revenues simply had to step up to keep the pace. The increase in tax revenue was a natural and unavoidable consequence. Second, even though the new tax burden was completely imposed on the agrarian economy, the population should still have been able to pay. The failure of the Ming court in these later days was due largely to its inability to enforce its own tax laws and to curb local abuses, which resulted in its fiscal deficit.

The history of the last years of the Ming dynasty provides page after page of most pathetic reading. After north China was in turn ravaged by bandits and ransacked by the infiltrating Manchu columns, the court in Peking became increasingly anxious as it waited for supplies from the far south. But no steady and substantial supplies were forthcoming. In early 1644 arrearages in army pay had accumulated to several million taels of silver, while tax payments from the south arrived only in small parcels of several tens of thousands. In his daily report Minister of Revenue Ni Yüan-lu kept Chuang-lieh-ti informed of such meager and scattered funds en route to Peking, giving the possible date of arrival for each consignment. The documents reflect the terrible anxiety of both the monarch and his chief fiscal administrator.[199] The imperial granaries were now practically empty. Unable to meet the ration requirements with husked rice, the Ministry of Revenue purchased small tonnages of miscellaneous beans in its place.[200] When Peking itself was besieged, the garrison had not been paid for five months. Troops were called to duty without cooking utensils. Each soldier was issued 100 copper cash and told to purchase food as he could. Morale and discipline sank to such a low point that a general reported: "When you whip one soldier, he stands up; but at the same time another is lying down." [201] It was not surprising that the dynasty was about to fall; it was a wonder indeed that it had survived until then.

CONCLUSION

But what does all this point to? What can we learn from this chapter of financial history?

With the information compiled on the preceding pages I hope I have presented a preliminary sketch of the Ming governmental machinery in action, even though my perspective has been limited to fiscal administration.

Inasmuch as the fundamental concept of government established by Ming T'ai-tsu had no place for economic checks and balances or for contractual settlements, the stability of the empire relied on the regulating power of the state. What consent the dynasty derived from the governed sprang exclusively from Confucian ideology, which was both formal and rigid. This basic design deprived later emperors and ministers of the ability to make adjustments. But in premodern times, without adequate statistical and other controlling methods, devoid of satisfactory transportation and communication facilities, and lacking sufficient administrative personnel, emperors and ministers were simply unable to freeze a country of China's size into a state of changelessness. Sooner or later a cleavage was bound to develop between the governmental organization and the state it meant to govern. In the Ming period we see both the marvel and the fallacy of a bureaucrat-manipulated economy. In the long run many segments of the economy managed to escape from regimentation. When this occurred, the Confucian administrators, bound by their sense of doctrinal integrity, refused to adapt to the new circumstances. On one side, formality and traditionalism were more than ever emphasized; on the other, compromises and irregularities were connived at behind the scenes. Such practices further widened the gap between the idealized order and the economic reality.

The effect of introducing silver as a common medium of exchange during the dynasty cannot be overlooked. A specialist has estimated that in the last 72 years of the Ming period more than 100 million foreign silver coins were imported into China, in addition to the production of domestic silver mines.[202] The Ming fiscal administration was in essence built on the foundation of a grain economy. With its diversified rates and measurements, self-supporting institutions, regional and departmental self-sufficiency, divided budget, separate channels of cash flow, numerous material and *corvée* labor impositions, and local tax captains, the fiscal machinery was grossly unfit for a new monetary economy. Here I have enumerated the many unsatisfactory features of the Ming fiscal administration. However, those features would not have been so appallingly evident had not the wide circulation of silver thoroughly changed the nation's economic out-look. The archaic fiscal structure became more outdated than ever because it was set against the background of a mobile and expanding economy.

After the middle period the Ming court retained its arbitrary power in handling individual cases but lacked strength in enforcing its law uniformly. Outwardly, the emperor's authority was not questioned at any moment, but his grip on the provincial units was clearly slipping. Power did not seep into the hands of provincial governors and military commanders, who could still be disciplined, or imperial clansmen, who, thanks to the two founding emperors, had never been allowed to become a dominant political force. Rather, the power vacuum was exploited by the local gentry and, in the case of taxation, by minor administrators. These two groups were too scattered to become power-conscious. Confucian indoctrination was too strong for them to de-velop any class ideology. No open revolt was expected from them. But they resorted to evasion, sabotage, passive resistance, and irregu-lar practices. The foundation of the dynasty was crumbled not by hard-hitting blows, but by gradual erosion.

In this connection, I do not feel wholly satisfied with the traditional cyclic interpretation of the rise and fall of dynasties. Toward the end of each dynasty, according to such interpretations, the rich and powerful landowners managed to falsify tax records, thus maintaining tax-free estates for themselves while the weak and inarticulate peasants had to bear the major share of the tax burden. Meanwhile, the appetite of the government for tax revenue remained unchecked, until hunger and desperation drove the overtaxed peasants to open uprisings, which caused the dynasty to fall. This interpretation may find more validity in the histories of other periods, such as the Han and the T'ang. Its application to the Ming is not at all convincing. In the late Ming period regular land taxes, even with the extras and increments, often constituted only a small fraction of the local collec-tion. The exorbitant rates that the contemporary writers complained about most were surcharges and unscheduled, irregular, and some-times unauthorized impositions, which for the most part did not appear on any tax ledger.[203] Nor did such malpractices first appear in the waning years of the dynasty; many of them had long historical standing.

During the reign of Chuang-lieh-ti the philosopher-statesman Liu Tsung-chou reported that in his native Shan-yin County, Chekiang Province, land taxes were collected two years ahead of time, while the delivery of the proceeds to Peking was one year behind schedule.[204] At the same time Supervising Secretary Sun Ch'eng-tse informed the emperor that officials in the Ministry of Revenue were unable to handle the fiscal reports submitted by the provinces. Orders of investigation seldom brought forth any reply.[205] From an administrative point of view, the institutional breakdown cannot be regarded as a result of overtaxation by the central government. On the contrary, it may be argued that in the later years of the dynasty the Ming court had too little taxing power. It could no longer generate enough revenue to provide an efficient and honest administration.

Sufficient condemnations of the Ming government for its overtaxation have been made by traditional writers. Curiously, criticism for its undertaxation can also from time to time be found in contemporary writings. But such criticism, unpopular by traditional Confucian standards, aroused little attention and gathered no following at all. Kuei Yu-kuang, an outstanding literary figure who in the later sixteenth century administered the Court of the Imperial Stud in Nanking, estimated that both land taxes and corvée labor levies in Su-chou Prefecture, then considered the most exorbitant across the nation, could in fact be doubled. In his essay he questioned the wisdom of government's "go-easy" policy toward the people. Failure in raising enough tax revenue to launch constructive projects, he charged, amounted to denying people the opportunity to find more means to improve their livelihood and to enrich themselves. The "benevolent" administrators in the end could do no better than hand out charity to their starving subjects.[206] Shen Te-fu, whose miscellaneous notes published in the early seventeenth century remain to this date a major source of social history in the Ming period, deplored that the Ming court was unable to derive enough tax income to match that of the Sung. Referring to the Southern Sung period, he said nostagically, "Fiscal administrators in those days must have been superior to ours by myriads and millions of times." [207]

As for "peasant rebellions" in the late Ming period, again, I cannot accept the interpretation that they resulted from overtaxation. In the regions where such uprisings became significant and gained momentum the land tax had either been exempted or reduced.[208] I feel that the breakdown of governmental machinery was much more to blame. Unable to raise sufficient funds from tax sources, the government had long neglected irrigation projects. Water control works remained unrepaired; granary reserves held against natural disasters were sold for cash. Recent research by many scholars provides abundant evidence that army deserters and unemployed postal carriers played a much more important role than the peasants in the nationwide rebellions. The mass desertion of soldiers has been mentioned above. The abolition of the imperial postal service was another consequence of the court's inability to meet expenditures. The dismissed carriers organized themselves into war bands. Joining deserters from the army, they took up banditry.[209] Peasants who joined them did so either because of coercion or because their homesteads had been destroyed. The famines in north China in the 1630s and 1640s might be considered a contributing factor. As for higher taxation, I admit it must have given the rebels a tremendous psychological and ideological advantage, but its economic effect was secondary. In an unsorted collection of 220 original documents concerning the late Ming rebellions published in 1954, sixteen documents complain about army pay arrearages and military supply shortages, eight cite army deserters as the origin of the insurgents, five mention the imperial postal service personnel, fifteen indicate that famine and general desperation among the people were causes of unrest, and eight bear witness that peasants were enlisted by the rebels under threats and duress. Only three documents blame taxation. Among the three, one speaks of the nationwide heavy taxation in a broad and general sense. The other two were petitions to the emperor requesting that land taxes in certain regions in Shansi and Honan be remitted. Appendixes indicate that these requests were subsequently approved by Chuang-lieh-ti.[210] Another modern study lists the causes of the rebellions in the following order: famine, banditry, taxation, and abolition of the postal system.[211]

In brief, the fall of the Ming involves too many factors for generalization. In terms of length of time, some of the factors could be traced back to the founding of the dynasty. In dimension, some of the factors touch regional particularities and local administrations. What I have so far done is merely venture in and out of the fringes of an immense land hitherto unexplored. The topic is wide. The source material in front of us is virtually inexhaustible. My survey can be carried much further, both in depth and in breadth.

TILEMANN GRIMM 明 *Ming*

Education Intendants

INSTITUTIONAL EVOLUTION OF
EDUCATION INTENDANCIES

Traditional China's unique system of civil-service examinations has attracted great Western interest ever since intimate contacts between China and the early modern West were established around 1600. The favorable impression that the system made on the great Jesuit missionary Matteo Ricci reverberated for two centuries in the West as a general belief in "China's wise government." [1] The system even played a role in the nineteenth-century development of a civil service in Great Britain at a time when nothing of the kind existed elsewhere in Europe, as S. Y. Teng has shown.[2] It was almost taken for granted that civil-service examinations, first instituted in the second century B.C. by the Han emperor Wu,[3] were an integral part of the Chinese state system throughout history—one aspect of the "unchanging China" that Westerners have been fond of visualizing. However, as modern scholarship has shown, the examination system was a highly diversified institution in the T'ang dynasty (618–907),[4] and thereafter it was reshaped almost totally by reforms in the eleventh century and in response to a great growth in the number of examinees and degree holders that actually had begun somewhat earlier.[5] Therefore, the Sung (960–1279) and Yüan (1260–1368) periods and the early years of the Ming dynasty—however late they may be in the perspective of China's over-all history—must be regarded as the formative years of a system that prevailed for half a millenium thereafter and forms part of the background from which modern China is emerging. This paper explores one aspect of the evolving system's maturation during the Ming dynasty.

Given the relative novelty of a regularized, standardized system of civil-service recruitment by examination, a special task quickly forced itself upon early modern China's policy makers. This was to establish control over the examination process at some intermediate point between the local level and the central level—or, put in other terms, to assert control over examinees and office candidates after they had left their home areas and before they entered the triennial examinations in their provincial capitals. On one hand, central government authorities could confidently feel that their control over the system reached down as far as the provincial examinations, which fed men of talent into the metropolitan and palace examinations in the capital. On the other hand, the magistrates and prefects who were responsible for schools and students at the local level were not well situated to guide their candidates into the province-wide contests. Here, then, was a void to be filled. Not unnaturally, line administrative agencies at the provincial level took on this responsibility for a time, but with only partial success. A new, specialized office consequently evolved. We call it the education intendant or education commissioner (*t'i-hsüeh kuan*).

There are some hints that an office of this sort emerged as early as 1103 (1105?) in Sung times [6]—that is, not very long after the emergence of newly regularized examinations. Further developments along these lines occurred during the Yüan period.[7] Although these matters deserve additional study, presently available data clearly suggest that education intendancies did not attain a regular, stable place in China's governmental structure until the Ming period, and then not in its earliest years. When they emerged in maturity they partly reflected a Sung conception and certain Yüan practices, but they represented much more than a resurrection of pre-Ming institutions.

A Yüan-style Confucian Schools Superintendency (*ju-hsüeh t'i-chü ssu*) was indeed established at the very beginning of the Ming dynasty, when the founding emperor, T'ai-tsu (1368–98), installed a Confucian school at his capital, Nanking, with his famed counselor Liu Chi as its superintendent. But Liu was little more than an imperial preceptor, who had "to transmit the classics to the crown prince." [8] There is no evidence that the office existed very long or that it had any responsibilities concerning the empire-wide school system that T'ai-tsu ordered into being in 1369. Presumably the students of T'ai-tsu's earliest years were supervised generally by the National University (*kuo-tzu chien*) at the capital.[9]

In T'ai-tsu's reign responsibility for supervision of schools through-out the empire gradually became fixed as a censorial responsibility and assigned, rather vaguely, to officials of the Provincial Surveillance Offices and to the metropolitan Censorate's own touring representa-tives, the regional inspectors *(hsün-an yü-shih)*. These were the officials collectively known as "guardians of the customs and laws" *(feng-hsien kuan)*. Such questions as Who had to guard what? and What is the limit between "customs" and "laws"? were eventually to become matters of institutional dispute of some consequence.

The vaguely defined censorial responsibility of supervising the em-pire's school system became the specific responsibility of specially designated education intendants in 1436, the first year of the boy emperor Ying-tsung's reign. This decision was provoked by complaints about conditions in the schools made by the minister of revenue Huang Fu, who suggested that officials of the Provincial Administra-tion Offices and the Provincial Surveillance Offices should make regu-lar semiannual inspection tours, "giving examinations in order to find genuine talents." A conference of Ministry of Rites officials recom-mended instead that specialized education intendants be designated, one surveillance commissioner for each province and one censor for each of the two metropolitan areas surrounding Peking and Nanking, where there were no regular provincial-level administrative establish-ments. In consequence, the Ministry of Personnel nominated persons to be appointed for such purposes in all areas except the southwestern frontier provinces of Yunnan and Kweichow.[10] This is the event that the *Ming-shih* (Ming history) cites as the "original establishment" *(shih-she)* of education intendants.[11]

Since the regular line officials in the provinces—not merely other officials of the Provincial Surveillance Offices, but officials of the Provincial Administration Offices, prefects, and local magistrates—had long been accustomed to exercising control of various sorts over the local schools, and since the new education intendants were re-ferred to as "officials in control of schools" *(t'i-tiao hsüeh-hsiao kuan)*, confusion soon arose about divisions of responsibility in the educa-tional realm, culminating in strong jurisdictional jealousies. One com-plaint submitted in 1445 by a Provincial Administration Office official in Kwantung Province may perhaps be representative of more wide-spread feelings. He reported that regular line officials resented the education intendant's encroachment upon their realms of authority, and he particularly objected that the education intendant was barely able to visit local areas once a year because of the difficulty of travel in the mountainous terrain of Kwangtung. Inasmuch as the education intendant believed extensive travel was unnecessary because he was solely concerned with examination papers (*wen-chü*), the memoralist suggested that the office ought to be abolished altogether.[12]

The veteran minister of rites Hu Yen (1361–1443) responded to this complaint with a defense of the new system:

> The education intendants have all been recommended by high officials and appointed through court deliberations. It would be very difficult now to do away with them. But if there really are those who neglect their duties they should be removed, and we request that such orders be issued. The administration and surveillance commissioners should of course supervise (*t'i-tu*) the examinations in their travels, and the responsible senior officials (*t'i-tiao cheng-kuan*) of prefectures and subprefectures should of course visit the schools every new moon and every full moon to determine who is diligent and who is lazy. But nowadays each expects the other to do it.

Ying-tsung, clearly upset by the charges, insisted that all three categories of persons be punished—the education intendants who permitted local schools to deteriorate, the local officials who persisted in their petty animosities, and also the Censorate's regional inspectors who failed to bring such problems to the court's attention. It was ordered that the matter be investigated thoroughly and criminal evidence assembled.[13]

Five years later, in 1450, after Ying-tsung had fallen captive to the Mongols in consequence of a foolish campaign and Ching-ti (1449–56) had been hastily enthroned, education intendancies were temporarily suspended. The court was in an agony of self-criticism occasioned by the national emergency, and the Hanlin Academy official Chou Hung-mo submitted twelve recommendations aimed at strengthening government and morale in the interior, which he felt must be strengthened before there could be any resolution of the frontier difficulties. One of his recommendations was to abolish the education intendants because "they did not really supervise instruction," [14] and such action seems indeed to have been taken. It is possible that supervisory officials were badly needed in other realms, but there is no escaping the conclusion that institutional frictions had continued to accumulate. Not for the first time in Chinese history, old established institutions stood opposed to a new one, pending clarification and narrowing of its proper sphere. To be sure, there was a void in educational control between the local and the central authorities, but filling this void appropriately required time for all interests to be suitably harmonized—or, in other words, for step-by-step adjustments of conflicting interests through organizational experiments. In this case, a wholly satisfactory resolution of the jurisdictional conflicts did not come about until Ch'ing times, when the provincial education intendant (the "Literary Chancellor") was put on an equal footing with other highest-level provincial authorities.

A brief comment about terminology is perhaps relevant here. The creation of education intendants in 1436 involved some ambiguities, inasmuch as the term I render as "control" (*t'i-tiao*) was used to refer to the duties of both the new education intendants and the "responsible senior local officials" (*t'i-tiao cheng-kuan*), the prefects and magistrates in the line administrative hierarchy. These latter officials had primary responsibility at the local level and were in a position to "control" school activities within their jurisdictions far more closely than any touring intendant could. They and the teaching officials (*chiao-kuan*) on the school staffs were most basically in charge of the everyday activities of students. The intendants could not really "control" the schools; they had to "supervise" (*t'i-tu*) schools throughout the whole province—and this is the very term that was used in reference to their duties once the intendancies were reestablished. I suggest that this terminological confusion in the early stage reflects an understandable confusion on the part of the central government about the role the new intendants were to play. Hu Yen's use of the term "supervise" (well known from military usage) in reference to the duties of provincial-level authorities probably suggests the beginning of needed clarifications between supervisory activities and what might be considered direct managerial activities in the educational realm.

Five years after Ying-tsung, released from his Mongol captivity, had been reinstalled on the Chinese throne, he revived the education intendancies. He recalled the conditions that had prompted such appointments in 1436, when it was complained that students in the schools "were unwilling to devote earnest study to the Four Books and the Five Classics or to discuss the commentaries but only memorized old compositions waiting for the next examination in anticipation of happy success." [15] "In the governance of the empire," he proclaimed to a group of newly appointed intendants, "the most important thing is to promote schools and foster talents; the flourishing or deterioration of education, the growth or decay of human capabilities, and the rise or fall of good government all depend upon this." He urged that the intendants rectify themselves so that they might presume to rectify others, establish strict regulations, and cause teachers and students alike "to uphold right doctrines, pursue right ways, abandon frivolous habits, and develop sincere attitudes." He also proclaimed a new set of guiding principles for school supervision, emphasizing two terms, "supervision" (*t'i-tu*) and "school governance" (*hsüeh-cheng*), that were to be prominent in the educational system until the end of the old examination order in 1905.[16]

The education intendancy system that was reestablished by Ying-tsung in 1462 remained in effect thereafter, throughout the remaining years of the Ming dynasty. The guiding principles that he then formulated, based upon a less detailed set of guidelines issued in 1436,[17] are the basis for our understanding how the system was intended to function. To a greater extent than the 1436 guidelines, they manifest a Neo-Confucianistic concern about learning processes and basic philosophical issues, probably reflecting the influence of Hsieh Hsüan, leader of the Ho-tung school of the rationalistic form of Neo-Confucianism, who had himself been one of the original education intendants in 1436 and had subsequently become a major influence on Ying-tsung's senior grand secretary, Li Hsien.[18] Ying-tsung's principles were modified somewhat in a reformulation of 1575, reflecting the somewhat Legalistic thought-control intentions of the famous grand secretary Chang Chü-cheng, then in the ascendancy.[19]

The differing tones of the 1436, 1462, and 1575 regulations appear in their opening paragraphs. The 1436 version simply says that students should not only devote themselves to reading and composition; they must first of all be given guidance in such matters as filial piety, brotherliness, loyalty, sincerity, propriety, righteousness, incorruptibility, and a sense of shame, "so that by observing the effects in conduct one can find evidence of the sources [in morality]." [20] In the 1462 version an emphasis on practical action cannot be missed: "As for their readings, students should stress knowing how to put them into action. They should first pore over and memorize the sages and the classics to the point of never forgetting them, and then they should accept the explanations and interpretations of their instructors, so that they may embody in their own conduct the precepts of the sages, giving priority to filial piety, brotherliness, loyalty, sincerity, propriety, righteousness, incorruptibility, and a sense of shame. They should not be allowed merely to pursue mouth-and-ear education [that is, "in one ear and out the other"].[21] Chang Chü-cheng's version is more stern and repressive: "The sages condescended to educate the nation through the classics and thus transformed mankind. If one were able to acknowledge the classics in his own person [to "internalize" them?], then why would he need to establish other affiliations by assembling colleagues for empty chat? Henceforth each education intendant should so supervise instructors and students that they sincerely seek after and personally exemplify the long-taught classical principles, terminating their past practices. They must not be permitted to form separate academies (*shu-yüan*) in which to assemble hosts of colleagues and summon local ne'er-do-wells to chatter emptily and neglect their occupations, thereby forming cliques of place seekers and establishing a pattern of patronage. Education intendants who offend in this regard should be impeached by regional inspectors, and place seekers should be arrested and turned in [for punishment]." [22]

In general, the different sets of guiding principles follow a common pattern. They begin with statements concerning the attitudes to be inculcated in the students. Then follow sections dealing with the competence of the instructors. Except for prefectural headmasters, members of the school staffs held positions outside regular officialdom, and the regulations abound in intimations that instructors were "negligent teachers," had only "rude and vulgar knowledge," and were even "corrupt and degenerate." Intendants were instructed to be lenient with those who were merely idle and crude; they were to be warned and exhorted to reform. Only if they persisted in their old ways were they to be punished in any fashion, and only if a third inspection showed no improvement were they to be dismissed. In any case, the traditional Confucian view that morality is more important than skill prevailed; the evaluation of instructors was always to emphasize their moral conduct. This emphasis on morality in such evaluations was perhaps a counterweight against the growing emphasis on technical literary skill in the school and civil-service examinations. The regulations also devote close attention to the procedures used for admission to the schools and for the subsequent selection of students to participate in the civil-service examinations. There were admonitions about adhering to fixed quotas and fulminations against the intrusion of personal feelings into selection considerations. Nevertheless, the regulations are not particularly specific as regards this whole realm, considering the possibilities for abuses and corruption that unquestionably existed in it.[23]

As has already been suggested, the successive regulations never resolved the matter of institutional frictions. The 1436 principles were notably vague in this regard. The 1462 regulations tried to clarify the matter as follows:

Officials of the Provincial Administration Offices and Provincial Surveillance Offices, and regional inspectors, are not permitted to encroach upon the sphere of duties of the supervisors [that is, the education intendants]. If, however, public business leads them to the prefectures, subprefectures, and districts, they should of course encourage the instructors and students to be diligent in their studies, and they are not permitted to shirk or disregard [this obligation]. If the education intendant's conduct is not correct, the regional inspector should report the facts in a memorial.[24]

The 1575 regulations say very little more. In general, the line administrative officials could not be denied their managerial responsibility and the education intendants could not be denied their supervisory responsibility; it was merely hoped that the managers and the supervisors could coexist satisfactorily.

There was more than institutional friction involved here. The overlapping of functions in the educational realm created a tension between two types of officials, on one hand those who might be categorized as bureaucrats and on the other those who might be characterized as intellectuals or scholars. To the extent that line administrative officials maintained control over education, some element of police control crept into the educational system. But it would be a gross oversimplification to suggest that such officials, as bureaucrats, represented state controls whereas the education intendants, as intellectuals, represented autonomous educational interests. The fact that education intendants were institutionally affiliated with censorial agencies, the metropolitan Censorate or the Provincial Surveillance Offices, gave them as great a concern for state control as existed among the administrative officials, if not a greater one. A more fundamental ambivalence existed in the education intendancy itself, since the requirement that one person must be both censor and scholar, or bureaucrat and intellectual, at the same time created incongruities that could only be resolved according to the backgrounds and personalities of the individuals concerned.

For Ming censors themselves to be scholars and intellectuals was not unusual. One of the very first education intendants, a censor appointed in 1435, Hsieh Hsüan, is recognized as one of the most notable philosophers of the early Ming period. Moreover, a quick survey of the most famous Ming intellectual history, Huang Tsung-hsi's *Ming-ju Hsüeh-an* (Teachings of the Ming Confucians) has discovered that no fewer than fourteen Censorate officials can be regarded as reputable Ming philosophers; six of them saw service as education intendants. But such data are not quite relevant. It was not required that education intendants be selected from among censorial officials. What happened was that anyone appointed to be an education intendant thereby automatically became a censorial official. Of the first group of thirteen intendants appointed in 1436, only two had previously held censorial posts. Two had been ministry officials, four had been assigned to the Hanlin Academy, three had been provincial or local administrative officials, and two had been teachers.[25] A sampling of 57 biographies of persons who at one time or another served as education intendants [26] gives the impression that intendants came principally from three groups. One comprises officials of the various ministries in the capital, primarily secretaries in either the Ministry of Justice or the Ministry of Revenue; 21 of the 57 samples belong in this group. Another group comprises Hanlin Academy officials, of whom another 21 are to be found in the sample. The remaining 15 cases in the sample represent censorial offices. Everything thus suggests that education intendants were not selected because of their reputations or qualifications as censors. The high proportion of Hanlin Academy appointees suggests, if nothing else, that appointees were chosen in large part because of their standing as scholars and intellectuals.

The performances of individual intendants, of course, need not have any correlation with their prior institutional affiliations; and performances need not have been influenced significantly by the fact that becoming an education intendant automatically made one a censorial official. But in practice there was nevertheless a clear distinction between intendants of the "bureaucrat" type, who examined students sharply, who always emphasized the regulations, who stood for orderliness above all, and on the other hand intendants of the "intellectual" type, who were interested in pedagogical matters, who befriended talented students, and who participated in the philosophical debates of the time. In Ming times the difference was commonly noted in such terms as strictness and correctness in behavior (*yen* and *cheng*) contrasted with liberality and generosity of mind (*k'uan* and *hou*).[27] I have found only one case, that of P'eng Hsü in the 1430s, in whose performance as education intendant it was noted that "liberality and strictness were both exemplified" (*k'uan yen te t'i*).[28] The man "who seldom laughed," who was regarded as an "ice mirror," [29] who was thought completely incorruptible,[30] or who obstinately stood on principle [31] was always a typological contrast to the man who possessed a profound understanding of the classics,[32] whose mind was "drunk" with literature,[33] who had students join him in singing and argumentation while touring the country,[34] or (in the words of a critic) who "walked with students to mountains and rivers and invited friends to read poetry and drink wine." [35]

The sixteenth century, of course, witnessed a significant rise of intellectualism generally in China, particularly manifested in the flourishing of private academies. The revised guiding principles for education intendants that were promulgated in 1575 reflect this situation. They were aimed at curbing what the authorities considered an all too intellectual atmosphere; they not only denounce "empty talk" in the philosophical realm but also inveigh against that "floating evasiveness" in literary style that is so hard for any examiner to tolerate. Chang Chü-cheng once wrote in a memorial, "If one considers recent years, [one finds that] these [education] officials have become more and more worthless; it is hardly possible to find persons of self-esteem among them. Since there are no lofty actions and no solid learning to hold the students' minds under control, they devote themselves to empty talk, seeking after praise and 'selling the law.' " [36] What especially annoyed the "bureaucratic" minds of the court was the forming of cliques, which is repeatedly warned against in the 1575 regulations. However, the more "intellectual" education intendants inevitably attracted followers, and they were often instrumental in the formation of private academies. Since their dedication to teaching and intellectual leadership inevitably produced more than their normal share of "talents" for the examinations and the civil service, it is men of this type who, ironically perhaps, are generally praised as model intendants by their subsequent biographers.

Even so, the "intellectual" intendants represented a losing cause and were constantly embattled. The stern, repressive attitudes reflected in Chang Chü-cheng's regulations constantly appeared in official documents of the sixteenth century, which were full of warnings about "guarding the proper style in compositions" and "keeping to the orthodox Ch'eng-Chu line" of Neo-Confucianism. In 1530 a memorialist complained about increases in "supernumerary students" (*fu-sheng*, those allowed to enter schools beyond the approved admissions quota): "Sons and younger brothers from among the people, evading the *corvée* labor service, strive to enter the schools; intendants often patronize them and so parade their goodness." [37] In 1544 a memorialist, pursuing the theme "Keep honoring the basic substance," wrote: "In selecting talents, literary form (*wen*) definitely comes first, although considerations of behavior should also be blended in (*i hsing hsiang-ts'an*)." [38] This was, after all, the very time when the notorious "eight-legged essay" (*pa-ku wen*) form was becoming the standard form in which examinations were to be written. It was not the intellectualism of the private academies that was perpetuated, but the repressive standardization of Chang Chü-cheng's 1575 regulations, which were echoed in the Ch'ing dynasty.[39]

ACTUAL FUNCTIONING OF THE
INTENDANCY SYSTEM

Principal characteristics of the actual activities of education intendants can be discerned partly in the successive regulations and, perhaps more fully, in the biographies of individual intendants. Some gradual changes obviously occurred between the fifteenth and the sixteenth centuries, but they suggest more an increasing regularization than a conspicuous departure from the past.

1. Establishing school regulations

Both guiding principles and biographies make it clear that, upon first arriving in his area of jurisdiction, an intendant normally promulgated school regulations (t'iao-yüeh) full of admonishments to the students. For the most part these are moral exhortations, since the intendants could not be expected to go beyond the regulatory patterns established by the central government. Their phrasings are somewhat tighter and simpler, as aphoristic directives aimed squarely at the students themselves: "Be determined," "stress modesty," "deny the self," "take root in the learning of the sages, take part in the government of the day." [40] Some detailed points of procedures were also commonly included.

2. Resisting private influences

Immediately upon arrival in any locality, an intendant was commonly besieged by petitioners urging some private cause relating to the schools. Although the materials I have used do not provide details about any such petitions, one source indicates that "slander and praise [of other persons]," "special requests," and "gifts [for the intendant or his associates]" were commonly involved. In this particular case it is reported that petitioners had no success because of the intendant's uprightness,[41] and other sources often speak of petitions being rebuffed or disregarded by intendants. It is said of one fifteenth-century intendant that "he did not let anyone know when he went on tour but just suddenly appeared in a single carriage. When students came to call he abruptly closed the doors and examined them, and on the same day he determined their grades. By the time the students got home from the examination the grade list was already posted in the street, so that favor seekers had nowhere to turn." [42] It is apparent that high officials of the central or provincial governments sometimes tried to influence education intendants on behalf of family members or friends. The fact that sources seldom refer to such incidents—only when intendants resisted such pressures [43] —should not obscure the probability that, in practice, irregular influences on intendants must have been common, and commonly effective.

3. Touring the province

The rule was that every education intendant must visit every locality in his jurisdiction at least once a year and preferably twice a year. The case just mentioned, of an intendant who traveled "in a single carriage," confirms the general impression that intendants normally traveled in some state, accompanied by at least one secretarial assistant. They were to use government post boats and government courier horses, and all their travel expenses were paid by the government.[44] That many intendants did in fact perform the assigned tours on schedule is indisputable, and perhaps touring on schedule was a fairly common practice when the intendancy system was new. But biographical sketches of sixteenth-century intendants mention touring far less commonly than fifteenth-century biographies lead one to expect. The late fifteenth-century writer Ch'iu Chün (1420–95) reported that the great distances involved made annual tours practically impossible, so that there were districts hardly visited in nine years.[45] The famous seventeenth-century commentator on Ming affairs Sun Ch'eng-tse (1592–1676), no doubt relying upon some late Ming memorial, wrote that intendants normally made their tours every two or three years, providing only the most superficial "supervising" of the district schools and concentrating primarily on scrutinizing students' written compositions, which were regularly collected and delivered to the intendant's office in the provincial capital.[46] The preference of some intendants for sitting in their offices in the provincial capitals and waiting for students' compositions to be submitted for evaluation probably increased the possibilities of special

influence or other abuses, but it must have minimized institutional
frictions with such other censorial officials as regional inspectors and
provincial surveillance commissioners whose special business was to
tour local areas ferreting out abuses of all kinds. In any event, the
ideal persisted that intendants should properly tour annually, as the
1575 regulations testify.

4. Resisting jurisdictional encroachments

As has already been indicated, the Ming government never distinguished the obligations and prerogatives of education intendants
from those of some other types of officials with complete success.
Therefore, it is not surprising to find that intendants were characteristically jealous of their powers and occasionally had to defend their
rights actively. One of the most jealous was Ch'en Hsüan, a famed
remonstrator who as education intendant in the 1470s was noted for
spending his nights in school buildings, pacing the corridors and
listening to the students recite their assignments. On one occasion
when he was on duty in Honan Province the powerful eunuch dictator Wang Chih came visiting, and all the officials present, including
a nominal censor-in-chief, offered him very obsequious attentions.
Ch'en merely gave a discreet bow. The eunuch asked what office he
held. Ch'en responded, "Vice [surveillance] commissioner in control
of schools." Wang asked, "Is this greater than censor-in-chief?" Ch'en
said, "How could an education intendant be compared to a censor-in-
chief! It is just that I am a teacher and dare not abase myself." The
Ming-shih reports that Ch'en's words and manner were so stern and
upright, and his students gathered about outside the yamen in such
a crowd, that Wang Chih was overawed and dismissed him politely.[47]
Ch'en Feng-wu similarly stood his ground resolutely when his jurisdiction was challenged, on one occasion getting imperial approval for
his right to rank examination candidates when a regional inspector
had ordered his rankings changed and on another occasion refusing to
reinstate students whom he had dismissed despite the urgings of a
grand coordinator and a regional inspector.[48] Some education intendants no doubt went too far in claiming their rights, as in the case of
the respected literary figure Li Meng-yang, whose pretensions and
encroachments while intendant in Kiangsi Province "sickened" censorial complainers.[49]

5. Upholding the orthodox rites

The whole educational system of Ming China was closely connected with the state cult of Confucius,[50] and it was natural for the education intendant to concern himself with the ceremonial rites that were the foundation of public morality. Biographies of intendants regularly note their activities in this regard, supplementing the work of local magistrates, who had primary responsibility. Ancestral halls were repaired, sacrificial offerings to this or that ancient worthy were reinstituted, sacrificial utensils were replaced, irregular local cults and superstitions were opposed, and locally supported community schools (*she-hsüeh*) were kept in operation or reinstituted. The intendants were also expected to make sure that lands set aside in every locality for the support of schools and public rites were properly utilized and tended.

6. Relations with private academies

The almost astonishing spread of private academies, stimulated largely by the great philosophical leaders Wang Shou-jen and Chan Jo-shui, was one of the remarkable phenomena of China's intellectual life in the sixteenth century,[51] and education intendants throughout the empire found themselves necessarily involved with this movement. The Ming court's guiding principles never gave intendants any specific responsibilities as regards private academies, except that in 1575 they were ordered to help suppress such irregular institutions. Until that time, intendants apparently assumed some responsibility for fostering the movement, which provided meeting places for free intellectual discussion as well as the training of young men preparing to take the civil-service examinations. After all, their principal charge was to foster human talents and safeguard sound learning, and they could hardly ignore the mushrooming of private establishments devoted to the same purposes. Consequently, education intendants participated in the work of private academies and often established academies themselves. Chu Hsi's own academy, the Pai-lu-tung, was a model for other developments and a natural focus of attention. One intendant had all his students memorize and observe the regulations of this famous academy,[52] and another was admittedly guided in his career as intendant by his prior experience as a teacher in the Pai-lu-tung.[53] Yang I-ch'ing (1454–1530), who eventually became a grand secretary and was subsequently adjudged to be the best education intendant of all Ming history, while intendant founded an academy called the Correct Learning Academy (Cheng-hsüeh Shu-yüan). "He selected the best students from all schools, assembled them for further study in the academy, and personally served as superintendent (*tu-chiao*). His principal creed was moral action first, only then literary skill. From the successive students of this academy came two first-place palace-examination graduates (*chuang-yüan*) and many others whose scholarship, character, and achievements were famous." [54] Other intendants similarly established academies, some bearing inspirational names such as the Literary Enlightenment Academy (Wen-ming Shu-yüan) or the Fostering Rectitude Academy (Yang-cheng Shu-yüan) and others named after their localities or after famous Sung dynasty Neo-Confucians. Some intendants are reported to have had intimate relations with Wang Shou-jen and Chan Jo-shui.

7. *The evaluation of students*

The principal activity of all education intendants, of course, had to do with the performance of students in the government schools, with the dominant purpose of seeing to it that students progressed properly toward candidacy for government appointments. There were two routes by which students could expect to develop official careers.[55] On one hand, every government school was expected annually, or at somewhat longer intervals, to submit qualified graduates for advanced study in the National University in the capital. Through the first half of the Ming dynasty, status as a National University student led regularly to an eventual appointment and official career. The other channel was of course the public examination process, in which qualified candidates successively stood for provincial examinations, then a metropolitan examination conducted by the Ministry of Rites, and finally a palace examination theoretically conducted by the emperor himself. Passers of these examinations became government-sanctioned degree holders, eligible for appointment; and in the latter half of the Ming dynasty holders of the highest degrees (*chin-shih*, passers of the metropolitan and palace examinations) thoroughly dominated all appointments of significance. Government-supported students in the local schools and National University students, as well as private scholars, could all present themselves for qualification to take the provincial examination and thus get on the staircase to eventual officialdom.

The education intendants, once appointed, became the critical focal points of advancement through either of these two channels. In 1480 it was specified unequivocally that "annual tribute" (*sui-kung*) students presented to the National University must be nominees of the education intendants,[56] and it had already been established, in 1444, that all candidates for the provincial examinations must also be nominees of the education intendants.[57] In 1532 it was ordered that an education intendant should be demoted if five or more of his nominees for the National University in any one year proved, on being examined in the capital, to be unfit for advanced study.[58] And in 1586 it was further ordered that an intendant's future career should also be made to depend in some measure on the Ministry of Rites' evaluations of provincial examination compositions written by students in his jurisdiction.[59] A censorial memorialist in 1546, as a matter of fact, blamed education intendants for deterioration of literary style—and, by inference, moral conduct—throughout the empire.[60]

Precisely how the education intendants managed these obviously heavy responsibilities is not wholly clear. It has been noted above that some intendants did indeed visit local schools and pay close attention to what the students were doing. In any event, it is clear that intendants were heavily dependent on groundwork done by the local magistrates and prefects, in whose offices were kept routine reports on the students' everyday progress; [61] the intendants probably paid attention only to those students who were pronounced ready by the local authorities and the school instructors. Matteo Ricci's firsthand observations of the system in operation around 1600 suggest that examination visits by the intendants (Ricci's *Tihio*, that is, *t'i-hsüeh*), at least in late Ming times and in some localities, were taking on the festive, formal character of first-level (*hsiu-ts'ai*) public competitions later, in Ch'ing times. And Ricci makes it clear that intendants examined only a few hundred students chosen by local magistrates and teachers out of thousands of hopefuls.[62]

On the other hand, there is abundant evidence, already referred to,

that many Ming intendants did not make regular examination tours—
or, at least, that many localities were not often visited by them—and
that some stayed in their offices in the provincial capital scrutinizing
student papers sent to them by the local authorities. Of one Ming
intendant, it is boasted that he read three hundred student papers
per day.[63]

It is known that some intendants promulgated examination rules
(*k'o-t'iao*) setting forth the standards and procedures in accordance
with which they would evaluate students; one such set of rules was
vigorously criticized by a grand secretary but was not amended by the
intendant.[64] As is to be expected, the biographies of intendants indicate that different individuals emphasized different things or had
different methods. One asked for reproduction of passages from the
classics; another was fond of inquiring into the students' knowledge
of philological details; others emphasized the writing of poetry. One
intendant so disapproved of poetry that "even if [students] in their
compositions emulated [the famous ancient poets] Yang Hsiung or
Ssu-ma Hsiang-ju or used words in the fashion of [the famous ancient
writings] *Chuang-tzu* or *Li Sao*," he still felt they were unacceptable.[65]

At all events, what is perfectly clear is that concern with literary
style had become predominant in the education intendants' work, as
in the civil-service examinations themselves, by the sixteenth century.
As the gradual development of the notorious "eight-legged essay"
form indicates, literary form had become the test of a proper "gentleman." Beginning in the sixteenth century, successful examination
compositions were published and circulated widely under government
auspices, and students increasingly devoted themselves to mastering
the art of slavishly imitating these successful models. Naturally, it was
easier to grade literary style, especially by the standards of such a rigid
prescription as the "eight-legged essay," than to evaluate morality in
conduct; it was easier to maintain a sense of objectivity in such
evaluations. One might therefore be excused for concluding that by
later Ming times "bureaucratism" had fully triumphed over "intellectualism," or that outward appearance had superseded inner quality
in the Ming value system generally. Such "bureaucratism" was perhaps the cost that Ming China had to pay for its attempts to institu-
tionalize the Chinese empire to a far greater extent than ever before.

But it must be kept in mind, also, that traditional Confucianism is rooted in the conviction that outer form necessarily flows from and reflects inner quality and, conversely, that inner quality necessarily manifests itself in outer form. Ming education intendants could therefore console themselves if need be with the thought that, although what was being tested on the surface was literary style, what was being probed and discovered by their evaluations, in a more profound actuality, was the complex of moral qualities (filial piety, brotherliness, and so forth) that characterized the true "gentleman." Thus, after all, they could believe they were indeed fulfilling their responsibilities as set forth in the guiding principles for education intendants promulgated in 1436 and 1462.

But institutional evolution does not, like a wheel, always come full circle. Substantial changes had actually occurred. On one hand, the evaluation of moral qualities in the recruitment system now rested very heavily on aesthetic judgments; literary considerations, not other kinds of considerations, had become paramount when the growing complexity of the system required some sort of standardization or formalization in examinations. No doubt there was concurrently a development of literary acumen in general. On the other hand, the education intendancies had clearly become specialized organs, and the career patterns of education intendants suggest at least partial career specializations. I do not think it would be going too far to suggest, consequently, that the persisting concept of a nonspecialized officialdom in early modern China should be used with increased caution.

JOHN MESKILL 明 *Academies and*
Politics in the Ming Dynasty

In modern times the academies (*shu-yüan*) of imperial China have attracted sympathetic attention, one scholar, for example, praising them as the highest seats of learning and the most vital centers of thought of the last premodern millenium.[1] In the Ming dynasty, on the contrary, a hostile opinion prevailed, and academies were attacked. The content of their learning was questioned, though its vitality was bitterly acknowledged. The effects of academies became an issue when they were indicted as disturbers of the peace in one way or another. As a result, a series of edicts called for their destruction.

The suppression of the academies showed them to have a political as well as educational side, their political significance lying in their organizing groups of educated men who thus acquired a certain feeling of common interest. The political experience of the academies is of course only one part of their history, a general account of which would require atention to several other subjects, especially their method of education. Yet their experience with politics went far toward defining their place in Chinese life, and more generally it suggested how independent organizations might gravitate toward political activities in a society as centered on government as China's, and how government in turn would respond to separate political organizations.

BACKGROUND

Briefly, three features of the earlier history of academies set the stage for events in the Ming dynasty. First was a preference for remote and secluded sites. Scholars tended to found academies as places for withdrawal from certain conditions that seemed unfavorable to the kind of education or self-development they sought. The turmoil of the Five Dynasties, for example, stimulated a desire for scholarly retreats.[2] By the time of Southern Sung, though life was more settled, some scholars, especially in the Chu Hsi school, had reservations about the conduct of official education and the effects of the examination system on scholarship.[3] In Yüan times, with many scholars remaining outside government either from disapproval of the Mongols or because of the suspension of the examination system, academies grew further.[4]

The seclusion of academies and their founding by individual scholars contributed to the idea, stressed later, that they were "private" schools. Some of the most prominent early academies were founded by men not acting as officials; some acquired private sources of income; and some had principals chosen by sponsors of the school, not the government, and privately enrolled students. To that extent the academies were private. On the other hand, they did not emphasize their independence as a necessary virtue. Even though the founders did not act in an official capacity, they often were or had been officials, sought imperial permission for what they did, received official endowments of land, and acquired teachers through agreement with the government.[5] The independence of the academies was sometimes implied, but not as a necessary condition in the way asserted by some modern Western schools. On the contrary, to describe an academy as independent was usually to condemn it. It was wrong, as was generally understood, to act privately at the cost of the general welfare and harmony, a fault of which a number of academies would be accused. Implicitly the way to correct the fault was to close the academy or bring it under state management. Privacy, therefore, was a particular and vulnerable characteristic. It will be convenient to think of it as symbolized by private directorship, in which the principal was not acting as a state official.

The second general feature was a growth of the rate at which academies were built. The following, based on crude figures, indicates the movement: [6]

Period	Academies Established, Repaired, or Restored	Approximate Rate
Northern Sung	39	1 in 4 years
Southern Sung [7]	140	1 a year
Yüan	227	2 a year

The growth depended greatly, no doubt, on intellectual forces working in ways still to be explained, but an increase of material facilities, printed books being the most striking example, helped. The region of growth was ever more the southeast—the valleys of the Yangtze and the Kan, leading toward Hunan and the southern coast.[8]

Third among features of general background was a movement by government, beginning with the Yüan dynasty, to supervise academies more closely. It began to urge the establishment of academies, granting lands to their support and supplying books. At the same time, it began to assign teachers, who were given a place in the tables of provincial education officials.[9]

EARLY MING

For the first century of the Ming dynasty, the long-range trend towards more academies seemed halted. Only in the following 40 years did it begin again. The approximate rates were as follows: [10]

Period	Academies Established, Repaired, or Restored	Approximate Rate
Hung-wu to T'ien-shun (96 years: 1368-1464)	69	1 a year
Ch'eng-hua to Hung-chih (40 years: 1465-1505)	125	3 a year

Though the reason for the setback is unclear, the establishment of a school system and a regular examination system may have directed the attention of most scholars to government service.[11] At any rate, the government adopted no policy opposing academies. The government established two itself—Ni-shan and Chu-ssu academies [12] —to show its respect for Confucius and his descendants, as the Yüan had done earlier. It helped to maintain or repair certain older academies, such as Hsiang-shan in Kiangsi.[13] Furthermore, it tolerated individuals' establishing academies in honor of their forebears or of great scholars [14] and maintaining or reviving some of the great old academies of Sung times.[15]

Chu Hsi scholarship remained dominant in the academies, as it had been since the late years of the Yüan era.[16] The great Sung school at which Chu Hsi had resided, Pai-lu-tung Academy in Nan-k'ang, Kiangsi, was restored.[17] Another of the great Sung academies, Pai-lu-chou, in Chi-an Prefecture, Kiangsi, was revived somewhat later.[18] A Lien-hsi Academy, one of several of that name, was established in the Hung-wu period (1368–98) to honor Chou Tun-i.[19]

Then as before, institutions of several different types and uses were called academies.[20] Some were simply libraries, which was what the term had signified in the T'ang dynasty, except that later it usually referred to private libraries. Others were schools, the more modest designed to educate the young of a clan or neighborhood and resembling private elementary schools or the Ming dynasty's local schools. Many, whatever other uses they may have had, also maintained shrines and sacrificed to great figures of the past. Still others seem to have served cultivated men of the region as a meetinghouse or club where they read and discussed great writing and practiced their own.

Among all the centers called academies, certain ones combined several features. They were dedicated to great men, almost always scholar-philosophers, of the past, contained libraries, served as meeting places for literati, and were centers of higher learning. In the times of their greatest vigor, prominent scholars supervised the students there. Their learning involved a training or self-cultivation which aimed at the achievement of personal virtue either in addition to success in the state examinations or regardless of it. The students followed a schedule of systematic study, regular lectures, discussions, and sometimes interviews with the principal, under an organization resembling that of a Ch'an monastery.[21] Academies of this kind, and organizations connected with them, became an issue in Ming government.

BURGEONING OF ACADEMIES

The modest growth of academies in the first half of the dynasty became luxuriant in its third quarter, in the sixteenth century.[22] Over one third of the academies of the whole dynasty were founded in the Chia-ching reign period (1522–66) alone. (See below, table on

p. 169.) The larger causes of this movement have yet to be made clear. If the early development of the school and examination systems had absorbed the literati at first, the ossification of the systems—the decline of the schools to little more than registration centers, and the standardized and formalized examinations—may have repelled many of them later.[23] Unquestionably a more immediate factor was the rise of new philosophical schools with unconventional attitudes, often criticizing the behavior of most of the educated and of those in government in particular. The most famous of the new schools was the Yang-ming, made up of followers of Wang Shou-jen (1472–1529), but there were others as well, such as the Pai-sha, which followed Ch'en Hsien-chang (1428–1560) and was involved in the apparently sudden reversal of official toleration.

THE CHIA-CHING PROHIBITIONS

With the mushrooming of academies came the first broad official disapproval. In Chia-ching 16 (1537), a censor, Yu Chü-ching, impeached Chan Jo-shui (1466–1500), the minister of personnel in Nanking, charging him with advocating perverse doctrines and ways and attracting the rootless from far and wide to an academy that he had established privately.[24] The Ministry of Personnel answered that Chan Jo-shui proposed only to follow in the footsteps of the ancients. Some of his interpretations differed from what was usual, but he had developed the classics and philosophical writings at many points. It was true, however, that his followers were many and included eccentrics, and his academies seemed to have violated regulations. They should be destroyed or changed.

The emperor, though he did not dismiss Chan Jo-shui, and acknowledged that he had permission to keep an academy, banned his books and those of the late Wang Shou-jen and ordered academies built privately (thereafter?) to be closed. Students were warned to stick to their task of preparing for the examinations in the places where they were registered.[25]

The next year, Chia-ching 17 (1538), the minister of personnel Hsü Tsan argued that academies established by officials, including those charged with pacifying aborigines, ought to be prohibited, as they diverted emphasis from the appropriate state offices and misused funds to support students and print books. The emperor issued such a prohibition.[26]

The variety of complaints and the repeated edicts of prohibition indicated that the issue was grave. Yet little seems to have happened. Some records imply that at least one of Chan Jo-shui's academies closed, a possibility that we may accept for the sake of simplicity, even though none of the relevant gazetteers confirms it.[27] Otherwise, nothing that I have seen in the local records—gazetteers or academy histories—shows any effects of the sweeping prohibitions.[28] Of course, there may have been adverse effects short of permanent closing; some academies may have reduced their activities just enough to mollify the authorities, for example. The weight of the evidence, however, inclines the other way. To note only a few instances of academies that continued to flourish, Pai-lu-tung Academy, boasting old connections with Chu Hsi, acquired more land and buildings during the Chia-ching period.[29] Pai-lu-chou apparently moved shortly after the prohibitions but continued to display its name-plaque and published its history in Chia-ching 25 (1546).[30] Nan-hsi Academy, which had been enlarged in the Hung-chih and Cheng-te periods, suffered no noted reversal.[31] At most, it would seem, a few academies of certain characteristics must have been the targets.

The particulars of the charges show that the offensive characteristics were probably unorthodox teaching and behavior and the irregular assembling of men. It was a fact, for instance, that Wang Shou-jen's teachings differed from Chu Hsi's, which were endorsed officially, as did those of Chan Jo-shui, who followed Ch'en Hsien-chang, founder of the meditative Pai-sha school.[32] Both Wang Shou-jen and Chan Jo-shui, however, had established academies years before the prohibitions, so that their unorthodoxy alone would not explain the timing of the attack. It is also true that some academy men behaved oddly, but whether their behavior was worse in 1537–38 remains unknown. It is unclear what mischief was done in academies in aborigine territories, where Wang Shou-jen had founded several without official objections years before, and how much truth was in the charge of improper use of state funds. More generally, however, the charges complained against a certain organizing activity. Academies, some of them private, were attracting students, some of them wanderers, from their regular assignment under the school system. More was involved than breaking the rules. A closer look at the two groups of academies in question will show them bound up with political rivalries.

THE CANTON GROUP

First, several of Chan Jo-shui's private academies were centered in the vicinity of Canton, the region where he had been born (Tseng-ch'eng) and studied under Ch'en Hsien-chang. By the time of the prohibitions he had privately established three academies: Yün-yü (in 1517), Ta-k'o (in 1519), and Kan-ch'üan (in 1537). All were close to Canton, the first two in the Hsi-ch'iao mountains and the third on Mt. Lo-fu, near his home.[33] Two others known to be his—Hsin-ch'üan and Hsin-chiang—were in the vicinity of Nanking and apparently drew the attention of officialdom to his teaching,[34] but at least one of them had imperial sanction and was not an issue in the prohibitions.

Furthermore, his academies observed in common the philosophical principles of Ch'en Hsien-chang, in whose memory Chan established the schools.[35] Several of the academies thus drew men together through both local ties and school ties.

As another thread of connection, Chan's academies had close neighbors; at least two Cantonese in addition to Chan—Fang Hsien-fu, a *chin-shih* and Hanlin bachelor in Chan's class (1505),[36] and Huo T'ao, a first-place *chin-shih* of 1514,[37] were studying and founding academies at about the same time in the Hsi-ch'iao mountains; Fang establishing Shih-ch'üan Academy there in 1517, the same year as Chan's first, and Huo T'ao establishing Ssu-feng Academy in 1523.[38] Thus, the Canton region included almost a complex of academies, drawing natives and perhaps others from farther afield together in similar intellectual pursuits.

Second, the men who shared some bond in establishing or patronizing academies also lined up together in a running political contest at the center of government. Like Chan Jo-shui, Fang Hsien-fu and Huo T'ao occupied offices of various prominence in court, Fang rising finally to be a grand secretary and Huo serving as a secretary in the Ministry of War, among other assignments. In 1521, about two decades before the prohibitions, a question had arisen about the proper terms to be applied to the emperor's forebears. As in other great rites disputes, officials at court split sharply over the issue. The advocate of the position that prevailed, in that it won the emperor's approval, was Chang Ts'ung (later Chang Fu-ching), a new *chin-shih* of 1521, who quickly rose to be grand secretary (by 1527) and the leader of a faction.[39] All three Cantonese men were in his camp.[40] When the emperor appointed Fang Hsien-fu grand secretary in 1532 a comet crossed the sky, convincing a censor that politics had gone sufficiently wrong to bring forth a portent. He appraised all the chief officials in a memorial, linking by his criticism Chang Ts'ung, Fang Hsien-fu, and Chan Jo-shui, as well as others.[41]

If the Canton academies seemed a distant appendage of the dominant Chang Ts'ung faction, they nevertheless felt some effects when the faction fell. In 1534 Fang Hsien-fu left the office of grand secretary; in 1535 Chang Ts'ung also left. In 1536 an opponent of Chang Ts'ung moved into the office, and in 1537 the academies came under attack.

With the departure of Chang Ts'ung and the appointment of Hsia Yen (*chin-shih* of 1517), who had opposed Chang on important issues since 1528, Chang's faction had fallen. Hsia Yen, his replacement, had differed sharply with two particular members of the old faction, Fang Hsien-fu and Huo T'ao, who were associated, like Chan Jo-shui, with academies.[42] Though the change of circumstances seemed not radical enough to drive Huo and Chan from office, the removal of the faction leaders Chang Ts'ung and Fang Hsien-fu had opened the way for harassment of the remainder and their organization.

THE YANG-MING SCHOOL

Wang Shou-jen and his school similarly linked factionalism with academies. In the first place, Wang had become a subject of dispute years before the prohibitions. After rising to fame as a general, he had been recommended for higher posts by two of the factionalists, Hu T'ao [43] and Chang Ts'ung, the support of the latter provoking a rankling disagreement. Chang Ts'ung, then a grand secretary, was preparing to nominate Wang Shou-jen to fill a vacant grand secretaryship. Two other grand secretaries blocked the nomination.[44] One, Kuei O (d. 1531), earlier an ally of Chang Ts'ung, had once tried to patronize Wang and had been rebuffed, to his lasting resentment.[45] The other, Yang I-ch'ing (1454–1530), was engaged with Chang Ts'ung in a long-drawn-out struggle for influence [46] and saw Wang's candidacy as a threat. The incident led to Kuei O's arguing in 1529, three months after Wang Shou-jen had died, that since he had extolled views opposed to Chu Hsi's and encouraged followers in holding distorted views, he should be divested of his hereditary rank and scholarship in his line should be prohibited. The emperor agreed.[47] The involvement of Wang Shou-jen in political controversy prefigured that of his followers, as will be noted later.

In the second place, Wang sponsored academies in even more places and with a greater sense of organization than Chan Jo-shui. During Wang's lifetime he founded or served academies throughout the southeast.[48] Soon after being banished to Kweichou, the result of a brush with the eunuch dictator Liu Chin in 1506, he was appointed headmaster (concurrently with his position as provincial education commissioner) of Kuei-yang Academy.[49] At that time he apparently saw academies as civilizing institutions, for he encouraged aborigines to build them.[50] Later in life he had academies built in southern Kiangsi, where he had put down bandits.[51] He seems to have thought academies also useful for inculcating unity and purpose of will: his following rose in the first place, in the view of the dynastic history, among troops who were served by academies.[52] He once spoke of academies as barracks for "picked troops." [53] Academies for educating tribesmen or inspiriting troops probably differed greatly from the places of advanced discourse and discussion he furthered elsewhere, but they shared the function of associating men under leaders with a program.

Wang Shou-jen also developed a plan to spread his teaching. Central to it was philosophical discussion, as he showed by his own example. Disciples in the hundreds gathered round him in schools in the early Chia-ching period (1522–66).[54] He expected the disciples to spread the teaching in a similar way, leading to the establishment of more academies.[55] He saw the academies as complementing the state schools, as achieving what the state schools did not.[56]

In the Cheng-te (1506–21) and early Chia-ching years he often led philosophical discussions, his presence spreading the fame of some academies, such as Lung-kang, Lien-hsi, Chi-shan, and Fu-wen.[57] His disciples did the same, perhaps even more energetically after his death in 1529, when academies began to erect shrines in his honor. Just before and after he died, a number of academies were established, Yang-ming Academy in Yüeh-nan, Fu-ku in An-fu, and others near Hang-chou, Hsiu-shui, Shao-hsing, and Yü-yao.[58] Some of them, far from being isolated shrines, apparently became sizable centers of learning with many students. The academy near Hang-chou could accommodate over 100 students.[59] Under Wang Shou-jen, moreover, those attracted to the academies came not from the immediate vicinity alone but from relatively distant places. In 1524, for example, Wang, teaching in Chekiang, drew more than 300 disciples, among them some from Hukwang, Kwangtung, Kiangsi, the Southern Metropolitan Area, and other places.[60]

Beyond serving as centers of study, some academies became headquarters for associations or clubs. Wang Shou-jen had discoursed before one of the earliest, a Time Misers' Association (*hsi-yin hui*), which met five days a month in An-fu District, Kiangsi.[61] Within a few years of his death similar associations, sometimes called Common Resolve Associations (*t'ung-chih hui*), formed in the capital (1532) and in the region of the southern capital (1533 and 1534). The Common Resolve Association of Peking included important officials. The Cantonese grand secretary Fang Hsien-fu was one, and others were editors in the Hanlin Academy and officials in the ministries and offices of scrutiny.[62] Thus through their connections with these associations, the academies were linked to court politics.

The Association of the Four Localities (*ssu-hsiang hui*) in the Nanking region illustrated another feature, the forming of several academies into an organization. It was based on three academies founded by, among others, the principal of the National University at Nanking. It held a grand meeting regularly in spring and autumn, and counted among its members literati of surrounding cities.[63] It was the second such association to be formed in the Southern Metropolitan Area, where the political connections of the academy movement seemed in some ways especially pronounced. Other associations were formed thereafter, the movement characteristically involving leadership or patronage of officials, regular programs of activity, and a membership of literati from a relatively wide surrounding region. Though academies and associations were charged several times with gathering the unsettled and the eccentric, their leadership also included a notable number of men who had placed high in the *chin-shih* examinations.

One more trait stood out. In 1534 an academy, or more exactly a lecture hall, was built in honor of Wang Shou-jen at a crossroads.[64] In a movement that had grown from Sung times in secluded mountains or river islands, the crossroads halls that came to be built in several places reflected a new interest in membership. The halls became stopping places for lecturers who traveled from one meeting to another. The Yang-ming movement was thus developing an organization more extensive than that of the Cantonese group.

With the appointment of Hsia Yen as grand secretary a year before the first prohibition, the balance of favor in high places swung away from some Yang-ming schoolmen as well as from Ch'en Hsien-chang's Cantonese followers. Hsia Yen, since he opposed Chang Ts'ung and those connected with him, opposed specifically at least two Yang-ming disciples in government—Tsou Shou-i, whom he had wanted removed from the Nanking Hanlin Academy,[65] and Wang Chi, whom he impeached when Wang was a director in the Nanking Ministry of War.[66] Both men had engaged in scholarly discussions with Chan Jo-shui,[67] and both were active in the academy movement.[68]

In sympathy with Hsia Yen in this respect was Yen Sung, who succeeded Hsia Yen as minister of rites when Hsia was promoted to be grand secretary. Yen Sung was said to hate all the philosophical speculation of the day.[69] Judging from the reputation he acquired later for repressive action, he could well have joined in the stifling of the academies; one scholar, indeed, has speculated that the indictment of 1538 was inspired by him.[70] Whether this is so or not, the prohibitions appeared consistent with the shift of political fortunes that had just occurred.[71]

LIMITATIONS ON THE SUPPRESSION

That only some, not all, academies were attacked pointed to some of the political factors involved. Even though Hsia Yen, who apparently preferred Chu Hsi scholarship, opposed some Yang-ming followers, he had no quarrel with the idea of academies, as is shown by his founding of one, Chung-li, about a month before the prohibition of 1537. True, Chung-li may have differed from the attacked academies in having the approval of the emperor and a library including imperial documents.[71] Yet later Hsia Yen, with money presented him by the emperor, built Wen-chiang Academy, where he held philosophical discussions with students [72] in the manner characteristic of the attacked academies. The academies, in addition, were close together, in the P'o-yang Lake basin of Kiangsi, Hsia Yen's native region, much as Chan Jo-shui's academies had been built near Canton and Wang Shou-jen's in the provinces in which he had been born or had done his major work. The Hsia Yen academies seemed to differ from the others mainly in the content of the teaching and the political weight of the founder. Political weight also implied closeness to the emperor, but the emperor neither approved nor disapproved of academies as such, as the variety of his actions showed.

The prohibitions of 1537–38 represented nothing so weighty as an official policy, if a policy may be measured by attempts to effect it. The ineffectiveness of the prohibitions suggested that no one in the center of government dominated it sufficiently to sustain a policy. A vagueness of direction was to be expected at the time, if only because life in high office was fleeting. Major officials held office for shorter periods in the Cheng-te and Chia-ching eras than in any part of the dynasty before, except the first 35 years.[73] In the first reign of the dynasty, brief appointments had reflected the domineering activity of the founding emperor, but in the Chia-ching era they reflected the opposite. Emperor Shih-tsung was a sickly man, preoccupied at times with the occult, whose reign critics later deplored for its vulnerability to factions. Major offices often went, it was complained, to those whose words lulled the emperor, not to those whom the emperor's word had bound.

As a result, no one appeared determined or entrenched enough to persevere in the attack on academies. The emperor's own attitude toward academies lacked special conviction, as is shown by his capacity for patronizing some even after prohibiting others. Hsia Yen, the more active grand secretary, may have opposed certain academies for their connection with political rivals but saw no harm in others and seemed not disposed to press a relentless attack, since we hear no more of prohibitions during his later years in office. A second grand secretary, Li Shih (d. 1538/9), was an old and apparently diffident man unlikely to do battle over the issue.[74] Of the seven other highest officials, the heads of the six ministries and the censor-in-chief, only two remained in office throughout the twelve months in which the issue seemed liveliest.[75] True, the two were Hsü Tsan, minister of personnel, and Yen Sung, minister of rites, whose names have been linked to the second prohibition; but Hsü Tsan apparently had no profound dislike of academies, as we do not hear from him again on the subject, though he rose to be a grand secretary. Yen Sung was the more implacable opponent, as has been mentioned, but he could not dominate government in his position at the time of the prohibitions. Why he did not act later, when he became grand secretary, remains unclear.

Moreover, regional officials and others found the prohibitions no reason to stop their patronage or encouragement. In Kiangsu, for example, the prefect of T'ung-chou established Wen-hui Academy in 1537, and an assistant magistrate of Yen-ch'eng District built Cheng-hsüeh Academy in 1538.[76] In Kiangsi an assistant surveillance commissioner established an academy at Wen-hu, north of Hsiu-shui District.[77] In Kwangtung even Chan Jo-shui may have persisted in his errant ways when he privately established Kan-ch'üan Academy in 1537, though that might have been just before the first edict, of course; and two other men, one acting officially and the other privately, founded academies in 1538.[78] At least five more academies were privately established by or for Chan Jo-shui in the next two decades.[79] Together with the larger number of others recorded only as founded "during the Chia-ching period," they suggest that the movement had suffered little.

SEQUEL TO THE CHIA-CHING PROHIBITIONS

In Kiangsi, especially, academies continued to prosper. A central figure there and in the whole movement later was Hsü Chieh (1494–1574), a man of Sung-chiang, Kiangsu, a region of several important academies in a later era. His actions illustrated that academy founders in the provinces disregarded the first prohibitions and even created conditions for a more severe attack later. Figuring prominently in his *chin-shih* class (he took third place in 1523), he had drawn young students to him even in the early days of his service. In his teaching he followed Wang Shou-jen.[80] When he was assigned as assistant commissioner for education in Kiangsi, he strongly supported the growth of the Yang-ming school, patronizing such disciples as Tsou Shou-i, Liu Pang-ts'ai, Lo Hung-hsien, and Li Sui, who came together for meetings at his arrangement, bringing with them other literati from their cities.[81] His patronage covered much of the growth of the associations mentioned earlier. His support apparently flagged not at all under the weight of the emperor's prohibitions, for in 1539 he built a shrine in honor of Wang in Nan-ch'ang Prefecture, Kiangsi.[82]

Hsü Chieh promoted academies and associations so wholeheartedly that by the time he became grand secretary in 1552 the ambitious on the political ladder below him also made it a point to found academies. Observers in the lower Yangtze valley sardonically called academies there the temporary residences of the governors.[83]

At the center of government he continued to support the academy movement, or its functional companion, the lecture movement, most concretely by lecturing at the Ling-chi Temple. His lectures, though apparently continuing for only a few years, drew "a thousand" (elsewhere "five thousand") students and led to the beginning of a Ling-chi Association.[84]

Politically, Hsü Chieh was considered to lead a faction of men who had been tied to him in any of several ways, such as being born in the same place, serving in the Hsü family's region, or crossing his path at some point in government.[85] Their rivals were another faction under Grand Secretary Yen Sung.[86] Unlike Yen, however, Hsü could also be placed at the head of a wide, though loose, organization of officials and literati whose membership in academies and associations suggested some measure of loyalty to their patron. Correspondingly the ties, though no doubt a source of strength on one hand, had defined the academies as political targets on the other.

THE WAN-LI PROHIBITION

No sooner had Hsü Chieh died than edicts appeared attacking academies once more and with far greater effect. In 1579 the prefect of Ch'ang-chou, Kiangsu, Shih Kuan-min (*chin-shih* of 1565), was found to have collected funds wrongfully from the people and built independently a Lung-ch'eng Academy in Wu-hsin District. He was dismissed, and an edict ordered the abolition of private academies throughout the empire. All were to be turned into state buildings and their lands returned to the community. Groups were forbidden to gather for idle purposes at the expense of localities, and regional inspecting censors were ordered to heighten their watchfulness over educational affairs.[87]

The effects of the edict were sweeping. According to the general account, 64 academies were converted to state uses in the Southern Metropolitan Area and neighboring regions.[88] Local sources that are silent on the effects of the 1537–38 prohibitions note a number of closings immediately after the 1579 edict.[89]

The greater effect of the 1579 prohibition was owed to the power and will of Chang Chü-cheng (1525–82), who dominated government in the first decade of the Wan-li era (1573–1620) and so hated the kind of philosophical discussion fashionable in the academies that to speak of it made him gnash his teeth.[90] He stated his reasons several times. Generally, he felt that scholars should devote themselves to the essentials of government rather than to literary practice and speculative philosophy.[91] He was disturbed at what he considered the laxity of the state education system and saw academies as working against a "unification" of education that was already impaired.[92] He loathed especially the latter-day exponents of the Yang-ming learning.[93] On several counts—his utilitarian view of education, his vision of a unified social order, and his specific dislike of some Yang-ming schoolmen—his convictions and temperament were inimical to academies. Political circumstances and events before the prohibition had sharpened his hostility.

After Hsü Chieh's fifteen-year term as grand secretary, academy men and their allies naturally held places throughout government. Chang Chü-cheng may have curbed a desire to take matters in hand earlier out of deference to Hsü Chieh, who had been his master and political tutor since the days when Hsü was principal of the Hanlin Academy and Chang a compiler there. Later, differences apparently grew up between the two, as is indicated by Hsü's passing over Chang several times in promoting officials,[94] and ultimately Chang Chü-cheng made clear his hostility to Hsü Chieh's philosophical practices and followers.[59] He dismissed some who had probably been close to Hsü Chieh. For example, Tsou Te-han (*chin-shih* of 1571) was a son of Tsou Shou-i, who figured above as a protégé of Hsü. When Chang Chü-cheng planned to suppress philosophical discussion and Tsou Te-han as an official in the Ministry of Punishments defended it, censors reported that Tsou was building a faction, and he was sent to a minor provincial post.[96] Lo Ju-fang (*chin-shih* of 1553), who had helped persuade Hsü Chieh to lecture in the Ling-chi Temple, conducted meetings of philosophical discussion attended by many court officials.[97] Thus incurring Chang Chü-cheng's anger, he was finally dismissed, as was an associate who tried to carry on after him.[98]

Although Chang Chü-cheng imposed his will upon many men for many different reasons, one issue particularly turned his anger against academicians, in that the issue revolved around his personal conduct, and academicians spoke out strongly against him. In 1577 his father died. An official in the Ministry of Revenue, perhaps toadying to Chang, proposed that he not go into full mourning. A powerful eunuch, Feng Pao, with whom Chang Chü-cheng maintained close relations,[99] supported the suggestion. A group in the Hanlin Academy, including Wang Hsi-chüeh, and others outside it, including Tsou

Yüan-piao, argued against it, with the result that five of their members were beaten in court and punished in other ways.

The furor against Chang Chü-cheng's conduct continued, marked in the sky by a flaming comet (so contemporaries believed) and in the streets by bills of denunciation. The emperor intervened, commissioning Chang's son and a eunuch to observe the mourning as substitutes, and threatening death to anyone who posted bills again. Even so, the crisis passed only slowly, and subsequent historians, recording the affair as Chang Chü-cheng's curtailment of mourning,[100] treated it as a benchmark of the period. It was even said that from the parties in the dispute grew the factions that continued to fight to the end of the dynasty.[101]

The political animosities exposed in the crisis appeared again in the attack on academies two years later. Among academies known to have been changed or closed, several were not only guilty of gathering groups, as the edict said, for idle purposes (such as philosophical discussion). Some were tied to the political opposition to Chang Chü-cheng. Lung-ch'eng, the academy founded by a relatively minor official whose misbehavior had provided the occasion for a prohibition that seemed disproportionately sweeping, was distantly related to Wang Hsi-chüeh, one of the major critics of Chang Chü-cheng when he curtailed mourning. The academy's most famous graduate, Sun Chi-kao (first place *chin-shih* of 1574), was associated with Wang Chiu-hsüeh, another Wu-hsin man and a *chin-shih* of 1586, who in turn was a disciple of Wang Hsi-chüeh.[102] The attack on Lung-ch'eng thus weakened a source of Wang's political support.

Another academy disturbed by the prohibition was Jen-wen in Chi-shui, Kiangsi. From it and its Yang-ming tradition had come Tsou Yüan-piao, another major protester against Chang Chü-cheng's offense. His criticism had brought down upon him first exile in a military camp and then an enforced retirement.[103] The prohibition closed the academy until Chang's death.

Also implicated through politics was Fu-ku Academy in An-fu, Kiangsi, which was forced to change its name to Three Sages Shrine (San-hsien Tz'u).[104] Fu-ku had been not only an important center of discussion in the Yang-ming movement but a member of the Association of the Four Localities organized by Tsou Shou-i and others. Tsou Shou-i's son, Te-han, had established his opposition to Chang Chü-cheng by obstinately defending philosophical discussion and was promptly labeled the organizer of a faction. The academy with which he was connected consequently was tied to the opposition.

For some of the academies that suffered under the prohibition, no direct link to central politics has appeared. A few were characterized by the philosophical interests or educational practices that Chang Chü-cheng opposed. One, for example, was Huai-yü in Kuang-hsin, Kiangsi, which was closed, though no evidence has appeared that would connect it directly with political rivals of Chang Chü-cheng. The fact that its founder had brought together other academies for lecture meetings shows that it was supporting educational practises Chang thought harmful.[105] Connections with the new philosophical movements were so incriminating, it seems, that even the most honorable intellectual origins could not save two old academies dating from Sung times. Pai-lu-tung was closed and stripped of all but 760 of its 2,300 *mou* of land.[106] Pai-lu-chou, receiving word of the prohibition, put up a new name sign, Hu-hsi Public Office, and waited.[107] Both schools, despite their orthodox backgrounds, had come under the influence of the Ming reform movements. Pai-lu-tung had invited Hu Chü-jen, a colleague of the teacher of Chan Jo-shui, to hold philosophical discussions. It owed its restoration, after Chang Chü-cheng died, to his enemy Tsou Yüan-piao.[108] Pai-lu-chou had been restored for the first time since the middle of the fourteenth century by Huang Tsung-ming, another disciple of Wang Shou-jen.[109]

A few other academies that were changed or closed have been identified,[110] but their activities and relationship to politics remain undiscovered. Nan-hsi Academy in Fukien, another old academy related to Chu Hsi, was required to change its name to Chu-shih Shrine; it sought permission to restore the old name.[111]

As the last instances mentioned above show, the political positions of some of the academies that suffered attack were uncertain. Opposition to Chang Chü-cheng came frequently enough from advocates of the new Ming philosophical movements, men who used academies to propound and develop their thought, to suggest that additional political connections may appear later, especially when the still un-identified majority of the 64 academies have been discovered.

Nevertheless, the evidence is neither simple nor complete enough to justify ignoring parts that are difficult to explain. Some academies, certainly, escaped unaffected. The only two that have been identified as untouched immediately [112]—Wan-sung Academy in Hang-chou and Chin-sheng in Jao-yang District, Hopei—enjoyed special circum-stances that might have afforded protection. Wan-sung, a rich academy much patronized by officials, followed rules laid down by Chu Hsi.[113] Despite the fact that Wang Shou-jen had been there, local officials argued that the true sources of its teaching were the ancient sages. Apparently sufficient official support and disavowal of the modern unorthodox practises exonerated it. Chin-sheng escaped owing to its remoteness. Not many miles south of Peking, it was not far from the capital in miles, but it may have been out of the way, and it was certainly removed from the Yangtze valley, where the full force of the attack fell.

By 1581, two years after the prohibition, when 64 academies in the southern region were reported changed or abolished, five others were noted to remain.[114] One, Tzu-yang Academy, which had been built in Anhwei in Sung times to commemorate the site at which Chu Hsi and his father had studied, had presumably maintained ties to orthodoxy strong enough to protect it. Another, Ch'ung-cheng Academy in Nanking, far from being able to claim that sanction, was associated with the Yang-ming teaching and even the patronage of Keng Ting-hsiang, a critic of Chang Chü-cheng's curtailment of mourning. Like Chang Chü-cheng, however, Keng Ting-hsiang ab-horred the more radical aspects of Ming intellectual movements, as is shown by his break with the famous iconoclast Li Chih.[115] Keng's more moderate views may have been reflected in the academy and spared it from attack, but no more definite information has come to hand. An academy of the same name in Hopei, also associated with men who had denounced Chang Chü-cheng, was forced to close.[116] The three other remaining academies—Chin-shan, Shih-men, and T'ien-ch'üan—were too obscure to have found a place in the ordinary sources. A clear picture of the effects of the prohibition, therefore, remains to be drawn, but that it must include Chang Chü-cheng's response to political opposition is certain.

One of Chang's victims described the power of his will almost prophetically. Ho Hsin-yin, a member of a radical branch of the Yang-ming teaching, met Chang in earlier days and sensed such hatred that he predicted he would die at Chang's orders.[117] He also told a friend that, while Yen Sung had meant to destroy Confucian learning and failed and Hsü Chieh to promote it and failed, Chang Chü-cheng would be able to do either.[118] In 1580 Chang, having received a report that Ho Hsin-yin was leading a private academy, heard parts of his teaching and put him in jail, where he died.[119]

SEQUEL TO THE WAN-LI PROHIBITION

Ho Hsin-yin had been right about dying at Chang Chü-cheng's hands, but he was wrong about the fate implied for academies. Even Chang Chü-cheng knew, from a survey taken shortly before he died, that he had failed to suppress all academies.[120] He had, however, done much to disarm a movement that had served other politicians in his lifetime, though it remains to be shown that, as one scholar has said, he reached power by destroying the academies supporting Hsü Chieh.[121] His targets obviously included many academies of the Yang-ming school, but they included others as well, and some academies, even one prominent in the Yang-ming school, escaped.

Chang's effort, though it went farther than most of the earlier prohibitions, was similarly his own, not part of a state-sustained policy. That became clear as soon as he died, when Tsou Yüan-piao, the old and hard-hit opponent, petitioned to restore both Jen-wen Academy in his own city and the old Pai-lu-tung Academy.[122] The petitions were granted, indicating that the pressure on academies had passed with their powerful enemy. Again, as in the earlier period, the emperor did not sustain the prohibition. In fact, Shen-tsung had awarded mottoes to certain academies at the very height of the repression.[123]

The 1579 repression nevertheless had much stronger and more sustained direction than the 1537–38 prohibitions, as the destruction of academies showed; and even with the revival afterwards, effects of the prohibitions remained. One immediate effect was a drop in the rate at which academies were founded. As was shown earlier, the rate of establishing, repairing, and restoring academies had risen in the first part of the Ming dynasty as follows:

Period	*Approximate Rate*
Hung-wu to T'ien-shun (1368–1464)	1 a year
Ch'eng-hua to Hung-chih (1465–1505)	3 a year
Cheng-te (1506–21)	6 a year
Chia-ching (1522–66)	8 a year
Lung-ch'ing (1567–72)	10 a year

The rates thereafter were as follows: [124]

Period	*Approximate Rate*
Wan-li (1573–1620)	4.7 a year
T'ien-ch'i (1621–27)	1.6 a year
Ch'ung-chen (1628–44)	3.5 a year

The Chang Chü-cheng repression, it would appear, had upset the academy movement so that by the T'ien-ch'i era, in which occurred a final repression, fewer academies were built than at any time during the previous century and a half. The rising rate at the end of the dynasty might suggest, on the other hand, that the prohibitions had only stunned the academies, not crippled them. Ch'ing dynasty rates would no doubt show a further rise in numbers.

A second probable effect, which was in keeping with a long-range trend, was a reduction of the proportion of academies founded privately. Roughly, the proportions were as follows: [125]

	Academies Established, Repaired, or Restored	
Period	*By Commoners (min)*	*By Regional Officials*
Sung	46%	22%
Yüan	37%	19%
Ming	15%	63%

Though a large number of Yüan academies are unclassifiable here, it may be assumed that officially sponsored academies held a greater place than is shown, in view of the Yüan policy of support and control.

In Kiangsi, which consistently had the greatest number of academies, the shifting proportions moved in conformity with the political events described above: [126]

Academies Founded in Kiangsi by Commoners

Sung		80%
Yüan		70%
Ming		70%
Until Cheng-te (1368–1505)		70%
Cheng-te to Chia-ching (1506–66)		50%
From Lung-ch'ing on (1567–1644)		30%

Chang Chü-cheng's brake on private academies stands out clearly against Hsü Chieh's encouragement of them.

The most detailed tabulation available for the Ming period, though applying only to Kwangtung Province, may represent tendencies in some of the other provinces where academies were prominent. Kwangtung ranked second or third in number of academies in Ming times.[127]

Period	Academies Established in Kwangtung [128]	
	Officially	Privately
Chia-ching 1-17 (1522–38) (To the prohibitions)	16	7
Chia-ching 18-45 (1539–66) (After the prohibitions)	35	20
Lung-ch'ing (1567–72)	4	0
Wan-li 1-10 (1573–82) (Chang Chü-cheng administration)	5	0*
Wan-li 10-47 (1582–1620)	32	6
T'ien-ch'i (1620–27)	1	0
Ch'ung-chen (1628–44)	13	3

*None definitely indicated; some of the following figure of 6 may be included.

These figures suggest, first, that an unusually large number of private academies was established, along with official academies, in Kwangtung in the latter part of the Chia-ching era. The period of growth, coinciding approximately with Hsü Chieh's rise to influence, contrasted strikingly with the small numbers for the rest of the dynasty (the Wan-li period, when six academies were established privately, ranked second in this respect). Second, the period corresponding approximately to the end of Hsü Chieh's dominance and the rise of Chang Chü-cheng reduced the figures for privately established academies to their usual small size. If other southern provinces showed a similar pattern, academies in the latter half of the Ming apparently followed a first delayed, then accelerated course toward bureaucratization.[129] In the long run, Chang Chü-cheng had probably been more successful than he realized in furthering the unification of education.

Bureaucratization, incidentally, means affiliation with officialdom, not especially with the emperor. Shen-tsung, like Shih-tsung before him, showed no strong views about academies. Even his nominal support, signified often by mottoes sent out in his name to be hung on the walls of the academies, conferred only a little protection against decisions of a premier as willful as Chang Chü-cheng. When, for example, a censor ordered Pai-lu-tung Academy to close and discovered that it had an imperial motto, he was impressed enough to negotiate with it, but in the end it retained only 760 of its original 2,300 *mou* to carry on its sacrifices.[130] The obstacle to reopening academies was Chang Chü-cheng, not the emperor.

THE T'IEN-CH'I PROHIBITION

Academies rose again, though at a slower rate than before. The records of the old Pai-lu-tung and Pai-lu-chou Academies note their revival in the latter part of Shen-tsung's reign. A teacher in the Chan Jo-shui line organized successful discussion meetings.[131] Even Lung-ch'eng Academy, the first target of the great repression, regained its land through the patronage of the prefect, Ou-yang Tung-feng, and a hall for discussions, though the term "academy" was avoided.[132]

Most famous of all the late academies were Tung-lin in Wu-hsi, about halfway between Ch'ang-chou and Su-chou on the Canal, and Shou-shan in Peking. The last Ming repression centering around them has been described at length, exposing the political motivations at work in 1625.[133] Here I shall merely mention a few features that illustrate the direction the academy movement had taken after its earlier experiences.

The past having shown that founding a "private" academy was dangerous, and that association with officials might provide protection, the reviver of Tung-lin, Ku Hsien-ch'eng (1550–1612), and his companions took great care to secure not only the support of prefect Ou-yang Tung-feng and the magistrate of Wu-hsi District but also the acquiescence of the governor, the regional inspector, and the education intendant. The petition to revive the academy came from students of the district school, emphasizing a supplementary role for the academy, and "public sentiment" was even sounded.[134] "Not without some misgivings did Ku and his friends accept public assistance. They were aware of the fact that there was no precedent in local history for doing so." [135] Their uneasiness arose as well, we may suspect, from knowledge that the use of public funds had incriminated others before. Yet tangible association with officials, dangerous though it might prove to be if the officials fell from favor, was safer than complete independence. Objectively, the notice in the *Ming-shih*, "The prefect of Ch'ang-chou . . . and the magistrate of Wu-hsi . . . built [the academy] for them," [136] may have been inaccurate, the state funds having been used for the shrine and private funds for the academy; but it represented political wisdom.

Once established, however, the academy set out on what our story shows to be a collision course with central authority. It joined with neighboring academies to hold meetings to which "the educated people in the southeast vied with each other in going." [137] It established ties with central officials, tolerating, in its political aspirations, one who was given to a "free use of public funds and . . . unscrupulous political methods," [138] and another who was a eunuch.[139] It became a part, in short, of a political faction and suffered the consequences.

If, then, caution dictated keeping one's distance from politics in addition to seeking the patronage of officials, Shou-shan Academy should have fared better. Like Tung-lin, it had been begun under high auspices, those of the censor-in-chief Tsou Yüan-piao and the vice censor-in-chief Feng Ts'ung-wu (*chin-shih* of 1589). Unlike Tung-lin, it ruled out political discussion,[140] a decision almost surely reflecting the experience of Tsou Yüan-piao, whose life had spanned a large part of the eighty-eight-year era of conflict. No matter, when a new repression was in the making, Shou-shan felt the first attacks. Three years before the repression, censors addressed charges against Tsou Yüan-piao and Feng Ts'ung-wu, questioning the value of their discussion meetings in answering current problems and suggesting that a faction might develop.[141] The latter danger was the excuse for the request in 1625 that the emperor suppress the academies "in order to cut out the party root." [142] The order of suppression that followed apparently being too narrow to satisfy the enemies of the academies, a more general order against academies of the Tung-lin group throughout the empire appeared a month later.[143] The memorial on which the second edict was based charged that all academies formed a closely knit organization, that their members helped one another in official advancement, that membership comprised people of various classes, that the academies wielded "the power of the court from afar," and that they agitated for political purposes.[144]

Among the academies known to have been abolished in the T'ien-ch'i repression, in addition to Shou-shan and Tung-lin, was Jen-wen in Chi-shui, which Tsou Yüan-piao had long patronized and revived before, after the 1579 repression. Five others were in northern Kiangsi, like Jen-wen in the drainage basin of Lake P'o-yang, so that a connection among them is possible, though not demonstrable, on the basis of proximity.[145] Another was Kuan-chung Academy, apparently associated with Feng Ts'ung-wu [146] and in Hui-chou,[147] and two others were in I District, Hui-chou Prefecture,[148] also suggesting a connection. An order was also given specifically to destroy all academies in Su-chou and Ch'ang-chou Prefectures, Kiangsu,[149] presumably because most were in the Tung-lin organization. Nevertheless, the number of academies destroyed apparently fell short of that in the 1579 repression.[150]

Almost wholly, the memorial for the prohibition cited above defined the danger of academies in terms of political power. True, an attack in 1625, when the eunuch dictator Wei Chung-hsien dominated the emperor (it was even asserted that Wei issued the order without permission) [151] might be expected to stress crude questions of control. Yet the charges of earlier times, though made by cultivated scholars instead of despised eunuchs, pointed toward the same issue. Then, complaints against the organizing of wanderers under private leadership had been a persistent theme. In 1625 the question was put more simply—the rootless had found roots in a party—but it was an old question. In view of the attack on Shou-shan, even a vow to shun political discussion would not suffice. The group in power at court had to guard against even the possibility of concerted rival action.

By implication, the issue went beyond questions of factional power and tested in general what forms were permissible in Ming political contests. Attackers of academies pretended to defend not merely their own selfish interests. The charges they made were public, not secret, and were addressed to the general opinion of what was right, which it was the emperor's mandate to uphold. They were arguing that it was not right in constitutional terms to form a separate political organization. Nothing demonstrates the strength of their argument more clearly than the silence on the other side. The court record, the record of government, contains no defense of the right of private academies to exist. A muted defense may be heard in occasional inscriptions and private writings, but at the political center nothing lasting was said. Instead of defending independence, the solution was to end it, assuming that academies were useful enough to be permitted to exist at all. Academies, rather than taking shelter under some official's wing or promising to stay away from politics, should be integrated into the one legitimate national polity.

When Wei Chung-hsien fell from power, academies rose once again, as has been shown. Though I have not examined their condition in the last reign of the dynasty, their role seemed to be implied in the order of the restoration itself (1628), when, instead of a mere edict of toleration, a specific charge to revive academies was given to education intendants. Their supervision would bring the academies more fully under the structure of government, which was to shape their future in the Ch'ing period, when they became official or semiofficial schools, some like Tung-lin gaining "greater external splendor and a better economic position" [152] than they had enjoyed for some time.

JAMES B. PARSONS 明 *The Ming Dynasty*

Bureaucracy: Aspects of Background Forces

INTRODUCTION

The present study is concerned with presenting certain major forces involved in the background of the Ming dynasty bureaucracy. The basis of the study was provided by some 23,000 officials who held office at various levels of the administration throughout the dynasty. For purposes of analysis, these levels were divided into five categories, given here in descending order of importance: (1) central government, (2) provincial, (3) prefectural (*fu*), (4) subprefectural (*chou*) and county (*hsien*) I, and (5) county II. Officials in the central government category include grand secretaries (*ta hsüeh-shih*) of the Grand Secretariat (*nei-ko*), ministers (*shang-shu*) of the Six Ministries (*liu-pu*), and censors-in-chief (*tu yü-shih*) of the Censorate (*tu ch'a-yüan*).[1] The provincial category includes, for all provinces, provincial governors (*hsün-fu*), regional inspectors (*hsün-an*), administration commissioners (*pu-cheng shih*), and surveillance commissioners (*an-ch'a shih*).[2] In the prefectural category are included the prefectural magistrates (*chih-fu*) of 136 prefectures (out of a total of 159).[3] Officials in the subprefectural and county I category include subprefectural magistrates (*chih-chou*) of 44 dependent subprefectures (out of a total of 208) and county magistrates (*chih-hsien*) of 105 counties (out of a total of 1,144).[4] The term "county II" was used to designate county offices below that of magistrate, and 41 of these subordinate offices from 40 counties were included. The specific offices in the county II category varied from county to county, the choice depending largely upon the completeness of the lists.[5] As for the geographical spread at the subprefectural and county I level, the 44 subprefectures and 105 counties were selected from all 15 provinces on the basis of roughly three subprefectures and seven counties per province. Furthermore, an effort was made to select them from different sections of the province.

The 41 county II level offices were also chosen, roughly equally, from all provinces with the exception of Kwangsi, Kweichow, and Yunnan, where the lists of such subordinate officials were so sketchy as to be virtually useless.

The chief sources for the study were the *Ming-shih* (Ming history), provincial gazetteers, and various levels of local gazetteers.[6] The central government officials were obtained from the *Ming-shih* (109–10), occasionally supplemented or corrected by more complete information in Lei Li's *Kuo-ch'ao lieh-ch'ing nien-piao* (Chronological tables of high officials of the [Ming] dynasty).[7] Provincial officials were taken from the provincial gazetteers, and in the case of every province except Shensi it was possible to check the lists in one edition of the gazetteers with those in another. In most instances, prefectural, sub-prefectural, county I, and county II officials were obtained from the various levels of local gazetteers. However, in some cases, prefectural officials were taken from provincial gazetteers, and subprefectural and county officials were taken from either provincial or prefectural gazetteers. In general, it was possible to check lists of prefectural magistrates obtained from one source with lists in another source, but it was not possible to do such checking for most subprefectures and counties.

In presenting the analysis of the various categories of officials, five major topics will be considered: (1) evidences of fluctuations in dynastic stability, (2) the role of regionalism, (3) clan connection, (4) patterns in the careers of central government officials, and (5) the question of official degrees. In addition, there is a final miscellaneous section in which several topics of secondary importance are treated.

As for the total number of individual officials and of the various official positions they occupied, there were approximately 23,300 of the former and 31,100 of the latter. Thus, the average individual official occupied roughly 1.3 positions. This 1.3 figure is considerably lower than had been anticipated, and in itself is already an indication of certain basic characteristics of the Ming bureaucracy. For example, from it one can deduce that the bureaucracy was quite broadly based and that the competition for offices was keen. It is true, of course, that there were instances of certain individuals who held numerous offices, even in a few cases reaching as high as ten. However, such individuals were quite exceptional, and usually succeeded in capping their careers by obtaining an office in the top echelons of the central government included in this study. On the average, though, the central government officials occupied only approximately two positions, which means that they were only slightly more fortunate in their careers than the members of the bureaucracy in general.

Finally, in the sections where there is a breakdown according to reign period, it will be noted that the 17 reign periods actually existing during the dynasty have been abbreviated to 14.[8] The Chien-wen period (1399–1402) has been combined with the preceding Hung-wu period, the Hung-hsi period (1425) with the subsequent Hsüan-te period, and the T'ai-ch'ang period (1620) with the subsequent T'ien-ch'i period. In the case of the Hung-hsi and T'ai-ch'ang periods, the reason for combining them with the subsequent periods was their brevity. As for the Chien-wen period, purely on the basis of length of time it would have been possible, and indeed desirable, to have given it separate consideration. However, there are very few lists of officials, except those for the central government, which contain any indication of the point of separation between Hung-wu and Chien-wen. Such a lack is due to the usurpation of the Yung-lo Emperor and his insistence that the Hung-wu period be considered to have continued down to his own accession in 1402.

EVIDENCE OF FLUCTUATIONS
IN DYNASTIC STABILITY

One of the early suggestions that some indication of fluctuations in the stability of the Ming dynasty could be obtained from an analysis of the bureaucracy was presented in an article by Otto van der Sprenkel. He feels that, on the basis of the length of official terms in the upper echelons of central government offices, the Ming dynasty can be divided into five periods of fluctuations in stability.[9] A slightly altered version of this same approach was advanced in an earlier article of my own.[10] In this article, it was proposed that the dynasty could be divided into the following six periods: Period i (1368–1402), Period ii (1403–49), Period iii (1450–1505), Period iv (1506–66), Period v (1567–

1620), and Period vi (1621–44). Period i might be characterized as one of initial instability, Period ii greatest stability, Period iii beginning decline, Period iv decided decline, Period v moderate recovery, and Period vi final decline.

Based on subsequent more detailed research, considerable doubt has arisen about the merits of attempting to be rather specific concerning major periodic divisions of the dynasty. Thus, in the present study, reign period divisions only have been used. Nevertheless, it is still felt that the bureaucracy can provide certain clues indicative of dynastic stability. The best evidence for this point is provided by Table i which presents the average length of official terms according to reign period and category of office.

TABLE I   *Length of Term in Office (Given in years according to type of office and reign period)*

	Central	Provincial	Prefectural	Subprefec-tural and County I	County II
Hung-wu	1.0	5.5	6.0	6.4	10.8
Yung-lo	4.5	4.2	7.4	8.8	13.6
Hsüan-te	3.5	3.6	8.5	8.4	11.9
Cheng-t'ung	4.3	3.7	7.5	7.5	10.5
Ching-t'ai	2.1	2.3	5.3	6.6	8.0
T'ien-shun	4.8	3.7	5.3	6.0	7.3
Ch'eng-hua	3.5	2.2	5.1	5.5	7.6
Hung-chih	4.1	1.9	4.8	4.3	5.9
Cheng-te	1.9	1.5	3.3	3.5	5.9
Chia-ching	2.0	1.3	3.2	3.1	4.4
Lung-ch'ing	1.6	1.2	3.0	3.2	3.8
Wan-li	2.8	2.0	3.3	3.5	3.5
T'ien-ch'i	.8	1.4	2.9	3.1	2.9
Ch'ung-chen	1.2	2.0	3.3	2.9	3.6

It will be noted that the figures in Table i demonstrate considerable consistency for all categories of offices. The general trend is that the figures for roughly the first half of the fifteenth century show an increase over those for the initial Hung-wu period. Subsequently, there is a progressive decline in the averages until the Wan-li period, when there is a slight upward swing. Finally, there is a resumption of the decline in the T'ien-ch'i and Ch'ung-chen periods, and in every category except one, either one or the other of these two terminal reign periods possessed the lowest averages for the entire dynasty. In fact, the T'ien-ch'i and Ch'ung-chen averages should probably be slightly lower, since there is evidence that the lists of officials (except for the central government) are not as complete as those for the immediately preceding periods.[11] As for the accuracy of the figures for the beginning reign periods, they, also, are undoubtedly slightly high due to the fact that the lists are not complete.[12] However, considering the over-all consistency which they demonstrate, it is doubtful if the margin of error is great enough to invalidate the general trends shown.

Comparing the figures for the very beginning and very end of the dynasty, one must modify the disposition to place the greatest instability of the dynasty in the initial Hung-wu period on the one hand and in the terminal T'ien-ch'i and Ch'ung-chen periods on the other. It is true that for the central government the greatest instability in tenure occurred during these three periods. However, there is a significant difference for the other categories of officials. Relative instability was shown at *all* levels of the bureaucracy during the T'ien-ch'i and Ch'ung-chen periods, while it was more confined to the central government level only during the Hung-wu period. Stability at the provincial and lower levels during Hung-wu was quite impressive, even when one remembers that the figures are probably somewhat too high.

Concerning the interesting phenomenon of the general moderate upswing in all the averages for Wan-li, the question arises as to whether these higher figures indicate a real dynastic resurgence or result from some less praiseworthy and perhaps even incidental causes. We do know that some quite vital developments occurred during the earlier Wan-li period. There was the era of reform and efficient administration dominated by Chang Chü-cheng, perhaps the most impressive single Ming statesman. In addition, one might cite the important alteration in fiscal policy,[13] and the major military campaign conducted to aid the Korean defense against the Japanese invasion. On the other hand, the subsequent picture darkened, particularly following 1600. The emperor secluded himself within the palace, creating an unusually tight bottleneck for the administrative processes; the situation was allowed to deteriorate in Manchuria; and the principal officials, far from living up to the standard of Chang Chü-cheng, were generally mediocre. Interestingly enough, two of the more frequent complaints voiced of the emperor and his administration were that requests to retire went unheeded and that offices were allowed to remain vacant for extended periods.[14] Thus, it is probable that more than a usual amount of administrative laxness and inattention were at least partly responsible for the higher Wan-li averages, and consequently the period becomes correspondingly less worthy of being considered an era of real resurgence.

Based on the foregoing, it becomes clear that the relationship between dynastic stability and length of tenure in office is certainly not absolute and automatic. It would be absurd to argue, for example, that the Hung-chih period was twice as stable as the Chia-ching because the tenure of central government officials in the former averaged 4.1 years while those in the latter averaged only 2.0. Furthermore, one might maintain that the very fact that the central government during T'ien-ch'i and Ch'ung-chen could replace its officials with such rapidity was evidence that its basic power and vitality were intact. However, although admitting definite limitations, I feel that the general

TABLE II   *Officials of Unknown Provincial Origins (Given in percentages of totals according to type of office and reign period)*

	Central	Provincial	Prefectural	Subprefectural and County I	County II
Hung-wu	22.6	34.1	46.4	40.8	25.6
Yung-lo	9.3	15.2	24.4	23.2	19.6
Hsüan-te	3.4	11.0	19.7	23.9	14.7
Cheng-t'ung		6.9	17.6	20.4	22.4
Ching-t'ai	3.3	3.0	15.6	9.7	15.6
T'ien-shun		3.5	9.8	10.8	21.0
Ch'eng-hua		2.9	8.0	8.2	10.6
Hung-chih		1.1	7.0	7.0	5.7
Cheng-te		1.8	4.3	6.4	4.6
Chia-ching		1.3	3.7	5.9	5.8
Lung-ch'ing		1.8	2.3	5.6	1.6
Wan-li	7.3	1.8	4.7	7.1	3.9
T'ien-ch'i	3.3	5.6	7.7	7.5	11.3
Ch'ung-chen	13.1	6.2	10.1	10.6	7.3

trends shown in Table I do serve as something of a weather-vane indicating fluctuations in dynastic stability.

Table II presents, according to reign period, the percentages of officials whose native provinces were not indicated in the official lists and were not discovered subsequently. There is the expected concentration of these officials of unknown origins at the beginning and end of the dynasty. These figures have historiographical connotations, serving as something of a rough indicator of the tidiness and completeness of bureaucratic records. In addition, since the figures confirm certain trends noted in connection with Table I, they are of some value in indicating fluctuations in dynastic stability, particularly in connection with the instability of the terminal T'ien-ch'i and Ch'ung-chen periods.

THE ROLE OF REGIONALISM IN THE BUREAUCRACY

The first question to be considered in discussing the role of regionalism is the relative political power of the various provinces.[15] Provincial ratings are presented, based on two different methods of calculation, in Tables III and IV. Table III is based on the calculation of provincial percentages of the total number of official positions included in the study,[16] and Table IV is based on the ratio between official positions and population.[17] In the final column of both tables, Chekiang, Kiangsi, and Pei-chihli occupy positions among the top four provinces. Thus, their claim to political prestige can hardly be questioned. Most of the remaining twelve provinces vary only one to three places in the two final lists. However, Nan-chihli varies particularly radically, dropping from first place in Table III to tenth place in Table IV. Moving in the opposite direction, Fukien rises from sixth place in Table III to supplant Nan-chihli in first place in Table IV.

Nan-chihli's fall in Table IV was due primarily to the unevenness in political importance among its various sections. Northern Nan-chihli, though populous, was a politically under-represented area, and the powerful southeastern counties could not make up for the unfavorable official-population ratio caused by the north. Fukien had an internal

TABLE III   *General Provincial Political Power (Given in percentages)*

	Central	Provincial	Prefec-tural	Subprefec-tural and County I	County II	Total
Chekiang	11.6(4)*	14.7(2)	14.0(2)	9.2(3)	11.7(1)	12.8(2)
Fukien	5.3(8)	6.7(7)	8.8(4)	6.5(6)	8.0(5)	7.4(6)
Honan	10.6(5)	6.9(6)	6.2(8)	5.6(11)	5.9(9)	6.4(8)
Hukuang	7.6(7)	6.5(8)	7.6(6)	8.1(4)	7.5(6)	7.5(5)
Kiangsi	14.1(1)	11.9(3)	11.1(3)	10.2(2)	10.3(3)	11.1(3)
Kwangsi	.6(13)	.9(13)	1.3(13)	3.0(13)	3.3(13)	1.8(13)
Kwangtung	2.1(12)	2.6(12)	3.7(12)	5.7(10)	4.6(12)	4.0(12)
Kweichow		.3(15)	.6(15)	1.8(15)	1.6(15)	.9(15)
Nan-chihli	14.1(1)	16.7(1)	15.1(1)	12.2(1)	11.6(2)	14.7(1)
Pei-chihli	12.5(3)	9.2(4)	7.8(5)	8.0(5)	9.0(4)	8.7(4)
Shansi	3.7(11)	5.1(10)	4.6(11)	5.4(12)	5.7(10)	5.1(11)
Shensi	4.1(10)	4.3(11)	5.3(10)	6.0(8)	6.4(8)	5.3(10)
Shantung	8.7(6)	7.6(5)	7.2(7)	6.5(6)	7.5(6)	7.3(7)
Szechwan	4.8(9)	5.9(9)	5.4(9)	6.0(8)	5.0(11)	5.7(9)
Yunnan	.2(14)	.7(14)	1.2(14)	2.3(14)	1.9(14)	1.4(14)

* (Figures in parenthesis are rankings)

TABLE IV   *Number of Official Positions Held Per Million Mean Population*

	Population	Central	Pro-vincial	Prefec-tural	Sub-prefec-tural and County I	County II	Total
Chekiang	10,700,000	12(3)*	117(1)	111(2)	72(10)	20(3)	332(3)
Fukien	5,000,000	8(6)	114(3)	149(1)	109(1)	34(1)	408(1)
Honan	6,200,000	15(2)	95(5)	84(5)	76(7)	16(8)	288(5)
Hukuang	11,100,000	6(10)	49(11)	57(10)	62(13)	12(13)	187(13)
Kiangsi	9,300,000	11(4)	109(4)	100(3)	92(4)	20(3)	331(4)
Kwangsi	4,400,000	7(14)	17(14)	25(15)	58(14)	14(12)	114(15)
Kwangtung	5,500,000	3(12)	40(12)	57(10)	87(5)	15(10)	201(9)
Kweichow	2,000,000	(15)	13(15)	27(14)	76(7)	15(10)	131(14)
Nan-chihli	20,500,000	8(6)	69(8)	62(9)	50(15)	10(15)	200(10)
Pei-chihli	6,700,000	19(1)	117(1)	98(4)	100(2)	25(2)	359(2)
Shansi	5,300,000	8(6)	83(6)	74(6)	84(6)	20(3)	268(6)
Shensi	6,800,000	7(9)	54(10)	65(8)	74(9)	17(6)	218(8)
Shantung	8,400,000	10(5)	77(7)	72(7)	65(11)	16(8)	242(7)
Szechwan	8,000,000	5(11)	63(9)	57(10)	64(12)	12(13)	200(10)
Yunnan	2,000,000	1.5(13)	30(13)	52(13)	98(3)	17(6)	198(12)

* (Figures in parenthesis are rankings)

unevenness in political power even more exaggerated than that of Nan-chihli. However, a few key counties along the coast were so spectacularly successful that, in view of Fukien's relatively low population, they were able to insure a high official-population ratio.[18]

Another fact which emerges from the two tables is that northern provinces were relatively more successful in placing officials at the central government level, while southern provinces were more successful at the lower levels. Fukien and Honan are the two best examples. Fukien's first-place position in Table IV was due primarily to its successes at the prefectural and lower levels, for the province placed only sixth at the central government level. On the other hand, Honan dropped from second place for the central government alone to fifth place generally. Thus, despite its obvious over-all political importance, Fukien was unable to overcome the geographical disadvantage of being distant from the capital, and could not equalize its power by attaining a position at the top level of the administration commensurate with its general political prestige. As for Honan's disproportionate power at the top, probably the major explanation was an advantageous location *vis à vis* the national capital, a factor which favored Pei-chihli even more heavily.

Attempting to arrive at an over-all assessment of provincial power ratings, it is obvious that both Table III and Table IV must be considered. Averaging the two, one might rate the provinces as follows: Group A (most powerful provinces)—Chekiang, Pei-chihli, Kiangsi, Fukien, and Nan-chihli; Group B (moderately powerful provinces)— Honan, Shantung, Shansi, Shensi, and Hukuang; and Group C (least powerful provinces)—Szechwan, Kwangtung, Yunnan, Kwangsi, and Kweichow. The key political areas, then, were the lower Yangtze region, the upper southern coast, and the upper north China plain. The major portions of the north China plain and the northwest, China's "classical" centers, had to be satisfied with a more modest political posture. And the far south and southwest, still not having compensated for a later arrival on the Chinese historical stage, was the politically depressed section par excellence.

To deal at least briefly with the manifestly complicated problem of discovering sources for the political power of the dominant areas, the easiest to account for is the position of Pei-chihli. Obviously its possession of the principal capital following 1421 provided the province with its major political advantage. Had the Ming capital remained at Nanking, it is doubtful if Pei-chihli's political importance would have been appreciably higher than that of its neighbors, Honan and Shantung. In addition, the quota system for *chin-shih* and *chü-jen* degrees, established early in the Ming, assured Pei-chihli, as well as all northern provinces, of somewhat larger numbers of higher degree holders (with good chances of successful political careers) than they probably would have obtained in free competition.[19] Fukien's position of success is more difficult to account for, though probably one of its single greatest advantages lay in its well-developed clan system, a question which will be dealt with in more detail subsequently. In addition, Fukien had economic advantages.[20] As for the lower Yangtze, it is by now well established that this area was China's key economic and cultural section, beginning at least with the Southern Sung. The well-known work of Chi Ch'ao-ting contains one of the earliest treatments of the area's economic importance, and this topic is considered briefly but cogently in the recent work of Professor Ping-ti Ho.[21] Specific evidence of its cultural significance is provided by Wu Kwang-tsing in his survey of China's great libraries. Dr. Wu states that Chekiang possessed 44 (21 percent) of the important Ming libraries, and Nan-chihli had 125 (61 percent).[22] The northern provinces (Pei-chihli, Shantung, Honan, Shansi, and Shensi) altogether had only 19 libraries.

Another issue which arises in connection with regionalism is whether or not particular areas tended to be especially dominant during certain periods. Tables v–vii present in as compact a fashion as possible the figures necessary to provide an answer to this question. It will be noted that, as a general rule, the provinces which we have already determined to have been politically most powerful manifested their strength from the beginning to the end of the dynasty. Nan-chihli, for example, was among the top four provinces for all fourteen reign periods at the provincial, prefectural, and subprefectural-county 1 levels. The performance of Chekiang and Kiangsi in these categories of offices was only slightly less impressive, though that of Pei-chihli and Fukien was more equivocal and spotty.

At the central government level, however, there was considerably more variation, with Nan-chihli again as the single most outstanding example of radical changes in stature. This province, being the nucleus area around which the dynasty formed, had the expected unusual success during the initial Hung-wu period, and attained an impressive 37 percent, a high point never reached by any other province. Subsequently, with the loss of the principal capital, Nan-chihli's central government percentages declined drastically during the Yung-lo and Hsüan-te periods, and though they recovered and remained reasonably high during the latter two thirds of the dynasty (following a nadir in Ch'eng-hua), never again did the province recapture the dominant position of the early years.

The other province which fluctuated in strength at the central government level almost as radically as Nan-chihli was Pei-chihli. Its

TABLE V *Variations in Provincial Power at the Central Government Level (Given in percentages)*

	Hung-wu	Yung-lo	Hsüan-te	Cheng-t'ung	Ching-t'ai	T'ien-shun	Ch'eng-hua	Hung-chih	Cheng-te	Chia-ching	Lung-ch'ing	Wan-li	T'ien-ch'i	Ch'ung-chen
Chekiang	10	12	3	1	13	17	19	13	8	12	19	9	15	14
Fukien	4	10	8	3		6	6	3	1	3	2	8	12	7
Honan	17	12	14	6	7	10	8	24	13	9	8	7	3	8
Hukuang	11	9	12	13		2	1	7	9	7	7	8	7	10
Kiangsi	2	23	15	19	23	15	10	10	4	23	10	14	3	6
Kwangsi									2	1	1	2		
Kwangtung	2						1	7	5	2		2		5
Kweichow														
Nan-chihli	37	6	4	16	23	12	2	16	12	19	12	11	15	19
Pei-chihli	5	7	4	16	20	33	22	9	12	9	6	13	27	10
Shansi	6					3		3	4	4	7	9	5	4
Shensi	4	6	1	3			5	3	4	1		9	11	2
Shantung	1	7	29	23	9	2	12	3	6	7	11	7	3	10
Szechwan		7	8		7	1	14	2	7	3	16	1		5
Yunnan												1		

early power was decidedly modest, and it was surpassed by five other provinces. Even the transfer of the capital to Peking in 1421 did not result in an immediate major enhancement of its political strength. A time lag of about a decade was necessary before the advantage of possessing the capital began to show a real effect. The province's most impressive period of power was from the middle to the late 1400s. Subsequently, there was a general decline until the 1620s when one of its less praiseworthy native sons, the eunuch Wei Chung-hsien, managed to seize virtual control of the court, and boosted Pei-chihli's percentage figure to 27 percent, the fourth highest for the entire dynasty.

There are a few more isolated examples of sudden enhancements in provincial political prestige at the central government level, reflecting transitory advantages in the power struggles. For example, Honan suddenly rose from 8 percent in Ch'eng-hua to 24 percent in Hung-chih, and Shantung moved from 7 percent in Yung-lo to 29 percent in Hsüan-te and 23 percent in Cheng-t'ung.

As for major and relatively long-lasting trends in provincial rise and fall, based on all categories of officials, there are suggestions of only

TABLE VI   *Variations in Provincial Political Power at the Provincial Government Level (Given in percentages)*

	Hung-wu	Yung-lo	Hsüan-te	Cheng-t'ung	Ching-t'ai	T'ien-shun	Ch'eng-hua	Hung-chih	Cheng-te	Chia-ching	Lung-ch'ing	Wan-li	T'ien-ch'i	Ch'ung-chen
Chekiang	11	11	21	17	18	15	14	15	13	16	10	14	15	14
Fukien	4	7	5	5	5	5	6	6	6	7	7	8	7	10
Honan	13	6	3	8	6	9	8	8	5	6	9	6	8	10
Hukuang	6	5	7	4	4	5	6	7	8	7	6	7	6	6
Kiangsi	14	15	17	18	16	17	13	12	9	13	12	10	7	7
Kwangsi	1	2	2	1	3			1	1	1	2	1		
Kwangtung	2	5	2	2	2	2	2	5	2	3	4	3	2	2
Kweichow										1	1		1	1
Nan-chihli	22	21	17	18	20	18	17	15	19	14	15	17	16	20
Pei-chihli	5	9	7	10	8	10	11	9	12	10	10	9	6	4
Shansi	5	3	3	4	5	3	6	7	5	4	7	6	7	5
Shensi	2	5	7	4	6	5	5	5	6	4	2	4	4	6
Shantung	13	6	7	7	2	6	6	7	7	9	9	7	11	6
Szechwan	4	5	3	3	5	6	7	6	7	6	4	6	5	2
Yunnan					1	1			1		2	1	2	2

TABLE VII   *Variations in Provincial Political Power at the Prefectural Government Level (Given in percentages)*

	Hung-wu	Yung-lo	Hsüan-te	Cheng-t'ung	Ching-t'ai	T'ien-shun	Ch'eng-hua	Hung-chih	Cheng-te	Chia-ching	Lung-ch'ing	Wan-li	T'ien-ch'i	Ch'ung-chen
Chekiang	17	16	13	16	21	11	12	17	14	14	14	14	13	11
Fukien	5	7	11	5	5	7	7	4	6	9	11	12	12	8
Honan	7	8	6	7	6	4	6	7	4	7	7	6	4	6
Hukuang	7	8	10	6	4	9	8	5	7	8	8	8	9	9
Kiangsi	11	12	18	15	14	14	13	12	11	10	11	10	7	12
Kwangsi	2		3	1	3	2		1	2	2	1	2	3	
Kwangtung	2	4	2	3	4	8	5	5	3	3	3	4	4	2
Kweichow							1			1		1	1	2
Nan-chihli	22	17	14	11	10	13	13	18	16	15	13	13	18	18
Pei-chihli	7	10	8	8	7	9	9	8	11	9	8	6	7	6
Shansi	5	3	2	5	7	6	7	5	4	4	7	5	4	5
Shensi	4	4	3	5	5	9	6	5	7	5	3	5	5	6
Shantung	8	9	9	11	6	3	6	7	8	7	7	8	6	7
Szechwan	2	2	1	6	6	6	6	7	5	5	6	5	5	3
Yunnan	1		1	1	1	1	1	1	1	1	2	1	2	3

two, neither of which is really spectacular. The two are Fukien and Kiangsi. Fukien's movement was generally upward beginning in the second half of the sixteenth century, while Kiangsi's trend during this same period was downward.[23] On the whole, however, the tables indicate that the politically dominant regions were reasonably successful in maintaining their positions of power rather steadily from the beginning of the dynasty to its fall.

Furthermore, the tables demonstrate that there was no real correlation between dominance in the central government and dominance at the lower levels, with the possible exception of the case of Nan-chihli during the initial Hung-wu period. In other words, power at the upper echelons of the bureaucracy was not automatically transferable to the lower echelons. This fact suggests a high degree of sophistication and complexity for the Ming bureaucracy with a system of checks and balances so intricate that regional cliques simply could not pack offices at all levels with their favorites. This is not to say that powerful individuals or groups were completely without means to obtain offices for favorites. The shifts in provincial power in the high central govern-

TABLE VIII *Variations in Provincial Political Power at the Subprefectural-County I Level (Given in percentages)*

	Hung-wu	Yung-lo	Hsüan-te	Cheng-t'ung	Ching-t'ai	T'ien-shun	Ch'eng-hua	Hung-chih	Cheng-te	Chia-ching	Lung-ch'ing	Wan-li	T'ien-ch'i	Ch'ung-chen
Chekiang	16	12	7	5	8	10	13	10	8	8	7	10	8	7
Fukien	5	5	8	5	7	6	4	5	5	8	9	8	8	7
Honan	4	6	3	4	5	5	6	7	7	5	7	6	6	5
Hukuang	6	9	9	9	11	6	9	8	8	9	7	8	10	8
Kiangsi	16	14	15	9	19	13	10	12	10	10	11	9	8	10
Kwangsi	2	3	2	3	2	1	2	3	3	4	5	3	3	4
Kwangtung	2	4	4	6	5	5	5	6	6	7	8	6	6	4
Kweichow							1	1	2	2	3	2	3	5
Nan-chihli	21	14	12	11	14	15	13	12	13	13	11	11	12	12
Pei-chihli	6	7	7	9	10	13	11	8	8	8	10	8	9	7
Shansi	8	8	6	7	3	3	5	5	7	6	2	5	6	5
Shensi	3	6	7	8	2	8	6	7	8	6	4	6	8	8
Shantung	6	7	12	7	6	7	8	9	9	7	5	6	5	5
Szechwan	4	6	7	7	5	6	5	6	5	6	7	8	8	4
Yunnan	1		2	1	1	4	1	2	2	2	3	3	4	4

ment offices just noted were undoubtedly partly due to favoritism, and powerful groups were possibly even more successful in placing friends and relatives in minor positions at the capital. Generally speaking, however, it would seem definite that whatever packing of offices occurred was extremely diffuse, reflected other influences in addition to regionalism, and did not stem from any tightly knit controlling faction.

The next sub-topic to be considered in connection with the role of regionalism in the bureaucracy is the question of key centers of power within provinces. That internal provincial concentrations of political strength were really vital factors in the world of Ming politics is amply demonstrated by the following statistic: 49 percent of all the official positions considered in this study were occupied by natives of only 146 counties, 13 percent of the total number. Table IX presents a province-by-province listing of these 146 counties whose native sons occupied from 40 to 494 official positions. Table X attempts to provide a view of the situation as a whole, and Maps I–IV were prepared to give a clearer

TABLE IX *Local Areas of Particular Political Significance (According to Province)*

Local Area		Number of official positions occupied by area natives	Percentage of provincial total	Local Area		Number of official positions occupied by area natives	Percentage of provincial total
Chekiang				Loyang	洛陽	91	5.1
Yü-yao	餘姚	327	9.1	An-yang	安陽	47	2.6
Yin-hsien	鄞縣	276	7.8	Hsiang-ch'eng	襄城	44	2.5
Tz'u-ch'i	慈谿	214	6.0	Ku-shih	固始	43	2.4
Shan-yin	山陰	172	4.8	Ch'i-hsien	杞縣	40	2.2
Jen-ho	仁和	151	4.3			Total %:	21.2
Ch'ien-t'ang	錢塘	142	4.0	*Hukuang*			
Lin-hai	臨海	120	3.4	Ma-ch'eng	麻城	112	5.4
K'uai-chi	會稽	109	3.1	Huang-kang	黃岡	94	4.5
Wu-ch'eng	烏程	98	2.8	Chiang-ling	江陵	75	3.6
Hsiu-shui	秀水	84	2.4	Chiang-hsia	江夏	69	3.2
Kuei-an	歸安	81	2.3	Pa-ling	巴陵	64	3.1
P'ing-hu	平湖	81	2.3	Shih-shou	石首	47	2.3
Shang-yü	上虞	78	2.2	Ch'i-chou	蘄州	46	2.2
Chia-hsing	嘉興	76	2.1	Ying-ch'eng	應城	42	2.0
Lan-ch'i	蘭谿	66	1.9	Wu-ling	武陵	41	2.0
Chin-hua	金華	53	1.5	Han-yang	漢陽	41	2.0
Huang-yen	黃巖	49	1.4			Total %:	30.3
Yung-chia	永嘉	46	1.3	*Kiangsi*			
Lin-an	臨安	45	1.3	Feng-ch'eng	豐城	208	6.7
Hai-ning	海寧	44	1.2	An-fu	安福	207	6.7
Hai-yen	海鹽	43	1.2	Nan-ch'ang	南昌	195	6.3
Shun-an	淳安	42	1.2	T'ai-ho	泰和	174	5.6
Li-shui	麗水	41	1.2	Chi-shui	吉水	160	5.2
Feng-hua	奉化	40	1.1	Lu-ling	廬陵	111	3.6
		Total %:	69.9	Lin-ch'uan	臨川	106	3.4
Fukien				Chin-hsien	進賢	93	3.0
P'u-t'ien	莆田	494	24.2	Wan-an	萬安	86	2.8
Chin-chiang	晋江	304	14.9	Hsin-chien	新建	84	2.7
Min-hsien	閩縣	171	8.4	Kuei-ch'i	貴溪	76	2.5
Fu-ch'ing	福清	81	4.0	P'o-yang	都陽	66	2.1
Hou-kuan	侯官	73	3.6	Kao-an	高安	57	1.8
Lung-ch'i	龍溪	73	3.6	Fu-liang	浮梁	55	1.8
Ch'ang-lo	長樂	68	3.3	Nan-ch'eng	南城	53	1.7
Chang-p'u	漳浦	59	2.9	Hsin-kan	新淦	49	1.6
T'ung-an	同安	58	2.8	Chin-ch'i	金谿	43	1.4
		Total %:	67.7	Hsin-yü	新喻	42	1.4
Honan						Total %:	60.3
Hsiang-fu	祥符	114	6.4	*Kwangsi*			
				Ch'üan-chou	全州	82	16.3

Name		No.	%
Lin-kuei	臨桂	47	9.4
Ma-p'ing	馬平	43	8.6
		Total %:	34.3
Kwangtung			
Nan-hai	南海	214	19.4
Shun-te	順德	91	8.2
Tung-kuan	東莞	90	8.1
P'an-yü	番禺	85	7.7
Hai-yang	海陽	45	4.1
Hsin-hui	新會	41	3.7
		Total %:	51.2
Nan-chihli			
Hua-t'ing	華亭	199	4.9
Wu-chin	武進	161	3.9
She-hsien	歙縣	156	3.8
Wu-hsi	無錫	151	3.7
Ch'ang-chou	長州	146	3.6
Ch'ang-shu	常熟	145	3.5
Wu-hsien	吳縣	133	3.2
Wu-yüan	婺源	117	2.9
K'un-shan	崑山	109	2.7
Wu-chiang	吳江	101	2.5
Shang-hai	上海	92	2.2
I-hsing	宜興	90	2.2
T'ai-ts'ang	太倉	86	2.1
Shang-yüan	上元	79	1.9
T'ung-ch'eng	桐城	76	1.9
Hsüan-ch'eng	宣城	73	1.8
Chiang-tu	江都	71	1.7
Tan-t'u	丹徒	63	1.5
Chiang-ning	江寧	62	1.5
Chin-t'an	金壇	55	1.3
Tang-t'u	當塗	54	1.3
Ho-fei	合肥	52	1.3
Chia-ting	嘉定	50	1.2
Shan-yang	山陽	50	1.2
Ching-hsien	涇縣	48	1.2
T'ai-chou	泰州	43	1.1
Hsiu-ning	休寧	43	1.1
Ch'i-men	祁門	42	1.0
Chiang-yin	江陰	40	1.0
Tan-yang	丹陽	40	1.0
		Total %:	64.2
Pei-chihli			
Jen-ch'iu	任邱	116	4.8
Chen-ting	眞定	70	2.9
Ch'ang-yüan	長垣	59	2.4
K'ai-chou	開州	56	2.3
Ch'ing-yüan	清苑	55	2.3
Cho-chou	涿州	49	2.0
Shun-t'ien	順天	47	1.9
Mien-i-wei	錦衣衛	45	1.9
Ta-hsing	大興	44	1.8
Ku-an	固安	40	1.7
		Total %:	24.0
Shansi			
P'u-chou	蒲州	98	6.9
Yang-ch'ü	陽曲	79	5.6
An-i	安邑	57	4.0
T'ai-yüan	太原	52	3.7
Tse-chou	澤州	45	3.2
Ta-t'ung	大同	43	3.0
Ch'ang-chih	長治	43	3.0
P'ing-ting	平定	41	2.9
Tai-chou	代州	41	2.9
		Total %:	35.2
Shensi			
Hsien-ning	咸寧	105	7.1
San-yüan	三原	77	5.2
Ching-yang	涇陽	61	4.1
Hsi-an	西安	43	2.9
		Total %:	19.3
Shantung			
Li-ch'eng	歷城	79	3.9
I-tu	益都	66	3.2
Te-chou	德州	63	3.1
I-hsien	掖縣	60	2.9
Pin-chou	濱州	54	2.7
Chi-ning	濟寧	51	2.5
Chang-ch'iu	章邱	49	2.4
Tung-p'ing	東平	48	2.4
Lai-yang	萊陽	45	2.2
Lin-ch'ing	臨清	40	2.0
		Total %:	27.3
Szechwan			
Nei-chiang	內江	135	8.5
Pa-hsien	巴縣	112	7.0
Nan-ch'ung	南充	90	5.6
Fu-shun	富順	70	4.4
Ch'eng-tu	成都	67	4.2
I-pin	宜賓	58	3.6
		Total %:	33.3
Yunnan			
K'un-ming	昆明	56	14.1

TABLE X   *Concentrations of Political Power in Counties within Provinces (Given in number of counties)*

Number of official positions held	Chekiang	Fukien	Honan	Hukuang	Kiangsi	Kwangsi	Kwangtung	Kweichow	Nan-chihli	Pei-chihli	Shansi	Shensi	Shantung	Szechwan	Yunnan
40 — 45	6		3	3	2	1	2		5	3	5	1	2		
45 — 50	2		1	2	1	1			3	2			2		
50 — 55	1				2				3	1	1		2		
55 — 60		2			1					2	1		1	1	1
60 — 70	1	1		2	1				2	1		1	2	2	
70 — 80	2	2		1	1				4		1	1	1		
80 — 90	3	1			2	1	2		2					1	
90 — 100	1		1	1	1		1		1		1				
100 — 125	2		1	1	2				3	1		1		1	
125 — 150	1								3					1	
150 — 175	2				2				3						
175 — 200		1			1				1						
200 — 250	1				2			1							
250 — 300	1														
300 — 350	1	1													
350 — 400															
400 — 450															
450 — 500		1													
Total no. of counties in 40+ category	24	9	6	10	18	3	6		30	10	9	4	10	6	1
Total no. of counties in province	75	57	96	108	77	50	75	13	97	116	78	96	89	111	31

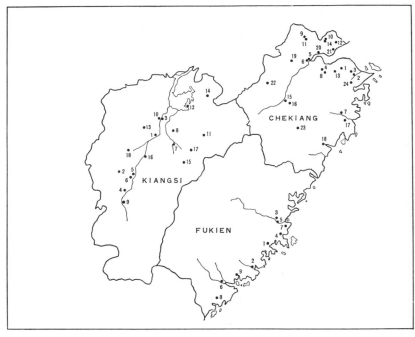

MAP I *Politically Significant Local Areas of Chekiang, Fukien, and Kiangsi (Numbered according to importance)*

Chekiang

1. Yü-yao 姚縣餘
2. Yin-hsien 鄞
3. Tz'u-ch'i 慈谿
4. Shan-yin 山陰
5. Jen-ho 仁和
6. Ch'ien-t'ang 錢塘
7. Lin-hai 臨海
8. K'uai-chi 會稽
9. Wu-ch'eng 烏程
10. Hsiu-shui 秀水
11. Kuei-an 歸安
12. P'ing-hu 平湖
13. Shang-yü 上虞
14. Chia-hsing 嘉興
15. Lan-ch'i 蘭谿
16. Chin-hua 金華
17. Huang-yen 黃嚴
18. Yung-chia 永嘉
19. Lin-an 臨安
20. Hai-ning 海寧
21. Hai-yen 海鹽
22. Shun-an 淳安
23. Li-shui 麗水
24. Feng-hua 奉化

Fukien

1. P'u-t'ien 田莆
2. Chin-chiang 江晉
3. Min-hsien 縣閩
4. Fu-ch'ing 清福
5. Hou-kuan 官侯
6. Lung-ch'i 溪龍
7. Ch'ang-lo 樂長
8. Chang-p'u 浦漳
9. T'ung-an 安同

Kiangsi

1. Feng-ch'eng 城豐
2. An-fu 福安
3. Nan-ch'ang 昌南
4. T'ai-ho 和泰
5. Chi-shui 水吉
6. Lu-ling 陵廬
7. Lin-ch'uan 川臨
8. Chin-hsien 賢進
9. Wan-an 安萬
10. Hsin-chien 建新
11. Kuei-ch'i 溪貴
12. P'o-yang 陽都
13. Kao-an 安高
14. Fu-liang 梁浮
15. Nan-ch'eng 城南
16. Hsin-kan 淦新
17. Chin-ch'i 溪金
18. Hsin-yü 喻新

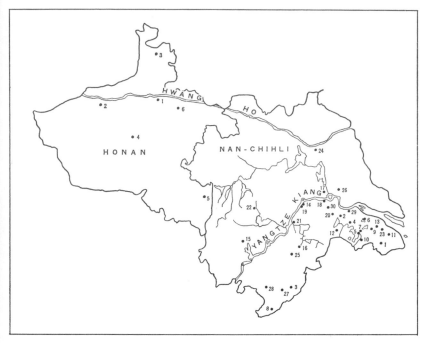

MAP II *Politically Significant Local Areas of Nan-chihli and Honan*
(*Numbered according to importance*)

1.	Hua-t'ing	華亭	16.	Hsüan-ch'eng	宣城
2.	Wu-chin	武進	17.	Chiang-tu	江都
3.	She-hsien	歙縣	18.	Tan-t'u	丹徒
4.	Wu-hsi	無錫	19.	Chiang-ning	江寧
5.	Ch'ang-chou	長州	20.	Chin-t'an	金壇
6.	Ch'ang-shu	常熟	21.	Tang-t'u	當塗
7.	Wu-hsien	吳縣	22.	Ho-fei	合肥
8.	Wu-yüan	婺源	23.	Chia-ting	嘉定
9.	K'un-shan	崑山	24.	Shan-yang	山陽
10.	Wu-chiang	吳江	25.	Ching-hsien	涇縣
11.	Shang-hai	上海	26.	T'ai-chou	泰州
12.	I-hsing	宜興	27.	Hsiu-ning	休寧
13.	T'ai-ts'ang	太倉	28.	Ch'i-men	祁門
14.	Shang-yüan	上元	29.	Chiang-yin	江陰
15.	T'ung-ch'eng	桐城	30.	Tan-yang	丹陽

1.	Hsiang-fu	祥符
2.	Lo-yang	洛陽
3.	An-yang	安陽
4.	Hsiang-ch'eng	襄城
5.	Ku-shih	固始
6.	Ch'i-hsien	杞縣

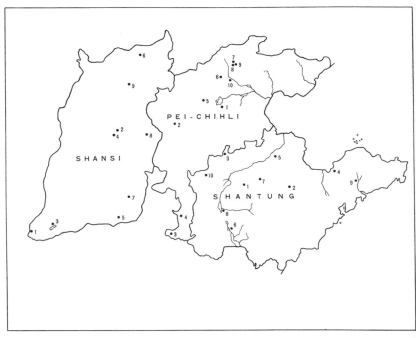

MAP III   *Politically Significant Local Areas of Pei-chihli, Shansi, and Shantung (Numbered according to importance)*

Pei-chihli			*Shansi*			*Shantung*		
1.	Jen-ch'iu	任邱	1.	P'u-chou	蒲州	1.	Li-ch'eng	歷城
2.	Chen-ting	眞定	2.	Yang-ch'ü	陽曲	2.	I-tu	益都
3.	Ch'ang-yüan	長垣	3.	An-i	安邑	3.	Te-chou	德州
4.	K'ai-chou	開州	4.	T'ai-yüan	太原	4.	I-hsien	掖縣
5.	Ch'ing-yüan	清苑	5.	Tse-chou	澤州	5.	Pin-chou	濱州
6.	Cho-chou	涿州	6.	Ta-t'ung	大同	6.	Chi-ning	濟寧
7.	Shun-t'ien	順天	7.	Ch'ang-chih	長治	7.	Chang-ch'iu	章邱
8.	Mien-i-wei	綿衣衛	8.	P'ing-ting	平定	8.	Tung-p'ing	東平
9.	Ta-hsing	大興	9.	Tai-chou	代州	9.	Lai-yang	萊陽
10.	Ku-an	固安				10.	Lin-ch'ing	臨清

conception of the geographical implications of the internal provincial concentrations. The most striking general fact which Table x makes clear is that political power was more evenly spread among the counties in provinces of the north China plain and the northwest, and that concentration was most prevalent in the far south. Nine of Fukien's

MAP IV   *General View of Politically Significant Local Areas*

57 counties produced 68 percent of the occupants of all the official positions held by Fukien natives, and six of Kwangtung's 75 counties produced 51 percent of the total for that province. Even Kwangsi, whose over-all political strength was extremely small, had three counties which reached an impressive combined total of 34 percent. The

single most powerful county in all China was P'u-t'ien of Fukien. Natives of this county held 494 positions, almost one fourth of the total for the entire province. The figure for this county was considerably more than the entire *provincial* totals of either Kweichow or Yunnan, and came within a mere nine positions of equaling the total for Kwangsi.

A major factor behind the concentration of power within provinces in the far south was the presence of powerful clans. For example, members of only 10 P'u-t'ien County clans occupied 310 of the 494 official positions held by natives of the county. The question of clan influence will be dealt with subsequently.

Another point to be considered in the discussion of regionalism is the question of trends in filling provincial, prefectural, subprefectural-county I, and county II offices. The disposition of the Chinese government to insist that no individual be appointed to fill an office within his native province is well known. And as the accompanying tables (Tables XI–XXV) demonstrate, this regulation against serving in one's native province was quite thoroughly implemented during the Ming. There were minor exceptions, many of which occurred at the beginning of the dynasty when procedures had not yet been regularized and immediate political needs had to be met. Other exceptions were perhaps the result of a person's still being registered as a native of a particular province even though his family had long actually resided elsewhere,[24] and a few were possibly due to incorrect identification of the native province. However, there were still exceptions which are of sufficient proportions to be noted specifically. Pei-chihli is the most notable example, for 9 percent of its provincial officials and 3 percent of its prefectural officials were actually Pei-chihli natives. Perhaps the fact that Pei-chihli was not considered to be a proper province was the main reason why the strictures against serving in one's native province were less rigidly observed in its case than elsewhere. Furthermore, it should be noted that a considerable percentage of the instructors in county schools, included for some provinces in the county II level offices, were natives of the same provinces in which they served.

The most significant general principle discovered by examining the tables dealing with service at provincial and lower levels is that regional considerations in appointments were present at all levels and

TABLE XI *Provincial Origins of Officials Serving in Chekiang (Given in percentages according to native province and type of office)*

	Provincial	Prefectural	Subprefectural and County I	County II
Chekiang	.2	.3	.3	.8
Fukien	10.2	15.0	15.3	13.6
Honan	7.9	4.5	2.0	1.7
Hukuang	8.1	8.2	9.2	9.3
Kiangsi	14.0	14.3	20.4	26.2
Kwangsi	1.2	1.9	2.0	1.7
Kwangtung	2.9	4.0	7.9	5.9
Kweichow	.2	.2	.8	
Nan-chihli	23.7	27.2	26.7	28.0
Pei-chihli	9.1	6.4	2.8	2.5
Shansi	4.9	1.9	2.1	1.7
Shensi	3.3	1.7	1.5	1.7
Shantung	7.7	7.6	4.0	4.2
Szechwan	5.7	6.2	4.0	1.7
Yunnan	.3	.8	1.2	.8

TABLE XII *Provincial Origins of Officials Serving in Fukien (Given in percentages according to native province and type of office)*

	Provincial	Prefectural	Subprefectural and County I	County II
Chekiang	25.2	25.3	23.6	26.2
Fukien	.2	.2	.2	9.9
Honan	6.3	1.5	.6	
Hukuang	6.1	7.6	4.6	2.9
Kiangsi	18.5	17.4	19.1	19.8
Kwangsi	1.7	1.3	4.8	2.9
Kwangtung	6.1	7.9	23.8	19.2
Kweichow			1.0	
Nan-chihli	20.8	28.6	17.2	14.0
Pei-chihli	5.2	3.0	.8	1.7
Shansi	1.8	.9	1.0	.6
Shensi	.2	.6	.2	.6
Shantung	2.4	.9	1.9	
Szechwan	5.0	4.0	1.0	1.7
Yunnan	.6	.7	.4	.6

TABLE XIII   *Provincial Origins of Officials Serving in Honan (Given in percentages according to native province and type of office)*

	Provincial	Prefectural	Subprefectural and County I	County II
Chekiang	13. 7	8. 5	6. 7	10. 7
Fukien	4. 8	2. 8	2. 3	4. 0
Honan			. 1	4. 7
Hukuang	4. 4	6. 3	8. 0	13. 4
Kiangsi	11. 8	6. 1	5. 1	4. 7
Kwangsi	. 5	. 8	. 9	. 7
Kwangtung	1. 1	1. 0	1. 1	
Kweichow	. 3	. 2	. 4	. 7
Nan-chihli	14. 4	13. 2	15. 8	15. 4
Pei-chihli	15. 1	16. 9	20. 4	10. 7
Shansi	10. 0	11. 4	10. 8	6. 0
Shensi	6. 1	11. 6	10. 0	14. 8
Shantung	12. 3	17. 7	13. 9	11. 4
Szechwan	5. 6	3. 2	2. 9	2. 0
Yunnan	. 2	. 4	1. 3	. 7

TABLE XIV   *Provincial Origins of Officials Serving in Hukuang (Given in percentages according to native province and type of office)*

	Provincial	Prefectural	Subprefectural and County I	County II
Chekiang	15. 4	16. 8	10. 4	10. 2
Fukien	9. 9	8. 7	8. 5	4. 7
Honan	5. 3	6. 4	5. 2	3. 9
Hukuang		. 1		10. 2
Kiangsi	15. 8	11. 8	17. 3	15. 6
Kwangsi	. 9	1. 1	5. 9	12. 5
Kwangtung	3. 0	3. 8	5. 9	3. 9
Kweichow	. 4	1. 2	2. 4	6. 2
Nan-chihli	18. 6	19. 7	16. 3	14. 8
Pei-chihli	9. 2	5. 7	3. 5	1. 6
Shansi	4. 4	2. 9	. 7	1. 6
Shensi	3. 9	4. 9	4. 0	
Shantung	5. 7	6. 5	1. 7	. 8
Szechwan	7. 1	9. 1	14. 9	11. 7
Yunnan	. 4	1. 2	3. 5	2. 3

TABLE XV *Provincial Origins of Officials Serving in Kiangsi (Given in percentages according to native province and type of office)*

	Provincial	Prefectural	Subprefectural and County I	County II
Chekiang	27.6	23.8	25.5	23.6
Fukien	7.0	13.3	11.1	7.7
Honan	5.3	4.1	1.7	2.4
Hukuang	7.6	8.1	11.4	11.8
Kiangsi	.1	.3	.6	1.2
Kwangsi	1.6	1.2	2.8	1.8
Kwangtung	2.4	5.0	7.2	4.1
Kweichow		.3	.9	1.2
Nan-chihli	23.0	26.5	25.0	23.6
Pei-chihli	6.3	4.0	2.0	3.0
Shansi	3.6	1.9	.6	1.8
Shensi	2.9	2.7	1.4	4.7
Shantung	6.3	2.7	3.7	5.3
Szechwan	5.9	5.6	4.8	7.1
Yunnan	.4	.4	1.4	.6

TABLE XVI *Provincial Origins of Officials Serving in Kwangsi (Given in percentages according to native province and type of office)*

	Provincial	Prefectural	Subprefectural and County I	County II
Chekiang	18.1	12.8	8.6	
Fukien	13.3	15.1	15.5	
Honan	2.7	2.8	1.0	
Hukuang	8.0	9.5	11.3	
Kiangsi	21.4	15.1	13.7	
Kwangsi	.2	1.2	1.0	
Kwangtung	4.0	17.9	27.5	
Kweichow	.4	1.4	2.7	
Nan-chihli	19.0	13.8	9.6	
Pei-chihli	2.5	2.1	.5	
Shansi	.4	.2	1.2	
Shensi	.4	.9	1.0	
Shantung	2.2	2.8	1.2	
Szechwan	5.1	3.0	2.9	
Yunnan	1.6	1.4	2.4	

TABLE XVII   *Provincial Origins of Officials Serving in Kwangtung (Given in percentages according to native province and type of office)*

	Provincial	Prefectural	Subprefectural and County I	County II
Chekiang	24.1	20.2	13.1	13.3
Fukien	14.1	23.2	23.0	27.6
Honan	1.9	1.1	.3	
Hukuang	7.1	9.0	7.8	5.5
Kiangsi	21.0	19.9	22.5	21.6
Kwangsi	2.3	4.7	12.9	9.9
Kwangtung	.2	.2	1.0	4.3
Kweichow	.6	.6	1.1	
Nan-chihli	19.7	12.8	11.3	10.5
Pei-chihli	1.9	2.2	1.8	.6
Shansi	.8	.6	.3	.6
Shensi	.4	1.1		.6
Shantung	.8	.6	1.1	
Szechwan	5.0	3.2	2.1	1.7
Yunnan		.5	1.6	

TABLE XVIII   *Provincial Origins of Officials Serving in Kweichow (Given in percentages according to native province and type of office)*

	Provincial	Prefectural	Subprefectural and County I	County II
Chekiang	15.8	10.2	9.5	
Fukien	7.9	8.9	4.0	
Honan	2.8	3.2	.7	
Hukuang	9.7	10.8	13.5	
Kiangsi	13.6	15.7	2.2	
Kwangsi	1.4	1.5	5.1	
Kwangtung	3.7	3.8	5.5	
Kweichow	.2			
Nan-chihli	16.6	10.6	7.3	
Pei-chihli	4.5	5.1	2.9	
Shansi	2.4	2.3	.4	
Shensi	2.8	2.5	3.7	
Shantung	1.6	6.8	2.6	
Szechwan	13.4	12.9	24.2	
Yunnan	3.4	5.7	18.3	

TABLE XIX *Provincial Origins of Officials Serving in Nan-chihli (Given in percentages according to native province and type of office)*

	Provincial	Prefectural	Subprefectural and County I	County II
Chekiang	13.6	21.1	18.5	24.7
Fukien	10.8	9.5	7.1	6.7
Honan	9.9	8.7	7.1	3.3
Hukuang	8.0	8.9	8.4	9.3
Kiangsi	15.5	12.2	18.7	18.7
Kwangsi	1.4	1.0	2.0	3.3
Kwangtung	4.2	3.0	2.6	2.7
Kweichow	.5	.4	.3	
Nan-chihli	1.9	3.6	1.2	1.3
Pei-chihli	11.3	10.1	7.9	5.3
Shansi	3.3	4.9	5.5	6.7
Shensi	3.3	4.0	4.8	4.0
Shantung	10.3	8.1	8.6	8.7
Szechwan	5.6	4.2	5.8	4.7
Yunnan	.5	.4	1.5	.7

TABLE XX *Provincial Origins of Officials Serving in Pei-chihli (Given in percentages according to native province and type of office)*

	Provincial	Prefectural	Subprefectural and County I	County II
Chekiang	8.4	10.5	4.3	3.4
Fukien	3.9	3.9	2.0	8.0
Honan	10.2	10.5	17.3	12.5
Hukuang	3.7	4.9	5.4	1.7
Kiangsi	6.2	7.3	4.0	2.3
Kwangsi		.8	.9	2.3
Kwangtung	1.1	1.2	2.3	2.8
Kweichow	.5	.5	.8	.6
Nan-chihli	14.1	14.5	10.2	6.8
Pei-chihli	9.1	3.0	.3	28.4
Shansi	7.6	13.5	14.4	7.4
Shensi	10.7	9.6	14.2	5.1
Shantung	20.4	14.7	20.2	13.1
Szechwan	3.7	3.4	2.8	3.4
Yunnan	.5	1.5	.9	2.3

TABLE XXI *Provincial Origins of Officials Serving in Shansi (Given in percentages according to native province and type of office)*

	Provincial	Prefectural	Subprefectural and County I	County II
Chekiang	9.6	4.5	1.9	2.7
Fukien	3.4	1.3	.5	2.1
Honan	12.0	16.6	17.4	17.5
Hukuang	5.6	4.0	2.5	1.1
Kiangsi	6.0	4.5	1.5	1.1
Kwangsi	.5			
Kwangtung	.8		.5	.5
Kweichow	.2	.3	.3	.5
Nan-chihli	11.5	9.5	5.7	2.7
Pei-chihli	19.2	23.5	26.3	20.1
Shansi	.1		.2	18.5
Shensi	9.5	16.1	23.1	21.2
Shantung	17.4	17.1	18.6	9.5
Szechwan	3.9	1.3	.9	1.1
Yunnan	.3	1.3	.5	1.6

TABLE XXII *Provincial Origins of Officials Serving in Shensi (Given in percentages according to native province and type of office)*

	Provincial	Prefectural	Subprefectural and County I	County II
Chekiang	8.6	4.0	1.3	
Fukien	2.1		1.0	
Honan	13.2	16.5	11.5	8.9
Hukuang	7.6	4.8	6.3	7.1
Kiangsi	7.6	3.0	2.1	1.8
Kwangsi	.3		.4	
Kwangtung	1.0	.3		1.8
Kweichow			1.3	1.8
Nan-chihli	10.4	6.4	2.7	1.8
Pei-chihli	15.9	20.1	19.1	16.1
Shansi	12.9	17.1	24.8	28.6
Shensi	.1	.3		1.8
Shantung	14.5	17.7	11.7	12.5
Szechwan	5.5	8.8	17.0	16.1
Yunnan	.4	.8	.8	1.8

TABLE XXIII   *Provincial Origins of Officials Serving in Shantung (Given in percentages according to native province and type of office)*

	Provincial	Prefectural	Subprefectural and County I	County II
Chekiang	14.9	12.4	7.6	12.7
Fukien	5.2	4.8	1.3	4.7
Honan	10.3	12.2	14.0	9.4
Hukuang	6.2	5.3	6.3	5.7
Kiangsi	10.1	7.6	4.1	3.8
Kwangsi	.3	.3	1.2	1.9
Kwangtung	1.3	1.0	1.8	.9
Kweichow		.3	.3	.5
Nan-chihli	15.8	17.0	16.1	15.6
Pei-chihli	11.4	17.3	23.5	12.7
Shansi	12.3	9.9	11.5	5.2
Shensi	6.2	9.9	9.7	5.2
Shantung	.1	.3	.2	20.3
Szechwan	5.4	1.8	2.0	.9
Yunnan	.4		.5	.5

TABLE XXIV   *Provincial Origins of Officials Serving in Szechwan (Given in percentages according to native province and type of office)*

	Provincial	Prefectural	Subprefectural and County I	County II
Chekiang	12.7	10.4	3.5	1.0
Fukien	8.3	5.4	1.6	
Honan	9.3	5.7	1.9	1.0
Hukuang	9.7	14.9	31.5	19.4
Kiangsi	13.1	13.1	9.7	11.2
Kwangsi	.8	1.6	3.5	2.0
Kwangtung	3.3	2.9	1.6	2.0
Kweichow	1.0	2.3	8.1	14.3
Nan-chihli	15.4	11.6	8.6	2.0
Pei-chihli	7.5	4.1	.8	
Shansi	4.4	4.5	2.4	1.0
Shensi	7.5	14.0	12.4	12.2
Shantung	4.6	5.4	1.3	
Szechwan	.2		.3	16.3
Yunnan	2.1	4.1	12.9	17.4

TABLE XXV   *Provincial Origins of Officials Serving in Yunnan (Given in percentages according to native province and type of office)*

	Provincial	Prefectural	Subprefectural and County I	County II
Chekiang	18.5	9.2	3.6	
Fukien	10.0	7.1	4.4	
Honan	5.9	2.1	.8	
Hukuang	9.8	10.6	13.3	
Kiangsi	19.0	12.4	10.5	
Kwangsi	1.0	1.4	5.5	
Kwangtung	6.2	5.3	7.2	
Kweichow	1.3	3.2	13.8	
Nan-chihli	23.1	15.5	6.9	
Pei-chihli	3.1	2.5	1.1	
Shansi	2.3	2.5	1.4	
Shensi	5.7	2.5	4.1	
Shantung	3.9	3.2	.8	
Szechwan	17.0	23.3	26.5	
Yunnan				

generally intensified at lower levels.[25] That is, officials at the provincial level and below tended to be natives of provinces in the same general area, and this tendency frequently increased the lower the level of the office. Shansi and Kiangsi provide two of the best examples. Pei-chihli, Honan, Shantung, and Shensi produced 58 percent of Shansi's provincial, 73 percent of its prefectural, and 85 percent of its subprefectural-county I officials. Similarly, Nan-chihli, Chekiang, Hukuang, and Fukien produced 65 percent of Kiangsi's provincial, 71 percent of its prefectural, and 73 percent of its subprefectural-county I officials.

It is in the politically depressed provinces of the far south and southwest that one finds some modification in the disposition to award provincial and lower level offices to persons from the same general area, though such modification does not really alter the basic principle. For example, not a single Kwangtung native served as subprefectural or county magistrate in Shensi. Furthermore, Kwangtung supplied no more than 2 percent, at most, of provincial and lower officials in any northern province. However, because of the weak political posture of Kwangtung, Kwangsi, Kweichow, and Yunnan, natives of these provinces had difficulty obtaining appointment at the provincial level. Thus, Fukien and particularly the powerful lower Yangtze provinces of Kiangsi, Nan-chihli, and Chekiang typically played a major role in supplying the provincial officials of these four provinces. On the prefectural and subprefectural-county ı levels, though, the southern and southwestern provinces exchanged officials in a fashion very much like other sections of the country. For example, Kwangtung supplied only 4 percent of Kwangsi's provincial officials, but supplied 18 percent of its prefectural and 28 percent of its subprefectural-county ı magistrates. Even Kweichow, the weakest of all the provinces politically, whose natives occupied only 261 official positions during the entire dynasty, was the source of 14 percent of neighboring Yunnan's subprefectural and county magistrates, a percentage higher than that of any other province except Szechwan.

In sum, the Ming administration, in making appointments to provincial and lower offices, sought to prevent possible corruption and favoritism by generally refraining from appointing an official to serve in his native province, but at the same time recognized the need for at least some acquaintance with the general area.

The final point concerning regional connotations deals with a more detailed breakdown of central government offices. One might pose the question as to whether or not there was any trend for certain of the Six Ministries to be dominated by officials from particular provinces. In general, there was no such trend. Strong provinces were fairly uniformly strong in all ministries, and, conversely, weak provinces uniformly weak. There were, however, a few interesting exceptions. Pei-chihli made the greatest contribution to the Ministry of War, reflecting its strategic military position. On the other hand, Nan-chihli, Chekiang, and Kiangsi, based on their prominence in the cultural sphere, were especially important as sources of ministers for the Ministry of Rites. The most unexpected weakness in the ministries occurs in the contributions of Chekiang and Kiangsi to the Ministry of Revenue. Although natives of these rich southeastern provinces had great success in other ministries, they were actively discriminated against as regards appointments to the fiscal administration, beginning with the founding emperor, who resented the support that the southeastern prefectures had given one of his rivals for the throne.

THE EXTENT OF CLAN CONNECTION
IN THE BUREAUCRACY

In calculating kinship, persons of the same surname who were natives of the same county were assumed to be members of a common clan. This method of calculation almost certainly introduces an element of exaggeration, and the figures undoubtedly err on the side of allowing for too much clan connection. However, considering the large number of individuals involved, it was impossible to adopt a more accurate method. It is true that in some cases there was specific mention of kinship in the sources or there was the existence of a common character in given names which indicates that the individuals were brothers or paternal first cousins. However, such cases were definitely in the minority, and of themselves would not provide an accurate gauge of clan membership.

Tables XXVI and XXVII really speak for themselves and do not require extensive comment. Table XXVI provides a general indication of how broadly based the Ming bureaucracy was by demonstrating that, even on the basis of a most liberal method of calculating kinship, 59 percent of the officials had no relatives who held office. At the same time, officials who were members of great gentry clans, say those placing 10 or more persons in office, comprised only 6 percent of the total number of officials. Again, Table XXVII makes even more definite the general condition of a broad bureaucratic base for the dynasty. Eighty-eight percent of the officials in the top echelons of the central government had no relatives who reached such official heights, and no clan placed more than four members at this level. Thus, one can say that dominant clans simply did not exist at the top level of the government.

Table XXVIII presents an over-all picture of the geographical distribution of clans placing six or more members in the bureaucracy, and Table XXIX provides a detailed listing of these clans province by province. The latter table is probably a relatively complete listing of the Ming political elite, insofar as one existed.

As one has been led to expect from a previous reference, the most

TABLE XXVI   *Estimate of Clan Connections for the Bureaucracy in General*

Number of individuals placed by clan	Number of individuals in category	Percentage of total figure	Number of individuals placed by clan	Number of individuals in category	Percentage of total figure
1	10,970	59.0	6	420	2.2
2	1,980	10.7	7	370	2.0
3	1,440	7.8	8	240	1.3
4	1,090	5.8	9	260	1.4
5	725	3.8	10 and over	1,140	6.2

TABLE XXVII   *Estimate of Clan Connections for Central Government Officials*

Number of individuals placed by clan	Number of individuals in category	Percentage of total figure	Number of individuals placed by clan	Number of individuals in category	Percentage of total figure
1	616	88.4	3	9	1.3
2	68	9.7	4	4	.6

powerful clans were concentrated in the lower Yangtze area and in the south, with Fukien definitely heading the list. The Lin clan of P'u-t'ien County, Fukien, placed 71 of its members in office, and they occupied 128 official positions. These figures are more than twice as high as those for any other clan in the country except for the Ch'en clan, also of P'u-t'ien. However, recalling the point made earlier that Fukien was proportionately considerably weaker in the central government than in lower level offices, it is significant that members of the powerful Lin clan served in a mere three central government positions.

To make the point even clearer concerning the stronger position of the clan in the south in contrast to the north, there is the example of Kwangsi. Despite its low rating in political power, Kwangsi had one clan which managed to place 22 members in office, considerably more than any northern province clan. This was the Chiang clan of Ch'üan-chou.

Turning now to look at the situation of clan connections from the opposite viewpoint, it is of value to note the provincial percentages of

TABLE XXVIII *Provincial Distribution of Politically Powerful Clans* (*Given in numbers of cases; e.g., there were ten cases of clans in Chekiang having six members who held official positions*)

Number of members holding office	Chekiang	Fukien	Honan	Hukuang	Kiangsi	Kwangsi	Kwangtung	Kweichow	Nan-chihli	Pei-chihli	Shansi	Shensi	Shantung	Szechwan	Yunnan
6	10	11		5	14	1	6		12	1	3	3	3		1
7	10	5		4	12	1	2		9	2	2		2	3	1
8	5	4	1	1	5		3		5		2		4		
9	7	1	1	2	7				5		2		2	2	
10	3	3	2		4				2	3				1	
11	1		1	1	3		2		2				1	1	
12	3	1			3						1	1			
13					2		1		2						
14	1	3			2				2						
15	1	2							1						
16	1														
17					1										
18	2	3			1		1								
19															
20—25		3			2	1									
25—30		1													
30—35		1			1										
35—40															
40—50		1													
50—60															
60—70															
70—80		1													

officials having no relatives who held office. These percentages are as follows: Chekiang, 42 percent; Fukien, 34 percent; Honan, 71 percent; Hukuang, 62 percent; Kiangsi, 46 percent; Kwangsi, 64 percent; Kwangtung, 52 percent; Kweichow, 95 percent; Nan-chihli, 59 percent; Pei-chihli, 73 percent; Shansi, 73 percent; Shensi, 74 percent; Shantung, 71 percent; Szechwan, 69 percent; and Yunnan, 84 percent. These figures contain no surprises and merely offer further substantiation of facts concerning the geographical variations of clan strength previously mentioned. Note the remarkable consistency in the figures for all the northern provinces.

TABLE XXIX *Politically Powerful Clans (According to province)*

Province	Number of individuals holding office	Family name		Native area		Number of positions held
Chekiang	6	Ch'a	查	Hai-ning	海寧	7
		Chang	張	Hsiu-shui	秀水	9
		Chang	章	Lan-ch'i	蘭谿	13
		Ch'ien	錢	Yin-hsien	鄞縣	10
		Ch'ien	〃	Jen-ho	仁和	9
		Ch'in	秦	Tz'u-ch'i	慈谿	16
		Chou	周	Tz'u-ch'i	〃 〃	8
		Liu	劉	Shan-yin	山陰	10
		T'u	屠	P'ing-hu	平湖	8
		Wang	王	Feng-hua	奉化	13
	7	Chang	張	Tz'u-ch'i	慈谿	12
		Chang	〃	Yin-hsien	鄞縣	14
		Hsü	徐	Yü-yao	餘姚	8
		Liu	劉	Tz'u-ch'i	慈谿	18
		Lu	陸	Yü-yao	餘姚	10
		Sun	孫	Yin-hsien	鄞縣	10
		T'u	屠	Yin-hsien	〃 〃	23
		Wang	王	Yung-chia	永嘉	11
		Wang	〃	Lin-hai	臨海	18
		Wang	〃	Tz'u-ch'i	慈谿	12
	8	Chang	張	Jen-ho	仁和	12
		Ch'en	陳	Shang-yü	上虞	17
		Hsü	徐	Shang-yü	〃 〃	9
		Li	李	Yin-hsien	鄞縣	11
		Sung	宋	Yü-yao	餘姚	10
	9	Ch'en	陳	Yin-hsien	鄞縣	14
		Chou	周	Yin-hsien	〃 〃	12
		Li	李	Chin-yün	縉雲	10
		Lu	盧	Tung-yang	東陽	12
		Yang	楊	Yin-hsien	鄞縣	15
		Yang	〃	Yü-yao	餘姚	11
		Wu	吳	Yü-yao	〃 〃	17
	10	Chang	張	Yü-yao	〃 〃	13
		Chu	朱	Shan-yin	山陰	18
		Shao	邵	Yü-yao	餘姚	13
	11	Ch'en	陳	Jen-ho	仁和	17
	12	Chang	張	Shan-yin	山陰	18
		T'ao	陶	K'uai-chi	會稽	20
		Wang	王	Shan-yin	山陰	23
	14	Lu	陸	P'ing-hu	平湖	32
	15	Hu	胡	Yü-yao	餘姚	20
	16	Ch'en	陳	Yü-yao	〃 〃	32
	18	Feng	馮	Tz'u-ch'i	慈谿	33
		Sun	孫	Yü-yao	餘姚	23

Fukien	6	Cheng	鄭	Hou-kuan	侯官	8
		Ch'iu	邱	P'u-t'ien	莆田	12
		Chou	周	Chin-chiang	晉江	11
		Chuang	莊	Chin-chiang	〃 〃	9
		Hsü	徐	P'u-t'ien	莆田	7
		Lin	林	Ch'ang-lo	長樂	10
		Su	蘇	Chin-chiang	晉江	9
		Wu	吳	P'u-t'ien	莆田	12
		Wu	〃	Lien-chiang	連江	10
		Wu	〃	Chang-p'u	漳浦	6
		Yang	楊	Chien-an	建安	8
	7	Chang	張	P'u-t'ien	莆田	7
		Ch'en	陳	Hui-an	惠安	7
		Hsü	許	Chin-chiang	晉江	10
		Lin	林	Chang-p'u	漳浦	8
		Lin	〃	Lung-ch'i	龍溪	7
	8	Ch'en	陳	Fu-ch'ing	福清	11
		Hung	洪	Nan-an	南安	10
		Wang	王	Hou-kuan	侯官	9
		Yeh	葉	Min-hsien	閩縣	10
	9	Ts'ai	蔡	Chin-chiang	晉江	15
	10	Lin	林	Hou-kuan	侯官	14
		Wang	王	Chin-chiang	晉江	13
		Yang	楊	Chin-chiang	〃 〃	12
	12	Chou	周	P'u-t'ien	莆田	12
	14	Chang	張	Chin-chiang	晉江	25
		Fang	方	P'u-t'ien	莆田	25
		Lin	林	Chin-chiang	晉江	17
	15	Li	李	Chin-chiang	〃 〃	20
		Lin	林	Fu-ch'ing	福清	15
	18	Ch'en	陳	Min-hsien	閩縣	27
		Cheng	鄭	Min-hsien	〃 〃	24
		Huang	黃	Chin-chiang	晉江	29
	21	Cheng	鄭	P'u-t'ien	莆田	24
Fukien	22	Ch'en	陳	Chin-chiang	晉江	29
	23	Ch'en	〃	Ch'ang-lo	長樂	33
	25	Lin	林	Min-hsien	閩縣	38
	32	Huang	黃	P'u-t'ien	莆田	36
	40	Ch'en	陳	P'u-t'ien	〃 〃	50
	71	Lin	林	P'u-t'ien	〃 〃	128
Honan	8	Wang	王	Hsiang-fu	祥符	13
	9	Hsü	許	Ling-pao	靈寶	26
	10	Chang	張	Hsiang-fu	祥符	11
		Chang	〃	Lo-yang	洛陽	13
	11	Li	李	Hsiang-fu	祥符	19
Hukuang	6	Chang	張	Chiang-ling	江陵	8
		Chang	〃	Chung-hsiang	鍾祥	6
		Li	李	Hsiang-yang	襄陽	7
		Liu	劉	Chiang-ling	江陵	7

Province		Surname		Place		
		Wang	王	Shih-t'ou	石首	9
	7	Ch'en	陳	Ch'i-chou	蘄州	7
		Liu	劉	Chiang-hsia	江夏	9
		Liu	〃	Shih-shou	石首	9
		Yang	楊	Pa-ling	巴陵	12
	8	Fang	方	Pa-ling	〃〃	11
	9	Liu	劉	Ma-ch'eng	麻城	17
		Wang	王	Huang-kang	黃岡	13
	11	Chou	周	Ma-ch'eng	麻城	14
Kiangsi	6	Chang	張	Nan-ch'ang	南昌	10
		Chang	〃	Nan-ch'eng	南城	6
		Ch'en	陳	Lu-ling	盧陵	8
		Ch'en	〃	Hsin-chien	新建	11
		Chou	周	Ning-chou	寧州	14
		Hsiao	蕭	Lu-ling	盧陵	7
		Hsü	徐	Kuei-ch'i	貴溪	9
		Lei	雷	Feng-ch'eng	豐城	12
		Kuo	郭	Wan-an	萬安	11
		Ou-yang	歐陽	An-fu	安福	21
		P'eng	彭	Lu-ling	盧陵	11
		Tseng	曾	Chi-shui	吉水	11
		Wang	王	Chi-shui	〃〃	9
		Wang	〃	Nan-ch'ang	南昌	7
	7	Ch'en	陳	Nan-ch'ang	〃〃	12
		Chou	周	Lu-ling	盧陵	9
		Chou	〃	An-fu	安福	10
		Chou	〃	Kuei-ch'i	貴溪	12
		Hsü	徐	Shang-jao	上饒	7
		Hu	胡	P'o-yang	鄱陽	10
		Jao	饒	Chin-hsien	進賢	10
		Kuo	郭	T'ai-ho	泰和	16
		Wu	吳	Nan-ch'ang	南昌	12
		Wu	〃	Lin-ch'uan	臨川	8
		Yang	楊	Nan-ch'ang	南昌	10
		Yüan	袁	Feng-ch'eng	豐城	9
	8	Ch'en	陳	T'ai-ho	泰和	16
		Huang	黃	Feng-ch'eng	豐城	10
		Li	李	T'ai-ho	泰和	10
		Lo	羅	Chi-shui	吉水	11
		T'u	涂	Nan-ch'ang	南昌	11
	9	Ch'en	陳	Kao-an	高安	20
		Hsiao	蕭	T'ai-ho	泰和	13
		Lo	羅	Nan-ch'ang	南昌	14
		Ou-yang	歐陽	T'ai-ho	泰和	12
		T'u	涂	Feng-ch'eng	豐城	14
		Wu	伍	An-fu	安福	16
		Yang	楊	Feng-ch'eng	豐城	14
	10	Chou	周	Chi-shui	吉水	15
		Hsiung	熊	Feng-ch'eng	豐城	17

		Li	李	Nan-ch'ang	南昌	11
		Liu	劉	T'ai-ho	泰和	10
	11	Liu	〃	Chi-shui	吉水	11
		Liu	〃	Lu-ling	廬陵	16
		P'eng	彭	An-fu	安福	17
	12	Ch'en	陳	Lin-ch'uan	臨川	20
		Wan	萬	Nan-ch'ang	南昌	20
		Wang	王	T'ai-ho	泰和	14
	13	Li	李	Chi-shui	吉水	19
		Tseng	曾	T'ai-ho	泰和	21
	14	Liu	劉	Nan-ch'ang	南昌	26
		Yang	楊	T'ai-ho	泰和	19
	17	Hsiung	熊	Nan-ch'ang	南昌	31
	18	Liu	劉	Wan-an	萬安	35
	20	Wang	王	An-fu	安福	26
	21	Li	李	Feng-ch'eng	豐城	30
	32	Liu	劉	An-fu	安福	57
Kwangsi	6	Teng	鄧	Ch'üan-chou	全州	6
	7	Chang	張	Lin-kuei	臨桂	9
	22	Chiang	蔣	Ch'üan-chou	全州	34
Kwangtung	6	Ch'en	陳	P'an-yü	番禺	9
		Ch'en	〃	Hai-yang	海陽	8
		Ch'en	〃	Tung-kuan	東莞	9
		Kuan	關	Nan-hai	南海	6
		Kuang	鄺	Nan-hai	〃 〃	9
		Wang	王	Tung-kuan	東莞	8
	7	Huang	黃	Nan-hai	南海	11
		Liang	梁	P'an-yü	番禺	7
	8	Chang	張	Shun-te	順德	9
		Chou	周	Nan-hai	南海	11
		Wu	吳	Nan-hai	〃 〃	12
	9	Ho	何	Shun-te	順德	18
	11	Liang	梁	Nan-hai	南海	14
		Liang	〃	Shun-te	順德	12
	13	Li	李	Nan-hai	南海	22
	18	Ch'en	陳	Nan-hai	〃 〃	24
Nan-chihli	6	Chang	張	T'ung-ch'eng	桐城	9
		Ch'en	陳	Wu-hsien	吳縣	12
		Chiang	江	Wu-yüan	婺源	13
		Chou	周	T'ai-ts'ang	太倉	9
		Chu	朱	K'un-shan	崑山	7
		Hsü	徐	Hua-t'ing	華亭	8
		Li	李	Hsing-hua	興化	9
		Liu	劉	Ch'ang-chou	長州	8
		Wang	汪	Hsiu-ning	休寧	6
		Wang	王	Chin-t'an	金壇	10
		Wu	吳	Wu-chiang	吳江	13
		Wu	〃	I-hsing	宜興	7

	7	Chao	趙	Ching-hsien	涇縣	11
		Ch'en	陳	Hua-t'ing	華亭	8
		Chiang	江	She-hsien	歙縣	9
		Ch'ien	錢	Ch'ang-shu	常熟	13
		Fang	方	T'ung-ch'eng	桐城	9
		Hsü	徐	Hsüan-ch'eng	宣城	
		Hu	胡	Chi-ch'i	績溪	15
		Lu	陸	Wu-hsien	吳縣	8
		Wu	吳	Hua-t'ing	華亭	10
	8	Ch'in	秦	Wu-hsi	無錫	12
		Hung	洪	She-hsien	歙縣	15
		Ku	顧	K'un-shan	崑山	12
		Li	李	Hua-t'ing	華亭	14
		Wang	王	Ch'ang-shu	常熟	11
	9	Chang	張	Ch'ang-chou	長洲	11
		P'an	潘	Wu-yüan	婺源	21
		Wu	吳	She-hsien	歙縣	11
		Wang	王	T'ai-ts'ang	太倉	26
		Wang	〃	K'un-shan	崑山	12
	10	Ch'en	陳	Ch'ang-shu	常熟	18
		Ch'eng	程	She-hsien	歙縣	16
	11	Chang	張	Hua-t'ing	華亭	24
		Wu	吳	Wu-chin	武進	18
	13	Wang	汪	Wu-yüan	婺源	33
		Chang	張	Shang-hai	上海	16
	14	Wang	汪	She-hsien	歙縣	23
		Wang	王	Hua-t'ing	華亭	23
	15	Fang	方	She-hsien	歙縣	20
Pei-chihli	6	Chang	張	Ku-an	固安	7
	7	Liu	劉	Ta-hsing	大興	11
		Liu	〃	Jen-ch'iu	任邱	11
	10	Li	李	Jen-ch'iu	〃 〃	13
		Wang	王	Ch'ing-yüan	清苑	16
		Wang	〃	K'ai-chou	開州	16
Shansi	6	Chou	周	Yang-ch'ü	陽曲	9
		Liu	劉	Hung-tung	洪洞	9
		Wang	王	Yang-ch'ü	陽曲	9
	7	Han	韓	Hung-tung	洪洞	10
		Kuo	郭	Kao-p'ing	高平	8
	8	Chang	張	Yang-ch'ü	陽曲	15
		Wang	王	T'ai-yüan	太原	15
	9	Li	李	Ch'ü-wo	曲沃	13
		Yang	楊	P'u-chou	蒲州	19
	12	Chang	張	P'u-chou	〃 〃	14
Shensi	6	Chang	〃	Ching-yang	涇陽	13
		Huang	黃	Hsien-ning	咸寧	7
		Li	李	Feng-hsiang	鳳翔	6
	21	Wang	王	Ning-chou	寧州	14

Shantung	6	Chang	張	Tsou-p'ing	鄒平	9
		Chang	〃	Shou-kuang	壽光	12
		Liu	劉	Shou-kuang	〃 〃	9
	7	Wang	王	Hsin-ch'eng	新城	17
		Wang	〃	I-hsien	掖縣	9
	8	Chang	張	Pin-chou	濱州	9
		Feng	馮	Lin-ch'ü	臨朐	9
		Wang	王	Ts'ao-hsien	曹縣	15
Shantung		Wang	王	Tzu-ch'uan	淄川	8
	9	Chao	趙	Li-ch'eng	歷城	11
		Hsieh	薛	Pin-chou	濱州	9
	11	K'ung	孔	Ch'ü-fu	曲阜	11
Szechwan	7	Hsieh	薛	Lung-an	龍安	7
		Kao	高	Nei-chiang	內江	17
		Li	李	Nei-chiang	〃 〃	12
		Yang	楊	Fu-shun	富順	8
	9	Liu	劉	Pa-hsien	巴縣	16
		Yang	楊	Nan-ch'ung	南充	15
	10	Wang	王	Nan-ch'ung	〃 〃	20
	11	Chang	張	Nei-chiang	內江	14
Yunnan	6	Yang	楊	Ta-li	大理	6
	7	Li	李	K'un-ming	昆明	7

TABLE XXX　*Clans with Political Power Extending through Substantial Portions of the Dynasty*

陳　莆　田
Ch'en of P'u-t'ien, Fukien.

At least one member holding office during all reign periods from Yung-lo through Ch'ung-chen (1403–1644) with the exception of Lung-ch'ing (1567–72). Concentration during Chia-ching (1522–66) which had 36% of the total number of offices occupied by members of the family.

林　莆　田
Lin of P'u-t'ien, Fukien.

At least one member holding office during all reign periods from Yung-lo through Ch'ung-chen (1403–1644) with the exception of Ching-t'ai and T'ien-shun (1450–64).

林　閩　縣
Lin of Min-hsien, Fukien.

At least one member holding office during all reign periods from Yung-lo through Ch'ung-chen (1403–1644) with the exception of Ching-t'ai and T'ien-shun (1450–64). Concentration during Chia-ching (1522–66) which had 35% of the total number of offices occupied by members of the family.

李　豐　城
Li of Feng-ch'eng, Kiangsi.

At least one member holding office from Hsüan-te through T'ien-ch'i (1425–1627) with the exception of Cheng-t'ung (1436–39). Concentration during Chia-ching which had 35% of the total number of offices occupied by members of the family.

熊　南　昌
Hsiung of Nan-ch'ang, Kiangsi.

At least one member holding office from Cheng-t'ung through Ch'ung-chen (1436–1644) with the exception of Ching-t'ai (1450–57), Ch'eng-hua (1465–87) and T'ien-ch'i (1421–27). Concentration during Chia-ching which had 41% of the total number of offices occupied by members of the family.

劉　安　福
Liu of An-fu, Kiangsi.

At least one member holding office during Hung-wu (1368–98) and from Ching-t'ai through Wan-li (1450–1620). Concentration during Cheng-te and Chia-ching (1506–66) which had 52% of the total number of offices occupied by members of the family.

劉　萬　安
Liu of Wan-an, Kiangsi.

At least one member holding office from Ching-t'ai through Ch'ung-chen (1450–1644) with the exception of Lung-ch'ing (1567–72) and T'ien-ch'i (1621–27). Concentration during Chia-ching which had 34% of the total number of offices occupied by members of the family.

陳　餘　姚
Ch'en of Yü-yao, Chekiang.

At least one member holding office during Cheng-t'ung (1436–49) and from Ch'eng-hua through Ch'ung-chen (1465–1644) with the exception of Lung-ch'ing (1567–72) and T'ien-ch'i (1621–27). Concentration during Chia-ching which had 38% of the total number of offices occupied by members of the family.

黃　莆　田
Huang of P'u-t'ien, Fukien.

At least one member holding office during Yung-lo (1403–24) and from Ch'eng-hua through Ch'ung-chen (1465–1644) with the exception of Lung-ch'ing (1567–72). Concentration during Chia-ching which had 42% of the total number of offices occupied by members of the family.

陳　長　樂
Ch'en of Ch'ang-lo, Fukien.

At least one member holding office during Hung-wu and Yung-lo (1368–1424) and from Cheng-te through T'ien-ch'i (1505–1627).

The next point to be considered in connection with the role of the clan in the bureaucracy is the time span during which the more powerful clans managed to remain important politically. After an analysis, according to reign period, of the official posts occupied by members of the same clan, it was discovered that there was not a single instance of a clan placing a member in office during each of the fourteen reign periods. In the overwhelming majority of cases, the political significance of a clan did not extend beyond a century at most, and there were found only ten clans whose power might properly be described as "dynastic" in scope. These ten clans are listed in Table xxx. The list is dominated by Fukien (with five) and Kiangsi (with four). Chekiang had only one, and Nan-chihli is not represented at all. Note that in eight of the ten cases there is a decided tendency toward a concentration of office-holding during the Chia-ching period (1522–66).

Finally, there is one curious instance of a relatively extended clan continuity in power which is not noted in Table xxx. The clan in question is the Hsieh of Lung-an Prefecture in Szechwan. The position of prefectural magistrate of Lung-an was occupied hereditarily by the Hsiehs for twelve generations. The practice of confining the office to members of the Hsieh clan began during the late Sung, continued throughout the Yüan, and remained in force until the early Cheng-te period (first decade of the sixteenth century). This is obviously a special case and, though interesting as a historical curiosity, has no general significance.

BACKGROUND PATTERNS IN THE CAREERS OF CENTRAL GOVERNMENT OFFICIALS

The most striking fact which emerges from Table xxxi is that the grand secretaries had relatively little experience in the other offices included in the survey. Ninety-five of the 157 (61 percent) individual grand secretaries suddenly appear in their exalted positions without having held offices at lower levels. This obviously does not mean that they had no prior official experience, but it does mean that such experience was decidedly confined to specific types of offices. It was a rare grand secretary indeed who came up through the lower offices which were surveyed. Note, for example, that only one grand secretary was found to have served as a subprefectural or county magistrate,[26] only five had served as prefectural magistrates, and only fourteen had occupied one of the various provincial offices. Even those who had served as ministers were in a decided minority (37 out of 157). Manifestly, one would have to obtain more definite information from other sources concerning the total career backgrounds of the grand secretaries before proposing any definitive conclusions, but the most logical preliminary conclusion to be drawn from Table xxxi is that an official should remain at the capital if he were to have the best chance of attaining the pinnacle of power and be appointed grand secretary. Probably the 95 grand secretaries who do not appear in any other office in the survey had a long background of service in lower central government offices. Thus, they built up their political position at the capital without risking what might happen to their careers if they went away for service in the provinces.

TABLE xxxi   *Background Patterns in the Careers of Officials Serving in the Grand Secretariat, Six Ministries, and Censorate (Given in numbers of cases)*

| | Grand Secretariat | Ministry | Censorate | Provincial | | Prefectural | Subprefectural and County I | No Service in Offices Included in Survey |
				1–2 offices	3 or more offices			
Grand Secretariat (157)*	16**	37	3	11	3	5	1	95
Six Ministries (529)*		113**	51	146	110	106	32	174
Censorate (110)*		19	8**	43	34	17	4	16

*   Total number of individuals serving in office
** Prior term(s)

The backgrounds of the ministers were quite different from those of the grand secretaries. There was still a sizable percentage (approximately one third) of the ministers who had no service in the other offices surveyed. However, a decided majority of the ministers did appear in lower offices, and there was much more of a progression from subprefectural and county magistrate [27] to prefectural magistrate to provincial offices and finally (perhaps after service in a lower central government office) to the headship of one of the Six Ministries. Thus, it would seem that ministers had a considerably wider range in their service backgrounds than grand secretaries.

Patterns in the careers of censors-in-chief did not differ substantially from those of ministers. There was an even smaller percentage of censors-in-chief than ministers (15 percent against 33 percent) who served in no other office considered in the study. Generally speaking, then, the censors had extensive past experience in county, subprefectural, prefectural, and provincial offices.

OFFICIAL DEGREES

The general situation of official degrees is presented in Table xxxii.[28] It will be noted that all the categories of officials exhibit the same general trends. Most importantly, the percentages of *chin-shih* degree holders were lower during the beginning reign periods, gradually increased during the second half of the fifteenth century, reached a pinnacle during the late 1400s and early 1500s, and underwent a gradual, though generally modest, decline subsequently. The opposite is true for holders of the lower degrees (that is, those who had not attained *chü-jen* status.)

The degree situation during the early reign periods reflects the fact that it took some time to rehabilitate the examination system after its neglect by the Mongols, and have it provide adequate numbers of higher degree holders. Consequently, prior to the second quarter of the fifteenth century, and particularly during the Hung-wu period, the shortage of *chin-shih* and *chü-jen* made it necessary to fill numerous offices with individuals who had been recommended for posts or

TABLE XXXII   *Degrees Held by Officials (Given in percentages)*

	Provincial			Prefectural			Subprefectural and County I			County II		
	Chin-shih	*Chü-jen*	Lower Degrees	*Chin-shih*	*Chü-jen*	Lower Degrees	*Chin-shih*	*Chü-jen*	Lower Degrees	*Chin-shih*	*Chü-jen*	Lower Degrees
Hung-wu	60	6	34	54	11	34	16	16	67	5	19	76
Yung-lo	72	15	13	53	24	24	24	18	57		42	58
Hsüan-te	79	15	6	76	15	10	30	28	43	6	41	53
Cheng-t'ung	78	14	8	63	31	6	19	31	50		41	59
Ching-t'ai	90	5	5	59	33	8	27	33	40	8	33	58
T'ien-shun	94	4	2	61	35	4	27	39	35	6	59	35
Ch'eng-hua	95	4	2	83	15	2	28	49	23	8	37	55
Hung-chih	99.6	.4		84	15	1	35	51	14	11	33	57
Cheng-te	99.4	.6		87	12	1	29	54	17	7	32	62
Chia-ching	98.9	.8	.3	80	17	3	28	55	17	4	19	77
Lung-ch'ing	99.3		.7	79	19	2	33	54	13	3	22	76
Wan-li	98.9	.9	.2	73	23	4	32	54	14	2	25	73
T'ien-ch'i	98.8	1.2		68	26	6	28	56	16	2	33	65
Ch'ung-chen	97.4	2.1	.5	45	40	15	29	51	20		21	79

who held only low degrees.[29] In fact, the ratio for Hung-wu between holders of *chin-shih* and *chü-jen* degrees on the one hand and holders of lower degrees on the other is probably decidedly exaggerated in favor of the former in Table XXXII, due to the fact that the calculations are based on only those officials whose degrees were indicated in the sources. And undoubtedly most of the officials lacking an indication of a degree were holders of lower degrees. By the mid-1400s, however, the *chin-shih* degree shortage had been rectified, and the possession of that degree became a *sine qua non* for an official career of real consequence.

Another interesting factor in regard to degrees was the situation during the terminal Ch'ung-chen period. The figures present certain evidence suggesting difficulty for the bureaucracy. Provincial administration was relatively unshaken, though the percentage of *chin-shih* holding office at the provincial level dipped slightly, and reached a point lower than it had been in more than a century and a half. On the other hand, prefectural administration was obviously in serious trouble. The *chin-shih* percentage of prefectural magistrates dropped to its lowest point in the entire dynasty, while the *chü-jen* percentage reached the highest point in the dynasty. Moving on to the county II level, the percentage of officials holding lower degrees was again the highest in the dynasty. Thus, we have in these Ch'ung-chen figures definite indications of a decline in bureaucratic quality. The figures provide more general confirmation of Li Wen-chih's contention in his study of the late Ming peasant rebellions that one of the causes of the rebellions was the ineptitude of local officials in northern Shensi, many of whom were incompetent lower degree holders.[30]

The object behind the calculation in Table xxxiii of the percentages of the various degrees held by subprefectural and county magistrates is to demonstrate that the degrees held by these officials generally varied from higher to lower depending upon the political importance of the area in which they served. Thus, we find the lowest *chin-shih* percentages for Kweichow and Yunnan subprefectural and county magistrates and the highest *chin-shih* percentages for Nanchihli (71 percent), Chekiang (47 percent), and Kiangsi (40 percent) magistrates. We have in these percentages, then, further evidence of the prestige of the lower Yangtze region.

MISCELLANEOUS TOPICS

Regional Concentrations of Family Names

One of the minor points sometimes referred to in Chinese social history is the tendency for certain family names to be concentrated in particular areas, the classic example being the case of the name Lin and its concentration in Fukien. As a side result of analyzing the provincial orgins of officials in the present study, it was possible, with only a small additional effort, to obtain evidence of regional concentrations of family names which perhaps has at least some validity. Admittedly, it is by no means certain that because, for example, 43 percent of the officials surnamed Ch'ien came from Chekiang, there was a corresponding general concentration of persons with that sur-

TABLE XXXIII   *Degrees Held by Subprefectural and County I Officials (Given in percentages according to provinces in which they served)*

	Chin-shih	*Chü-jen*	Lower Degrees		*Chin-shih*	*Chü-jen*	Lower Degrees
Chekiang	47	40	13	Nan-chihli	71	21	8
Fukien	28	46	26	Pei-chihli	29	53	18
Honan	28	47	25	Shansi	39	45	15
Hukuang	21	60	19	Shensi	13	55	33
Kiangsi	40	44	16	Shantung	20	60	20
Kwangsi	11	67	22	Szechwan	22	56	22
Kwangtung	27	52	23	Yunnan	9	65	26
Kweichow	5	62	33				

name in Chekiang. However, it is likely that there would be some correspondence between the geographical distribution of the surnames of officials and that of the general population. Thus, Table XXXIV was prepared. Note the expected concentration of Lins (65 percent) in Fukien.

TABLE XXXIV   *Evidences of Regional Concentrations of Family Names*

Family Name		Province	Percentage of total	Family Name		Province	Percentage of total
Chang	章	Chekiang	35	Chiang	姜	Chekiang	25
		Nan-chihli	30			Nan-chihli	20
		Kiangsi	20			Kiangsi	19
Cheng	鄭	Fukien	29	Ch'ien	錢	Chekiang	43
Ch'eng	程	Nan-chihli	35			Nan-chihli	39
Ch'en	陳	Fukien	20	Chin	金	Chekiang	35
Chia	賈	Pei-chihli	24			Nan-chihli	28
		Shansi	22	Ch'in	秦	Nan-chihli	30
		Honan	17	Chou	周	Kiangsi	18
Chiang	江	Honan	31			Hukuang	15
		Kiangsi	16	Chu	朱	Nan-chihli	21
Chiang	蔣	Nan-chihli	24	Chung	鍾	Kwangtung	25
						Kiangsi	22

Fang	方	Nan-chihli	29	Shen	沈	Chekiang	45
		Chekiang	19			Nan-chihli	27
		Fukien	14	Shih	石	Pei-chihli	19
Fu	傅	Kiangsi	23	Shih	史	Nan-chihli	23
Feng	馮	Chekiang	20	Su	蘇	Pei-chihli	18
Hsia	夏	Nan-chihli	27			Kwangtung	17
		Kiangsi	19	Sun	孫	Chekiang	18
Hsiao	蕭	Kiangsi	28			Shantung	16
		Hukuang	17	Sung	宋	Pei-chihli	18
Hsieh	謝	Kiangsi	17			Shantung	12
Hsieh	薛	Shantung	21	Tai	戴	Fukien	21
Hsiung	熊	Kiangsi	46			Kiangsi	17
		Hukuang	15	T'ang	唐	Nan-chihli	24
		Szechwan	14			Hukuang	14
Hsü	徐	Chekiang	23	T'ao	陶	Chekiang	37
		Nan-chihli	22	Teng	鄧	Kiangsi	23
Huang	黃	Fukien	25			Hukuang	23
Hung	洪	Fukien	31			Kwangsi	13
		Chekiang	19			Kwangtung	12
Jen	任	Szechwan	20	Ts'ai	蔡	Fukien	19
		Shansi	18	Ts'ao	曹	Nan-chihli	23
		Shensi	15	Tseng	曾	Kiangsi	37
Ku	顧	Nan-chihli	57			Kwangtung	14
		Chekiang	20			Hukuang	14
Kung	龔	Nan-chihli	26	Tsou	鄒	Kiangsi	31
		Kiangsi	20			Hukuang	17
Kuo	郭	Kiangsi	16	Ts'ui	崔	Pei-chihli	29
		Shansi	15			Honan	16
Liang	梁	Kwangtung	31			Shantung	19
Lin	林	Fukien	65	Tung	董	Chekiang	23
		Kwangtung	14	Wan	萬	Kiangsi	43
Lo	羅	Kiangsi	27	Wang	汪	Nan-chihli	55
		Kwangtung	12	Wu	吳	Nan-chihli	24
Lu	陸	Chekiang	43	Yao	姚	Chekiang	35
		Nan-chihli	36	Yeh	葉	Chekiang	32
Lu	盧	Chekiang	21			Fukien	20
Lü	呂	Chekiang	22	Yen	嚴	Chekiang	38
		Pei-chihli	15	Yin	尹	Kiangsi	23
Mao	毛	Nan-chihli	24	Yü	于	Shantung	36
Ma	馬	Pei-chihli	18			Pei-chihli	19
		Shantung	14	Yü	俞	Chekiang	42
Pai	白	Shensi	18			Nan-chihli	31
P'an	潘	Nan-chihli	36	Yü	余	Fukien	16
P'eng	彭	Kiangsi	43			Szechwan	14
Shao	邵	Chekiang	34			Hukuang	13

The Imperial Clan and the Bureaucracy

The present study provides quite definite confirmation of the recognized fact of the imperial clan's political impotence. The Ming practice of insuring the economic security of younger sons of the emperors by providing them with large princely estates is well known. On these estates, the princes lived in idle luxury and were accorded some social recognition,[31] but the great majority of their descendants rapidly were reduced to modest circumstances and obscurity. The financial burden resulting from supporting the princes on a lavish scale and their descendants on a progressively declining scale had become a heavy one by the end of the dynasty when the Jesuit observer, Semedo, estimated that they numbered 60,000.[32] In an attempt to help solve the problem of the imperial clansmen, they were allowed, following 1595, to participate in the state examinations and become officials.[33]

It is doubtful, however, if this attempted solution was at all effective, for among the many thousands of officials surveyed in the present study, only two members of the imperial clan were discovered. It is significant that both of them held office during the terminal Ch'ung-chen period. Furthermore, neither of them held a position of any importance. One served as magistrate of Hsü-chou in Nan-chihli and the other as magistrate of Ch'üan-chou in Kwangsi.

Natives of Liaotung and Foreigners Serving in the Bureaucracy

Natives of Liaotung occupied only 49 of the official positions surveyed. With a single exception for an earlier period, this official service was scattered fairly evenly from Ch'eng-hua through Ch'ung-chen (1465–1644). Thus, what little political importance Liaotung had was concentrated in the last three fourths of the dynasty. None of the Liaotung natives rose to occupy one of the high central government positions. Eighteen of the 49 offices they occupied were provincial, 11 were prefectural, 17 were subprefectural and county i, and three were county ii.

Two foreign groups, Annamese and Mongols, appeared in the official lists, though both were insignificant numerically and highly limited in time span. Annamese held ten positions, all concentrated during the Cheng-t'ung, Ching-t'ai, and T'ien-shun reign periods (1436–64). This was the period immediately following the collapse of Chinese intervention in Annam when the area had elicited considerable attention and interest. The highest position held by an Annamese was minister of the Ministry of Works. He was the son of the Annamese king, and undoubtedly the appointment was nothing more than an honorary gesture. The other nine offices occupied by Annamese were probably functioning appointments. Four of these were provincial offices, two were prefectural, and one was a county II post.

Four positions were held by Mongols, all of whom served during the Hung-wu period. Three of the Mongols were prefectural magistrates, and one was a county II official.

This survey of foreigners in the Ming bureaucracy obviously does not present the entire picture of the dynasty's employment of non-Chinese. The role of Moslems and Europeans as astronomers in Peking is well known. However, it seems definite that foreigners in the more "regular" bureaucratic positions were rarities indeed.

SUMMARY

It is possible to make deductions concerning fluctuations in the general stability of the Ming dynasty based on periodic variations in the length of tenure in office. In virtually every category of the official positions surveyed, the shortest tenures occurred during the terminal T'ien-ch'i and Ch'ung-chen reign periods. Thus, the downfall of the dynasty in 1644 did not occur because its fortunes during the previous two decades were in the hands of a tightly knit clique dominated by motives of narrow self-advantage. Rather, the fall was attended by an intensified and general bureaucratic chaos with officials, especially in the top positions, being replaced with bewildering rapidity. The unfortunate bureaucrat serving during the last decades of the dynasty simply did not have an opportunity to formulate viable policies, and there was no hard core of officials who enjoyed a sufficiently long tenure to permit them to put into effect programs either wise or foolish. In addition, the decline in bureaucratic quality, suggested by the degrees held by Ch'ung-chen officials, adds further evidence indicative of terminal chaos and incompetence.

Extending this basis of judging the stability of the dynasty to earlier periods, the study offers evidence for considering the first half of the fifteenth century as the "golden age" of the dynasty. Subsequently, there was a general gradual decline until the modest recovery occurring in the Wan-li period.

The key Ming centers of political power were the lower Yangtze Valley (Nan-chihli, Kiangsi, and Chekiang), the upper north China plain (Pei-chihli), and the upper southern coast (Fukien). These areas were successful in maintaining their strong positions relatively steadily throughout the dynasty, the only particularly notable evidence of long-range variation being the decline of Kiangsi and the rise of Fukien following the mid-sixteenth century. Thus, Ming political power generally coincided with economic strength and cultural dominance. The exception was Pei-chihli, whose political prestige probably was due mainly to its possession of the principal national capital following 1421.

Examining the political situation in more detail within provinces, we find that there was a definite tendency for power to be concentrated in particular local areas. Such concentration was greatest in the lower Yangtze Valley and especially in the south. For example, Nan-chihli's dominant counties were concentrated in the southeastern corner of the province, and Fukien's were all located along the coast. Political success in northern provinces was more evenly distributed.

As for regional connotations in official appointments at provincial, prefectural, subprefectural, and county levels, there was general observance of the rule that persons should not serve in their native provinces. At the same time, the existence of such factors as distinctive regional problems and differences in language made it impractical to assign officials at random to serve in provincial and lower posts. The result was a decided tendency to appoint officials who were natives of nearby provinces to fill these positions. In this fashion, the Ming administration sought to diminish corruption, while taking advantage of special competence and knowledge.

How successful were clans and special groups in exerting pressure upon the bureaucracy in favor of their own interests? The evidence overwhelmingly suggests the maintance of a high degree of bureaucratic integrity. A decided majority of the officials were from clans that placed only one member in office. Members of great gentry clans who obtained posts constituted no more than a small fraction of the total, and only a mere handful of these strong clans succeeded in achieving a continuity in power which was of sufficient extent to be worthy of the term "dynastic." In particular areas in the lower Yangtze Valley and especially in the south, with Fukien providing the prime example, clan power was of some importance. However, generally speaking, it was the bureaucracy which bent the clan to its own interests, and not the reverse. In a similar vein, there is nothing in the study to confirm the existence of powerful and long-continuing cliques which managed to dominate the bureaucracy and fill it with their favorites. Whatever favoritism existed, whether confined or extensive, seems to have been extremely diffuse. Thus, one might say that a real Ming political elite, narrowly based and enjoying an extended grasp on power, simply did not exist. The Ming situation, then, provides a considerable contrast to earlier periods of Chinese history when, as noted by Eberhard, great clans held power throughout long periods. The contrast is equally great with the elitist conditions of Republican Rome and eighteenth-century England which have been presented in the works of Syme and Namier.

Concerning the matter of patterns in official careers, the present study permits only a preliminary assessment. Ministers and censors seem to have had relatively varied official experience prior to attaining these offices. However, grand secretaries appear to have had most of their experience concentrated in the capital, where they undoubtedly had the advantage of being able to nurture their political images and careers with great care at the very center of power.

As for the question of official degrees, concrete evidence is presented to support the long-recognized circumstance that, by around the third decade of the fifteenth century, the *chin-shih* degree was essential for a really significant political career.

In sum, the Ming bureaucracy, erected on a broadly based foundation, presents a picture of enormous complexity and balance. Espousing its own interests and containing within itself its reason for existence, it was remarkably successful in maintaining integrity against pressures which would bend it toward particularistic ends. It was one of the political marvels of the premodern world, and was not unworthy of the high esteem it elicited from certain of the Europeans who were privileged to witness its operation.

APPENDIX I
Ming Reign Periods

1. Hung-wu and Chien-wen (1368–1402)
2. Yung-lo (1403–1424)
3. Hung-hsi and Hsüan-te (1425–1435)
4. Cheng-t'ung (1436–1449)
5. Ching-t'ai (1450–1456)
6. T'ien-shun (1457–1464)
7. Ch'eng-hua (1465–1487)
8. Hung-chih (1488–1505)
9. Cheng-te (1506–1521)
10. Chia-ching (1522–1566)
11. Lung-ch'ing (1567–1572)
12. Wan-li (1573–1620)
13. T'ai-ch'ang and T'ien-ch'i (1620–1627)
14. Ch'ung-chen (1628–1644)

APPENDIX II
Subprefectural and County Magistrates Included in Study

Chekiang
  Subprefectures:
    An-chi   安吉
  Counties:
    Chia-hsing   嘉興
    Chien-te   建德
    Chu-chi   諸暨
    Hai-ning   海寧
    Hsi-an   西安
    Hsiang-shan   象山
    Lung-yu   龍游
    P'ing-yang   平陽
    T'ien-t'ai   天臺

Fukien
  Counties:
    Ch'ang-lo   長樂
    Ch'ang-t'ai   長泰
    Ch'ing-liu   清流
    Hui-an   惠安
    Lien-chiang   連江
    Lung-ch'i   龍溪
    Nan-an   南安
    Ning-te   寧德
    Shou-ning   壽寧
    Yu-ch'i   尤溪

Honan
  Subprefectures:
    Hsü   許
    Kuang   光
    Yü   裕
  Counties:
    Ch'i   杞
    Hsin-yeh   新野
    Huo-chia   獲嘉

T'ung-hsü 通許
Wen 溫
Yen-ling 鄢陵
Yung-ch'eng 永城

Hukuang
  Subprefectures:
    Yüan 沅
    Kuei-yang 桂陽
    Feng 澧
  Counties:
    An-lu 安陸
    Ch'i-shui 蘄水
    Ch'i-yang 祁陽
    Chien-li 監利
    Hsin-ning 新寧
    I-ch'eng 宜城

Kiangsi
  Counties:
    Chin-hsien 進賢
    Ch'ung-jen 崇仁
    Fen-i 分宜
    I-huang 宜黃
    Jui-ch'ang 瑞昌
    Lung-ch'üan 龍泉
    T'ai-ho 泰和
    Tu-ch'ang 都昌
    Yü-shan 玉山
    Yung-feng 永豐

Kwangsi
  Subprefectures:
    Ch'üan 全
    Heng 橫
    Pao 竇
    Shang-ssu 上思
    Tso 左
    Yang-li 養利
    Yü-lin 鬱林
  Counties:
    Lin-kuei 臨桂

Ling-ch'uan 靈川
Wu-yüan 武緣

Kwangtung
  Subprefectures:
    Ch'in 欽
    Hua 化
    Lien 連
    Te-ch'ing 德慶
  Counties:
    Chieh-yang 揭陽
    Hsing-ning 興寧
    Hui-t'ung 會同
    Ju-yüan 乳源
    Tung-kuan 東莞

Kweichow
  Subprefectures:
    Chen-ning 鎮寧
    Huang-p'ing 黃平
    Ma-ha 麻哈
    P'u-an 普安
    Tu-shan 獨山
    Yung-ning 永寧
  Counties:
    Chen-yüan 鎮遠
    Shih-ping 施秉
    Wu-ch'uan 婺川
    Yin-chiang 印江
    Yung-ts'ung 永從

Nan-chihli
  Subprefectures:
    Kao-yu 高郵
    Shou 壽
    Wu-wei 無爲
  Counties:
    Ch'ang-chou 長州
    Chiang-tu 江都
    Chü-jung 句容
    Hua-t'ing 華亭
    Shang-hai 上海

Wu-chin 武進
Wu-yüan 婺源

Pei-chihli
  Subprefectures:
    Luan 灤
    Ts'ang 滄
  Counties:
    An-su 安肅
    Ch'ü-yang 曲陽
    Han-tan 邯鄲
    Huo-lu 獲鹿
    Lai-shui 淶水
    Lo-t'ing 樂亭
    Tung-an 東安
    Wei 魏

Shansi
  Subprefectures:
    Hun-yüan 渾源
    P'ing-ting 平定
  Counties:
    Ch'ang-tzu 長子
    Chi-shan 稷山
    Chieh-hsiu 介休
    Ch'ü-wo 曲沃
    Fen-yang 汾陽
    Kao-p'ing 高平
    Ta-t'ung 大同
    Yü-tz'u 榆次

Shensi
  Subprefectures:
    Chia 葭
    Ho 河
  Counties:
    Ch'ang-an 長安
    Chen-ning 眞寧
    Ch'i-shan 岐山
    Hsün-yang 洵陽
    Lan-t'ien 藍田
    Lüeh-yang 略陽

Mien 沔
Shang-nan 商南

Shantung
  Subprefectures:
    Kao-t'ang 高唐
    P'ing-tu 平度
    Wu-ting 武定
  Counties:
    Ch'ang-i 昌邑
    Ch'ang-lo 昌樂
    Chiao 膠
    Fu-shan 福山
    Li-ching 利津
    T'ang-i 堂邑
    Tsou 鄒

Szechwan
  Counties:
    Chih-chiang 執江
    Fu-shun 富順
    Hsin-tu 新都
    K'ai 開
    Ming-shan 名山
    Nan-ch'ung 南充
    P'eng-ch'i 蓬溪
    Wan 萬
    Ying-shan 營山
    Yung-ch'uan 永川

Yunnan
  Subprefectures:
    An-ning 安寧
    Chien-ch'uan 劍川
    Chien-shui 建水
    Chin-ning 晉寧
    Ning 寧
    O-mi 阿迷
    Shih-p'ing 石屏
    Sung-ming 嵩明
  Counties:
    Huang-kung 皇貢
    Kuang-t'ung 廣通

APPENDIX III
County II Offices Included in Study

Chekiang
   Vice-magistrate (*hsien-ch'eng* 縣丞) of Hsi-an 西安
   Vice-magistrate of Lung-yu 龍遊
   Warden (*tien-shih* 典史) of Ch'ang-shan 常山

Fukien
   Vice-magistrate of Nan-an 南安
   Vice-magistrate of Ning-hua 寧化
   Instructor (*chiao-yü* 教諭) of Lo-yüan 羅源
   Assistant Instructor (*hsün-tao* 訓導) of Shou-ning 壽寧

Honan
   Warden of Ch'ang-ko 長葛
   Warden of Hsi 息
   Instructor of Ch'ang-ko 長葛

Hukuang
   Vice-magistrate of Liu-yang 劉陽
   Instructor of Ch'i-yang 祁陽
   Instructor of Hsin-ning 新寧

Kiangsi
   Vice-magistrate of I-huang 宜黃
   Vice-magistrate of Wu-ning 武寧
   Assistant-magistrate (*chu-pu* 主簿) of Nan-feng 南豐

Kwangtung
   Vice-magistrate of Wen-ch'ang 文昌
   Assistant-magistrate of Ying-te 英德

   Instructor of Ju-yüan 乳源
   Warden of Hsing-ning. 興寧

Nan-chihli
   Vice-magistrate of Chü-jung 句容
   Assistant-magistrate of Wu-hsi 無錫
   Assistant-magistrate of Wu-yüan 婺源

Pei-chihli
   Instructor of Ch'ü-yang 曲陽
   Instructor of Chi-tse 雞澤
   Instructor of Wei 威
   Instructor of Yen-shan 鹽山

Shansi
   Instructor of Ch'ü-wo 曲沃
   Instructor of Fen-yang 汾陽
   Instructor of Yang-ch'eng 陽城
   Vice-magistrate of Chi-shan 稷山

Shensi
   Vice-magistrate of Ch'i-shan 岐山
   Instructor of Lo-nan 雒南
   Warden of Ch'ang-an 長安

Shantung
   Instructor of Fu-shan 福山
   Instructor of Li-ching 利津
   Instructor of Lin-i 臨邑
   Instructor of T'ang-i 堂邑

Szechwan
   Instructor of Fu-shun 富順
   Instructor of Ying-shan 營山
   Warden of P'eng-ch'i 蓬溪

Notes

LIEN-SHENG YANG *Ming Local Administration*

1. Chu Hsi, *Chu-tzu Yü-lei* (1876 ed.), 108.2a.
2. She I-tse, *Chung-kuo T'u-ssu Chih-tu* (Chungking, 1944), pp 158–71; Huang K'ai-hua's article on the Ming *t'u-ssu* system and the development of the Southwest in *Hsin-Ya Hsüeh-pao*, VI, no. 2 (1964), pp. 484–93. On page 486, Huang errs in labeling the *li-mu* and the *tien-shih* as *tso-erh* or assistant magistrates. They were *shou-ling-kuan* or chief officers of *chou* and *hsien* respectively. The collective term for both *tso-erh* and *shou-ling* was *tso-ling*. See *Ta-Ming Hui-tien* (*Wan-yu Wen-k'u* ed.), 4.80–82; and T'ung-tsu Ch'ü, *Local Government in China under the Ch'ing* (Cambridge, Mass., 1962), pp. 8–9.
3. *Wen-hsien T'ung-k'ao* (*Shih-t'ung* ed.), chs. 265–77.
4. Charles O. Hucker, "Governmental Organization of the Ming Dynasty," *Harvard Journal of Asiatic Studies*, XXI (1958), 8–10.
5. Wm. Theodore de Bary, *et al.*, *Sources of Chinese Tradition* (New York, 1960), pp. 611–12.
6. Ch'ing scholars include Chao I, Hung Liang-chi, and Yao Nai; modern scholars include Derk Bodde, H. G. Creel, Masubuchi Tatsuo, and Cho-yün Hsü.
7. Ts'ao's *Liu-tai Lun* (Discourses on the six dynasties [Hsia, Shang, Chou, Ch'in, Han, Wei]) can be found in *San-kuo Chih, Wei-chih* (*T'ung-wen* ed.), 20.13b–16a, commentary quoting the *Wei-shih Ch'un-ch'iu*; and in *Wen-hsüan* (*Wan-yu Wen-k'u* ed.), 52.95–101.
8. Lu's *Wu-teng Chu-hou Lun* (Discourses on feudal lords of the five ranks) is in *Wen-hsüan*, 54.24–30; and in *Chin-shu* (*T'ung-wen* ed.), 54.10a–13a.
9. Since the essays by Ts'ao and Lu are both preserved in the *Wen-hsüan*, it can be assumed that their contents were familiar to T'ang T'ai-tsung, who composed the biography of Lu Chi in the *Chin-shu*.

   T'ang T'ai-tsung appointed Chang-sun Wu-chi and others as hereditary prefects (*shih-hsi tz'u-shih*). Since all the appointees declined to go to their posts, T'ai-tsung soon abolished the institution. The appointment was not completely an innovation because hereditary prefects had existed in the period of disunion. In the early years of the Southern Sung, Kao-tsung planned to introduce a program of hereditary governors by first making their appointments for life. This plan was thwarted by the revolt led by the governor Li Ch'eng.
10. *T'ung-tien* (*Shih-t'ung* ed.), 31.177a-b.

11. Tu Yu, however, was not exclusively for the modern, because he also admitted the value of ancient ideals, particularly in peaceful times. (*T'ung-tien*, 4.25a-b.)
12. *Ibid.*, 195.985a.
13. *Ibid.*, 31.177a-b, 185.985a.
14. Liu Tsung-yüan, *Liu Ho-tung Chi* (sppy ed.), 3.1a-7b.
15. Hsiao Kung-ch'üan, *Chung-kuo Cheng-chih Ssu-hsiang Shih* (Taipei, 1954), pp. 408–9.
16. Notably Hu Yin (1121 *chin-shih*), *Tu-shih Kuan-chien*, 1.19b-20b.
17. Hsiao Kung-ch'üan, *Chung-kuo Cheng-chih Ssu-hsiang Shih*, pp. 408–12.
18. Liu Tsung-yüan, *Liu Ho-tung Chi*, 3.7a-7b.
19. W. T. de Bary, *et al.*, *Sources of Chinese Tradition*, p. 588.
20. Liu Tsung-yüan, *Liu Ho-tung Chi*, 3.7b.
21. Hsiao Kung-ch'üan, *Chung-kuo Cheng-chih Ssu-hsiang Shih*, pp. 466–69. An early example is the interesting conversation between Sung Shen-tsung and Wang An-shih recorded in the *Hsü Tzu-chih T'ung-chien Ch'ang-pien* (Taipei, 1961), ch. 223, under the year 1071. The emperor remarked that the "prefectural soldier" (*fu-ping*) system and the *tsu-yung-tiao* system of taxation of T'ang were mutually dependent (*hsiang-hsü*). In reply, Wang said that the militia of Sung known as *i-yung* also could be effective if the soldiers were well paid and treated with decency. Here one can discern both an awareness of the interlocking nature of institutions and an analysis in terms of *t'i* and *yung*.
22. Hsiao Kung-ch'üan, *Chung-kuo Cheng-chih Ssu-hsiang Shih*, pp. 461–69.
23. Lo Pi, *Lu Shih, Kuo-ming Chi* (Shanghai, 1933), 4.55a-56b, 7.65b-67b, 8.1a-20b.
24. Hozumi Nobushige, *Gonin Gumi Seido Ron* (Tokyo, 1921), pp. 466–98.
25. *Wu Yüan-ying Chi* (sptk ed.), 8.5a, 12.8b-11b.
26. *Ta-Ming Hui-tien*, 13.315–316.   27. *Ibid.*, 13.316.
28. Lü K'un, *Shih-cheng Lu, Ming-chih* (Ch'ung-wen ed.), 1.30a-31a.
29. Meng Sen, *Ming-tai Shih* (Taipei, 1957), pp. 126–27; Chang Ts'un-wu's article on Ming eunuchs in *Yu-shih Hsüeh-pao*, III, no. 2 (1964), 13–15.
30. *Wei-shu* (T'ung-wen ed.), 113.4b. Yen Keng-wang in his *Chung-kuo Ti-fang Hsing-cheng Chih-tu Shih*, part II, vol. 2 (Taipei, 1963), pp. 603–4, has suggested that the Northern Wei system of having three heads in one local government probably existed for only a short period.

31. Meng Sen, *Ming-tai Shih*, pp. 110–11. That Ming T'ai-tsu was deeply concerned with local administration is evidenced by two of his imperial compilations: the *Tao-jen Hsü-chih* and the *Tse-jen T'iao-li*, quoted in *Ta-Ming Hui-tien*, vols. 9 and 10 respectively. These were handbooks to guide local government officials.
32. T'ung-tsu Ch'ü, *Local Government in China under the Ch'ing*, p. 20.
33. *Chu Chih-shan Shou-hsieh Hsing-ning chih Kao-pen* (Peking, 1962), 4.1a-2a.
34. Ping-ti Ho, *The Ladder of Success in Imperial China: Aspects of Social Mobility, 1368–1911* (New York, 1962), pp. 32–33.
35. *Nan-yung Chih* (Nanking, 1931), 4.63a; Lung Wen-pin, *Ming Hui-yao* (1887 ed.), 64.5b-6a.
36. *Ming-shih* (T'ung-wen ed.), 164.23b-24a, 207.16b-17a.
37. Lung Wen-pin, *Ming Hui-yao*, 41.7a, 10b-11b. This is reflected even in literature, e.g., in the story about the old candidate Hsieh-yü T'ung in *Ching-shih T'ung-yen* (Peking, 1956), vol. 18.
38. Lung Wen-pin, *Ming Hui-yao*, 41.10b.
39. Ko Shou-li, *Ko Tuan-su-kung Chi* (1802 ed.), 1.17b.
40. Chao I, *Kai-yü Ts'ung-k'ao* (Shanghai, 1957), 16.296–299; Yen Keng-wang, *Chung-kuo Ti-fang Hsing-cheng Chih-tu Shih*, part I, vol. 1 (Taipei, 1961), pp. 77–79, 221–23.
41. Yen Keng-wang, *Chung-kuo Ti-fang Hsing-cheng Chih-tu Shih*, part I, vol. 2, pp. 345–57.
42. T'ung-tsu Ch'ü, *Local Government in China under the Ch'ing*, pp. 93–96, 258.
43. *Chou-hsien Shih-i* (1886 ed.), 27b.
44. Chao I, *Kai-yü Ts'ung-k'ao*, 17.331–35.
45. *Ming-ling*, 40b.
46. Chao I, *Kai-yü Ts'ung-k'ao*, 16.303–305; Shen Chia-pen, "Li-tai Hsing-kuan K'ao," in *Shen Chi-i Hsien-sheng I-shu*, A.20a-21b, B.15a-b; A. F. P. Hulsewé, *Remnants of Han Law*, I (Leiden, 1955), 10, 81–82.
47. *Ming-shih*, 94.1a.   48. *Ibid.*, 93.12b-13a.
49. Lung Wen-pin, *Ming Hui-yao*, 64.7a.
50. Chai Hao, *T'ung-su Pien* (Shanghai, 1937), V, 109; Chu Li, *Han T'ang Shih-chien Hou-chi* (1822 ed.), 4.4a–5a.
51. Yen Keng-wang, *Chung-kuo Ti-fang Hsing-cheng Chih-tu Shih*, part I, vol. 1, p. 93.
52. *Ta-Ming Hui-tien*, ch. 166.
53. *Ibid.*, 78.1818, 79.1826–1827, 93.2127.
54. Fascinating details on local finance can be found in the writings of Hai Jui and Shen Pang, both of whom served as district magistrates

in the second half of the sixteenth century. Hai was renowned for his reforms in local government on various levels. See *Hai Jui Chi* (Peking, 1962) and Shen Pang, *Wan-shu Tsa-chi* (Peking, 1961).

55. D. C. Twitchett, *Financial Administration under the T'ang Dynasty* (London, 1963), pp. 30–31, 132–34.

   In addition, officials under the T'ang and the Sung after their retirement continued to receive half salary; even officials of lower ranks enjoyed the "protective" (*yin*) privilege of having a son enter the civil service without passing an examination. Under the Ming, the *yin* privilege was restricted to officials of the third and higher ranks, and only exceptionally were individual officials granted a pension after their retirement.

56. For a short period under Ming T'ai-tsu, nobles were also permitted to collect rent from state land as salary. (*Ta-Ming Hui-tien*, 38.1095–99.)

57. There were, however, no *kung-shih k'u* in the *hsien* government, where office expenses had to be shared by the clerks.

58. *Ta-Ming Hui-tien*, 39.1106–1114.

59. *Chia-ching Hai-ning-hsien Chih* (1898 ed.), 2.10b–12b; Hai Jui, *Hai Jui Chi*, pp. 48–51; Shen Pang, *Wan-shu Tsa-chi*, pp. 27, 49, 133–36.

60. Liang Fang-chung, *Ming-tai Liang-chang Chih-tu* (Shanghai, 1957) is a valuable study. On page 92, Liang erroneously breaks the compound *chung-nan* "heavy and difficult" (a term that dates back to Sung times) into two parts of a sentence.

61. Hai Jui, *Hai Jui Chi*, pp. 48–57, 118–19; Lü K'un, *Shih-cheng Lu, Ming-chih*, 1.18b–19a.

62. Hai Jui, *Hai Jui Chi*, p. 40; Ko Shou-li, *Ko Tuan-su-kung Chi, Chia-hsün*, B.20b.

63. Hai Jui, *Hai Jui Chi*, p. 181.

64. *Ta-Ming Hui-tien*, 8.199–200; Hai Jui, *Hai Jui Chi*, *pp.* 40–41, 49, 54.

65. *Ta-Ming Hui-tien*, 22.608–11, 28.836, 30.889–92; Lien-sheng Yang, *Les Aspects Économiques des Travaux Publics dans la Chine Impériale* (Paris, 1964), p. 47.

66. Ko Shou-li, *Ko Tuan-su-kung Chi, Chia-hsün*, B.21a; Hai Jui, *Hai Jui Chi*, pp. 93–94.

67. Hai Jui, *Hai Jui Chi*, pp. 93–94.

68. *Ta-Ming Hui-tien*, 30.892.

69. E.g., Chu Hsi, *Chu-tzu Yü-lei*, 128.7b.

70. Ku Yen-wu, *Jih-chih Lu Chi-shih* (Shanghai, 1930), 12.17b.

71. Chung-li Chang, *The Chinese Gentry: Studies on Their Role in Nineteenth-Century Chinese Society* (Seattle, 1955), pp. 51–70; Lien-

sheng Yang, *Les Aspects Économiques des Travaux Publics dans la Chine Impériale*, pp. 8–12.
72. Fu I-ling, *Ming-ch'ing Nung-ts'un She-hui Ching-chi* (Peking, 1961), pp. 68–189.

ROMEYN TAYLOR *Yüan Origins of the Wei-so System*

1. Reported strength was 1,198,442 in 1392, 3,150,000 in the mid-1440s, and more than 4,000,000 in late Ming times. The numbers may have decreased greatly in mid-Ming times. See Charles O. Hucker, "Governmental Organization of the Ming Dynasty," *Harvard Journal of Asiatic Studies*, XXI (1958), 57.
2. *Ta-Ming Hui-tien* (Wan-li ed.), 18.1a–8a, gives the "present quotas" of *t'un-t'ien* totaling 2,138,407 *ch'ing* (with *mou* excluded from the sum). The reported total cultivated area in 1602 was 11,618,949 *ch'ing* (total rounded off to nearest *ch'ing*). The latter figure is cited in Ping-ti Ho, *Studies on the Population of China, 1368–1953* (Cambridge, Mass., 1959), p. 102. Professor Ho warns against excessive trust in totals reported for tax purposes, however, since they were commonly understated.
3. *Ming-shih* (Po-na ed.), 89.1a.   4. *Ibid.*, 128.3b.
5. Wu Han, "Ming-tai ti Chün-ping," in his *Tu-shih Cha-chi* (Peking, 1956), pp. 94–95.
6. *Ming T'ai-tsu Shih-lu* (photolithographic reproduction, 1940), 24.3a–b.
7. Henry Serruys, "Remains of Mongol Customs in China during the Early Ming Period," *Monumenta Serica*, XVI (1957), 144–46.
8. Wei Ch'ing-yüan, *Ming-tai Huang-ts'e Chih-tu* (Peking, 1961), pp. 12–13.
9. Wang Yü-ch'üan, "Ming-tai Chün-t'un Chih-tu ti Li-shih Yüan-yüan chi ch'i T'e-tien," *Lishi Yanjiu*, no. 59 (1959), pp. 45–55.
10. Charles O. Hucker, "The Yüan Contribution to Censorial History," *Bulletin of the Institute of History and Philology*, Academia Sinica, extra vol. no. 4 (1960), 219–27.
11. Ch'en Yin-k'o, "Fu-ping chih Ch'ien-ch'i Shih-liao Shih-shih," *Bulletin of the Institute of History and Philology*, Academia Sinica, VII (1937), 275–86. Ch'en held that the *fu-ping* from the time of its origin in the Western Wei era until the establishment of the Sui dynasty was a Hsien-pi institution composed of full-time soldiers. The *fu-ping*, in his view, became a military-agricultural Chinese institution only in the Sui dynasty, and it retained this character in the T'ang period. Ch'en's views are noted in Robert des Rotours,

trans., *Traité des Fonctionnaires et Traité de l'Armée* (2 vols.; Leiden, 1947), I, xxvi–xxx. Des Rotours stated that he was hesitant to accept Ch'en's conclusion. If Ch'en is correct, however, at least in regarding the *fu-ping* as originally a Hsien-pi institution rather than a Chinese one, this would roughly parallel a Mongol origin of the Yüan-Ming *wei-so* system.

12. Serruys, "Remains of Mongol Customs . . . ," pp. 142–43. H. F. Schurmann has also drawn attention to this division between the Chinese bureaucracy and the steppe-originated military system during the Yüan period. See his "Problems of Political Organization during the Yüan Dynasty," in *International Congress of Orientalists* (Moscow, 1963), V, 26–30.

13. B. Vladimirtsov, *Le Regime Social des Mongols: Le Feodalisme Nomade* (Paris, 1948), pp. 133, 142–43.

14. *Ibid.*, p. 134.   15. *Ibid.*, pp. 141–42.

16. *Ibid.*, p. 132.   17. *Ibid.*, p. 134.   18. *Ibid.*, p. 135.

19. K. A. Wittfogel, "Public Office in the Liao Dynasty and the Chinese Examination System," *Harvard Journal of Asiatic Studies*, X (1947), 36.

20. Vladimirtsov, *Le Regime Social des Mongols*, pp. 156–57. Kesig denotes a duty taken in rotation (*ibid.*, p. 209, n. 11). In this context, the term refers to the practice of dividing the *kesig* into units that stood watches.

21. *Ibid.*, pp. 152–55.

22. H. F. Schurmann, *Economic Structure of the Yüan Dynasty* (Cambridge, Mass., 1956), pp. 2–4, 7.

23. Paul Ratchnevsky, *Un Code des Yuan* (Paris, 1933), p. x.

24. Schurmann, *Economic Structure of the Yüan Dynasty*, pp. 3–5.

25. For a list of offices having *ta-lu-hua-ch'ih* and for ethnic origins of the seal-holders, see Yanai Watari, *Yüan-tai Meng-Han-Se-mu Tai-yü K'ao*, trans. into Chinese by Ch'en Chieh and Ch'en Ch'ing-ch'üan (Taipei, 1963), pp. 47–65. On recruitment of officials from among the *noyan*, see Vladimirtsov, *Le Regime Social des Mondols*, p. 183. On recruitment of officials from the *noyan* and the *kesig*, see Meng Ssu-ming, *Yüan-tai She-hui Chieh-chi Chih-tu* (Peking, 1938), pp. 46–47. Although membership in the *kesig* was generally hereditary, there were some *se-mu-jen* and *Han-jen* officers until the reign of Ying-tsung (1321–23), when the *Han-jen* were removed. See Yanai Watari, *Yüan-tai Meng-Han-Se-mu Tai-yü K'ao*, pp. 67–69.

26. *Li-tai Chih-kuan Piao* (Shanghai, 1937), 55.15b.

27. Cheng Kuang-yü and Hsü Sheng-mu, *Chung-kuo Li-shih Ti-t'u Chi* (Taipei, 1955), II, 75.

28. *Yüan-shih* (Po-na ed.), 92.7b.
29. *Hsü T'ung-chih* (Shanghai, 1936), p. 4061.
30. K'o Shao-min, *Hsin Yüan-shih* (1922 ed.), 55.29b–33a.
31. *Yüan-shih*, 91.4b.
32. K'o Shao-min, *Hsin Yüan-shih*, 55.19b–21a.
33. *Ibid.*, ch. 57; *Li-tai Chih-kuan Piao*, 52.22a.
34. Ratchnevsky, *Un Code des Yuan*, p. 146, n. 5; Yanai Watari, *Yüan-ch'ao Chih-tu K'ao*, trans. into Chinese by Ch'en Chieh and Ch'en Ch'ing-ch'üan (Taipei, 1963), p. 36.
35. Yanai Watari, *Yüan-ch'ao Chih-tu K'ao*, pp. 28–29; Meng Ssu-ming, *Yüan-tai She-hui Chieh-chi Chih-tu*, pp. 33–34.
36. Vladimirtsov, *Le Regime Social des Mongols*, p. 183.
37. Yanai Watari, *Yüan-tai Meng-Han-Se-mu Tai-yü K'ao*, pp. 56–59.
38. Wang Yü-ch'üan, "Ming-tai Chün-t'un Chih-tu," pp. 44–49.
39. Huang Yü-chia, "Sung-Yüan T'u-ti Ssu-yu-chih Fa-chan," *Chin-ling Hsüeh-pao*, IX (1939), 5. Huang's figure is 172,000 *ch'ing*, 21 *mou*, which Schurmann has misread as 172,221 *mou*, thereby greatly understating the size of this sector of the economy. See Schurmann, *Economic Structure of the Yüan Dynasty*, p. 29.
40. Fan Wen-lan, *Chung-kuo T'ung-shih Chien-pien* (Shanghai, 1947), p. 478.
41. *Yüan-shih*, 100.7a–11a.
42. *Ibid.*, 100.13b–28b.
43. Ratchnevsky, *Un Code des Yuan*, pp. 241–42.
44. Wang Yü-ch'üan, "Ming-tai Chün-t'un Chih-tu," pp. 50–52.
45. Meng Ssu-ming, *Yüan-tai She-hui Chieh-chi Chih-tu*, pp. 25–36; Yanai Watari, *Yüan-tai Meng-Han-Se-mu Tai-yü K'ao*, pp. 6–29.
46. *Hsü Wen-hsien T'ung-k'ao* (Shanghai, 1936), p. 3885.
47. *Yüan-shih*, 98.2a–b.
48. *Hsü Wen-hsien T'ung-k'ao*, p. 3884.
49. Chang Ch'i-yün, *Chung-kuo Chün-shih Shih-lüeh* (Taipei, 1956), p. 35, says the *t'an-ma-ch'ih chün* were registered as "classified peoples." However, the lists of elements among *se-mu-jen* provided in Yanai Watari, *Yüan-tai Meng-Han-Se-mu Tai-yü K'ao*, and Meng Ssu-ming, *Yüan-tai She-hui Chieh-chi Chih-tu*, do not include Ch'i-tan, Nü-chen, and Chinese, although Meng Ssu-ming shows that in unofficial usage the term *se-mu-jen* might be stretched to cover Ch'i-tan and Nü-chen (p. 32). The *t'an-ma-ch'ih chün* must therefore have been counted as *Han-jen*, for the most part.
50. Ratchnevsky, *Un Code des Yuan*, p. lvii.
51. Regulations concerning inheritance of military offices are discussed in Ratchnevsky, *Un Code des Yuan*, pp. xliii–xliv.
52. Yanai Watari, *Yüan-tai Meng-Han-Se-mu Tai-yü K'ao*, pp. 42–48.

53. Meng Ssu-ming, *Yüan-tai She-hui Chieh-chi Chih-tu,* p. 45.
54. Ratchnevsky, *Un Code des Yuan,* p. xlvi. The author's word is *étranger,* which apparently is intended to mean "foreigner." In any case, the rule made it impossible for a Chinese family to increase the number of offices under its control by winning promotions.
55. Meng Ssu-ming, *Yüan-tai She-hui Chieh-chi Chih-tu,* pp. 45–46.
56. *Yüan-shih,* 98.3a.
57. Meng Ssu-ming, *Yüan-tai She-hui Chieh-chi Chih-tu,* p. 44.
58. *Ibid.,* pp. 87 ff.
59. Ratchnevsky, *Un Code des Yuan,* pp. 141–42.
60. *Ibid.,* p. lxvii.   61. *Ibid.,* p. lxiii.
62. *Hsü Wen-hsien T'ung-k'ao,* p. 3886.   63. *Ibid.,* p. 3888.
64. See Romeyn Taylor, "Social Origins of the Ming Dynasty, 1351–1360," *Monumenta Serica,* XXII (1963), 31–32.
65. K'o Shao-min, *Hsin Yüan-shih,* 47.14a.
66. *Ming T'ai-tsu Shih-lu,* 3.3a. The new office was the *hsing-kuo i yüan-shuai-fu.* The word *i,* meaning "wing," was commonly used in Yüan times to designate part of an army.
67. *Ming T'ai-tsu Shih-lu,* 4.2a–2b.
68. *Ibid.,* 4.3b.   69. *Li-tai Chih-kuan Piao,* 46.1a–3a.
70. *Ming T'ai-tsu Shih-lu,* 6.8a.   71. *Ibid.,* 14.5a.
72. Wu-chou, Wu-yüan, Ch'u-chou, Chen-chiang, and Yang-chou. See *Ming T'ai-tsu Shih-lu,* 6.7a, 6.7b, 7.7a, 5.2a, and 8.1b, respectively.
73. *Ibid.,* 14.5a–14.6a.   74. *Ibid.,* 14.10a.   75. *Ibid.,* 19.2a.
76. *Ming-shih,* 76.18a–19a.
77. *Li-tai Chih-kuan Piao,* 57.12a–14b; Hucker, "Governmental Organization of the Ming Dynasty," pp. 62–63.
78. *Ming T'ai-tsu Shih-lu,* 14.5a.   79. *Ibid.,* 27.2b.
80. *Hsü T'ung-chih,* p. 4061.
81. *Ta-Ming Hui-tien,* 118.2a.
82. K'o Shao-min, *Hsin Yüan-shih,* 86.3b–4b.
83. Lung Wen-pin, *Ming Hui-yao* (Peking, 1956), p. 769.
84. Huang Chin, *Huang Ming K'ai-kuo Kung-ch'en Lu* (Ming Cheng-te ed.), 13.24a.
85. *Yüan-shih,* 91.8a.   86. *Ming T'ai-tsu Shih-lu,* 4.3b.
87. *Ibid.,* 6.2a.   88. *Ibid.,* 6.1b.   89. *Ibid.,* 12.1b.
90. Hsia Hsieh, *Hsin-chiao Ming T'ung-chien* (Taipei, 1962), p. 113.
91. Wang Yü-ch'üan, *Ming-tai ti Chün-t'un* (Peking, 1965), pp. 29–33.
92. *Ta-Ming Hui-tien,* 18.1a–8a.
93. K'o Shao-min, *Hsin Yüan-shih,* 86.3b–4b.
94. *Ming T'ai-tsu Shih-lu,* 17.4a–b.
95. *Hsü Wen-hsien T'ung-k'ao,* p. 2891.
96. Wei Ch'ing-yüan, *Ming-tai Huang-ts'e Chih-tu,* p. 14.

97. For Ming "yellow register" procedures, see Ping-ti Ho, *Studies on the Population of China, 1368–1953*, pp. 3–23; and Wei Ch'ing-yüan, *Ming-tai Huang-ts'e Chih-tu*, especially pp. 54–72 on military registration.
98. Ratchnevsky, *Un Code des Yuan*, pp. xxv–xxvii.
99. *Ta-Ming T'ai-tsu Yü-chih Chi* (Ming palace ed.), 1.6a–7a.
100. Chief Councilor Hsü Ta, Chief Administrators Ch'ang Yü-ch'un, Liao Yung-chung, and Censor-in-chief T'ang Ho.
101. *Ta-Ming Hui-tien*, 118.8a.
102. *Ming-shih*, 69.17b.
103. *Ming T'ai-tsu Shih-lu*, 183.3a.
104. Wei Ch'ing-yüan, *Ming-tai Huang-ts'e Chih-tu*, p. 62.
105. See *Ming-shih*, ch. 105.
106. Lu Jung, *Shu-yüan Tsa-chi Chai-ch'ao* (*Chi-lu Hui-pien* ed.), 184.21b–22a.
107. Wei Ch'ing-yüan, *Ming-tai Huang-ts'e Chih-tu*, pp. 54–72.
108. Cf. the table on p. 25 of Taylor, "Social Origins of the Ming Dynasty, 1351–1360"; the number should be reduced by 25 (the number of nonhereditary titles) and increased by three, representing Chang Wen, Na-ha-ch'u, and Chang Ch'üan.
109. Taylor, "Social Origins of the Ming Dynasty, 1351–1360," pp. 24–35.
110. Serruys, "The Mongols in China during the Hung-wu Period," *Mélanges Chinois et Bouddhiques*, XI (1956–1959), 1–328.
111. *Yüan-shih*, 98.1a–b, before proceeding to a description of the Yüan military organization, purported to show that the flourishing or decline of dynasties had been tied to the success or failure of their military systems. After recounting the Mongols' conquests, it asks, "How was this not a flourishing?"

JUNG-PANG LO *Policy Formulation and Decision-Making on Issues Respecting Peace and War*

1. Richard C. Snyder, H. W. Bruck, and Burton Spain, *Foreign Policy Decision Making: An Approach to the Study of International Politics* (Glencoe, Ill., 1962), pp. 1 and 10. The studies were initiated as a consequence of American involvement in the Far East: the decision to intervene in the Korean War in 1950 and the conclusion of the Japanese Peace Treaty in 1951.
2. Snyder *et al.*, *Foreign Policy Decision Making*, p. 197.
3. Richard C. Snyder, "A Decision-making Approach to the Study of Political Phenomena," in Roland Young, ed., *Approaches to the Study of Politics* (London, 1958), p. 10.

4. Snyder *et al.*, *Foreign Policy Decision Making*, pp. 43 and 94; Snyder, "A Decision-making Approach," p. 16.
5. Herbert McClosky, "Concerning Strategies for a Science of International Politics," in Snyder *et al.*, *Foreign Policy Decision Making*, p. 189.
6. Arthur F. Wright, "On the Uses of Generalization in the Study of Chinese History," in Louis Gottschalk, ed., *Generalizations in the Writing of History* (Chicago, 1962), pp. 36–58; and Arthur F. Wright, "Sui Yang-ti: Personality and Stereotype," in Arthur F. Wright, ed., *The Confucian Persuasion* (Stanford, 1960), pp. 47–76.
7. Karl A. Wittfogel, *Oriental Despotism: A Comparative Study of Total Power* (New Haven, 1957), p. 106.
8. Wittfogel, *Oriental Despotism*, pp. 106–7.
9. *Hsün-tzu* (sptk ed.), 9.14a.
10. *Shang-tzu* (or *Shang-chün Shu*; sptk ed.), 31.10b.
11. On using the judgment of history to prescribe the action and behavior of the rulers, see *Ta-Tai Li-chi* (sptk ed.), 3.3a–5a, 8.7b–9b. From the official historiographer *(shih-kuan)* of Early Chou came the grandee secretary *(yü-shih ta-fu)* of Former Han, who had the duty of remonstrance, and the imperial censors *(yü-shih)* of later times. See Liu I-cheng, *Kuo-shih Yao-i* (Shanghai, 1948), pp. 33–34.
12. See statements in *Tso-chuan* under the 11th year of Duke Yin and the 11th year of Duke Hsi; Li Kou, *Li Chih-chiang Wen-chi* (sptk ed.), 2.7b–13b; and Chang Ping-lin, "Chien-lun," in *Chang-shih Ts'ung-shu* (Hangchow, 1919), 2.6b and 2.13b.
13. See Ku Yen-wu, *Jih-chih Lu* (*Wan-yu Wen-k'u* ed.), 9.6. Wang Ch'in-jo, ed., *Ts'e-fu Yüan-kuei* (reprint ed.; Hong Kong, 1960), chs. 469–70 and 477 *passim*, lists many instances of ministers using their prerogatives of *feng-po* to block improper actions of the emperor. An early, well-known case was that of chancellor Wang Chia, who repeatedly rejected the edict of the Han Emperor Ai ennobling his favorite Tung Hsien in the year 1 b.c. See *Han-shu* (Po-na ed.), 86.7a–17a; cf. Homer H. Dubs, *History of the Former Han Dynasty*, III (Baltimore, 1955), 5.

Besides *feng-po*, another device was refusal by members of the Secretariat *(chung-shu sheng)* to draft imperial decrees even on the direct order of the emperor. A third way was to cross out key words in decrees and return them to the emperor *(t'u-kuei)*. This was the way by which the supervising secretary Li Fan blocked the appointment of a bribe-taking official as chancellor by the T'ang emperor Hsien-tsung. Crossing out the word "chancellor," he wrote "no" beside it. See Chu Kuo-chen, *Yung-chuang Hsiao-p'in* (reprint ed., 1959), 3.54; and Ku Yen-wu, *Jih-chih Lu*, 9.6.

The duty of the supervising secretaries, as stated in the *T'ang Liu Tien* (reprint ed.; Kyoto, 1935), 8.14a, was to use their power of *feng-po* (sealed dissent) to check on the acts and policies of the emperor. The T'ang emperor T'ai-tsung constantly reminded his ministers that he did not want men who knew only how to correct the wording of official documents; he wanted men who would correct him and reject his decrees when he was wrong. See *Cheng-kuan Cheng-yao* (SPPY ed.), 1.12a. Thus, as a modern authority on Ming history has observed, "Before the time of the first Ming emperor, under the system of the Three Departments, the power of the emperor was actually limited." See Wu Han, *Ming T'ai-tsu* (reprint ed.; Peking, 1953), pp. 108–11 *passim*; quotation on p. 109.

14. This was the case at least in the Han period. The *t'ing-i*, a full-scale conference of ministers in the court to decide on major questions of state, perhaps operated similarly in later dynasties. The *Han-shu* mentions many occasions when important issues were debated in court, sometimes by small groups of high officials in the presence of the emperor and sometimes in plenary meetings of ministers convened by the chancellor on instructions from the emperor, where decisions were reached by majority vote. The question of war or peace with the Hsiung-nu in 120 B.C. (*Han-shu* 52.15b–19a) and the question of sending more troops to Chu-yai (Hainan island) or evacuation in 46 B.C. (*Han-shu* 64B.14a) were decided by such court sessions. In 33 B.C., when the question of transferring the Kan-ch'uan Shrine to the capital was debated and the vote was fifty in favor and eight against, the grandee secretary (in charge of policy review) Chang T'an declared, "Your minister has heard that to consult widely and to follow the view of the majority is to conform with the will of Heaven. 'The Great Plan' (*Hung-fan*, a section of the ancient classic *Shu-ching*) states, 'When consulting three men, accept the opinion of two.' In other words, the principle is for the few to accept the view of the many." See *Han-shu* 25B.11a.

The quotation from "The Great Plan" refers to the making of decisions about important matters of state. "When consulting three men, accept the opinion of two. When you (the ruler) have an important question (to decide), consult your own mind, consult the officials, consult the people, and consult the tortoise [shell] and the milfoil." The questions to be resolved were both domestic and external, the external questions being peace and war. In his annotated translation, *Shoo King* (*The Chinese Classics*, 1960 reprint; III, Book 4, pp. 335–38 and note 25 on p. 337), James Legge calls this practice a form of divination and scoffs at it as superstitious. In a way this was true. The ancient Chinese used the tortoise shell and the milfoil, just as modern men might toss a coin, to help them make up their minds in difficult decisions.

On decision-making in the Han period, see Yang Shu-fan, "Hsi-Han Chung-yang Cheng-fu I-shih Chih-tu," *Ta-lu Tsa-chih*, XVI, no. 9 (May 15, 1958), 9–13.

15. "According to practice, in all major matters of war and the state, each of the members of the Secretariat wrote his opinion and signed his name. This was known as 'five-flowers decision' *(wu-hua p'an-shih)*. It was then studied by the presidents and vice presidents of the Secretariat and criticized and corrected by the supervising secretaries before promulgation as an order by the emperor. Thus, there were seldom errors of policy" (*Cheng-kuan Cheng-yao*, 1.12a). Yeh Meng-te, in his *Shih-lin Yen-yü (Ts'ung-shu Chi-ch'eng* ed.), 3.25–26, states that this was the system from Han to T'ang. During the Sui-T'ang period, while the secretaries of the Hanlin Academy drafted routine orders, "important and major matters of frontier defense" were in most cases decided by the chancellors, who themselves drafted the decrees (Yeh Meng-te, *Shih-lin Yen-yü*, 5.48). Besides Yeh Meng-te (1077–1148), Ku Yen-wu (1613–82), and other historians of the past, modern Chinese scholars have also pointed out that in the T'ang period the authority of the emperor was restricted and that it was balanced by the authority of the bureaucracy. As Ch'ien Mu has written, "In the Sui and T'ang periods, when they were in the Chancellery and were subordinates of the chancellor, the remonstrating officials checked and restrained the Son of Heaven; they did not check and restrain the chancellor" (*Kuo-shih Ta-kang*, 1947 reprint; II, pt. 6, ch. 31, p. 392). Tseng Fan-k'ang has written, "In conclusion, during the T'ang period, the supervisory powers of the Chancellery were mainly aimed at checking the policies of the rulers' orders and decrees . . . and thus placed legal restraint on imperial power." See his *Chung-kuo Cheng-chih Chih-tu Shih* (Taipei, 1954), p. 223.

16. *Ming T'ai-tsu Shih-lu* (photolithographic reprint, 1940), 29.6a–7b; *Ming-shih* (1884 ed.), 72.1a. According to Huang Tso, "In decisions over important matters and major questions, the ministers only made their reports and received their orders." See his *Han-lin Chi (Ts'ung-shu Chi-ch'eng* ed.), 2.17–18.

17. Huang Tso, *Han-lin Chi*, 2.11–12, 8.100. Cf. *Ming-cheng T'ung-tsung*, ch. 7, cited in Wu Chi-hua, "Ming Jen-Hsüan Shih Nei-ko Chih-tu chih Pien yü Huan-kuan Chien-yüeh Hsiang-ch'üan chih Huo," in *Chung-yang Yen-chiu-yüan Li-shih Yü-yen Yen-chiu-so Chi-k'an*, XXI (December, 1960), 383.

18. Huang Tso, *Han-lin Chi*, 2.18, 8.109–110; *Ming-shih*, 72.1b; *Hsü T'ung-tien (Wan-yu Wen-k'u* ed.), 25.1269, col. 1; and Chao I, *Nien-erh-shih Cha-chi* (reprint ed., 1962), 33.701–2.

19. *Hsü T'ung-tien*, 25.1269.
20. *Ming-shih*, 72.1b.
21. Harold D. Lasswell and Abraham Kaplan, *Power and Society: A Framework for Political Inquiry* (rev. ed.; New Haven, 1961), pp. 75–76.
22. Wu Chi-hua, "Ming Jen-Hsüan Shih Nei-ko Chih-tu," p. 392.
23. *Ming-shih*, 196.21a. Earlier, in 1495, during a debate on the question of Annam, "the Grand Secretary Hsü Po declared: '. . . Moreover, in major issues, the court has never failed to consult the ministers.' . . . The emperor (Hsiao-tsung, 1487–1505) agreed and thereupon accepted the view of the majority." Chang Ching-hsin, *Yü-Chiao Chi* (*Ts'ung-shu Chi-ch'eng* ed.), 8.111–12.
24. Chao I, *Hai-yü Ts'ung-k'ao* (1796 ed.), 18.24a.
25. H. D. Lasswell and A. Kaplan, *Power and Society*, pp. 134, 138.
26. Charles O. Hucker, "Governmental Organization of the Ming Dynasty," *Harvard Journal of Asiatic Studies*, XXI (1958), 63–64.
27. *Ming-shih*, 72.1b; Chao I, *Nien-erh-shih Cha-chi*, 33.702–3.
28. *Ming-shih*, 73.6b.
29. *Ibid.*, 164.26a–b; Chao I, *Nien-erh-shih Cha-chi*, 35.737.
30. *Ming-shih*, 72.4a.
31. *Ibid.*, 73.19b–20a.
32. Huang Tso, *Han-lin Chi*, 2.20.
33. Chu Kuo-chen, *Yung-chuang Hsiao-p'in*, 8.180.
34. Inaba Kunsan, *Shinchō Zenshi* (Chinese translation; 1914), I, ch. 12, p. 134.
35. Charles O. Hucker, "Confucianism and the Chinese Censorial System," in Arthur F. Wright, ed., *Confucianism and Chinese Civilization* (New York, 1964), pp. 50–76.
36. Ku Yen-wu, *Jih-chih Lu*, 9.6a. Also see *Yüan-chien Lei-hsien* (Shanghai, 1883 ed.), 86.10a.
37. Ku Ying-t'ai, *Ming-shih Chi-shih Pen-mo* (1936 ed.), 28.57; Chao I, *Nien-erh-shih Cha-chi*, 35.737.
38. Ku Yen-wu, *Jih-chih Lu*, 9.5b.
39. Ch'iu Chün, *Ta-hsüeh Yen-i Pu* (1605 ed.), 8.9a–b.
40. Chao I, *Nien-erh-shih Cha-chi*, 36.737.
41. Huang Tso, *Han-lin Chi*, 8.113–114.
42. Ku Yen-wu, *Jih-chih Lu*, 9.7; Huang Tso, *Han-lin Chi*, 6.71; *Hsü Wen-hsien T'ung-k'ao* (*Wan-yu Wen-k'u* ed.), 52.3261, col. 3. For views of some modern scholars see Yü Teng, "Ming-tai Chien-ch'a Chih-tu Kai-shu," *Chin-ling Hsüeh-pao*, VI, no. 2 (November 1936), 227–28; and Tseng Fan-k'ang, *Chung-kuo Cheng-chih Chih-tu Shih*, p. 229.
43. Yen Ts'ung-chien, *Shu-yü Chou-tzu Lu* (reprint ed., 1930), 16.1a; Ku Ying-t'ai, *Ming-shih Chi-shih Pen-mo*, 14.80.

44. *Huai-nan-tzu*, "T'ai-tsu Hsün," based on *Tso-chuan*, 23d year of Duke Chao.
45. T'an Hsi-ssu, *Ming Ta-cheng Tsuan-yao* (late Ch'ing reprint), 21.36a.
46. See *Shou* in *Dai Kan Wa Jiten* (Tokyo, 1955), III, 902.
47. *Ming T'ai-tsu Shih-lu*, 68.4b–5a. Also in Ch'en Jen-hsi, *Huang-Ming Shih-fa Lu* (Ming ed.), 6.31a–b. T'an Hsi-ssu (*Ming Ta-cheng Tsuan-yao*, 3.14a–b) declares that the event took place after T'ai-tsu read a passage in the *Ta-hsüeh Yen-i* by Chen Te-hsiu (1178–1235) suggesting that a ruler had the duty of preserving life and should not indulge in war. Cf. *Ming T'ai-tsu Shih-lu*, 68.2a–b.
48. Huang Chang-chien, "Lun Huang-Ming Tsu-hsün-lu Pan-hsing Nien-tai ping Lun Ming-ch'u Feng-chien Chu-wang Chih-tu," *Chung-yang Yen-chiu-yüan Li-shih Yü-yen Yen-chiu-so Chi-k'an*, XXXII (1961), 119–20.
49. The passage on T'ai-tsu's foreign policy may be found in *T'u-shu Chi-ch'eng*, "pien-i," 3.2b–3b; in Wu Han, "Shih-liu Shih-chi Ch'ien chih Chung-kuo yü Nan-yang," *Tsing-hua Hsüeh-pao*, XI, no. 1 (1936), 148–49; and Ishihara Michihiro, "Kō-Min So-kun no Sei-ritsu," in *Shimizu Hakushi tsuitō Kinen Mindaishi Ronsō* (Tokyo, 1962), pp. 5–6. Hsi-yang may be Chola on the east coast of India.
50. For a list of Ming works that quoted the Ancestral Instructions on policies toward Japan, see Ishihara Michihiro, "Kō-Min So-kun no Seiritsu," pp. 7–9.
51. Yen Ts'ung-chien, *Shu-yü Chou-tzu-lu*, 2.2b.
52. T'an Hsi-ssu, *Ming Ta-cheng Tsuan-yao*, 13.20b.
53. Mao Yüan-i, ed., *Wu-pei Chih* (1617 ed.), 223.1b.
54. T'ai-tsu's proclamation to neighboring states in 1368, found in Li Wen-feng, ed., *Yüeh Ch'iao Shu* (preface 1540; mimeographed ed.), 2.9b–10a, and Chang Ching-hsin, *Yü-Chiao Chi*, 3.33.
55. T'an Hsi-ssu, *Ming Ta-cheng Tsuan-yao*, 6.25a.
56. Ch'en Jen-hsi, *Huang-Ming Shih-fa Lu*, 6.28b.
57. Ho Ch'iao-yüan, *Wang-heng Chi*, 1.1a–b, in his *Ming-shan Ts'ang* (Ming ed.).
58. Wu Han, "Shih-liu Shih-chi Ch'ien chih Chung-kuo yü Nan-yang," p. 148.
59. Yen Ts'ung-chien, *Shu-yü Chou-tzu Lu*, 15.1b–2a. Also see Haneda Toru, "Timur to Eiraku Tei (Timur no Shina Seibatsu Keihaku)," *Geibun*, III, no. 10 (1912), 343–60.
60. Hsü Yü-hu, "Cheng Ho Hsia Hsi-yang Yüan-yin chih Hsin-t'an," *Ta-lu Tsa-chih*, XVI, no. 1 (January 15, 1958), 19–23.
61. *Ming-shih*, 321.3b.
62. Ngo Si-lien, *Dai-Viet Su-ky Toan-tho*, cited in Yamamoto Tatsuro, *Annanshi no Kenkyū* (Tokyo, 1950), p. 285.

63. Yen Ts'ung-chien, *Shu-yü Chou-tzu Lu*, 5.8a–b; T'an Hsi-ssu, *Ming Ta-cheng Tsuan-yao*, 14.13a–b; Ku Ying-t'ai, *Ming-shih Chi-shih Pen-mo*, 22.3.

64. *Ming-shih*, 7.7b–8b, 149.6b–7a, 151.10b; Yen Ts'ung-chien, *Shu-yü Chou-tzu Lu*, 17.6b; T'an Hsi-ssu, *Ming Ta-cheng Tsuan-yao*, 16.16a–18a.

65. Ku Ying-t'ai, *Ming-shih Chi-shih Pen-mo*, 22.10.

66. *Ming Jen-tsung Shih-lu* (photolithographic reprint, 1940), 2.2b–3a.

67. *Ming Hsüan-tsung Shih-lu* (photolithographic reprint, 1940), 16.1a–3a; Ho Ch'iao-yüan, *Wang-heng Chi*, 2.13b–14b; Ku Ying-t'ai, *Ming-shih Chi-shih Pen-mo*, 22.11.

68. Hsia Hsieh, *Ming T'ung-chien* (1896 ed.), 19.4a–b.

69. *Ming Hsüan-tsung Shih-lu*, 24.5b–6a.   70. *Ibid.*, 32.12a–b.

71. Yen Ts'ung-chien, *Shu-yü Chou-tzu Lu*, 5.22a–b; Li Wen-feng, *Yüeh Ch'iao Shu*, 6.13b–14b; Ho Ch'iao-yüan, *Wang-heng Chi*, 2.13b–14b; T'an Hsi-ssu, *Ming Ta-cheng Tsuan-yao*, 18.23b–24a; Ku Ying-t'ai, *Ming-shih Chi-shih Pen-mo*, 22.14; *Ming-shih*, 148.5b. Also see *San-ch'ao Sheng-lun Lu*, purported to be by Yang Shih-ch'i, in *Sheng-ch'ao I-shih Erh-pien* (1842 ed.), 1.30b–33a.

72. Yen Ts'ung-chien, *Shu-yü Chou-tzu Lu*, 5.22b–23a.

73. Ku Ying-t'ai, *Ming-shih Chi-shih Pen-mo*, 22.21.

74. The identification is made in D. G. E. Hall, *A History of Southeast Asia* (London, 1955), pp. 38–39.

75. Ku Ying-t'ai, *Ming-shih Chi-shih Pen-mo*, 30.3.

76. *Ming-shih*, 304.8a; Ku Ying-t'ai, *Ming-shih Chi-shih Pen-mo*, 29.72.

77. Ku Ying-t'ai, *Ming-shih Chi-shih Pen-mo*, 30.6.

78. Yen Ts'ung-chien, *Shu-yü Chou-tzu Lu*, 5.26a; T'an Hsi-ssu, *Ming Ta-cheng Tsuan-yao*, 32.19a.

79. T'an Hsi-ssu, *Ming Ta-cheng Tsuan-yao*, 32.19a; Yen Ts'ung-chien, *Shu-yü Chou-tzu Lu*, 5.26a; and Huang Tso, *Han-lin Chi*, 8.109–110.

80. *Ming-shih*, 321.25a; Yen Ts'ung-chien, *Shu-yü Chou-tzu Lu*, 6.4a–b; Li Wen-feng, *Yüeh Ch'iao Shu*, 12.1a–2b; Ho Ch'iao-yüan, *Wang-heng Chi*, 2.20a; T'an Hsi-ssu, *Ming Ta-cheng Tsuan-yao*, 52.21b.

81. Yen Ts'ung-chien, *Shu-yü Chou-tzu Lu*, 6.5a; Li Wen-feng, *Yüeh Ch'iao Shu*, 12.2b–4b.

82. Yen Ts'ung-chien, *Shu-yü Chou-tzu Lu*, 6.6a; T'an Hsi-ssu, *Ming Ta-cheng Tsuan-yao*, 52.21a–b.

83. Yen Ts'ung-chien, *Shu-yü Chou-tzu Lu*, 6.4b–5a.

84. *Ming-shih*, 203.6b, 7a–8b; T'an Hsi-ssu, *Ming Ta-cheng Tsuan-yao*, 52.22a–23b.

85. *Ming-shih*, 321.26a; Ho Ch'iao-yüan, *Wang-heng Chi*, 2.20a–b; T'an Hsi-ssu, *Ming Ta-cheng Tsuan-yao*, 52.23a. Texts of the memorials by P'an Chen and P'an Tan are in *Ming-shih*, 203.9a–b, 10a.

86. *Ibid.*, 321.27a; Yen Ts'ung-chien, *Shu-yü Chou-tzu Lu*, 6.9a.
87. T'an Hsi-ssu, *Ming Ta-cheng Tsuan-yao*, 52.25a.
88. *Ming-shih*, 321.27b, 198.17a.
89. *Ibid.*, 321.28a.
90. *Ibid.*, 149.27b.
91. Ku Ying-t'ai, *Ming-shih Chi-shih Pen-mo*, 58.78.
92. *Ibid.*; T'an Hsi-ssu, *Ming Ta-cheng Tsuan-yao*, 54.31b–32b; *Ming-shih*, 149.27b–28a.
93. *Ming-shih*, 252.4b.
94. *Ibid.*, 257.20a. For the whole story, see Chao I, *Nien-erh-shih Cha-chi*, 39.739–740.
95. *Sun-tzu* (SPTK ed.), 1.1a.
96. Theodore Abel, "The Element of Decision in the Pattern of War," *American Sociological Review*, VI, no. 6 (December, 1941), 854–55. A study of 25 major wars showed that the decision to wage war is usually based on careful weighing of chances and anticipation of consequences and is reached far in advance of the actual outbreak of hostilities.
97. Hucker, "Governmental Organization of the Ming Dynasty," pp. 65–66.

RAY HUANG   *Fiscal Administration During the Ming Dynasty*

1. Marianne Rieger, "Zur Finanz und Agrargeschichte der Ming-Dynastie, 1368–1643," *Sinica*, XII (1937), 130–43, 235–52.
2. *Ming-shih* (Po-na ed.), 206.24.
3. *Ibid.*, 224.21.
4. Shen Pang, *Wan-shu Tsa-chi* (reprint; Peking, 1961), pp. 86–90.
5. *Ibid.*, p. 48.
6. *Hui-chou-fu Fu-i Ch'üan-shu* (1620 ed.; Library of Congress microfilm), p. 4.
7. *Ch'ing-shih* (Taipei, 1961), II, 1464.
8. *Ming-shih*, 72.11, 72.13.
9. That the salaries of Ming officials were unreasonably low has been commented upon by many historians. See *Ming-shih*, 82.16; Chao I, *Nien-erh-shih Cha-Chi* (*Ts'ung-shu Chi-ch'eng* ed.), 32.686.
10. *Ming-shih*, 82.20.
11. Sun Ch'eng-tse, *Ch'un-ming Meng-yü Lu* (Ku-hsiang-chai pocket ed.), 35.15.
12. *Ming-shih*, 157.8.
13. *Ming-shih* 111 lists 91 ministers of revenue. However, two of them are known never to have assumed office. This reduces the number of officials who actually acted as ministers to 89. Biographies of 51 of

these can be found in the *Ming-shih*. Lung Wen-pin, *Ming Hui-yao* (reprint; Taipei, 1956), I, 514, mentions that Yang Ssu-i (appointed 1368) and Teng Te-mou (appointed 1370) also were ministers of revenue, but these names do not appear in the *Ming-shih* list.

14. *Ming-shih*, 150.1; Lung Wen-pin, *Ming Hui-yao*, I, 515.
15. *Ming-shih*, 157.8.
16. *Ibid.*, 149.5, 198.8.   17. *Ibid.*, 149.6–7.
18. *Ibid.*, 151.6–7; cf. 8.6.
19. Ku Yen-wu, *Jih-chih Lu* (*Wan-yu Wen-k'u* ed.), 4.50.
20. *Ming-shih*, 160.5.
21. *Ibid.*, 202.7, 256.7. For Pi Tzu-yen's arrest, see also Chiang P'ing-chieh, *Pi Shao-pao-kung Ch'üan* (early Ch'ing ed.), p. 22.
22. *Ming-shih*, 194.15, 214.7, 220.9–10, 241.11.
23. *Ibid.*, 220.24, 222.26.
24. Chiang P'ing-chieh, *Pi Shao-pao-kung Ch'üan*, p. 26.
25. Sun Ch'eng-tse, *Ch'un-ming Meng-yü Lu*, 25.27.
26. See Lu Shan-chi, *Jen-chen Ts'ao* (*Ts'ung-shu Chi-ch'eng* ed.), chs. 1 and 2. Lu was in charge of the Ministry's Honan and Kwangtung bureaus in 1619.
27. Ni Hui-ting, *Ni Wen-cheng-kung Nien-p'u* (Yüeh-ya-t'ang ed.), 4.8–9.
28. *Ming-shih*, 225.3; Lung Wen-pin, *Ming Hui-yao*, I, 521.
29. For instance, Li Nü-hua, while minister, acted as the head of the Honan Bureau. See Lu Shan-chi, *Jen-chen Ts'ao*, 1.7.
30. Shen Pang, *Wan-shu Tsa-chi*, pp. 49–50.
31. *Ibid.*, pp. 146–47.
32. *Ta-Ming Hui-tien* (*Wan-yu Wen-k'u* ed.), 29.867.
33. For the origin of the *Fu-i Ch'üan-shu*, see Pi Tzu-yen's 1628 memorial that appears in Sun Ch'eng-tse, *Ch'un-ming Meng-yü Lu*, 35.24–28.
34. *Ch'ung-chen Ts'ung-shih So-chiao* (photolithographic reproduction, 1934), I, 100.
35. Details about Ni's fiscal reforms are dealt with in my article, "Ni Yüan-lu: Realism in a Neo-Confucian Scholar-Statesman," in Wm. Theodore de Bary, ed., *Self and Society in Ming Thought* (New York).
36. Ni's attitude toward issuing government notes is not quite clear. His son, Ni Hui-ting, claims that he was never enthusiastic about issuing notes. But Ku Yen-wu indicates that Ni "insisted on" issuing them. See Ni Hui-ting, *Ni Wen-cheng-kung Nien-p'u*, 4.23–24; and Ku Yen-wu, *Jih-chih Lu*, 4.103.
37. For tax captains, see *Ming-shih*, 78.7, 78.14; and Lung Wen-pin, *Ming Hui-yao*, II, 953–56. The most comprehensive study on the

topic is Liang Fang-chung's *Ming-tai Liang-chang Chih-tu* (Shang-hai, 1957).

38. Ku Yen-wu, *Jih-chih Lu*, 3.63–64.
39. For the differences between fiscal *mou* and actual *mou* in Ming times, see Ping-ti Ho, *Studies on the Population of China, 1368–1953* (Cambridge, Mass., 1959), pp. 102–23.
40. *Ming Shen-tsung Shih-lu* (photolithographic reproduction, 1940), 106.2–3.
41. *Ibid.*, 126.3–4.   42. *Ibid.*, 116.3.
43. *Ming-shih*, 77.7. The increases in the two military districts, Hsien-fu and Ta-t'ung, amounted to about one third of the earlier assessments. See *Ming Shen-tsung Shih-lu*, 120.3, 126.1.
44. *Ta-Ming Hui-tien*, 24.627, 24.641–644, 25.669–673.
45. For surcharges see *Ta-Ming Hui-tien*, 27.797–800; *Ming-shih*, 79.3–5; and Ku Ying-t'ai, *Ming-shih Chi-shih Pen-mo* (*Wan-yu Wen-k'u* ed.), 24.27–28.
46. Ku Yen-wu, *T'ien-hsia Chün-kuo Li-ping Shu* (SPTK ed.), 12.95.
47. For Gold-Floral-Silver see *Ming-shih*, 78.3–4; *Ta-Ming Hui-tien*, 30.878; and Lung Wen-pin, *Ming Hui-yao*, II, 1082. See also Horii Kazuo, "Kingagin no Tenkai," *Toyoshi Kenkyu*, V, no. 2 (November, 1939).
48. This is based on many entries found in various sources. Certainly, the price sometimes fluctuated. In Hukwang Province husked rice could be bought for less than 0.35 taels per picul in years of good harvest around 1600; but the price could be double or triple that in other regions in time of shortage. In general, the price remained relatively stable.
49. See my doctoral dissertation, *The Grand Canal During the Ming Dynasty* (University of Michigan, 1964), p. 108.
50. *Ming-shih*, 79.10. For the exact quotas assigned to the provinces see *Ta-Ming Hui-tien*, 26.738–776.
51. *Hsü Wen-hsien T'ung-k'ao* (Shanghai, 1936), p. 3085.
52. Each year 100,000 wine jars were baked by factories operated by the Ministry of Works and delivered to the Court of Imperial Entertainments. See *Ta-Ming Hui-tien*, 194.3918. The amount of salt used by the court is estimated at 100,000 catties or seventy short tons a year; see *Ming Shen-tsung Shih-lu*, 26.8.
53. Charles O. Hucker, *The Traditional Chinese State in Ming Times (1368–1644)* (Tucson, 1961), p. 11.
54. *Ta-Ming Hui-tien*, 30.878; Lung Wen-pin, *Ming Hui-yao*, II, 1082.
55. This calculation is based on unedited data in *Ta-Ming Hui-tien*, 26.738–776.
56. *Ming-shih*, 79.15.

57. *Ibid.*, 185.1–2; Lung Wen-pin, *Ming Hui-yao*, II, 1067.
58. *Ta-Ming Hui-tien*, 28.836–848 *passim*.
59. Huang, *The Grand Canal During the Ming Dynasty*, pp. 105–6.
60. *Ibid.*, pp. 310–13.
61. *Ta-Ming Hui-tien*, 29.873.
62. This is based on unedited data in *Ta-Ming Hui-tien*, 26.738–776.
63. *Hsün-te-hsien Chih* (1585 ed.), 3.24.
64. Liang Fang-chung, "The Scope of Land Taxation of the Ming Dynasty," *Studies in Modern Economic History of China*, III, no. 1 (May, 1935), 61.
65. *Hsiang-ho-hsien Chih* (1620 ed.), 4.3.
66. This is based on a Ministry of Revenue report reproduced in *Ch'un-ming Meng-yü Lu*, 35.21.
67. *Wen-shang-hsien Chih* (1608 ed.), 4.3-10; *Hang-chou-fu Chih* (1579 ed.), 30.44, 31.65–70; *Hsün-te-hsien Chih*, 3.21–22.
68. *Ming-shih*, 80.104; *Hsü Wen-hsien T'ung-k'ao*, 2955-2958; *Ta-Ming Hui-tien*, 33.925–945; C. O. Hucker, "Governmental Organization of the Ming Dynasty," *Harvard Journal of Asiatic Studies*, XXI (1958), 46.
69. This calculation is based on *Ming-shih*, 80.1–4; *Hsü Wen-hsien T'ung-k'ao*, 2955–2958; and *Ta-Ming Hui-tien*, 33.925–945.
70. *Ming-shih*, 80.7; *Hsü Wen-hsien T'ung-k'ao*, 2958; *Ta-Ming Hui-tien*, 34.947.
71. *Ming-shih*, 80.7–8, 11; *Hsü Wen-hsien T'ung-k'ao*, 2958, 2960.
72. Ku Yen-wu, *T'ien-hsia Chün-kuo Li-ping Shu*, 36.50, 38.38, 39.74, 39.93, 40.41.
73. This calculation is based on *Ta-Ming Hui-tien*, 26.738–776.
74. *Ming-shih*, 80.5; Lung Wen-pin, *Ming Hui-yao*, II, 1051; *Hsü Wen-hsien T'ung-k'ao*, 2958, 2964; *Ta-Ming Hui-tien*, 34.949–951.
75. *Ming-shih*, 80.7–11, 14; Lung Wen-pin, *Ming Hui-yao*, II, 1055.
76. *Ming-shih*, 80.6–7. The promissory note could be inherited only by close relatives under most stringent conditions. See *Ta-Ming Hui-tien*, 34.952.
77. *Ibid.*, 34.947; *Ming-shih*, 80.8.
78. *Ming-shih*, 80.11–12; *Ta-Ming Hui-tien*, 32.909.
79. *Ta-Ming Hui-tien*, 32.908.
80. *Ming-shih*, 80.15; *Hsü Wen-hsien T'ung-k'ao*, 2962.
81. This is based on a memorandum cited in *Hsiang-ho-hsien Chih*, 11.11.
82. Ping-ti Ho, "The Salt Merchants of Yang-chou: A Study of Commercial Capitalism in Eighteenth Century China," *Harvard Journal of Asiatic Studies*, XVII (1954), 132.
83. This is based on a 1468 memorandum cited in Chu T'ing-li, *Yen-*

cheng Chih (1529 ed.), 7.3. Fujii Hiroshi considers that the so-called dealership originated from a corrupt practice within official-dom. Those who bribed the officials in charge were able to obtain the barter trade privilege before the legitimate merchants; then they sold their trading quotas to the latter. See Fujii Hiroshi, "The Origin and Significance of Chan-wo," in *Shimizu Hakase Tsuitō Kinen Mindaishi Runsō* (Tokyo, 1962), pp. 551–75.

84. *Ming Shen-tsung Shih-lu*, 568.6–7; *Hsü Wen-hsien T'ung-k'ao*, 2970–71; Sun Ch'eng-tse, *Ch'un-ming Meng-yü Lu*, 35.46–48; Ping-ti Ho, "The Salt Merchants of Yang-chou," p. 136; Ou Ts'ung-yu, *Chung-kuo Yen-cheng Hsiao-shih* (*Wan-yu Wan-k'u* ed.), 35. There is also a brief entry in *Ming-shih*, 80.16.

85. This is derived from unedited data in *Ta-Ming Hui-tien*, 32.903–924, 33.925–945; and *Hsü Wen-hsien T'ung-k'ao*, 2955–58. There are minor differences between the two sources.

86. This calculation is derived from the same sources given above in note 85.

87. Sun Ch'eng-tse, *Ch'un-ming Meng-yü Lu*, 34.45.

88. *Ming-shih*, 80.16; *Hsü Wen-hsien T'ung-k'ao*, 2970; *Ming Shen-tsung Shih-lu*, 439.1.

89. *Hsü Wen-hsien T'ung-k'ao*, 2970–71.

90. *Ming-shih*, 81.17–18; *Hsü Wen-hsien T'ung-k'ao*, 2931; *Ta-Ming Hui-tien*, 35.977. Note that originally the Ch'ung-wen Gate of Peking City was not designated an inland duty station. Rather, collections at the gate were considered part of the sales tax revenue. Eventually, however, the station became part of the inland customs system in effect. Its income was audited together with receipts at other inland duty stations. See *Ming-shih*, 81.20–21; *Hsü Wen-hsien T'ung-k'ao*, 2935, 2937; Sun Ch'eng-tse, *Ch'un-ming Meng-yü Lu*, 35.42.

91. With the exception of the collections at Lin-ch'ing and Pei-hsin-kuan. See *Ming-shih*, 81.17; *Hsü Wen-hsien T'ung-k'ao*, 2931; *Ta-Ming Hui-tien*, 35.980–81.

92. *Ta-Ming Hui-tien*, 35.977–78

93. Chang Tu, *et al.*, *Lin-ch'ing Chih-li-chou Chih* (1782 ed.), 9.2.

94. Some such malpractices are dealt with in Huang, *The Grand Canal During the Ming Dynasty*, pp. 178–83.

95. *Hsü Wen-hsien T'ung-k'ao*, 2937–38; Sun Ch'eng-tse, *Ch'un-ming Meng-yü Lu*, 35.42; *Ming Shen-tsung Shih-lu*, 376.10.

96. Wu Chao-ts'ui, *Chung-kuo Shui-chih Shih* (Shanghai, 1937), I, 169.

97. This calculation is based on *Ta-Ming Hui-tien*, 35.1014–18.

98. Such deliveries are recorded in *Ta-Ming Hui-tien*, 35.1014–18.

99. For the collection of commodity taxes, see Chou Chih-lung, *Ts'ao-ho I-pi* (1609 ed.; Library of Congress microfilm), *passim*.

100. For collecting points, see *Ming-shih*, 81.15. The amount of collections is mentioned in Chou Chih-lung, *Ts'ao-ho I-pi*, ch. 11.
101. Ho Shih-chin, *Kung-pu Ch'ang-k'u Hsi-chih* (*Hsüang-lan-t'ang Ts'ung-shu* ed.), 9.41–45, 12.41–47.
102. *Ming Shen-tsung Shih-lu*, 373.8.
103. This is derived from the unedited data in Ho Shih-chin, *Kung-pu Ch'ang-k'u Hsi-chih*, chs. 9 and 12.
104. *Ibid.*, 12.48.
105. *Ibid.*, ch. 9; *Ming Shen-tsung Shih-lu*, 373.8.
106. Sun Ch'eng-tse, *Ch'un-ming Meng-yü Lu*, 53.3.
107. *Ming Shen-tsung Shih-lu*, 383.12; *Ming-shih*, 216.16.
108. *Ming Hsi-tsung Shih-lu* (photolithographic reproduction, 1940), 7.25, 32.5; *Ming Ch'ung-chen Shih-lu* (photolithographic reproduction, 1940), 53.9.
109. *Ming-shih*, 82.19. Cf. Sun Ch'eng-tse, *Ch'un-ming Meng-yü Lu*, 35.8.
110. *Ming-shih*, 82.20.
111. Sun Ch'eng-tse, *Ch'un-ming Meng-yü Lu*, 35.10.
112. This is my estimate, based on *Ming-shih*, 82.20.
113. Ku Yen-wu, *T'ien-hsia Chün-kuo Li-ping Shü*, 38.33–34, 39.100–1. For the opening of the port see Katayama Seijiro, "The Twenty-four Leaders at Yüeh-chiang," in *Shimizu Hakase Tsuitō Kinen Mindaishi Runsō*, pp. 389–419.
114. *Ming Hsi-tsung Shih-lu*, 62.5.
115. These data are found in *Ming-shih*, 82.19–20; *Hsü Wen-hsien T'ung-k'ao*, 3086; *Ming Shen-tsung Shih-lu*, 20.8, 144.4–5, 234.3, 416.13; *Ta-Ming Hui-tien*, 26.738–76; Sun Ch'eng-tse, *Ch'un-ming Meng-yü Lu*, 31.32, 35.8–10.
116. *Ming-shih*, 78.4; Lung Wen-pin, *Ming Hui-yao*, II, 1009–10.
117. *Ming-shih*, 78.4.
118. Huang, *The Grand Canal During the Ming Dynasty*, ch. 5.
119. *Ming-shih*, 78.3.
120. Lien-sheng Yang, *Money and Credit in China* (Cambridge, Mass., 1952), p. 67.
121. *Ming-shih*, 78.3.   122. *Ibid.*, 81.4.
123. Huang, *The Grand Canal During the Ming Dynasty*, pp. 67–68. Cf. Harold C. Hinton, "The Grain Tribute System of the Ch'ing Dynasty," *The Far Eastern Quarterly*, XI, no. 3 (May, 1952), 342; and Hoshi Ayao, *Mindai Sōun no Kenkyū* (Tokyo, 1963), pp. 64–68.
124. *Ming-shih*, 153.10.
125. This calculation is based on *Ta-Ming Hui-tien*, 19.498–516.
126. To name only a few: Fu I-ling, *Ming-tai Chiang-nan Shih-min Ching-chi Shih-tan* (Shanghai, 1957), *passim*; Chou Liang-hsiao, "Ming-tai So-sung Ti-ch'ü ti Kuan-t'ien yü Chung-fu Wen-t'i,"

Lishi Yanjiu, X (1957), 65–66; Chü Tung-yün, *Chang Chü-cheng Ta-chuan*, pp. 175–77, 307; Li Chieng-lung, *Sung Yüan Ming Ching-chi Shih-kao*, pp. 207–8. A traditional source is Ku Yen-wu, *T'ien-hsia Chün-kuo Li-ping Shu*, 6.94, 7.4, 8.52.

127. *Ming-shih*, 153.10.

128. *Ming-shih*, 78.5, 153.11.

129. Ho Liang-ts'un, *Ssu-yu-chai Ts'ung-shuo Tsa-ch'ao* (*Ts'ung-shu Chi-ch'eng* ed.), 3.169; *K'un-shan-hsien Chih* (1576 ed.), 2.22.

130. T'ung-tsu Ch'ü, *Local Government in China under the Ch'ing* (Cambridge, Mass., 1962), p. 133.

131. See note 126 above.

132. By comparing the statistics of 1391 and those of 1502 in *Ta-Ming Hui-tien*, 24.627–628.

133. Sun Ch'eng-tse, *Ch'un-ming Meng-yü Lu*, 36.3–4.

134. *Ming-shih*, 81.17–18; *Hsü Wen-hsien T'ung-k'ao*, 2931–32.

135. *Ming-shih*, 79.14.

136. *Ibid.*, 185.1–3. Cf. Lung Wen-pin, *Ming Hui-yao*, II, 1053–54.

137. Fu I-ling, *Ming-tai Chiang-nan Shih-min Ching-chi Shih-tan*, *passim*; Miyazaki Ichisada, "Min-Shin Judai no Soshū to Keikōgyō no Hatten," *Toho Gaku*, no. 2 (August, 1951), 64–73; Nishijima Sadao, "Shina Shoki Engyō Shijō no Kōsatsu," *Toyo Gaku*, XXXI, no. 2 (October, 1947), 262–88; Shang Yüeh, "Chung-kuo Tsu-pen Chu-i Sheng-ch'an Yin-su ti Meng-ya chi ch'i Ts'eng-chang," *Lishi Yanjiu*, III (1955), 89–92; Liu Yen, "Ming-mo Ch'eng-shih Fa-chan hsia-ti Ch'u-ch'i Shih-min Yün-tung," *Lishi Yanjiu*, VI (1955), 29–59.

138. Ni Yüan-lu, *Ni Wen-chung-kung Ch'üan-chi* (1772 ed.), Memoranda, 9.5. For increasing trading activities, also see *Ming-shih*, 81.23; *Ming Shen-tsung Shih-lu*, 210.7.

139. That the northwest suffered an acute economic depression was mentioned by many contemporary writers. Of these, Ku Yen-wu presented the most convincing descriptions and some analysis. See Ku Yen-wu, *T'ing-lin Shih-wen-chi* (SPTK ed.), 1.13, and other essays. Ni Yüan-lu made similar observations. See Ni Yüan-lu, *Ni Wen-chung-kung Ch'üan-chi*, Memoranda, 6.2.

140. *Ming-shih*, 78.10.

141. Ku Yen-wu, *T'ien-hsia Chün-kuo Li-ping Shu*, 33.118; *Ching-hua-fu Chih* (late 16th century ed.), 8.13. This is also noted in many other local histories.

142. This calculation is based on *Ta-Ming Hui-tien*, 28.839–861.

143. Sun Ch'eng-tse, *Ch'un-ming Meng-yü Lu*, 35.18; *Ming-shih*, 235.14–15; Wang Shih-chen, *Feng-chou Tsa-pien* (*Ts'ung-shu Chi-ch'eng* ed.), 1.3.

144. This is based on Wang Shih-chen, *Feng-chou Tsa-pien*, 1.3–9. Wang's data are believed to have been obtained from the files of the Ministry of Revenue.
145. This calculation is based on *Ta-Ming Hui-tien*, 28.839–61.
146. The 1577 and 1578 figures are based on a report written by Chang Chü-cheng, reproduced in Sun Ch'eng-tse, *Ch'un-ming Meng-yü Lu*, 35.31–33. The 1583 figure is based on *Ming Shen-tsung Shih-lu*, 144.4–5. The 1593 figure is based on *Ming Shen-tsung Shih-lu*, 262.7–8. The 1607 figure is based on Ch'eng K'ai-hu, ed. *Chou-Liao Shih-huo* (1620 ed.), 8.27.
147. *Ming-shih*, 78.10.
148. *Ming Shen-tsung Shih-lu*, 178.22.
149. *Ibid.*, 383.12; *Hsü Wen-hsien T'ung-k'ao*, 3086; Ku Yen-wu, *Jih-chih Lu*, 5.5–6.
150. A brief analysis of Shen-tsung's personality can be found in Charles O. Hucker, "The Tung Lin Movement of the Late Ming Period," in J. K. Fairbank, ed., *Chinese Thought and Institutions* (Chicago, 1957), pp. 133–34.
151. *Ming-shih*, 79.15.
152. *Ming Shen-tsung Shih-lu*, 261.1.
153. *Ibid.*, 570.15–16.
154. *Ming-shih*, 81.20–21.
155. Sun Ch'eng-tse, *Ch'un-ming Meng-yü Lu*, 35.24–25; *Ming-shih*, 78.14–15.
156. Liang Fang-chung, *The Single-Whip Method of Taxation in China*, trans. by Wang Yü-ch'üan (Cambridge, Mass., 1956), p. 14.
157. Lung Wen-pin, *Ming Hui-yao*, II, 1018–20.
158. *Ming Hsi-tsung Shih-lu*, 70.18–19; *Ming Shen-tsung Shih-lu*, 36.649, 584.10; *Ming-ch'en Tsou-i* (*Ts'ung-shu Chi-ch'eng* ed.), 35.673–76.
159. *Ming Shen-tsung Shih-lu*, 571.4, 584.10.
160. *Ming-Ch'ing Shih-liao*, series B (Shanghai, 1936), 5.424.
161. *Ming Hsi-tsung Shih-lu*, 15.13–14.
162. *Ming Shen-tsung Shih-lu*, 441.19.
163. Li Hua-lung, *P'ing-Po Ch'üan-shu* (*Ts'ung-shu Chi-ch'eng* ed.), 1.18, 6.361–362; Ch'eng K'ai-hu, ed., *Chou-Liao Shih-huo*, 3.68.
164. *Ming Shen-tsung Shih-lu*, 254.5; Ku Yen-wu, *T'ien-hsia Chün-kuo Li-ping Shu*, 33.118.
165. Ch'eng K'ai-hu, ed., *Chou-Liao Shih-huo*, 7.17.
166. *Ming Shen-tsung Shih-lu*, 383.12.
167. *Ibid.*, 437.6.
168. These memoranda appear in Ch'eng K'ai-hu, ed., *Chou-Liao Shih-huo*.

169. These memoranda are reproduced in Ch'eng K'ai-hu, ed., *Chou-Liao Shih-huo*, 26.28–31, 30.8–12, 31.10–12, 32.25–27, 32.37–39, 33.17–20. See also *Ming Shen-tsung Shih-lu*, 580.13.
170. *Ibid.*, 569.12, 580.24; Ch'eng K'ai-hu, ed., *Chou-Liao Shih-huo*, 4.46.
171. *Ming-shih*, 21.12; *Ming-shih Kao* (Wen-hai Book Co. ed.), 1.104; *Ming T'ung-chien* (Chung-hua Book Co. ed.), 76.2955; T'an Ch'ien, *Kuo Ch'üeh* (reprint; Peking, 1958), 84.5156, 5158.
172. *Ming Kuang-tsung Shih-lu* (photolithographic reproduction, 1940), p. 26.
173. *Ming Hsi-tsung Shih-lu*, 1.2.
174. *Ming-shih*, 256.8.
175. Ch'eng K'ai-hu, ed., *Chou-Liao Shih-huo*, 44.46.
176. *Ibid.*, 44.24.
177. *Ibid.*, 44.29.
178. Ch'ien Mu, *Kuo-shih Ta-kang* (2d ed.; Shanghai, 1947), II, 587.
179. These rates appear in *Ming-shih*, 78.11–12, and *Hsü Wen-hsien T'ung-k'ao*, 2794–95. Lung Wen-pin, *Ming Hui-yao*, II, 1033–34, carries the same information, but the figures differ slightly from the other two sources. The lack of clarity in the original text led me at one time to believe that extras ordered in 1637, at 0.0048 taels per *mou* and 0.01409 taels per *mou*, were two consecutive orders, one on top of the other, both applying to all taxable land. I am grateful to Professor Lien-sheng Yang for pointing out that the rate of 0.01409 taels per *mou* could not have been applied uniformly without bringing in income far exceeding the amount reported. I believe that my present interpretation—that the rate of 0.0048 taels per *mou* was applicable to land *under previous registration*—can be supported by evidence in the sources. See *Ming-shih*, 252.2, and *Hsü Wen-hsien T'ung-k'ao*, 2975. But that the rate of 0.01409 taels per *mou* was applicable to land *hitherto untaxed* is not verifiable in the contemporary sources. *Ming-shih*, 78.12, mentions the rate of 0.01409 taels per *mou* but does not indicate how it was applied. *Ming-shih*, 252.2, and *Hsü Wen-hsien T'ung-k'ao*, 2975, mention taxes on land hitherto untaxed but do not specify a rate. I link these bits of evidence together, realizing that my interpretation is questionable and hoping that subsequent investigators may correct or verify it.
180. Among many others, Wang Yü-ch'üan condemns this collection, saying "The agricultural economy of China was bled to exhaustion by special land taxes levied on the peasantry . . . ." See Wang Yü-ch'üan, "The Rise of Land Tax and the Fall of Dynasties in Chinese History," *Pacific Affairs* (June, 1936), p. 201.

181. Ch'eng K'ai-hu, ed., *Chou-Liao Shih-huo*, 11.15.
182. *Ming Shen-tsung Shih-lu*, 574.14. Cf. Ch'eng K'ao-hu, ed. *Chou-Liao Shih-huo*, 11.13–17, 15.41.
183. This calculation is based on Ch'en Jen-hsi, *Huang-Ming Shih-fa Lu* (reprint; Taipei, 1965), ch. 34. Note that *Ming-shih*, 78.11, and *Hsü Wen-hsien T'ung-k'ao*, 2794, both claim the total quota was 5.2 million taels. But Ch'en's detailed account was copied from the files of the Ministry of Revenue and seems to be thorough and consistent.
184. Lu Hsiang-shang, *Lu Chung-su-kung Chi* (1755 ed.), 4.3; *Hsü Wen-hsien T'ung-k'ao*, 2795.
185. *Ming-shih*, 252.2; *Hsü Wen-hsien T'ung-k'ao*, 2795.
186. *Hsü Wen-hsien T'ung-k'ao*, 2795.
187. The total quota for 1641 was 21,330,735 taels. See Sun Ch'eng-tse, *Ch'un-ming Meng-yü Lu*, 35.12. The figure was obtained from the files of the Ministry of Revenue.
188. This calculation is based on Ch'en Jen-hsi, *Huang-Ming Shih-fa Lu*, pp. 958–96.
189. Sun Ch'eng-tse, *Ch'un-ming Meng-yü Lu*, 36.48.
190. *Ibid.*, 35.29.
191. Ping-ti Ho, *Studies on the Population of China, 1368–1953*, pp. 3–23, 277.
192. *Ta-Ch'ing Shih-tsu Shih-lu* (Man-chu Kuo-wu-yüan ed., 1937), 61.6–7, 70.31–32, 79.23–24.
193. Wang Hsien-ch'ien, *Tung-hua Lu* (Shanghai, 1891), K'ang-hsi era, 42.8.
194. *Ibid.*, Hsün-chih era, 15.1.
195. *Ta-Ch'ing Sheng-tsu Shih-lu* (Man-chu Kuo-wu-yüan ed., 1937), 4.9.
196. This can be seen in the official memoranda appearing, for example, in *Ta-Ch'ing Shih-tsu Shih-lu*, 118.8, 119.13.
197. In 1665 the governor of Anhwei Province urged that the land survey be discontinued, arguing that it only created disturbances. See *Ta-Ch'ing Sheng-tsu Shih-lu*, 15.6–7.
198. *Ibid.*, 3.3.
199. Ni Yüan-lu, *Ni Wen-cheng-kung Ch'üan-chi*, Memoranda, 11.11. For descriptions of the difficult conditions under which the silver payments arrived from the south, see also *Ming-Ch'ing Shih-liao*, series B, 10.948, 977–78, 987.
200. Ni Hui-ting, *Ni Wen-cheng-kung Nien-p'u*, 4.11.
201. Ku Ying-t'ai, *Ming-shih Chi-shih Pen-mo*, 79.84–85.
202. Liang Fang-chung, "Ming-tai Kuo-chi Mou-i yü Yin ti Shu-ch'u-yü," *Chung-kuo She-hui Ching-chi Shih Chi-k'an*, VI, no. 2 (December, 1939), 324.

203. Sun Ch'eng-tse, *Ch'un-ming Meng-yü Lu*, 35.37, 36.56; Ni Yüan-lu, *Ni Wen-cheng-kung Ch'üan-chi*, Memoranda, 8.6–7; Ku Yen-wu, *T'ing-lin Shih-wen-chi*, 1.15–16.
204. Liu Ts'ung-chou, *Liu-tzu Wen-chi* (incorporated in *Ch'ien-k'un Cheng-ch'i Chi*), 415.4.
205. Sun Ch'eng-tse, *Ch'un-ming Meng-yü Lu*, 25.29–30.
206. Kuei Yu-kuang, *San-Wu Shui-li Lu* (*Ts'ung-shu Chi-ch'eng* ed.), 1.5, 1.7.
207. Shen Te-fu, *Yeh-hu-pien Pu-i* (Fu-li Shan-fang ed.), 2.37.
208. For instance, the land taxes in Honan and north Hukwang Provinces were remitted. See Ni Yüan-lu, *Ni Wen-cheng-kung Ch'üan-chi*, Memoranda, 8.7–17.
209. Cheng T'ien-t'ing, *et al.*, *Ming-mo Nung-min Ch'i-i Shih-liao* (2d ed.; Shanghai, 1954), p. 27; Ch'ien Mu, *Kuo-shih Ta-kang*, II, 591.
210. Cheng T'ien-t'ing, *et al.*, *Ming-mo Nung-min Ch'i-i Shih-liao*, passim.
211. Li Wen-chih, *Wan-Ming Min-pien* (Shanghai, 1948), pp. 15–25.

TILEMANN GRIMM   *Ming Education Intendants*

1. See Matteo Ricci, *China in the Sixteenth Century: The Journals of Matthew Ricci, 1583–1930*, trans. by L. J. Gallagher (New York, 1953); on the examination system, see pp. 34 ff.
2. Ssu-yü Teng, "Chinese Influence on the Western Examination System," *Harvard Journal of Asiatic Studies*, VII (1943), 267–312. Note Teng's conclusion (p. 305, n. 92), more cautious than that of Y. Z. Chang.
3. For a more recent view, see E. O. Reischauer and J. K. Fairbank, *East Asia: The Great Tradition* (Boston, 1960), pp. 106 ff.
4. Robert des Rotours, trans., *Le Traité des Examens* (Paris, 1932); see especially appendix, pp. 289 ff. For an evaluation, see Reischauer and Fairbank, *East Asia: The Great Tradition*, p. 164.
5. Beginning in 977 the numbers tended to rise above 300 per annum, an all-time high of 1,538 being reached for the year 1000. See *Wen-hsien T'ung-k'ao* (Taipei, 1965), 32.305; 30.282, dealing with figures of the Five Dynasties period, shows a certain rise above the T'ang average of 30 to 50 (see 19.276 ff.) toward 100 and more for the years 932, 941, 944, and thereafter.
6. *Sung-shih* (Hong Kong, 1959), 167.4886a, 20.4531d.
7. *Yüan-shih* (Hong Kong, 1959), ch. 91, and K'o Shao-min, *Hsin Yüan-shih* (Hong Kong, 1959), 62.6752b, 64.6757 (the latter *chüan* offers some details on subsequent developments).
8. *Ming-shih* (Hong Kong, 1959), 75.7257b. Cf. Fu Wei-lin, *Ming-shu* (Shanghai, 1937), p. 1230. The biographies of Liu Chi in *Ming-shih*,

128.7399, and Chiao Hung, *Kuo-ch'ao Hsien-cheng Lu* (Ming ed.), 9.1a ff, do not confirm this. Liu had served under the Yüan dynasty as assistant school intendant (*fu t'i-chü*) for Chiang-Che (the present Chekiang and Fukien) and as a provincial examination officer (*k'ao-shih kuan*). But in the *Ming-shih* biography of Sung Lien (128.7400) this is explicitly confirmed in connection with Chu Yüan-chang's conquest of Chekiang, whence he summoned famous literati to serve in his court. But it is clear that appointments of school intendants prior to 1368 should not be taken too seriously.

 9. Wu Han, "Ming-ch'u ti Hsüeh-hsiao," *Tsinghua Hsüeh-pao*, XV (1948), 33–61; Tilemann Grimm, *Erziehung und Politik im Konfuzianischen China der Ming-Zeit, 1368–1644* (Hamburg, 1960), pp. 50–56.

10. *Ming Ying-tsung Shih-lu* (photolithographic reproduction, 1962), 17.12b.

11. *Ming-shih*, 75.7257b.

12. *Ming Ying-tsung Shih-lu*, 128.2a–b.   13. *Ibid.*, 128.82a–b.

14. *Ibid.*, 191.10b–13a.   15. *Ibid.*, 17.12b.

16. *Ibid.*, 336.3a–6a.   17. *Ibid.*, 17.12b–24b.

18. See Li Hsien's biography in Chiao Hung, *Kuo-ch'ao Hsien-cheng Lu*, 13.45a.

19. Ying-tsung's guiding principles of 1462 are to be found in *Ming Ying-tsung Shih-lu*, 191.10b–13a, and also in *Ta-Ming Hui-tien* (*Wan-yu Wen-k'u* ed.), 78.1812–15. The 1575 reformulation is reproduced in *Ta-Ming Hui-tien*, 78.1815–18.

20. *Ming Ying-tsung Shih-lu*, 17.13a–b.

21. *Ta-Ming Hui-tien*, 78.1813.   22. *Ibid.*, 78.1815.

23. Abuses related to examinations were clearly perceived in Ming times, as a classical drama (*tsa-chü*) by Feng Wei-min (1511–80), titled *Pu Fu Lao* (Not subdued by age), clearly reveals. See *Ming-jen Tsa-chü Hsüan* (Peking, 1958), pp. 297 ff.

24. *Ta-Ming Hui-tien*, 78.1814.

25. *Ming Ying-tsung Shih-lu*, 17.12b.

26. Biographies found in Chiao Hung, *Kuo-ch'ao Hsien-cheng Lu*; *Ming-shih*; and *Ku-chin T'u-shu Chi-ch'eng* (Taipei, 1964), especially ch. 608.

27. E.g., see the biographies of Ch'en Hsüan in *Ming-shih*, 161.7465b, and Lu Kuo in Chiao Hung, *Kuo-ch'ao Hsien-cheng Lu*, 95.83b.

28. Biography of P'eng Hsü in Chiao Hung, *Kuo-ch'ao Hsien-cheng Lu*, 95.56b.

29. See the biographical extract on Hsü Jen-lung in *Ku-chin T'u-shu Chi-ch'eng*, 608.867b; or that of Chung Hsing (early 17th century), *ibid.*, or *Ming-shih*, 288.2800a (incorporated in the biography of Yüan Hung-tao).

30. See the biographies of Chiang Hsin in Chiao Hung, *Kuo-ch'ao Hsien-cheng Lu*, 103.67b, Yao Wen-hao, *ibid.*, 88.109a, or Chang Yung in *Ku-chin T'u-shu Chi-ch'eng*, 608.866b.
31. See the biography of Censor-in-chief Ch'en Feng-wu (1475–1541) in Chiao Hung, *Kuo-ch'ao Hsien-cheng Lu*, 59.37b; also see the biography of Wang Ying-chen, *ibid.*, 86.122a.
32. See the biographical extract on Hsieh Shao-nan in *Ku-chin T'u-shu Chi-ch'eng*, 608.866c.
33. See the biographical extract on Wei Huan-ch'u in *Ku-chin T'u-shu Chi-ch'eng*, 608.867b: "There were hardly examination officials who were his equal, so infatuated was he with literature all his life, and so unaware was he of toil and weariness."
34. See the biography of Yen Ch'ing in Chiao Hung, *Kuo-ch'ao Hsien-cheng Lu*, 88.99a.
35. Mentioned in item 6 of the 1575 edict; see *Ta-Ming Hui-tien*, 18.1816.
36. *Ming Shen-tsung Shih-lu* (photolithographic reproduction, 1940), 38.3a–b.
37. Hsü Hsüeh-chü, *Kuo-ch'ao Tien-hui* (Ming ed.), 130.5b.
38. *Ibid.*, 130.7a.
39. Cf. collected extracts from documents in *Ku-chin T'u-shu Chi-ch'eng*, 608.863c–864c: the section on "Education Commissioners—Ch'ing Dynasty." It can easily be shown that the early Ch'ing ordinations follow the documents of Ming Shen-tsung's time rather closely, often in complete sentences and paragraphs. Measures taken in the K'ang-hsi reign no longer copy the Ming model; rather, they call for what Chang Chü-cheng had wanted—strict regulation under firm leadership.
40. See the biographies of Yen Ch'ing and Yao Wen-hao in Chiao Hung, *Kuo-ch'ao Hsien-cheng Lu*, 88.99a, 109a.
41. See the biography of Yao Wen-hao cited above in n. 40.
42. See the biography of Sun Ting in *Ming-shih*, 161.7464d (in section on P'eng Hsü).
43. E.g., Hsiao Ming-feng; see Chiao Hung, *Kuo-ch'ao Hsien-cheng Lu*, 99.111b.
44. See item 8 of the 1462 edict, repeated in an abridged form as item 6 of the 1575 version.
45. Ch'iu Chün, *Ta-hsüeh Yen-i Pu* (1605 ed.,), ch. 69.
46. Sun Ch'eng-tse, *Ch'un-ming Meng-yü Lu*, cited in *Ku-chin T'u-shu Chi-ch'eng*, 608.871a–b.
47. See Ch'en Hsüan's biography in *Ming-shih*, 161.7465a–b.
48. See Ch'en Feng-wu's biography in Chiao Hung, *Kuo-ch'ao Hsien-cheng Lu*, 59.37a–b.

49. See his biography in Chiao Hung, *Kuo-ch'ao Hsien-cheng Lu*, 86.68b.
50. Grimm, *Erziehung und Politik*, pp. 28 ff and 104 ff.
51. This is discussed in Grimm, *Erziehung und Politik*, pp. 137 ff. In spite of the impression given by Ping-ti Ho, *The Ladder of Success in Imperial China* (New York, 1962), p. 200, I prefer to uphold my warning against considering the academy activities too revolutionary in character. As early as the sixteenth century, just as later in the eighteenth century, most academies merely offered better opportunities to prepare for taking the examinations; only a few became centers of "free" discussion. It was only the latter at which the government struck in 1537–38, 1579–82, and 1624–25. On the other hand, it is evident that many remonstrators complained about decay in local government schools and about the negligence of local officials, who ignored government schools but spent large sums constructing private academies. The danger that the educational system might drift out of centralized control was imminent. Anti-Chu Hsi attitudes troubled the government as well, but only for a short time, and then without any specific relevance to academies. See Hsü Hsüeh-chü, *Kuo-ch'ao Tien-hui*, ch. 132, which is devoted to matters of scholarship and learning. Also see a discussion of this point in Tilemann Grimm, "Some Remarks on the Suppression of Shu-yüan in Ming China," *Transactions of the International Conference of Orientalists in Japan*, II (1957), 14.
52. See the biographical extract on Shao Jui (T. Ssu-i) in *Ku-chin T'u-shu Chi-ch'eng*, 608.869c.
53. See the biography of Assistant Censor-in-chief Chou Meng-chung (1437–1502) in Chiao Hung, *Kuo-ch'ao Hsien-cheng Lu*, 55.16b–17a.
54. See the biography of Grand Secretary Yang I-ch'ing (1454–1530) in Chiao Hung, *Kuo-ch'ao Hsien-cheng Lu*, 15.71a. Cf. Hsü Hsüeh-chü, *Kuo-ch'ao Tien-hui*, 130.3a.
55. See *Ming-shih*, chs. 69–70, and *Ta-Ming Hui-tien*, ch. 77.
56. *Ta-Ming Hui-tien*, 77.1784.
57. *Ibid.*, 77.1798.   58. *Ibid.*, 77.1788.
59. Lung Wen-pin, *Ming Hui-yao* (1887 ed.), 47.16a–b.
60. *Ibid.*, 47.8a–b. It should be added that literary skill was to be reformed toward "literary truth." The change affected form rather than content. Compositions had become the sole criterion of judgment, but "correct behavior" was still what educational control was to guard.
61. Grimm, *Erziehung und Politik*, pp. 49, 88.
62. Ricci, *China in the Sixteenth Century*, pp. 34–35.
63. See the biographical extract on Hsü Hen-lung in *Ku-chin T'u-shu Chi-ch'eng*, 608.867b.

64. See the biography of Wang Ying-chen in Chiao Hung, *Kuo-ch'ao Hsien-cheng Lu*, 86.122a.
65. See the biography of Hsiao Ming-feng in Chiao Hung, *Kuo-ch'ao Hsien-cheng Lu*, 99.111b.

JOHN MESKILL   *Academies and Politics in the Ming Dynasty*

1. Hu Shih, "Shu-yüan-chih Shih-lüeh," *Tung-fang Tsa-chih*, XXI, no. 3 (February, 1924), 142.
2. Ch'en Tung-yüan, *Chung-kuo K'o-chü Shih-tai chih Chiao-yü* (Shanghai, 1934), p. 67.
3. Ch'en Tung-yüan, *Chung-kuo K'o-chü Shih-tai chih Chiao-yü*, pp. 69–70.
4. *Ibid.*, p. 74; Taga Akigorō, *Chūgoku Kyōiku-shi* (Tokyo, 1955), p. 77.
5. See Ch'en Tung-yüan, *Chung-kuo K'o-chü Shih-tai chih Chiao-yü*, pp. 64–66, 69, 71.
6. Figured from Ts'ao Sung-yeh, "Sung Yüan Ming Ch'ing Shu-yüan Kai-k'uang," *Yü-yen Li-shih-hsüeh Yen-chiu-so Chou-k'an* (Kuo-li Chung-shan Ta-hsüeh), vol. 10, no. 111 (1929) and vol. 10, nos. 112–15 (1930), particularly no. 111, p. 17, and no. 112, p. 20. His figures come from provincial gazetteers, the names of which he has not given. Presumably the figures would err from incompleteness, rather than exaggeration. They do not, however, distinguish among academies of different sizes.
7. Since the Southern Sung figures apply to only a part of China, the rate for the whole would be higher. The south, however, includes the regions of the greatest development of academies.
8. See Ts'ao, "Shu-yüan Kai-k'uang," *passim*, and Ho Yu-shen, "Yüan-tai Shu-yüan chih Ti-li Fen-pu," *Hsin-ya Hsüeh-pao*, II, no. 1 (August, 1956), 361–62.
9. Ch'en Tung-yüan, *Chung-kuo K'o-chü Shih-tai chih Chiao-yü*, p. 74; Sheng Lang-hsi, *Chung-kuo Shu-yüan Chih-tu* (Shanghai, 1934), pp. 63–67; Hayashi Tomoharu, "Gen-Min Jidai no Shoin Kyōiku," in Hayashi Tomoharu, ed., *Kinsei Chūgoku Kyōiku-shi Kenkyū* (Kokudo-sha, 1958), pp. 7, 9.
10. Ts'ao Sung-yeh, "Shu-yüan Kai-k'uang," no. 113, pp. 19–20.
11. Ch'en Tung-yüan, *Chung-kuo K'o-chü Shih-tai chih Chiao-yü*, pp. 74–75.
12. See *Ming T'ai-tsu Shih-lu* (Taipei, Academia Sinica photoreproduction), 36A.4a–5a.
13. *Hsü Wen-hsien T'ung-k'ao* (*Kuo-hsüeh Chi-pen Ts'ung-shu* ed.), 50.3246.

14. See, e.g., Hayashi Tomoharu, "Gen-Min Jidai no Shoin Kyōiku," p. 12.
15. *Ibid.*, p. 13.
16. Sheng Lang-hsi, *Chung-kuo Shu-yüan Chih-tu*, p. 67.
17. See, e.g., Hayashi Tomoharu, "Gen-Min Jidai no Shoin Kyōiku," p. 13.
18. *Pai-lu-chou Shu-yüan Chih* (8 ch.; 1878 ed.), 2.8a.
19. Hayashi Tomoharu, "Gen-Min Jidai no Shoin Kyōiku," p. 12.
20. See Sheng Lang-hsi, *Chung-kuo Shu-yüan Chih-tu*, p. 47; Hayashi Tomoharu, "Gen-Min Jidai no Shoin Kyōiku," p. 18.
21. The similarities to Ch'an organization and procedure are noted in Sheng Lang-hsi, *Chung-kuo Shu-yüan Chih-tu*, pp. 21–24, and Taga Akigorō, *Chūgoku Kyōiku-shi*, p. 70. Hu Shih ("Shu-yüan-chih Shih-lüeh," pp. 142, 145) stresses rather the individual and independent method of study, seeing the headmasters as consultants.
22. Ts'ao Sung-yeh, "Shu-yüan Kai-k'uang," no. 113, pp. 19–20. The figures are inexact but illustrate the trend.
23. See, e.g., Sheng Lang-hsi, *Chung-kuo Shu-yüan Chih-tu*, p. 77.
24. *Ming Shih-tsung Shih-lu* (photolithographic reprint, 1940), 199.10b; *Hsü Wen-hsien T'ung-k'ao*, 50.3246.
25. *Ming Shih-tsung Shih-lu*, 199.10b.
26. *Ibid.*, 212.1a, 2a; *Hsü Wen-hsien T'ung-k'ao*, 50.3246; Sheng Lang-hsi, *Chung-kuo Shu-yüan Chih-tu*, p. 85.
27. See notes from gazetteers of the Nanking region in Liu I-cheng, "Chiang-su Shu-yüan-chih Ch'u-kao," *Kiangsu Sinological Library Annual*, no. 4 (1931), p. 19; and notes on academies in the Canton region, where Chan Jo-shui founded several, in *Kuang-tung T'ung-chih* (Shanghai, 1864), vol. II, *passim*.
28. Unfortunately, I have not found any histories of Yang-ming academies or those connected with the Pai-sha school.
29. *Pai-lu-chou Shu-yüan Chih* (17 ch.; late Ming ed.), 2.2b ff.
30. *Ibid.*, 2.8a ff, 8.26a.
31. *Nan-hsi Shu-yüan Chih* (1716 ed.), 2.6a–b.
32. See *Ming-shih* (Kuo-fang Yen-chiu-yüan ed.; Taipei, 1962), 283.3181–3183.
33. Liu Po-chi, *Kuang-tung Shu-yüan Chih-tu Yen-ko* (Shanghai, 1939), pp. 27–29.
34. See Liu I-cheng, "Chiang-su Shu-yüan-chih Ch'u-kao," p. 19; *Ming Shih-tsung Shih-lu*, 199.10b–11a.
35. *Ming-shih*, 283.3183.   36. *Ibid.*, 196.2284.
37. *Ibid.*, 197.2294.
38. Liu Po-chi, *Kuang-tung Shu-yüan Chih-tu Yen-ko*, pp. 27–28.

39. For a resumé, see Meng Sen, *Ming-tai Shih* (Taipei, 1957), pp. 220–26. Cf. *Ming-shih*, 196.2279–80.
40. See, e.g., Meng Sen, *Ming-tai Shih*, pp. 220–26; *Ming-shih*, 196.2279, 2280, 2286.
41. *Ibid.*, 209.2425 (biography of Feng En). Feng criticized others who may not have been in the Chang Ts'ung faction, but I mean to note only the association of the Cantonese.
42. *Ibid.*, 197.2296.   43. *Ibid.*, 197.2294, 2296.
44. Chang Yü-ch'üan, "Wang Shou-jen as a Statesman," *Chinese Social and Political Science Review*, XXIII, no. 1 (April–June, 1939), 30–99; no. 2 (July–September, 1939), 155–252; no. 3 (October–December, 1939), 319–88; no. 4 (January–March, 1940), 473–522; especially pp. 97–98.
45. *Ming-shih*, 196.2283.   46. *Ibid.*, 196.2280.
47. T'an Ch'ien, *Kuo Ch'üeh* (Peking, 1958), IV, 3395.
48. See, e.g., Shen Te-fu, *Wan-li Yeh-hu-pien* (Peking, 1959), 24.608.
49. Chang Yü-ch'üan, "Wang Shou-jen as a Statesman," p. 44.
50. *Ibid.*, p. 43.   51. *Ibid.*, pp. 199–200.
52. Sheng Lang-hsi, *Chung-kuo Shu-yüan Chih-tu*, p. 78.
53. See Ch'en Tung-yüan, "Lu-shan Pai-lu-tung Shu-yüan Yen-ko K'ao," part II, in *Min-to Tsa-chih*, VII, no. 2 (1937), 2.
54. Chang Yü-ch'üan, "Wang Shou-jen as a Statesman," pp. 192–93.
55. *Ibid.*, pp. 203–4.
56. See Sheng Lang-hsi, *Chung-kuo Shu-yüan Chih-tu*, p. 77.
57. *Ibid.*, p. 78.
58. *Ibid.*, pp. 82–83; Chang Yü-ch'üan, "Wang Shou-jen as a Statesman," pp. 203–4.
59. Sheng Lang-hsi, *Chung-kuo Shu-yüan Chih-tu*, p. 82.
60. *Ibid.*, p. 79.
61. Wang Shou-jen, *Wang Yang-ming Ch'üan-chi* (Hong Kong, 1959), 35.681.
62. *Ibid.*, 35.680–81.   63. *Ibid.*, 35.681.   64. *Ibid.*, 35.681–82.
65. *Ming-shih*, 283.3184.   66. *Ibid.*, 283.3185.
67. *Ibid.*, 283.3184.
68. *Ibid.*, 283.3184–85.
69. Jung Chao-tsu, *Ho Hsin-yin Chi* (Peking, 1960), p. 125.
70. Ch'en Tung-yüan, *Chung-kuo Chiao-yü Shih* (Shanghai, 1926), p. 367.
71. *Ming Shih-tsung Shih-lu*, 198.3a.
72. *Chiang-hsi T'ung-chih* (1880–81 ed.), 82.2a.
73. James B. Parsons, "Preliminary Remarks Concerning a Statistical Analysis of Ming Dynasty Officials," *Transactions of the International Conference of Orientalists in Japan*, III (1958), 19.

74. *Ming-shih*, 110.1376, 193.2254.
75. *Ibid.*, 112.1432–33.
76. Liu I-cheng, "Chiang-su Shu-yüan-chih Ch'u-kao," pp. 20–21.
77. Wang Shou-jen, *Wang Yang-ming Ch'üan-chi*, 35.684.
78. Liu Po-chi, *Kuang-tung Shu-yüan Chih-tu Yen-ko*, p. 29.
79. *Ibid.*, pp. 30–31.
80. *Ming-shih*, 213.2474.
81. Wang Shou-jen, *Wang Yang-ming Ch'üan-chi*, 35.684.
82. *Ibid.*
83. Shen Te-fu, *Wan-li Yeh-hu-pien*, 24.608.
84. Huang Tsung-hsi, *Ming-jü Hsüeh-an* (Shanghai; Wen-tuan-lou ed.), 27.1b. See also *Ming-shih*, 283.3187.
85. See, e.g., *Ibid.*, 210.2444, 216.2503, 298.3346–47.
86. For members of Yen's faction, see *Ibid.*, 308.3487.
87. *Ming Shen-tsung Shih-lu* (photolithographic reproduction, 1940), 83.5b; *Ch'ang-chou-fu Chih* (1886 ed.), 21.17a.
88. *Ming Chi* (Shanghai, 1924), 40.6b.
89. See, e.g., *Chiang-hsi T'ung-chih* (late Ch'ing ed.), chs. 81–82.
90. Shen Te-fu, *Wan-li Yeh-hu-pien*, 8.219.
91. Robert B. Crawford, *The Life and Thought of Chang Chü-cheng, 1525–1582* (University Microfilms MIC 61–2098, 1961), pp. 129–30.
92. Ch'en Tung-yüan, *Chung-kuo Chiao-yü Shih*, pp. 370–71.
93. Liang Ou-ti, "Ming-tai ti Shu-yüan Chih-tu—Chung-kuo Shu-yüan Chih-tu Tzu-liao," *Hsien-tai Shih-hsüeh*, II, no. 4 (1935), 9, citing Shen Te-fu, *Wan-li Yeh-hu-pien*. Chang Chü-cheng had expressed some of his ideas against private academies as early as 1575. See Ch'en Tung-yüan, *Chung-kuo K'o-chü Shih-tai chih Chiao-yü*, pp. 74–78.
94. Robert B. Crawford, *Chang Chü-cheng*, p. 139.
95. Shen Te-fu, *Wan-li Yeh-hu-pien*, 8.215.
96. *Ming-shih*, 283.3184.
97. Huang Tsung-hsi, *Ming-ju Hsüeh-an*, 34.1a.
98. *Ming-shih*, 283.3186.
99. *Ibid.*, 213.2479.
100. *Ibid.*, 213.2480. Curtailment of mourning (*to-ch'ing*) was a technical term for cutting off mourning for a parent and returning to office at the command of the emperor. The literal meaning, "to violate one's feelings," reflected the question of filial piety involved, but the phrase had no pejorative content.
101. *Ibid.*, 229.2633–34.
102. *Ch'ang-chou-fu Chih*, 21.17a; *Ming-shih*, 234.2675.
103. *Ming-shih*, 243.2763–64.

104. Pan Shu-ko, "Ming-chi Hui Shu-yüan K'ao," *Jui-ho Chi-k'an*, II (1930), 133–41, particularly p. 138.
105. Pan Shu-ko, "Ming-chi Hui Shu-yüan K'ao," p. 137; Sheng Lang-hsi, *Chung-kuo Shu-yüan Chih-tu*, p. 108.
106. Ch'en Tung-yüan, "Lu-shan Pai-lu-tung Shu-yüan Yen-ko K'ao," part II, p. 1.
107. *Pai-lu-chou Shu-yüan Chih*, 1.8b.
108. Ch'en Tung-yüan, "Lu-shan Pai-lu-tung Shu-yüan Yen-ko K'ao," part II, p. 1.
109. *Pai-lu-chou Shu-yüan Chih*, 1.8a.
110. See Pan Shu-ko, "Ming-chi Hui Shu-yüan K'ao," pp. 136–38.
111. *Nan-hsi Shu-yüan Chih*, 2.6a.
112. Pan Shu-ko, "Ming-chi Hui Shu-yüan K'ao," pp. 136–38.
113. Wang Shou-jen, *Wang Yang-ming Ch'üan-chi*, "Wan-sung Shu-yüan Chi," p. 64.
114. T'an Ch'ien, *Kuo Ch'üeh*, V, 4397.
115. See *Ming-shih*, 288.3237, 221.2553.
116. Pan Shu-ko, "Ming-chi Hui Shu-yüan K'ao," pp. 136–38.
117. Jung Chao-tsu, *Ho Hsin-yin Chi*, p. 123, citing Huang Tsung-hsi, *Ming-ju Hsüeh-an*.
118. Jung Chao-tsu, *Ho Hsin-yin Chi*, p. 125.
119. T'an Ch'ien, *Kuo Ch'üeh*, V, 4353, 4360.
120. *Hsü Wen-hsien T'ung-k'ao*, 50.3246.
121. Ts'ao Sung-yeh, "Shu-yüan Kai-k'uang," no. 113, pp. 6–7.
122. Pan Shu-ko, "Ming-chi Hui Shu-yüan K'ao," p. 137.
123. See *Ming Shen-tsung Shih-lu*, 95.3b; T'an Ch'ien, *Kuo Ch'üeh*, V, 4380, 4393.
124. Figured from Ts'ao Sung-yeh, "Shu-yüan Kai-k'uang," no. 113, pp. 19–20. The roughness of figures in this source has already been noted.
125. Ts'ao Sung-yeh, "Shu-yüan Kai-k'uang," no. 112, pp. 27–28; no. 111, pp. 22–24; no. 113, p. 29. The figures for each dynasty do not total 100 percent because the auspices under which some academies were founded are unknown.
126. Tilemann Grimm, "Some Remarks on the Suppression of Shu-yüan in Ming China," *Transactions of the International Conference of Orientalists in Japan*, II (1957), 8–16; particularly p. 10.
127. Ts'ao Sung-yeh, "Shu-yüan Kai-k'uang," no. 115, p. 8.
128. Tabulated from Liu Po-chi, *Kuang-tung Shu-yüan Chih-tu Yen-ko*, pp. 28–38.
129. Internal bureaucratization as well as integration into the state structure is indicated by Shen-tsung's time (1572–1620). See Ch'en Tung-yüan, *Chung-kuo Chiao-yü Shih*, pp. 367–68.

130. Ch'en Tung-yüan, "Lu-shan Pai-lu-tung Shu-yüan Yen-ko K'ao," part II, p. 1.
131. Huang Tsung-hsi, *Ming-ju Hsüeh-an*, 41.1b.
132. *Ch'ang-chou-fu Chih*, 15.13b.
133. Heinrich Busch, "The Tung-lin Shu-yüan and Its Political and Philosophical Significance," *Monumenta Serica*, XIV (1949–1955), 1–163; and Charles O. Hucker, "The Tung Lin Movement of the Late Ming Period," in J. K. Fairbank, ed., *Chinese Thought and Institutions* (Chicago, 1957), pp. 132–63.
134. Busch, "The Tung-lin Shu-yüan," p. 28.
135. *Ibid.*, p. 29.   136. *Ibid.*, pp. 29–30.   137. *Ibid.*, pp. 44–45.
138. *Ibid.*, p. 55.   139. *Ibid.*, p. 58.   140. *Ibid.*, pp. 61–62.
141. *Ibid.*, p. 62.   142. *Ibid.*, p. 63.   143. *Ibid.*
144. *Ibid.*, pp. 63–64.
145. See Liang Ou-ti, "Ming-tai ti Shu-yüan Chih-tu," p. 12.
146. Busch, "The Tung-lin Shu-yüan," p. 66.
147. Sheng Lang-hsi, *Chung-kuo Shu-yüan Chih-tu*, p. 106, identifies Kuan-chung Academy as Tzu-yang Academy, located by Ts'ao Sung-yeh ("Shu-yüan Kai-k'uang," no. 111, p. 30) in Hui-chou.
148. Busch, "The Tung-lin Shu-yüan," p. 66.
149. *Ibid.*
150. Ch'en Tung-yüan, *Chung-kuo K'o-chü Shih-tai chih Chiao-yü*, pp. 77–78.
151. *Hsü Wen-hsien T'ung-k'ao*, 50.3246.
152. Busch, "The Tung-lin Shu-yüan," p. 71.

JAMES B. PARSONS *The Ming Dynasty Bureaucracy: Aspects of Background Forces*

1. Only the officials serving in the paramount central government have been included, i.e. those officials who served at Nanking until 1421 when Peking became the principal capital and those who served in Peking after 1421. Officials who served in the secondary capital at Nanking following 1421 have not been included because no complete lists are readily available. Lists in Lung Wen-pin, *Ming-shu*, and in Lei Li, *Kuo-ch'ao Lieh-ch'ing Nien-piao*, end in the early Wan-li period (1580s) and the task of completing the lists from the *Ming Shih-lu* would be too exacting. The censor-in-chief position was a double one, with a left and a right censor-in-chief. Beginning in the Wan-li period, however, the position of right censor-in-chief was usually not filled. Official terminology generally follows Charles O. Hucker, "Governmental Organization of the Ming Dynasty," *Harvard Journal of Asiatic Studies*, XXI (1958), 1–66.

2. The only exceptions occur in the two directly administered areas or metropolitan areas, which here are given the Chinese designations Pei-chihli (modern Hopei) and Nan-chihli (modern Kiangsu and Anhwei); these had only the first two of these provincial offices. Strictly speaking, Pei-chihli and Nan-chihli were not considered true provinces, but for purposes of convenience they are treated here in the same fashion as the thirteen "proper" provinces: Chekiang, Fukien, Honan, Hukuang (modern Hupeh and Hunan), Kiangsi, Kwangsi, Kwangtung, Kweichow, Shansi, Shensi (including modern Kansu), Shantung, Szechwan, and Yunnan. The administration commissioner position was a double one, with a left and a right administion commissioner.

3. Also included at the prefectural level were 20 (out of a total of 32) independent subprefectures. The difference between an independent and a dependent subprefecture was simply that the former was not subordinate to a prefecture, but was directly attached to a province. In addition, it should be noted that 14 of the missing 23 prefectures were in Yunnan, four were in Szechwan, two were in Kwangsi, one was in Hukuang, and one was in Kiangsi. Thus, the survey includes virtually all the important prefectures.

4. Obtaining completely accurate figures for the total numbers of Ming prefectures, subprefectures, and counties is a difficult task. Obviously, the figures varied to some extent during the dynasty. An added complication is the existence of special areas of administration, particularly in the southwest. Thus, the general figures given here, which are cited at the beginning of the geographical section of the *Mingshih,* do not entirely agree with the detailed province-by-province breakdown.

5. A detailed listing of offices and counties included in the county II category will be found in Appendix III. Appendix III is a listing of the names of subprefectures and counties whose magistrates were considered on the subprefectural county I level.

6. Gazetteer collections utilized were mainly those in the Institute of Humanistic Sciences of Kyoto University and in the Academia Sinica, Taiwan.

7. See Otto van der Sprenkel, "The Chronological Tables of Lei Li, an Important Source for the Study of the Ming Bureaucracy," *Bulletin of the School of Oriental and African Studies,* University of London, XIV (1952), 325–34, for a discussion of this work.

8. A list of the abbreviated reign periods will be found in Appendix I.

9. Mr. van der Sprenkel's article is "High Officials in the Ming, a Note on the *Ch'i Ch'ing Nien Piao,*" *Bulletin of the School of Oriental and African Studies,* University of London, XIV (1952), 87–114. This

is one of the pioneer articles dealing with the Ming dynasty bureaucracy. The five main phases of the dynasty that he proposes are: 1368–1402, 1402–87, 1487–1572, 1572–1620, and 1620–44.

10. James B. Parsons, "A Preliminary Analysis of the Ming Dynasty Bureaucracy," *Occasional Papers of the Kansai Asiatic Society*, VII (May, 1959), 5–6.

11. Most of the lists of officials, except for the central government, are divided only according to reign period without indicating precise years within the period during which a particular individual served. Thus, the average length of tenure was obtained simply by dividing the number of officials into the number of years in the reign period. Consequently, if the list was deficient, the average tenure would appear in the calculations higher than it actually was.

12. The chief factors indicating incompleteness in the official lists at the beginning and end of the dynasty are unusual variations in numbers (for example, from province to province) which are not so notable for other periods, and the incidence of cases where the lists completely omit the very early or very late reign periods. In the event of complete omissions, that particular office would not be included in the final calculations for the reign period averages.

13. This was particularly the consolidation of the land taxes into one payment, referred to popularly as the "single whip." Cf. Huang Han-liang, *The Land Tax in China*, (Columbia University, *Studies in History, Economics, and Public Law*, no. 187, 1918), p. 53.

14. Meng Sen, *Ming-tai Shih* (Taipei, 1957), pp. 295–96, 300. There are cases cited of officials, despairing of having their requests for retirement acted upon, finally abandoning their offices without the usual formalities. Also, at one point, there was only one functioning grand secretary, and even he refused to leave his bed for several weeks.

15. The provincial origins of roughly 12 percent of the officials are unknown; consequently, they could not be used in the regionalism calculations. In addition, for about 7 percent of the officials there are indications of their native provinces only, with no indications of their native local areas. Calculations requiring a knowledge of native local areas are therefore based on the approximately 81 ·percent of officials for whom complete information exists.

16. Percentages for the central government are based primarily on length of service. Because of the relatively small numbers of central government officials, it was felt that length of service would provide a better index to political importance than mere numbers of officials. Anyway, there are only minor differences in the results obtained from the two methods of calculation.

17. The population figures are those appearing in Ping-ti Ho, *The Ladder of Success in Imperial China* (New York, 1962), p. 225. Professor Ho's work in a real landmark in the social history of the Ming and Ch'ing periods.
18. The question of political power within provinces will be considered subsequently.
19. Short treatments of the Ming quota system for official degrees have appeared in Ping-ti Ho, *The Ladder of Success in Imperial China*, pp. 184–87; E. A. Kracke, Jr., "Region, Family, and Individual in the Chinese Examination System," in J. K. Fairbank, ed., *Chinese Thought and Institutions* (Chicago, 1957), pp. 251–53; and in Otto van der Sprenkel, "The Geographical Background of the Ming Civil Service," *Journal of Economic and Social History of the Orient*, IV, part 3 (1961), 302–36. All these are based primarily on *Ming-shih*, (Po-na ed.), 70.5b–6a. Briefly stated, the *chin-shih* quotas were distributed among three major areas (South, North, and Center), based on a ratio of 55:35:10. The southern area consisted of Chekiang, Fukien, Kiangsi, Hukuang, Kwangtung, and most of Nan-chihli; the northern, of Pei-chihli, Shantung, Honan, Shansi, and Shensi; and the central, of Szechwan, Kwangsi, Yunnan, Kweichow, and a portion of Nan-chihli. The system was formulated by the famous elder statesman Yang Shih-ch'i and others in 1425. It remained in force with minor temporary exceptions until the end of the dynasty. The *chü-jen* quota system was provincial and varied roughly according to population.
20. Ping-ti Ho, *The Ladder of Success in Imperial China*, pp. 234–35, points out Fukien's widespread commerce and quite diversified economy.
21. Ping-ti Ho, *The Ladder of Success in Imperial China*, pp. 231–33; and Chi Ch'ao-ting, *Key Economic Areas in Chinese History* (London, 1936), pp. 9–11, 35–45, 147–48.
22. Wu Kwang-tsing, *Scholarship, Book-production, and Libraries in China* (unpublished University of Chicago Ph.D. dissertation, 1944), p. 218. When the location of the 125 Nan-chihli libraries is analyzed in more detail, it is noteworthy that they are concentrated in precisely the same general section which was most important as a source of officials. The Nan-chihli area that became modern Anhwei, which was politically underrepresented, possessed only one of the 125 great libraries. Furthermore, according to Dr. Wu's figures, neither Fukien nor Kiangsi was at all comparable to Nan-chihli and Chekiang as regards libraries. Fukien had only eight and Kiangsi only five. Finally, in my own work on the late Ming peasant rebellions, there emerged from the very outset the bibliographic fact that the most extensive

and valuable of the primary sources were not compiled by eyewit-
nesses to the rebellions from the areas most directly affected. Instead,
most of the sources were the products of Nan-chihli and Chekiang
scholars, following in the well-established scholarly tradition of their
native areas. Even one of the most significant eyewitness accounts
(*Huang-shu,* by Fei Mi) was not written until after the author had
moved from his native Szechwan to Nan-chihli.

23. The indications of decline for Kiangsi confirm a point made by Ping-ti
Ho, *The Ladder of Success in Imperial China,* p. 231, where it is
stated that Chekiang replaced Kiangsi in academic success during the
sixteenth century. As for Fukien's upward trend beginning around
1550, one of the possible explanations might be the declining strength
of the Wakō (Japanese coastal raiders) and the subsequent recovery
of Fukien's politically dominant coastal area from Wakō depredations. Mr. Benjamin Hazard has been kind enough to provide me
with certain pertinent facts concerning the Wakō based on his own
extensive research. In a personal communication he stated that,
although Fukien was especially hard hit by raids from 1558 to 1563,
a sharp decline occurred subsequently.

24. In certain cases two native areas would be indicated for an official—
the traditional ancestral home plus the area in which the family was
registered and actually resident. Such cases were not significant
numerically, comprising certainly less than one percent of the total
number of officials. The area of actual residence was used in all
calculations.

25. This trend was demonstrated in a preliminary fashion in J. B. Parsons, "A Preliminary Analysis of the Ming Dynasty Bureaucracy."
Also, it was considered for provincial officials by Otto van der Sprenkel in "The Geographical Background of the Ming Civil Service."

26. The subprefectures and counties included in the survey amounted to
11 percent of the combined total, and only one grand secretary was
discovered to have served as a subprefectural or county magistrate.
Based on this ratio, one could estimate that only nine or ten grand
secretaries ever served in any subprefecture or county as magistrate.

27. Since 32 ministers were found to have served as subprefectural or
county magistrates on the basis of the 11 percent of these offices
included in the survey, by extension it could be estimated that a
total of around 300 of the ministers had served at this level.

28. The calculations for the official degrees are based on approximately
two thirds of the officials. The degrees held by the remaining third
were not indicated. The central government officials were not included
in the calculations of degrees because, following the Yung-lo period,
there was virtually no exception to the rule that all were *chin-shih.*

29. The official lists mention several bases upon which persons were recommended and appointed to office during the Hung-wu period. Some of the more commonly mentioned bases were: *lao-jen* (elder person), *ku-kuan* (former official), *ts'ai-neng* (ability), *jen-ts'ai* (human talent), and *ming-ching* (versed in the classics).
30. Li Wen-chih, *Wan Ming Min-pien* (Shanghai, 1948), pp. 8–9.
31. One of the more poignant brief descriptions of the exalted state of isolation and boredom in which the district princes lived was made by the Portugese Pereira in the sixteenth century: "Howbeit, not one of these [district princes] hath as long as he liveth, any charge of government at all. They give themselves to eating and drinking, and be for the most burly men of body. . . . They be nevertheless very pleasant, courteous and fair-conditioned, neither did we find, all the time we were in that city, so much honor and good entertainment anywhere as at their hands. . . . Notwithstanding the good lodging these gentlemen have so commodious that they want nothing, yet they are in this bondage, that during life they never go abroad. The cause, as I did understand, wherefor the king so useth his cousins is that none of them at any time may rebel against him." C. R. Boxer, ed., *South China in the Sixteenth Century* (London, 1953), pp. 40–41.
32. F. Alvares Semedo, *The History of That Great and Renowned Monarchy of China* (London, 1655), pp. 122–23.
33. Ping-ti Ho, *The Ladder of Success in Imperial China*, p. 22.

Glossary of Terms

an-ch'a shih 按察使
chang-ch'ien tsung-chih ch'in-ping tu chih-hui shih ssu 帳前總制親兵都指揮使司
ch'ang-li 常例
ch'ao-chin 朝覲
chen-shou 鎮守
chen tsai-hsiang 真宰相
cheng 正
Cheng-hsüeh Shu-yüan 正學書院
cheng-kuan 正官
cheng-shih t'ang 政事堂
ch'eng-hsiang 丞相
chi-mi chou 羈縻州
chi-mi fu-chou 羈縻府州
chi-shih-chung 給事中
ch'i-yün 起運
chiang 匠
chiao-kuan 教官
ch'ieh-hsieh 怯薛
chien-kuan 諫官
chien-sheng 監生
ch'ien-hu 千戶
ch'ien-hu so 千戶所
chih-chou 知州
chih-fen t'ien 職分田
chih-fu 知府
chih-hsien 知縣
chih-hui shih 指揮使
chih-shu 紙贖
chih-t'ien 職田
chin-hua-yin 金花銀
Chin-i wei 錦衣衛
chin-shih 進士
ch'in-ch'in 親親
ch'in-chün 親軍

ch'in-chün wei 親軍衛
ch'in-wang 親王
ching-piao 旌表
ching-t'ien 井田
ch'ing 頃
ch'iung-ping tu-wu 窮兵黷武
chou 州
chu-kung 助工
chü-jen 舉人
chuang-yüan 狀元
chün (soldier) 軍
chün (commandery) 郡
chün-hsien 郡縣
chün kuo ta-shih 軍國大事
chün-wang 郡王
chün-wei 郡尉
chung-nan 重難
chung-shu sheng 中書省
fen shu-mi yüan 分樞密院
fen yüan-shuai fu 分元帥府
feng-chien 封建
feng-hsien kuan 風憲官
feng-po 封駁
fu 府
fu-an 撫按
fu-i ch'üan-shu 賦役全書
fu-ping 府兵
fu-sheng 附生
fu-shih 府試
fu t'i-chü 副提舉
hai-wai 海外
Han chün 漢軍
Han-jen 漢人
hou 厚
hsi-yin hui 惜陰會
hsiang-hsü 相習

hsiang-yüeh 鄉約

hsiao-lien 孝廉

hsien 縣

hsien-hsien 賢賢

hsien-shih 縣試

hsing chung-shu sheng 行中書省

hsing-kuo i yüan-shuai fu 興國翼元帥
　府

hsing-sheng 行省

hsing shu-mi yüan 行樞密院

hsing tu-tu fu 行都督府

hsing yü-shih t'ai 行御史臺

hsiu-ts'ai 秀才

hsüan-wei ssu 宣慰司

hsüan-wei tao 宣慰道

hsüeh-cheng 學政

hsün-an 巡按

hsün-an yü-shih 巡按御史

hsün-fu 巡撫

Hu 胡

hui-pi 廻避

i 翼

i hsing hsiang-ts'an 以行相參

i-ping 義兵

i-t'iao-pien fa 一條鞭法

i-yung 義勇

jen-ts'ai 人才

ju-hsüeh 儒學

ju-hsüeh t'i-chü ssu 儒學提舉司

Jung 戎

kai-t'u kuei-liu 改土歸流

k'ao-ch'a 考察

k'ao-shih kuan 考試官

k'o 科

k'o-t'iao 科條

ku-kuan 故官

k'uai-chi lu 會計錄

k'uan 寬

k'uan yen te t'i 寬嚴得體

kung-hsieh ch'ien 公廨錢

kung-hsieh t'ien 公廨田

kung-shih k'u 公使庫

kuo 國

kuo-hsiang 國相

kuo-tzu chien 國子監

lao-jen 老人

li 禮

li-mu 吏目

liang 糧

liang-chang 糧長

liu-kuan 流官

liu-pu 六部

lu 路

men-hsia sheng 門下省

Meng-ku 蒙古

min 民

ming-ching 明經

mou 畝

mu-ping 募兵

Nan-jen 南人

nei-ko 內閣

pa-ku wen 八服文

Pai-lu-tung 白鹿洞

p'iao-i 票擬

ping-ma chih-hui shih ssu 兵馬指揮使
　司

ping-pu 兵部

po-hu 百戶

p'o-chia hsien ling, mieh-men tz'u-shih
破家縣令滅門刺史

pu-cheng shih 布政使

pu-i 部議

San-hsien Tz'u 三賢祠

San-pien 三邊

Se-mu jen 色目人

shang-shu 尚書

shang-shu sheng 尚書省

she 社

she-hsüeh 社學

sheng 省

sheng-yüan 生員

shih 使

shih-chin fei-ku 是今非古

shih-hsi tz'u-shih 世襲刺史

shih-hsüan 世選

shih-kuan 史官

shih-she 始設

shou 守

shou-ling kuan 首領官

shou tsai ssu-i 守在四夷

shu-mi yüan 樞密院

shu-yüan 書院

ssu-hsiang hui 四鄉會

ssu-li t'ai-chien 司禮太監

su-cheng lien-fang ssu 肅政廉訪司

sui-kung 歲貢

ta hsüeh-shih 大學士

ta-lu-hua-ch'ih 達魯花赤

ta tu-tu fu 大都督府

ta yüan-shuai fu 大元帥府

t'ai-chien 太監

tan 石

T'an-ma-ch'ih 探馬赤

tao 道

t'i 體

t'i-hsüeh 提學

t'i-hsüeh kuan 提學官

t'i-tiao 提調

t'i-tiao cheng-kuan 提調正官

t'i-tiao hsüeh-hsiao kuan 提調學校官

t'i-tu 提督

t'iao-chih 條旨

t'iao-pien-yin 條鞭銀

t'iao-yüeh 條約

ting 丁

t'ing-i 廷議

to-ch'ing 奪情

t'ou-huang 投荒

tsai-hsiang 宰相

ts'ai-neng 才能

tsu-fu 租賦

tsu-hsün 祖訓

tsu-yung-tiao 租庸調

ts'un-liu 存留

tsung-ping kuan 總兵官

tsung-tu 總督

tu ch'a-yüan 都察院

tu-chiao 督教

tu-chih 獨制

tu chih-hui shih 都指揮使

tu chih-hui shih ssu 都指揮使司

t'u-kuei 塗歸

t'u-ssu 土司

tu wei chih-hui shih ssu 都衛指揮使司

tu yü-shih 都御史

t'un-t'ien 屯田

t'un-t'ien ch'ien-hu so 屯田千戶所

t'un-t'ien wan-hu fu 屯田萬戶府

t'ung-cheng 通政

t'ung-cheng ssu 通政司

t'ung-chih hui 同志會

wan-hu 萬戶

wei 衛

wen 文

wen-chü 文具

Wen-ming Shu-yüan 文明書院

wu-ai 無礙

wu-hua p'an-shih 五花判事

Yang-cheng Shu-yüan 養正書院

yen 嚴

yen-lu 言路

yin 廕

ying-t'ien ssu 營田司

yu-t'ieh 由貼

yü-chung chün 禦中軍

yü feng-chien yü chün-hsien 寓封建於郡縣

yü-shih 御史

yü-shih ta-fu 御史大夫

yü-shih t'ai 御史臺

yüan-shuai fu 元帥府

yung 用

Index

Aborigines, 8, 153–54, 157; *see also* *T'u-ssu*

Absolutism, 43, 70

Academies (*shu-yüan*), 135, 138, 139, 143; military, 38; seclusion of, 149–50; growth of, 150 (table), 151 (table), 167 (table); education in, 152; prohibitions on, 153–54, 160, 162–63; Canton, 155–56; name changes, 166; repressions of, 168–69, 173; public funds for, 172; restoration order for, 174

Agricultural colonies, *see* *T'un-t'ien*

Altan Khan, 67, 111–12

An-ch'a shih (surveillance commissioner), 11

Animal fodder, 92

Annam, 55–56, 56–60, 62–66

Annamese, 223–24

Appointments, 15, 144–45, 272*n*

Aristocrats, 98; military, 37, 38–39; Mongol, 25–26, 29, 31; *see also* Gentry

Arms, laws on, 30

Army, 115, 117–18, 121, 123; Han, 28–30; newly submitted, 28–30; *see also* Soldiers

Association of the Four Localities (*ssu-hsiang hui*), 158–59, 166

Burma, 62

Capital, appointments to, 15

Censorate, 27, 48

Censors, 11, 131, 137, 272*n*

Censors-in-chief, 218 (table)

Census, 29–30, 37

Central government, 184–86, 185 (table), 206, 207 (table)

Centurions, 26, 35

Ceremonial rites, 142

Chan Jo-shui, 153–55, 161

Chancellery, 45, 244*n*

Chang Ch'ang, 23

Chang-ch'ien tsung-chih ch'in-ping tu chih-hui shih ssu (commandery before the tent in charge of the personal guard), 33

Chang Ching (Ts'ai Ching), 65

Chang Chü-cheng, 46, 86; on education officials, 139; and 1575 regulations, 134, 135; and academicians, 163–65; and prohibitions on academies, 166; reforms of, 179–80

Chang Fu, 46, 56, 57, 59, 61

Chang T'an, 243*n*

Chang Tsan, 63–64

Chang Ts'ung, 156, 157

Chang Yüeh, 65

Chao Shih-ch'ing, 80, 113

Chen-shou (grand defender), 13, 35

Ch'en Feng-wu, 142

Ch'en Hsin-chia, 68–69

Ch'en Hsüan, 142

Ch'en Liang, 8–9

Cheng-hsüeh Academy, 161

Cheng-shih t'ang (Hall of State Affairs), 45

Ch'eng hsiang (chief councilor), 44–45

Ch'eng-tsu, Emperor, 2, 46, 55–56, 79

Chi-mi chou (prefectures under loose rein), 2

Chi-shih–chung (supervising secretaries), 45, 49–50, 243n

Ch'i-yün (checked-out) funds, 83, 88, 89

Chia I, 5

Chiang clan, 207

Chien I, 57, 58, 59

Chien-kuan (remonstrating officials), 44

Chien-sheng (National University students), 14–15

Ch'ien-hu (chiliarch), 26, 35

Ch'ien-hu so (chiliads), 23, 27–29

Chih-chou (subprefectural magistrates), 11, 228

Chih-fen t'ien (land pertaining to office), 18

Chih-fu, see Prefects

Chih-hsien, see County magistrates

Chih-t'ien (office land), 18, 19

Chin-hua-yin (Gold-Floral-Silver), 89, 91, 104, 108

Chin-i wei (Embroidered-uniform Guard), 33

Chin Lien, 79

Chin-shih (metropolitan graduates), 13–14, 144, 184, 270n

Ch'in Ching, 80

Ch'in chün (personal troops), 35

Ch'in-chün wei (personal army guards), 34

Ch'in-wang, see Princes, imperial

Ching-ti, Emperor, 79

Ching-t'ien (well-field system), 10

Chinggis Khan, 25, 28

Chou Hung-mo, 132-33

Chou Sheng, 107

Chu Hsi, 2, 6, 9, 143–44, 151, 154

Chu Yüan-chang, Emperor, 23, 31–32; elevation of, 34; on colony-fields, 36; on military elite, 38, 40; on civil offices, 37

Chu Yüan-ming, 14

Chü-jen (provincial graduates), 13–14, 15, 184, 270n

Chuang-lieh-ti, Emperor, 68–69

Chün, see Soldiers

Chung-li Academy, 160

Chün-hsien lun (Discourses on the prefectural system) (Ku Yen-wu), quoted, 3–4

Chün-wang (prince of second degree), 3

Chün-wei (military governor), 17

Chung-li Academy, 160

Chung-shu sheng (Secretariat), 45

Civil-service examinations, 18, 37, 83, 129, 136, 144, 259n; see also Chin-shih; Chü-jen; Education Intendants; Eight-legged essay '

Clan: imperial, 5, 223; and Mongol communities, 25; in Fukien, 184; and bureaucracy, 206, 207 (table); distribution by province, 208 (table); political power of, 209–15 (tables), 216, 226; and family names, 221–22 (table)

Colony-fields, see T'un-t'ien

Common Resolve Association (t'ung-chih hui), 158

Confiscations, 103, 105, 107

Confucianism, 4; and fiscal administration, 74–75, 124, 126; and learning, 134; Ch'eng Chu line of, 139

Conscription, 30

Correct Learning Academy (Cheng-hsüeh Shu-yüan), 144

Corruption, 76–77, 205

Corvée labor, 98, 103, 139

County (hsien), 27, 87, 191 (table); magistrates (chih-hsien), 11, 87, 228; government, 220–21, 220 (table)

Court conferences, 49, 70

Court of Imperial Entertainments, 90–91
Court of the Imperial Stud, 102–3, 116
Customs duties, 99–100, 109

Daruhaci (head officials), 26–27
Degree-holders, 129
Desertions: military, 31, 39, 117; of salt producers, 96
Discipline, 12, 16, 132
Dynasty, length of, 6–7

Education: regulations on, 134–35, 136, 139; jurisdiction for, 136–37; *see also* Academies; *Ju-hsüeh*; National University; School System; *She-hsüeh*
——intendants (*t'i-hsüeh kuan*): 130; original establishment of, 131; and inspection tours, 131, 141–42; and *t'i-tu* (supervision), 132, 133, 134; guides for, 135–36; jurisdiction of, 136, 142; source of, 137–38; censorial office of, 138; seeking favor from, 140–41; and private academies, 143; and nomination of candidates, 145
Eight-legged essay (*pa-ku wen*), 16, 139, 146
Embezzlement, 102
Emperor: appointments by, 11–12; authority of, 44; restraints upon, 44–45; and ministers, 47; and public opinion, 48; personal income of, 89, 91
Enfeoffment, 2, 3, 5, 6, 8
Eunuchs: political influence of, 47–48; as army supervisors, 57; and foreign policy, 61, 62; and revenue ministers, 80; number of,

91; and salt production abuses, 98; as tax commissioners, 113
Examinations, *see* Civil-service examinations
Executions, 16–17, 78

Famine, 92, 127
Fang Hsien-fu, 155–56
Fang Pin, 56
Favoritism, 188, 205, 226
Fen yüan-shuai fu, 31
Feng-chien Hou-lun (Further discourses on the feudal system) (Lo Pi), 9
Feng-chien lun (Discourses on the feudal system) (Liu T'sung-yüan), 7–8
Feng-hsien kuan (guardians of the customs and laws), 131
Feng-po (sealed dissent), 44, 49, 50, 242n, 243n
Fiefs, Mongol, 25
Fines, 20, 103
Fiscal policies, 18–19, 77, 80–81
Flogging, 16, 17
Foreigners, 2, 224
Fu (prefectures), 1, 32
Fu-i ch'üan-shu (Comprehensive book on taxation and services), 84
Fu-ku Academy, 158, 165
Fu-ping (prefectural soldier), 24, 234n, 237–38n
Fu-sheng (supernumerary students), 139
Fu-shih (second qualifying tests), 18
Fukien: officials in, 182 (table), 183; and clan system, 184, 207, 216; local power in, 192 (map); origins of officials, 197 (table)

Gentry, 21, 108, 125

Gift-making, 20
Governors, 87–88; general, 12; provincial, 12; commandery, 17–18
Grain tribute, 89, 91
Granaries, imperial, 91, 123
Grand Canal, 93, 99, 107
Grand Court of Revision, 49
Grand secretaries, 216–17

Han-jen (Chin descendants), 29, 30, 238n
Han Lin-erh, 32
Hereditary authority, 2
Ho Hsin-yin, 168
Ho (Le), regime, 55–56
Ho-tung school, 134
Ho Wen-yüan, 61
Horses, supplying of, 102
Hsia Yen: quoted, 46–47; on war policy, 63, 66, 67; and academies, 156, 159, 160
Hsia Yüan-chi, 56, 57, 58, 78–79
Hsiang-yüeh (community contracts), 9–10
Hsiao Kung-ch'üan, 10
Hsieh clan, 216, 217 (table)
Hsieh Hsüan, 134, 137
Hsieh Sheng, 68–69
Hsien-shih (first qualifying tests), 18
Hsing (chung-shu) sheng (Branch Secretariats), 11, 27
Hsing-ning-hsien Chih (Gazetteer of Hsing-ning district) (Chu Yün-ming), 14
Hsing tu-tu fu (Branch Military Commissions), 34
Hsiu-ts'ai (first level) public competitions, 145
Hsiung T'ing-pi, quoted, 117
Hsu Tsan, 153–54, 161
Hsü Chieh, 162–63, 164
Hsüan-tsung, Emperor, 57, 58, 79

Hsüan-wei ssu, 31
Hsüan-wei tao (pacification circuits), 27
Hsüeh-cheng (school governance), 134
Hsün-an (regional inspector), 11, 12
Hsün-fu (grand coordinators), 12
Hu Chü-jen, 166
Hu Wei-yung conspiracy, 54
Hu Yin, 132
Huai-yü Academy, 166
Huang Fu, 131
Huang Tsung-hsi, 8, 10
Hui-pi (avoidance), 16
Hung-fan (The Great Plan), 243n
Huo T'ao, 155–56, 157

I-ping (militia), 31, 94, 111
I-t'iao-pien fa (single-whip method), 84, 93
I-yung (militia), 234n
Impeachment, 75, 135
Imperial palace, 93–94, 113
Inland duty stations, 252n

Japan, 52, 53, 54, 271n
Jen-tsung, Emperor, 57, 79
Jen-wen Academy, 165, 168, 173–74
Jih-chih lu (Record of daily learning) (Ku Yen-wu), 10
Ju-hsüeh (classical academies), 38
Ju-hsüeh t'i-chü ssu (Confucian Schools Superintendancy), 130

Kan-ch'üan Academy, 155, 161
K'ang Mao-ts'ai, 36
K'ao-ch'a (special evaluation), 12
Kesig (personal guard), 25, 26, 27, 30, 238n
Ko Shou-li, 15
K'o (offices of Scrutiny), 47, 85
Ko Tse, 79

K'o-t'iao (examination rules), 146
K'uai-chi Lu (fiscal records), 84
Kuan-chung Academy, 173
Kubilai, 26, 28
Ku Ch'eng, 53
Ku Hsien-ch'eng, 172
Ku Yen-wu, 3–5, 10, 20–21, 49–50
Kuei O, 157
Kuei-yang Academy, 157
Kuei Yu-Kuang, 126
Kuo Tzu-hsing, 31

Land: allotment, 28, 29, 36; assessments, 87, 119–20; surveys, 86, 121; reclamation, 101–2
Lao-jen (older person), 272n
Le Loi, 57–60
Le Ninh, 63–64, 66
Le (Ho) Qui-ly, 55
Levies, 18, 87, 92–93, 94, 111
Li (propriety), 44
Li Fan, 242n
Li Hsi-yüan, 65–66
Li Meng-yüan, 142
Li Ming, 109
Li-mu (chiefs of police), 3, 233n
Li Nü-hua, 82, 99
Li Pin, 57
Li Po-yao, 6
Liang, see Tax, grain
Liang-chang, see Tax captains
Liaotung, 223–24
Libraries, 152, 184
Lien-hsi Academy, 152
Lin clan, 207, 221
Ling-chi Association, 162
Liu Chi, 130
Liu Ch'iu, 61–62
Liu Chung-fu, 77–78
Liu Sheng, 58–59
Liu Sung, 6
Liu Ta-hsia, 62
Liu Tsung-chou, 126

Liu T'sung-yüan, 7–8
Lo Ju-fang, 164
Lo Pi, 9
Lu brothers, 9–10
Lu Chi, 5–6
Lu-ch'uan, 60–62
Lu Jung, 62
Lu-shih (Great History) (Lo Pi), 9
Lü K'un, 12
Lung-ch'eng Academy, 163, 165, 171

Ma Shen, 80
Ma Tuan-lin, 3
Mac Dang-dung, 63, 65, 66
Magistrates: power in Yüan dynasty, 10; qualifications of, 13–14; promotion of, 14; age limit for, 15; authority of, 15–16; judicial power of, 16–17; discipline of, 17; supervision of students by, 145; see also Officials
Manchurian campaign, 115
Manchus, 68–69, 76, 121, 122 (table)
Marriage, law on, 30
Maw Shans, 60, 62
Men-hsia sheng, see Chancellery
Meng-ku, see Mongols
Metals, precious, 106
Migrations, forced, 105
Military: authority of, 17; service families in, 23–24; circulating offices in, 37–38; hereditary offices in, 37–38; intelligence of, 70; expenses of, 115; see also Army; Officers; Soldiers; T'un-t'ien; Wei
Min (ordinary civilians), 37
Ming-i Tai-fang Lu (A plan for the prince) (Huang T'sung-hsi), 10
Ming-shih, 13, 17, 23, 131
Ming Shih-lu, 23, 59

Ming T'ai-tsu, Emperor: 2, 10, 19; and bureaucracy, 46; on eunuchs, 48; on frontier defenses, 51–53; and Annam, 55; and revenue ministers, 78; and land taxes, 86; and school system, 130–31

Ministers, 217–18, 217 (table)

Ministers of revenue: salary of, 76; role of, 77; punishments for, 77–78; leaving of office by, 78, 79–80; answers to criticism of, 80–81; staff of, 81–82; number of, 248–49n

Ministry of Revenue: appointments to, 79; and eunuchs, 80; organization of, 81–82; and fiscal planning, 82; and budget, 83–84; available revenue of, 91–92; and unscheduled commutations, 92; cash receivables, 104 (table); staffing of, 105; officials in, 205

Ministry of Rites, 48, 70, 144–45, 205

Ministry of War, 48, 70

Ministry of Works, 101–2

Mongols: military organization of, 24–26; settlement by, 26; and 1421 expedition, 56; Tumed, 67–68; as officials, 223–24

Moral conduct, 135–36, 140, 147

Mourning, curtailment of (to-ch'ing), 165–66, 265n

Mu Shao-hsün, 64

Mu Ying, General, 2

Myriads, 25, 27, 30

Nan-jen, 29, 30

Nan-hsi Academy, 154

National University (kuo-tzu chien), 14–15, 130, 145

Ni Yüan-lu, 81, 85

Noyan (masters), 25–26, 28

Occupation, and census, 29

Office of Transmission, 48, 49

Officers, military, 11, 12, 13, 23–24, 26, 28, 30, 31, 32, 33–34, 35, 38

Offices of Scrutiny, 49

Officials: accountability of, 17; prosecution of, 75; payment of, 76; arrests of, 79–80; regional, 169 (table); positions occupied by, 176–77; length of tenure of, 177–79, 188 (table); place of origin of, 180 (table), 197–204 (tables); non-native appointment of, 196; degree-holding by, 218–20, 221 (table); imperial clansmen as, 223; see also Appointments; Magistrates; Ministers; Prefects

Opinion, public, 48

Ordos, 67–68

Ou-yang Hsiu, 50

Pai-lu-chou Academy, 152, 154

Pai-lu-tung Academy, 143–44, 152, 154, 166, 168

Pai-sha school, 153, 154

P'an Chen, 64

P'an Tan, 64–65

Paper currency, 95, 100, 106

P'eng Hsü, 138

Philosophical discussions, 157, 158, 159, 160, 163

Pi Chiang, 80

Pi Tzu-yen, 80, 81, 84, 121

P'iao-i (suggested rescripts), 47

Ping-ma chih-hui (shih) ssu, 33

Ping-pu, see Ministry of War

Piracy, 110–11

Po-hu (centurion), 26, 35

Population, 182 (table); registers, 24, 29, 36–37

Postal service, 93, 127

Prefects: power in Yüan dynasty, 10; treatment of, 13; authority of, 15–16; judicial power of, 17; discipline of, 17; tax authority of, 87–88; supervision of students by, 145; hereditary, 233n

Prefectural government, 187 (table)

Princes, imperial, 2–3, 5, 25, 223, 272n

Promissory note, 251n

Provinces, 11, 182 (table), 183, 186 (table), 189 (table)

Provincial Administration Offices, 131

Provincial Surveillance Offices, 131

Pu-cheng-shih (administration commissioner), 11

Public works, 20–21

Rebellion, peasant, 7–8, 126–27, 220, 270–71n

Reigns, period of, 228

Remonstrance, 44, 50, 242n

Residence, official, 19, 20

Retirement, 180

Revenues, 20–21, 102

Ricci, Matteo, 129, 145

Salaries, 18–19, 55n, 76

Salt: revenue, 94, 99; quotas, 94; manufacture, 94–95; "payment for rationed," 95; reserve stock of, 96; nonquota, 96–97; monopoly, 98–99

School system, 131; *see also* Education

Secretaries: private, 16; grand, 46, 47, 71, 217, 218 (table); supervising, *see* Chi-chih-chung

Se-mu jen (classified peoples), 29, 30, 238n, 239n

Shao Ching-pang, 74–75

Shang-shu sheng (Department of State Affairs), 45

She (community-registration units), 30

She-hsüeh (local community schools), 143

Shen Pang, 75

Shen Te-fu, 126

Shen-tsung, Emperor, 112–13, 116

Sheng-yüan (candidates for the first degree), 18

Shih-ch'üan Academy, 155

Shih-kuan (official historiographer), 242n

Shih Kuan-min, 163

Shih-tsung, Emperor, 66, 160–61

Shou-ling kuan (principal subordinates), 16

Shou-shan Academy, 171, 172–73

Shu-mi yüan (Bureau of Military Affairs), 45

Shu-yüan, see Academies

Silver, 109–10, 124–25

Smuggling, 97, 103

Soldier-farmer, 36

Soldiers, 1, 26, 31, 37; *T'an-ma 'ch'ih*, 28, 30, 239n; *see also* Conscription; Desertions; *Fu-ping*; *I-ping*; *I-ying*

Ssu-feng Academy, 155

Ssu-jen-fa, 60

Ssu-li t'ai-chien (eunuch director of ceremonials), 47

Subordinates, selection of, 16, 17

Su-chou, 107–8

Su Shih, 8

Sui-kung (annual tribute) students, 145

Sun Ch'eng-tse, 81, 126

Sung T'ai-tsu, 9

Szechwan, 203 (table)

Ta-k'o Academy, 155

Ta-lu-hua-ch'ih (head officials), 26–27, 28

Ta-Ming Hui-tien, 36, 77

Ta tu-tu fu (Chief Military Commission), 27, 33–34, 35

T'ai-chien, see Eunuchs

T'ai Ts'ang Vault, 109, 112 (table), 113, 116

Tamerlane, 54–55

T'ang T'ai-tsung, 6, 243*n*

T'ang Wei, 64

Tax: quotas, 74–75, 86–87; commodity, 74–75, 101; racketeering, 75; assessment, 75–76; arrears, 84; captains, 85, 87, 88; grain, 85, 88, 106, 107; supervisors, 87; delinquencies, 87, 107, 108, 113–14, 118, 122; commutation of, 88–89; collection, 94, 114, 121; sales, 100–1; remission of, 114–15; *see also* Customs duties; Levies; Salt revenue

Tax, land: collection and distribution of, 90 (table); exemption from, 98, 120; reduction of, 107; arrears, 114; for war finance, 118; and registration, 256*n*

Thonganbwa, 60, 62

T'iao-chih (suggested rescripts), 47

T'i-hsüeh Kuan, see Education intendants

Time Misers' Association (*hsi-yin hui*), 158

Ting (service levy unit), 19, 92–93

T'ing-i (court conferences), 48–49, 243*n*

Trade, foreign, 99, 110

Tran Cao, 58, 60

Tran rulers, 56–57

Tsai-hsiang (prime minister), 44

Ts-ao Chiung, 5

Ts'eng Hsien, 66, 67

Tsou Te-han, 164

Tsou Yüan-piao, 168

Tsu-fu (rent and tribute), 85

Tsu-hsün (Ancestral Instructions), 52, 54, 57, 63, 64

Ts'un-liu (staying-in) funds, 83, 88, 89

Tsung-ping kuan (regional commanders), 35

Tsung-tu (supreme commanders), 12

Tu chih-hui shih ssu (Regional Military Commissions), 11, 34–35

T'u-ssu (chieftains serving as local officials), 2

T'un-t'ien (colony-fields), 10, 24, 28–29, 36, 39, 108–9

Tung Hsien, 242*n*

Tung-lin Academy, 172–73

T'ung-cheng ssu (Office of Transmission), 47

T'ung tien (Comprehensive canon) (Tu Yu), 6–7

Tzu-yang Academy, 167

Viceroys, 12

Wakō, 271*n*

Wan-hu (myriarch), 26, 28, 35

Wan-hu fu, 35

Wan Piao, 91

Wan-sung Academy, 167

Wang Chen, 61

Wang Chi, 61

Wang Chia, 242*n*

Wang Chih, 62–63, 142

Wang Ch'iung, 78–79

Wang I-chi, 67

Wang Kou, 80, 91

Wang Kuo-kuang, 82

Wang Lin, 80

Wang Shou-jen, 156–58

Wang T'ung, 57, 58, 59

Wang Wen-sheng, 65
Wang Yang-ming, *see* Wang Shou-jen; Yang-ming school
Wang Yin-chiao, 80
Water control projects, 101
Wei (guards), 23; at capital, 26; and colony-fields, 28, 29; officers of, 30; military organization, 34; Yüan organization, 35
Wei Chung-hsien, 173–74, 186
Wen-chiang Academy, 160
Wen-hsien t'ung-k'ao (Comprehensive inquiry into documentary sources) (Ma Tuan-lin), 3
Wen-hui Academy, 161
Weng Wan-ta, 65
White Lotus Society, 23, 31, 32
Wu Chih-yü, 121
Wu Chung, 56
Wu-hsi Academy, 171
Wu Lai, 10
Wu-pei chih (Treatise on military preparations, 1617), 53

Yang I-ch'ing, 144, 157
Yang Jung, 46, 57–58, 59, 60
Yang-ming Academy, 158

Yang-ming school, 153, 156–60, 162, 164–65, 167
Yang Shen, 8
Yang Shih-ch'i, 46, 57–58, 59–60; on barbarians, 57; on Lu-ch'uan rebellion, 61
Yang Ssu-ch'ang, 68
Yeh Ch'i, 109
Yeh Shih, 8–9
Yen Sung, 46, 64, 67–68, 159–60, 161
Yin (protective privilege), 236*n*
Yin Cheng-mou, 80
Ying-t'ien ssu (office for promotion of agriculture), 36
Ying-tsung, Emperor, 46, 61, 89, 132, 133–34
Yu Chü-ching, 153
Yu-t'ieh (tax bill), 93
Yü Kuang, 65
Yü-shih ta-fu (grandee secretary), 272*n*
Yü Tzu-chün, 62
Yüan-shuai (military commander), 31, 32–33
Yüan-shuai fu (local military commands), 27, 31, 32, 33, 34
Yün-yü Academy, 155